PACIFIC PASSIONS

Also by Frank Sherry

Raiders and Rebels: The Golden Age of Piracy

FRANK SHERRY

PACIFIC PASSIONS

The European Struggle for Power in the Great Ocean in the Age of Exploration

William Morrow and Company, Inc.
New York

Library of Congress Cataloging-in-Publication Data

Sherry, Frank, 1934–
    Pacific passions : the European struggle for power in the Great
Ocean in the age of exploration / Frank Sherry.
        P.   cm.
    Includes Bibliographical references and index.
    ISBN 0-688-07518-5
    1. Pacific Area—Discovery and exploration.   I. Title.
DU19.S488   1994
996.9'02—dc20   93-22612
                                                                                      CIP

Printed in the United States of America

First Edition

1 2 3 4 5 6 7 8 9 10

This book is for Stephen

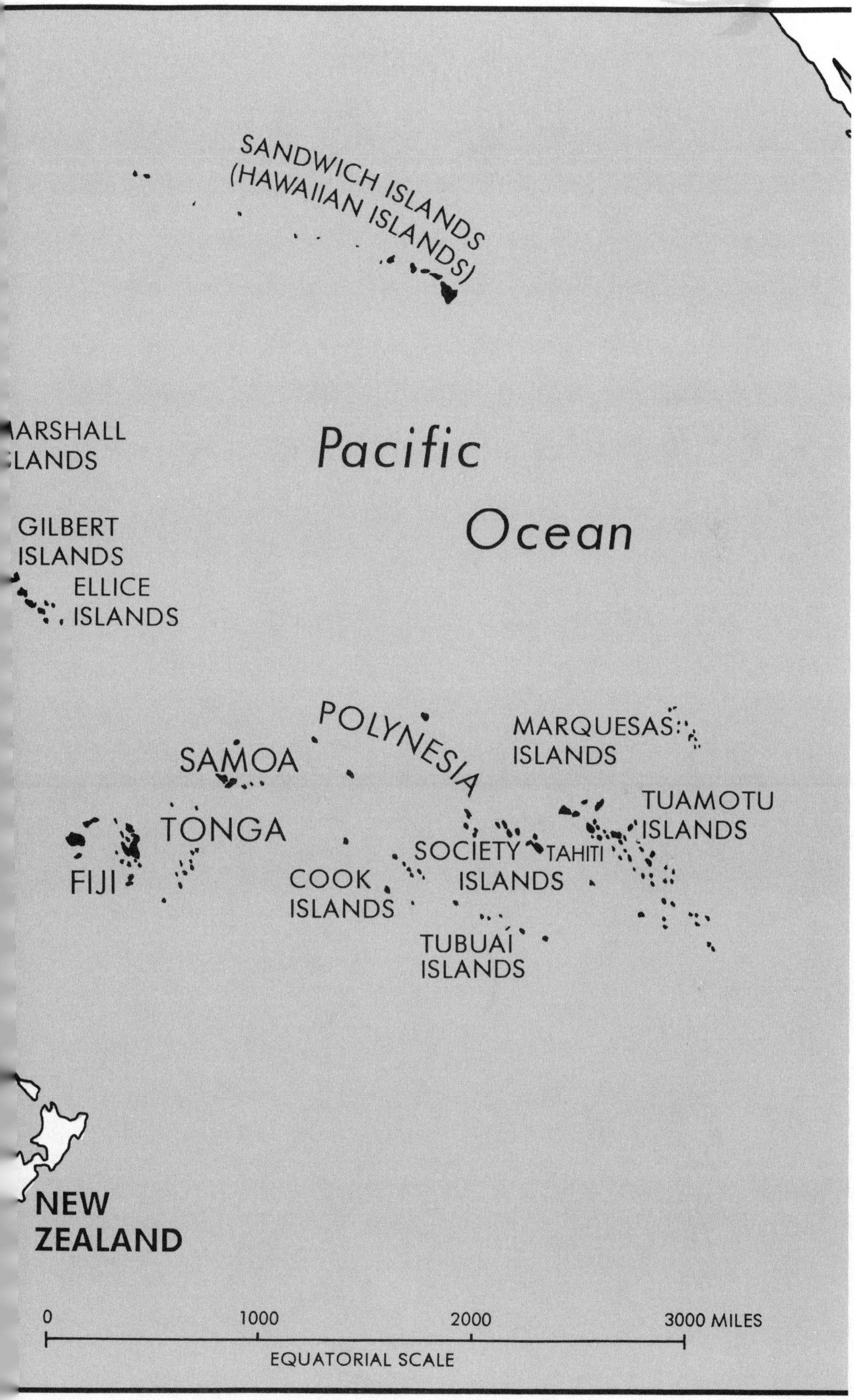

SANDWICH ISLANDS
(HAWAIIAN ISLANDS)

Pacific

Ocean

MARSHALL
ISLANDS

GILBERT
ISLANDS
ELLICE
ISLANDS

POLYNESIA

MARQUESAS
ISLANDS

SAMOA

TUAMOTU
ISLANDS

TONGA

SOCIETY   TAHITI
ISLANDS

FIJI

COOK
ISLANDS

TUBUAÍ
ISLANDS

NEW
ZEALAND

| 0 | 1000 | 2000 | 3000 MILES |

EQUATORIAL SCALE

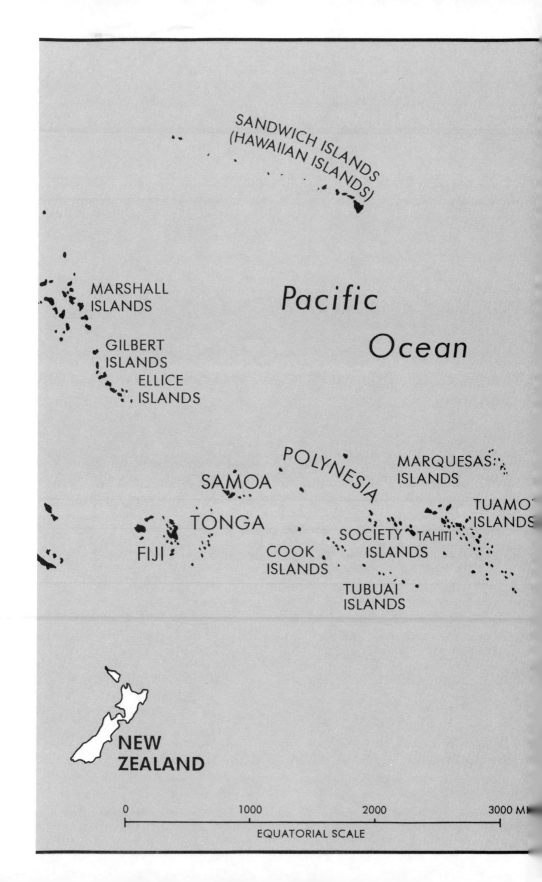

SANDWICH ISLANDS
(HAWAIIAN ISLANDS)

Pacific

Ocean

MARSHALL
ISLANDS

GILBERT
ISLANDS
ELLICE
ISLANDS

POLYNESIA

MARQUESAS
ISLANDS

SAMOA

TUAMO
ISLANDS

TONGA

SOCIETY
ISLANDS

TAHITI

FIJI

COOK
ISLANDS

TUBUAI
ISLANDS

NEW
ZEALAND

0   1000   2000   3000 M
EQUATORIAL SCALE

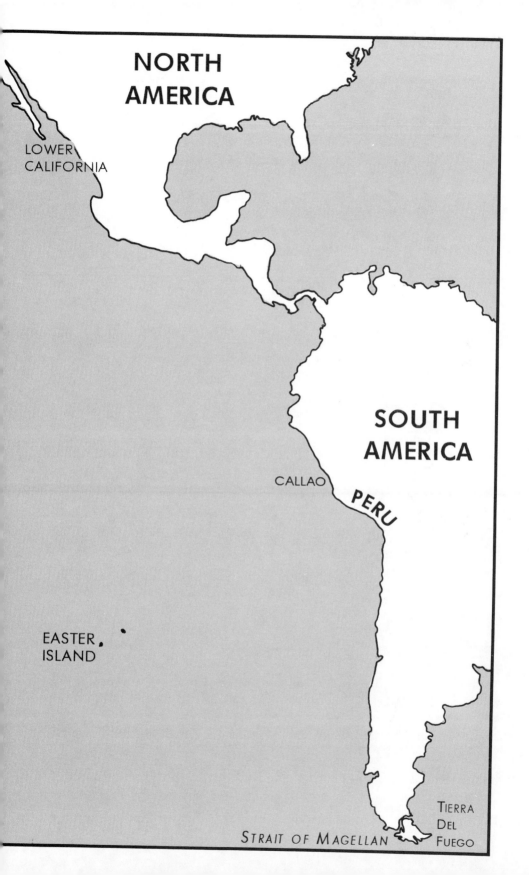

CONTENTS

12   Contents

PREFACE

The general purpose of this narrative is to tell in a single volume not only *how* but also *why* Europeans came to the Pacific during the two and a half centuries between Balboa's first sighting of the ocean and Cook's second voyage of exploration.

More particularly my intent is to show how the voyages described in these pages form a coherent chain of cause and effect because they were all linked to each other and to the great political and social movements of their times. In pursuit of this goal I have not sought to add new scholarly information to the world's store, but rather to give fresh perspective and clarity to the underlying pattern of the Pacific story. For this reason I have chosen to focus not only on those Pacific voyagers whose aim was exploration but also on the many others (naval officers, pirates, and merchants) who sailed the Pacific on missions of war or plunder or profit and furthered, even if inadvertently, western understanding of the great ocean.

In attempting to establish the political and social context in which the Pacific voyages took place I have stressed those events such as the bankruptcy of Philip II and the Dutch revolt, which (in my opinion) provided the chief impetus to the Pacific journeys, and I have paid correspondingly less attention to movements such as the Protestant Reformation that, for all their importance to history, had less impact on European actions in

13

the ocean. Although I have tried to achieve a proper balance in doing this, I realize that reasonable people may disagree with those aspects of the historical record that I have chosen to emphasize.

In order to tell this story in a single volume it has been necessary to condense some accounts of the voyages as well as some of the European events recounted here. I have tried to do this while preserving both accuracy and dramatic detail. The reader must judge if I have succeeded.

A word on names is also in order. To avoid confusion I have chosen to use the most familiar forms of all names pertinent to this narrative even if, in doing so, the result is a certain amount of inconsistency. Thus the first Hapsburg king of Spain is called Charles in these pages instead of the Spanish Carlos because that is how he is now known in the English-speaking world. For the same reason his Spanish mother is referred to as Juana instead of Johanna. I have followed the same pattern with regard to the voyagers, choosing the names that appear most often in the journals and chronicles, even if they are not strictly accurate. Thus the Spaniard Pedro Sarmiento de Gamboa is called Sarmiento here while another, Ruy Lopez de Villalobos, has come down to us as Villalobos rather than Lopez. I have adhered to this procedure with regard to ship names as well. For example, where the sources give the names of certain ships in English instead of their original language, I have retained the English form. On the other hand when a ship's name is given in the original language, I have used it throughout.

Finally I want to thank my dear wife and partner, Su, for her patience, good humor, and hard work during the composition of this book. I hope she knows how much her encouragement has meant to me.

—F. S.

PROLOGUE
A NEW AGE BEGINS

In fifteenth-century Europe anyone who possessed a barrel of cloves—or pepper, or ginger, or cinnamon—was rich. In that era before refrigeration, Europeans had learned that "powdering" foods with these aromatic substances not only would preserve them but would transform the blandest fare into a savory feast.

In addition to preserving and enhancing food, the redolent products of the far-distant Orient were prescribed as cures for such disorders as plague, edema, and epilepsy. They were made into aphrodisiacs and love potions. They were the basic ingredients in perfumes. They were also essential to the embalmer.

As a consequence, spices were the most sought-after commodity of Renaissance Europe. They were actually worth their weight in gold, largely because demand always far outstripped supply.

The spices originated in the mysterious Molucca Islands, the Spice Isles located somewhere in the misty waters beyond India.* From those distant parts the fragrant merchandise made its way westward by a process that had developed over centuries.

---

*Renaissance Europe had only the vaguest notion of the geography of Asia. Though Europeans knew that their spices came from the Moluccas, they had little idea of the location of these islands. In fact, the five major islands of the Moluccas lie almost directly under the equator in the island-dotted seas between Borneo and New Guinea at the western extremity of the Pacific Ocean.

First, far-ranging merchants of India sailed on the monsoon winds to the Moluccas. They carried the products of those paradisical isles via the Strait of Malacca to the Malabar Coast of southwestern India. Then Arab traders, sailing their dhows along routes as old as the pyramids, transported the spices from India to Egypt. There Europeans—particularly the merchants of Venice—received the precious goods, for which they paid enormous prices. The spices then were retailed at huge markups to an eager Europe. The Serene Republic of Venice grew rich on the European craving for spices.

Then, in 1453, a cataclysmic event threatened to end this time-honored trade: The Ottoman Turks took Constantinople. With the capture of the ancient city, standing at the juncture of Europe and Asia, the Turks became the most powerful force in the Muslim world, dominating the eastern Mediterranean from the Bosporus to the Nile. Moreover, the sultan made it clear he meant to continue his war on Christian Europe, including the Serene Republic of Venice. Inevitably the result would be disruption of the spice trade.

In far-off western Europe the Portuguese observed these developments in the Mediterranean with special interest. The hardy mariners of Portugal, their nautical skills sharpened by the harsh demands of Atlantic winds and waves, had long dreamed of seizing the spice trade for themselves by opening a water route around Africa to the source of the spices in Asia. Although such a sea route, if it existed, would entail great risk to the small ships of the time, the potential gain far outweighed the dangers. Spices took up little shipboard space in relation to their worth. If only a few vessels succeeded each year in making such a journey, the result would be huge profits for merchants and political power for the nation.

For decades, long before the fall of Constantinople, Portuguese navigators had been venturing southward along the coast of Africa in search of such a route. Supported by the royal house, especially by the famed Prince Henry (known as the Navigator because of his enthusiasm for exploration), Portuguese expeditions had reached the Azores, about eight hundred miles out in the open Atlantic, in 1427. Their ships had landed on the northwestern shoulder of the African coast as early as 1434. By the 1440s Portuguese captains had journeyed as far south as Senegal, the beginning of black Africa.

With the Turkish conquest of Constantinople and the threat to the Venetian spice trade, the Portuguese pressed southward with renewed vigor. In 1454, the year of the first printed Bible and a year after the Turks took Constantinople, a bull from Pope Nicholas V granted the Portuguese the exclusive rights to exploration and conquest on the road to the Indies "south and east." Portugal now claimed legal authority to bar other countries from seeking a sea route to India around Africa.

In 1462 Portuguese ships reached Sierra Leone and began exploring the Guinea coast of Africa. Soon Lisbon's caravels passed south of the Congo. Then, in 1488, Bartholomew Diaz rounded the Cape of Good Hope. The Portuguese stood poised for a thrust across the Indian Ocean itself.*

Although the Portuguese had now proved the feasibility of the southward route, some geographers thought it might actually be easier to reach India by sailing *westward* across the Atlantic. These speculations rested on uncertainty about the circumference of the earth. Many, relying on the calculations of the second-century Alexandrian astronomer Ptolemy, believed that the globe was no more than eighteen thousand miles around. Others thought the distance greater. In any case, it was often theorized that a ship might more easily reach the Orient by voyaging directly westward across the Atlantic than by following the projected Portuguese route around Africa.

A stubborn and proud navigator from Genoa, Christopher Columbus, was possessed by this thesis. Wandering from court to court with his maps and charts, he spent years trying to convince Western monarchs to finance such a transatlantic voyage under his leadership.

Then, in 1492, events came together that allowed Columbus to realize his dream. The Catholic monarchs Ferdinand and Isabella, who had united their two realms of Aragón and Castile by their marriage, had recently succeeded in driving the Moors from Granada, thus drawing all Spain under their sway.†

Ferdinand and Isabella were intrigued by the prospect of

---

*Meanwhile, the Venetians and Turks fought their inevitable war, resulting in a humiliating and costly defeat for Venice.
†"Spain" existed at this time more as a concept than as a political fact. Although Ferdinand and Isabella had unified, by marriage and by conquest, various regions of the country, it took another generation before Spaniards began to view themselves as a nation in the political sense. Still, for the sake of clarity, I shall use the term "Spain."

seizing the spice trade for themselves before the Portuguese could
reach India. Precluded by the papal bull of 1454 from infringing
on Portugal's African franchise, they decided to underwrite the
westward expedition proposed by Columbus. Accordingly the
Genoese navigator sailed, and upon his return to Spain in March
1493, Columbus announced that he had reached islands at the
eastern extremity of Asia, thus naming them the Indies.

Columbus's apparent success was a bitter pill for the Portuguese, who had not yet made their own final voyage to India
around Africa. If Columbus had indeed reached the East, Spain,
not Portugal, would reap the wealth of the spice trade. Ferdinand
and Isabella, following custom, obtained a series of papal bulls
that, in effect, drew a north-south boundary line in the Atlantic,
345 miles west of the Azores, and set aside everything west of it
for Spain alone to exploit.

The Portuguese were furious, even though they had obtained similar papal dispensations thirty-nine years earlier to
guard *their* claims to the African sea route. Threatening war, the
Portuguese demanded from Spain a general adjustment that
would protect their "right" to India.

Spain, not yet a great power, had to agree. Meeting at Tordesillas in northwestern Spain, the diplomats drafted a treaty that
reaffirmed the pope's Atlantic division but moved the demarcation 930 miles farther west. The result—though no one realized
it at the time—was a boundary line that struck the mainland of
South America about the mouth of the Amazon. This Treaty of
Tordesillas, signed in 1494, assigned to Spain all territory west of
that line and to Portugal all lands to the east.

The Portuguese declared themselves content. The treaty left
them sea-room in the South Atlantic to develop their African
route. It did not specifically mention trade with India, thus leaving them free to pursue their goal of seizing the spice trade. The
Portuguese may have also suspected that Columbus had not
reached India after all but only some lesser islands.*

Ferdinand and Isabella, relying on Columbus's assurances

*Although the framers of the Tordesillas accord intended only to establish "spheres of
influence" in the Atlantic, later statesmen used the document to justify dividing the entire
globe between Spain and Portugal. As Spanish power grew, Spain was to claim the right
to exclude all other nations from voyaging westward "beyond the line" established by
Tordesillas. The agreement also provided the basis for the Portuguese claim to Brazil,
which bulged east of "the line."

that he had opened a western path to the East, approved the Treaty of Tordesillas in the happy expectation that Spanish caravels would soon be touching on the shores of India and Cathay to take on cargoes of spices and silks. Their hopes soon turned to frustration.

For the next decade and more, navigators explored the coasts and islands across the Atlantic. Columbus himself made three more journeys. The mariners, searching for the splendid cities and fragrant pepper groves of the East, found only a primitive landscape. These early voyages in the wake of Columbus seemed to many to suggest that instead of India, the Spaniards had discovered only a savage wasteland.

By the time Columbus died in 1506, many geographers were convinced that the admiral had discovered a "New World." The influential Florentine, Amerigo Vespucci, did the most to advance this idea.

Vespucci, himself a navigator and, for many years, an agent of the great commercial house of the Medici, was sure that Columbus had stumbled on to a new continent—in reality a *barrier* between Europe and the East. Named chief pilot of Spain in 1508, Vespucci promoted his New World conception in his writings, and it quickly gained acceptance. The famed cosmographer Martin Waldseemüller applied the name Amerige or America to what is now South America, in honor of Vespucci, the first man to recognize the true nature of Columbus's discovery.*

As the concept of the New World took hold, mariners began seeking a passage through the obstacle of America. After all, they reasoned, if the earth was really only eighteen thousand miles around, the Spice Isles and India had to lie only a few hundred miles beyond this wild America. Though several expeditions sought a channel to the west, no strait was found.

Spain, frustrated in its quest for Eastern wealth, vigorously exploited the lands that had come under its sway. The island of Hispaniola (now Haiti and the Dominican Republic) became the center of Spanish life in the New World. The Spaniards searched assiduously for gold. Finding none of the precious metal at first, they established plantations. They developed a lively trade be-

---

*By 1538 the mapmaker Gerardus Mercator was applying the name America to all the Western Hemisphere.

tween Seville and the new colonies. They established the laws of Spain, and the church, in their New World. Still, their empire produced little.

Meanwhile, the Portuguese, continuing on their African course, succeeded in reaching the *real* India. In 1497 Vasco da Gama rounded the Cape of Good Hope and sailed to India's western coast, where he initiated relations with the powerful local rulers. Soon the Portuguese began establishing fortified trading posts in the East and filling their ships with spices. By 1512 they were well along in creating a commercial empire and in driving their Muslim and Indian competitors from Eastern seas. Their ships and strategic forts guarded the routes to the Moluccas and kept all other nations from entering African and Indian waters.

Wealth poured into Lisbon. European monarchs referred to the Portuguese king Manuel as the Fortunate. This sovereign also gave himself a title: Lord of the Conquest, Navigation, and Commerce of India, Ethiopia, Arabia, and Persia. The appellation summed up the splendor of a triumphant Portugal.

Then a Spanish adventurer, thirty-eight-year-old Vasco Núñez de Balboa, made a discovery that reignited Spain's own dream of Eastern wealth. Late in 1512 Balboa, who had been knocking about the New World for more than a decade, heard from friendly Indians that "a land of gold, washed by a vast sea," lay just over the jungle-covered mountains of the Spanish colony of Darién (today's Panama). Balboa responded to this news by leading a column of tough Spanish troopers into the jungles in search of "the other sea" reported by the Indians.

On September 25, 1513, after three weeks of trekking through gloomy jungle, Balboa and his men emerged onto an open mountaintop. From this height they beheld a sight that no European had ever seen. Below, foaming breakers rolled against a curving sandy shore, and beyond, a seemingly endless expanse of calm water shone beneath a tropic sun.

Kneeling and giving thanks for the glory before him, Balboa named his discovery Mar del Sur—the South Sea—because he had followed a southward route across the Isthmus of Panama and, to his eyes, the sea lay in that direction.* Four days later

---

*This moment of discovery has long fascinated poets. John Keats wrote perhaps the most famous description although he mistakenly identified the discoverer as Cortés: "He stared at the Pacific—and all his men looked at each other with a wild surmise—silent, upon a

Balboa reached the shores of his South Sea and, finding the sparkling water salty, rejoiced. He had found a new ocean that certainly washed against the much-desired East. Exultant, Balboa took possession of the great water and all it contained "in the names of the kings of Castile, present and future."

The news of his find was received in Spain with great excitement. King Ferdinand, now an ailing widower of sixty-four, recognized at once that Balboa's South Sea offered Spain a magnificent new opportunity at empire. All the world knew that the Portuguese, despite their far-flung trading stations, had not yet touched on the Moluccas themselves. Spain might still wrest the spice trade from the Portuguese by sailing farther west on Balboa's South Sea. Moreover, Spain might accomplish this aim without violating the Tordesillas agreement if the Spice Isles lay in Spain's half of the globe. Whether they did or not, however, Ferdinand was not one to allow a treaty to thwart his ambition.

Ferdinand and his advisers must have also seen that in addition to providing a route to the Spice Isles, Balboa's South Sea might lead Spaniards to the most fabled land of all: Terra Australis Incognita. This was the great unknown southern continent, incredibly rich and strange, that scholars had long postulated for the southern half of the globe.

Ignorant of the nature of gravity, Renaissance geographers believed that to maintain its equilibrium, the earth required a counterweight to the massive continents of the Northern Hemisphere. They theorized that some still-unknown southern continent had to exist well below the equator in order to keep the world from turning over like a top-heavy ball. This notion of a huge southern landmass had become an article of faith among geographers.*

Marco Polo's account of his travels in Asia, a printed version of which was widely distributed in 1477, spoke of a country called Lokach, to the south of Java. According to Polo, the gold of Lokach was "so plentiful that no one who did not see it could believe it."

---

peak in Darien." One of those who accompanied Balboa was Francisco Pizarro, future conqueror of the Inca Empire.

*The existence of the Americas, still only partially mapped at this time, merely made a southern continent more essential in the minds of scholars. By contributing their mass to the great northern continental areas, the Americas seemed only to add to the requirement for a counterbalancing land in the southern reaches of the globe.

With Balboa's discovery of a new South Sea beyond the mountains of Darién, it suddenly seemed likely that Lokach, which was no doubt Terra Australis Incognita, also lay within reach of Spanish mariners. But first a passage through America would have to be found.

Spain began a new hunt for a strait to the South Sea. The search proved fruitless until a Portuguese soldier and navigator named Fernão de Magalhães took up the quest.

Later ages would call him Ferdinand Magellan.

1
MAGELLAN*

The Magellan family lived on a small farm in Portugal's wild Tráz-os-Montes district, far from the sea ("a country," the natives liked to say, "that has nine months of winter and three months of hell").

Though the family belonged to the minor Portuguese nobility, the Magellans possessed only a modest estate and little wealth. They did, however, take great pride in their forebears, who had come to Portugal from Normandy in the twelfth century and had helped secure the throne for the ancestors of Portugal's ruling dynasty.

Ferdinand Magellan, the second son, entered the world in 1480 at his family's farm. After an unremarkable boyhood, Ferdinand left home at the age of ten to join his older brother Diogo as a page in the royal court in Lisbon. There he received instruction in letters, mathematics, music, and, most important, the profession of arms. At fifteen Magellan became a junior officer in the Portuguese Army, but he remained attached to the household of the sovereign, King Manuel.

On the basis of later physical descriptions, it is possible to picture how the future navigator probably looked as a young knight: short of stature, but broad and strong—a fighting bull—

*To avoid confusion, we shall use the anglicized version of the name throughout.

23

with thick black hair and dark eyes full of intensity. Only much later did he grow the full sable-colored beard depicted in portraits.*

In 1499, when Magellan was nineteen, an event took place that set Portugal on fire with excitement. Vasco da Gama returned from India, successful in opening the first sea route from Europe to the East. Portugal's long struggle to reach India by sailing around Africa had finally borne fruit.

Now, encouraged by reports of Muslim weakness in the Indian Ocean, King Manuel and his leading nobles embarked on a remarkably bold course: Portugal would send ships and men eastward to drive the Muslims from Africa, India, and beyond and to establish an impregnable Portuguese commercial empire in the East based on the spice trade. Portugal's daring enterprise also had a second, less mercenary purpose: the advancement of Christianity in the world. Thus the Portuguese thrust into the East would be part exploration, part imperialist grab, and part religious crusade. So many of the country's youth clamored to sail eastward that a Portuguese poet proudly proclaimed: "God has given the Portuguese only a little country to live in, but the whole world to die in."

Young Magellan failed to gain a place in the first invasion fleets that established Portuguese beach heads in the East. But in 1505, at the age of twenty-five, he embarked for India with the flotilla of Viceroy Francisco de Almeida, a grandee whose mission was to achieve permanent Portuguese control of the Indian Ocean.

Magellan, accompanied by his cousin Francisco Serrão, soon found himself in the forefront of remarkable Portuguese conquests. For the next four years he and Serrão participated in bloody battles, both on land and at sea, that drove the Muslims from their ancient enclaves in eastern Africa, Zanzibar, the Gulf of Aden, and the western coast of India.

Despite their scant numbers (Almeida, for example, led only

---

*A number of paintings, supposedly of Magellan, exist. All of them date from periods well after his death, and all differ from one another both in detail and in style. Yet they agree on basic characteristics. All portray Magellan as dark and bearded, with a hint of sensuality in the face, especially around the eyes and mouth. Some give him a sinister expression. Whether the artists based their portraits on previous paintings, on written descriptions, or on tradition remains unknown. We can only say with any degree of certainty that we have an idea of what Magellan looked like in general terms. His particular features, however, like many other details of his life, remain elusive.

two thousand men and twenty-five ships eastward), the Portuguese, with their superior cannon, tactics, and warships, crushed their Muslim foes and seized ports where, just a few years earlier, they had first appeared as humble traders.*

Many a Portuguese conquistador paid a price in blood for his country's ambition, however. One of these was Magellan, who in 1509 sustained a near-fatal stab wound in a major sea battle off the Arabian coast. It took five months for the young officer to recuperate sufficiently to rejoin his comrades. He then participated in the first, tentative Portuguese advance toward the Spice Islands themselves: a disguised reconnaissance, in September 1509, of the famed Malayan port of Malacca. During this operation the Malays mounted a surprise attack on the Portuguese ships, and Magellan helped rescue a number of his companions—among them his cousin Serrão—trapped ashore by Malayan forces.

Although he won praise and promotion for his heroism at Malacca, Magellan now decided that it was time to return home. He was weary of incessant combat. He had accumulated much booty. His commander and patron, the courtly Almeida, had been replaced by the fierce and ambitious Afonso de Albuquerque, who had brought his own officers out from Portugal.

In January 1510 Magellan joined a Lisbon-bound convoy. On the very first leg of the voyage his ship and another in the convoy ran aground on Padre Shoals near the Maldive Islands south of India. In the wreck Magellan lost all his property, except a young Malayan slave whom he had named Enrique.

Managing with others to get ashore on the barren islands, Magellan took charge of the situation. Choosing to stay behind with the seamen, he sent a party of officers for help in a ship's boat. Through Magellan's leadership the castaways survived until a relief vessel arrived several weeks later. Having lost all his property, Magellan, once more a hero, went back to India, where the white-bearded Albuquerque, short of experienced officers, gave him employment as captain of a caravel.

Thus it was that in 1511 Magellan took part in the final

---

*The Portuguese established the classic pattern of later European imperialism in Asia, Africa, and the Pacific. First came trade. Then came military occupation of key places, ostensibly to protect merchants and their installations. Finally came conquest of the native populations and incorporation within an "empire." With some variations all the later European imperialists followed this path.

conquest of Malacca. This sprawling city on the Malay Peninsula commanded the strait that formed the main sea route to and from the Spice Isles, which still lay some fifteen hundred miles farther to the east. All the spices that flowed to India and then to Europe had to pass through Malacca. Whoever held Malacca controlled the spice trade. The port fell to Albuquerque's forces in six weeks.

Once again, however, Magellan's personal fortunes suffered a serious blow. The ship carrying his share of Malaccan loot back to India sank en route, and for the second time Magellan lost his wealth.

Although poor again, Magellan once more determined to depart the East for Portugal. He seems to have resolved on this course because of a growing inability to get on with the acerbic Albuquerque. He set sail for Lisbon early in 1512.

Meanwhile, Albuquerque dispatched three of his vessels farther east to reconnoiter the Spice Islands. Magellan's cousin Serrão was the captain of one of these vessels.* After a number of adventures in the Spice Islands, Serrão and his crew fetched up at the island of Ternate, one of the lushest of the Moluccas. Serrão fell in love with the island and decided to spend the rest of his days there.

Most of his men eventually found their way back to Malacca. But Serrão himself settled down with a native wife and became a trusted adviser to the ruler of the island, a circumstance that was to have profound consequences for Magellan.

Magellan arrived home in Lisbon in June 1512. He had been away seven years and was now a grizzled veteran of thirty-two. Yet he owned little except his weapons, his clothing, and the young Malayan slave, Enrique, whom he treated more as a companion than a bond servant. Nevertheless, with his knowledge of the East and his skill in navigation, Magellan had high hopes of repairing his fortunes in the king's service.

Magellan must have marveled at the changes in the once-

---

*Some accounts say Magellan also commanded one of these ships, but this is highly unlikely. Not only was the timing improbable, considering Magellan's departure for home in 1512, but Albuquerque would be little disposed to entrust such a mission to Magellan, whom he disliked. Moreover, at no later time did Magellan ever give any indication that he possessed personal knowledge of the Moluccas. If, in fact, he had made this first journey to the Spice Isles, it seems probable that he would have said so in later years.

torpid Portuguese capital. New churches, sprawling warehouses, gorgeous private mansions, and bustling jetties, all products of the spice trade, lined the banks of the muddy Tagus River. Merchant vessels from all over Europe crowded the docks, waiting to take on cargoes of spices for shipment to other Christian capitals. The narrow streets teemed with exotic people of every race and nationality and rang with foreign speech. In seven years Lisbon had become one of the world's great commercial centers. Magellan must have felt confident that he had much to offer the ruler of such a cosmopolitan capital.

His expectations were soon thwarted. King Manuel received him with mysterious coolness and offered him no employment. Though given a nominal promotion in rank and a modest increase in his *moradia*, the stipend that officers of the king's household were allowed for their expenses, it was employment that Magellan wanted, a new chance at glory and fortune. But as the months passed, the king ignored him.*

It was probably about this time that a vaulting ambition seized Magellan: He wanted to lead an expedition to the Moluccas, the next logical step in Portugal's eastern conquests. By this time Magellan had received a number of letters from his cousin Francisco Serrão, now well established in a position of power on the island of Ternate. Serrão urged Magellan to journey to him as either a merchant or a conqueror. Magellan must have felt himself uniquely qualified to direct the coming Portuguese thrust toward the Spice Isles. But nothing came of his suit. The puzzled soldier continued to cool his heels at court.

In an apparent attempt to regain the king's favor, Magellan late in 1513 enlisted in a Portuguese expedition to Morocco. Though he distinguished himself in battle and took a serious wound in the thigh that caused him to limp for the rest of his life, Magellan's effort backfired. He was accused of selling army booty for personal gain. Enraged by the baseless charge, Magellan stormed back to Lisbon to protest his innocence in person to King Manuel, who coldly ordered his troublesome captain back to Morocco. In the end nothing came of the charges, and Magellan returned to court, to find the king more distant than ever.

---

*Though only a pittance, the moradia had symbolic importance since the relative amount determined rank at court. Magellan certainly ranked low, even after his small raise.

Despite almost two years of frustration, Magellan was still eager to travel to his cousin in the Moluccas. But by now, early in
1515, his plan had taken on a new wrinkle. He seems to have begun contemplating a scheme to reach the Spice Isles by sailing *west*
across the South Sea recently discovered by the Spaniard Balboa.

By this time all mariners had heard of the new ocean beyond
America, and all surmised that the Spice Isles had to lie some
relatively short distance across that water. From the Portuguese
point of view, a westward journey across this newly discovered
South Sea offered two great advantages. First, it would establish
a much shorter route to the Spice Isles than the one currently
followed. Second, and more important, such a voyage would establish a Portuguese claim to the Moluccas until Albuquerque
was ready to take them by force.

To any objections that such a westward enterprise by Portugal would trespass on Spain's half of the world, as defined by
the treaty of Tordesillas, Magellan could give a compelling reply:
National necessity dictated the voyage. All the world knew by now
that the Spanish monarch, Ferdinand, had given the Portuguese-
born mariner Juan Diaz de Solís (Vespucci's successor as Spain's
chief pilot) the task of finding a passage to the South Sea so that
Spain might seize the Spice Isles from the west. Was Portugal to
lose its prize at this late date for the sake of an outmoded agreement, a treaty made in geographic ignorance?*

Moreover, Magellan might well point out, no one could say
if the Spice Isles lay on the Portuguese or Spanish side of the
Tordesillas line of demarcation, as extended around the world.
Only by voyaging there could anyone know for certain, and even
then questions might remain if the islands lay close to the line,
for no reliable method existed to fix longitude. The surest way
to deal with the problem, therefore, would be to sail to the islands and simply claim them.

Magellan must have felt confident that he could locate a
passage through the barrier of America. As a member of the
Portuguese king's household he had access to the charts, reports,
and logs of Portuguese pilots who had clandestinely reconnoi-

*Of course, Magellan, like all mariners of the day, was ignorant of the most important
geographic fact of all: the 8,000 miles of ocean that lay between America and the Moluccas. His willingness to break the Tordesillas agreement on behalf of his sovereign very
likely stemmed from a mixture of national loyalty and personal ambition. Probably he
also knew that Portugal had already broken the treaty with a number of secret voyages
"beyond the line."

tered along the coast of South America. He knew that this intelligence, regarded as a state secret and kept under lock and key in the royal map room, indicated the possibility of a strait at several places along that rugged coast.

Although accounts differ, it appears that the blunt Magellan attempted to broach these ideas to the king at a public assembly. This was a breach of etiquette for a soldier in the king's service, one so serious that it infuriated the monarch and caused him to turn away from Magellan with a distaste obvious to all who witnessed it.

Hurt and rejected by the sovereign he had served well for many years, Magellan fled from Lisbon to the seaside town of Oporto, where he took lodgings in a waterfront tavern. For many weeks he brooded over his wrongs. Without honor or fortune—or the prospects of either—he seems to have fallen into a deep melancholy. But even during this black interlude Magellan, the master mariner, maintained an interest in the geographic problems posed by recent Portuguese and Spanish discoveries.

He often discussed these with a fellow exile from King Manuel's court: Ruy Faleiro, a famed Portuguese geographer and astrologer who had taken refuge in Oporto when the king had refused him the position of royal geographer. Brought together by common bitterness against their sovereign, Magellan and Faleiro spent many hours together discussing geographic theory. Faleiro—touchy, morose, and self-important—had a reputation as a necromancer. But he had worked out a method of calculating longitude that deeply impressed Magellan.* Together Faleiro and Magellan made plans for a voyage to seek a westward passage to the South Sea, should the opportunity arise.

As Magellan's exile stretched on into 1516, Spain entered a period of political turmoil, precipitated by the death of King Ferdinand in January of that year at the age of sixty-four. Ferdinand, who had ruled for forty-two years, was succeeded by his sixteen-year-old grandson Charles, the elder child of his mentally ill daughter Mad Queen Juana and her deceased husband, Philip of Burgundy. Although Ferdinand's legitimate heir, young Charles was also a Hapsburg, a "German" who could not even speak Spanish. Many Spaniards, therefore, opposed his succession. Rebellion threatened the political unity that Ferdinand and

*Faleiro's system was so flawed that it later proved useless.

Isabella had imposed on Spain, as young Charles tried to establish his sovereignty.

During this turbulent period it became known that Spain's latest effort to find a strait through America, led by Chief Pilot Juan Diaz de Solís himself, had ended tragically. The expedition, consisting of three small ships carrying a complement of sixty men, had put to sea in October 1515. In February 1516 de Solís, after coasting Brazil, had reached a great waterway (now called the Rió de la Plata) that seemed to offer the long-sought westward passage. Solís's three vessels had entered the broad stream. But the water had soon grown fresh, a certain sign that they had not entered a strait after all. Before the ships could turn back, however, the Spaniards had spied a group of Indians onshore who beckoned Solís to join them. The chief pilot, apparently seeking information, had rowed to land in a ship's boat with a few companions. All at once the "friendly" Indians had set upon the little party, killing them and devouring them while their horrified shipmates watched from their vessels. The survivors had fled downstream. Two of Solís's three ships eventually made it home to Spain. One was wrecked on the way.

With the failure of the Solís expedition, the death of Ferdinand, and the chaotic conditions in Spain upon the accession of Charles, Spanish interest in finding a strait to Balboa's new ocean all but disappeared. Many Spanish mariners, looking back on years of fruitless searching, speculated that the longed-for strait did not exist and that the South Sea might prove an enticing prize but forever out of reach.

From his place of exile in Oporto, however, it seemed to Magellan that in time Spain would renew attempts to reach Balboa's South Sea and the Moluccas. When that time came, it would need an outstanding navigator to lead the effort.* Having been rejected by his own sovereign, Magellan now considered offering his services to Spain. He had probably been weighing such a course for some time, for he had written to Serrão months earlier, saying he might join his cousin soon "if not by Portugal, then by way of Spain."

---

*In far-off Darién Balboa himself managed to carry out some tentative exploration of his South Sea, journeying to a few nearby islands in boats carried across the isthmus. But before he could organize a major expedition, Balboa ran afoul of the royal governor of Darién. The aged governor, who hated Balboa as a rival, had the younger man arrested on a flimsy charge of treason. The first European to look upon the Pacific was eventually beheaded in a public square in Darién in January 1519.

Service to a foreign monarch was common among mariners of that era. Columbus, Vespucci, Cabot—all had sailed for foreign kings. The late chief pilot of Spain, Solís, was Portuguese. Spanish authorities welcomed foreigners—provided they offered ability in navigation. Magellan, however, faced a somewhat more complicated situation than had Columbus and other seafarers. As a nobleman and a member of the Portuguese royal household he could not simply leave his king to serve another without incurring charges of treason. If he meant to lead a Spanish expedition to the Moluccas, he first had to free himself of his obligations to Manuel.

According to one account, Magellan obtained an audience with Manuel at which he formally asked the king's leave "to go and live with someone who would reward his services." Manuel answered that Magellan could do as he wished. Having obtained his sovereign's indifferent permission, Magellan departed his native land forever, taking with him a number of other Portuguese pilots. His colleague Faleiro planned to join him later.

Arriving in Seville, headquarters of the Spanish maritime industry, on October 20, 1517, Magellan renounced his Portuguese citizenship and prepared to embrace a new life.*

---

*In view of later developments, it seems likely that Portuguese expatriates living in Spain made the necessary arrangements for Magellan's defection. Probably these were private merchants, speculators who hoped to convince Spanish authorities to employ Magellan for a voyage to the Spice Isles.

2
THE SPANISH
ENTERPRISE

In Seville Magellan resided at the palatial home of a wealthy and influential Portuguese exile, Diogo Barbosa, who had served the Spanish crown for fourteen years and had become a figure of importance in his adopted country. Barbosa's son, Duarte, had earlier served in India with Magellan. The Barbosas probably played a large part in bringing Magellan to Spain. In any case Magellan's personal life now took a remarkable turn for the better: He fell in love with Barbosa's beautiful seventeen-year-old daughter, Beatriz.

Probably the elder Barbosa had betrothed the Portuguese navigator to his daughter, according to the custom of the day, even before Magellan left his homeland. But when Magellan met Beatriz in person, he immediately lost his heart. She readily returned his love, and in December 1517 they were married.

If Magellan found happiness in one sphere of life, however, he found only more frustration in another. Spanish maritime authorities, although impressed by the Portuguese defector, hesitated to provide the backing needed for his proposed voyage. With young King Charles still not firmly established on his throne, most officials thought it prudent to adopt a wait-and-see posture toward any new explorations.

Magellan had to bide his time. Meanwhile, Faleiro had arrived in Seville, and he flew into a rage when he learned that

Magellan, in meeting with the Spanish, had revealed hitherto secret details of their plan to seek a strait in the southern latitudes. Although Magellan soon made it up with Faleiro, it was now clear that the astrologer clearly would be an unstable element in their endeavor.

At last, in February 1518, with the new monarch gaining politically, Magellan's opportunity came. Spanish officials arranged for him and Faleiro to present their proposal to the king at Valladolid.

The seventeen-year-old Charles seemed to many a very unprepossessing figure. Of medium height, thin, pale, stooped, with an aquiline nose and bulging eyes, Charles of Spain had a protruding Hapsburg jaw so pronounced as to seem a caricature. The boy seldom spoke, and when he did, his voice lacked authority. Although those closest to him regarded him as affable, even kindly, Charles maintained a distant and grave bearing in public. This, together with his habit of silence, led some observers to think him feebleminded.

Charles's heritage seemed to support the view that he lacked the mental and physical attributes necessary for successful kingship. His Hapsburg father, Philip the Handsome, of Burgundy, had died at twenty-eight, a failure at almost everything he tried, from politics to war. His mother, Mad Juana, now lived out her life in mental darkness.

However, Charles was far from witless. He knew history, loved tales of chivalry, and had a genuine love of music. He had already proved his shrewdness as ruler of the Netherlands. With his recent inheritance of Spain and its possessions—Sardinia, Naples, and the New World—Charles reigned over one of the world's most extensive realms. Moreover, he expected to come into even greater territories upon the death of his paternal grandfather, Maximilian, the Holy Roman Emperor.*

In spite of his far-reaching possessions, Charles was money-poor. This circumstance made his realm vulnerable to attack in that age of mercenary armies when hard cash was needed to buy

---

*The Holy Roman Empire, founded A.D. 962 with the crowning of Otto I by the pope, consisted of a loose confederation of mostly German states in central and western Europe led by Austria. A patchwork of tiny principalities, ecclesiastic city-states, and duchies of various sizes and interests, the empire was powerful to the degree that its various components united on policy. The emperors were not hereditary monarchs but were chosen by seven Electors. Traditionally, however, Hapsburgs were chosen for the throne.

military power. Moreover, lack of coin was a barrier to Charles's own lofty ambitions. Although he never said so explicitly, the young Hapsburg, like his forebears, dreamed of uniting all Christendom under his rule and then leading a final, victorious crusade against the Muslim powers. He was realistic enough to understand, however, that to achieve universal Christian monarchy, he first had to make himself militarily powerful and that soldiers and cannon cost money.*

King Charles was therefore much intrigued by Magellan's proposal to claim the Moluccas for Spain, seeing in it the key to the wealth he needed to buy power. If successful, Magellan's voyage would give Spain control of the spice trade and perhaps the southern continent as well. With the spice monopoly in his hands, Charles would be one of the richest—and therefore one of the mightiest—monarchs in Europe. Impressed by Magellan and his proposition, Charles ordered a panel of his advisers to examine the plan and determine its feasibility.

Magellan and Faleiro now put their arguments to a commission of the king's ministers. The famed missionary priest Bartolomé de Las Casas was in Spain at this time to plead the cause of the natives, and he attended Magellan's presentation. Las Casas wrote:

> Magellan brought with him a well-painted globe showing the entire world, and thereon traced the course he proposed to take, save that the Strait was purposely left blank so that nobody could anticipate him. . . . I asked him what route he proposed to take, he replied that he intended to take that of Cape Santa Maria . . . and thence follow the coast south until he found the Strait. I said, "What will you do if you find no strait to pass into the other sea?" He replied that if he found none he would follow the course that the Portuguese took (around Africa via the Cape of Good Hope).

Las Casas added that though Magellan was "small of stature," he seemed "valiant in thought and for undertaking great things."

---

*Charles's ancestors, the Hapsburg rulers of Austria, had long flaunted the acrostic AEIOU, initials for the Latin motto *Austria est imperare orbi universo* ("Austria is destined to rule the world"). At the start of his long reign this sentiment clearly lay at the heart of Charles's policies. Though he denied it often enough in later life, Charles' enemies believed, with good reason, that he sought universal rule.

The ministers recommended the voyage to Charles, who decided to outfit the expedition at the crown's expense. On March 22, 1518, the king's ministers issued a complex contract for the voyage. Among other things the agreement provided that Magellan and Faleiro would each receive a 5 percent share of any long-term profits arising from their discoveries. It stipulated that each would bear the hereditary title of Governor and would wield absolute power, in the king's name, over any new nations they claimed for Spain. The king named Magellan and Faleiro captains general of the enterprise, conferring on them the power of life and death over all who sailed with them. But Charles reserved the right to appoint fiscal officers who would control the expenditures of the enterprise.

Now the Portuguese got wind of the planned expedition. King Manuel ordered his ambassador to Spain, Pedro da Costa, to stop it. Costa approached Magellan directly and suggested that King Manuel had had a change of heart and would now show his former captain much favor if he returned to the service of Portugal. The ambassador also argued that in accepting Spanish employment, Magellan was committing treason. It was one thing for a commoner, like Barbosa, to work for Spain, Costa noted, but when a nobleman like Magellan turned his coat, it was an offense against God and king. Magellan pointed out to Costa that King Manuel had rejected *him*. Now, he said, honor required him to fulfill his obligation to King Charles of Spain. Costa reported to King Manuel that he had failed to move Magellan. (He apparently did not concern himself much with Faleiro, whom he described as "half-crazy.")

Ambassador da Costa now tried to undermine Magellan's relations with his royal sponsor. He told Charles's ministers that the voyage by Magellan could have dire consequences for a contemplated royal marriage between Charles's sister Elinor and King Manuel. Nothing much came of this intrigue, however. Charles wrote to Manuel, blandly reassuring him that the intended voyage would not interfere with Portuguese rights and so should not disrupt the royal marriage.

On July 20, 1518, Charles ordered the Casa de Contratación (the Spanish board of trade) to prepare an armada as directed by Magellan and Faleiro. To emphasize his deep personal commitment to the enterprise, Charles made both Magellan and Faleiro knight commanders of the Order of Santiago, a signal honor.

At the end of July 1518 Magellan and Faleiro departed for Seville to undertake the fitting out of their fleet. Magellan stood on the brink of realizing his dream. To cap his happiness, his young wife, Beatriz, was pregnant. Magellan's fortunes were now flourishing beyond anything he could have imagined during the dark days of the previous year in Oporto.

Now the detailed labor of fitting out got under way in Seville. Spanish officials had purchased five ships for the voyage: *Trinidad*, the flagship of 110 tons; *San Antonio*, 120 tons; *Concepción*, 90 tons; *Victoria*, 85 tons; and *Santiago*, only 75 tons. The ships needed much work to make them seaworthy. As Sebastián Álvarez, a Portuguese agent in Seville, reported in a letter to King Manuel: "They are very old and patched . . . their ribs are as soft as butter."

As the expedition slowly progressed in Seville, young King Charles faced an unexpected political crisis that was to have far-reaching consequences for decades to come. It began in January 1519, when Charles's grandfather, the Holy Roman Emperor Maximilian, died. Instead of succeeding smoothly to the emperor's throne, Charles discovered that he had rivals. Both Francis I of France and Henry VIII of England announced that they were candidates for the imperial crown. Though Henry, as monarch of a relatively weak island nation, had little chance to win election, Francis—young, handsome, vigorous, and king of a resurgent France—was a serious opponent. Francis also had strong motivation for trying to block Charles. He saw that if Charles gained the imperial throne, the Hapsburg would control a vast domain, one that would virtually surround France.

For Charles the imperial power was essential if he was to carry out his aims. He concluded that there was only one way to assure himself the emperor's crown: He would bribe the imperial electors with sums that his rivals could not match. He set about borrowing vast amounts from the German banking house of the Fuggers, mortgaging his domains to do so. For six months prior to the imperial election Charles distributed this money where it would do the most good.

The strategy paid off on June 28, 1519, when Charles won election as emperor. It had cost him some 850,000 florins in bribes to make himself, at nineteen, the titular head of all central and western Europe except France, England, Portugal, and the

Papal States. Though he had gained his political end, the unhappy fact was that he had put himself deeply in debt at the very outset of his reign. From now on Emperor Charles V would require regular, large infusions of money just to service his debts. In addition, he now had an implacable enemy in Francis of France, and he desperately needed to increase his revenues to pay for mercenary troops to defend his lands. The hoped-for annexation of the Moluccas now took on even greater importance.*

In Seville the expedition was nearing readiness. To reach this point, Magellan had had to contend with a series of obstacles that might have daunted a lesser man. At one point, as shipwrights toiled on the armada, a mob, probably incited by Portuguese agents, had threatened Magellan for "insulting" Spain by flying personal banners of Portuguese origin on his flagship. The lack of money to pay for workmen and supplies had also caused long delays. Spanish pride and suspicion had hampered Magellan, as well. On one occasion the king, succumbing to pressure from Spanish officials, forbade Magellan to enlist more than five Portuguese in any of his crews. The king had relented only when Magellan pointed out that he already had trouble securing sailors for so difficult a journey, and that strictures on nationality might make the task impossible. Another problem had been the constant friction between Magellan and the Spanish officers who had been assigned, over his head, to most of the important posts in the fleet.

Despite all these handicaps, however, Magellan, trusting in Charles's continuing support, had pressed on with the project. He had also rejoiced with Beatriz at the birth of their son, Rodrigo, in March 1519.

By the summer of 1519 the day of departure was approaching, and now Portugal's agent in Seville, Sebastián Álvarez, made a last-ditch effort to persuade Magellan to abandon the Spanish enterprise. Álvarez warned that the fleet's Spanish officers had formed a cabal against Magellan and planned to take over the expedition when they found the opportune moment.

---

*Hard pressed financially, Charles now encouraged private investment in Magellan's project. This was the policy he was to follow from now on.

Magellan rebuffed Álvarez, saying he had no reason to desert King Charles, who had shown him much favor.* Álvarez then tried his wiles on Magellan's colleague Faleiro and had better luck, promoting a quarrel between Faleiro and Magellan, the exact nature of which remains unknown. In any event the King dismissed Faleiro from the fleet in late July 1519, ordering that the astrologer remain behind to organize a second armada to the Moluccas. This was only an excuse for ridding the project of the troublesome Faleiro, who soon afterward returned to Portugal and obscurity.

With Faleiro's removal Magellan was sole commander of the fleet in name as well as in fact. Many of his Spanish subordinates, however, insisted on regarding one of their number—Juan de Cartagena, captain of the *San Antonio*—as Magellan's co-commander, a circumstance the Portuguese captain general resolutely ignored.

By the end of August 1519 the expedition was ready. Some 260 men constituted the fleet's complement. Most of them were Spanish, but 37 Portuguese sailors and navigators made up the second-largest contingent. Magellan had also signed aboard a number of Asians whom he hoped to use as interpreters when the ships reached the Spice Islands. One of these was his personal servant, the twenty-six-year-old Malayan Enrique. A variety of other nationals, including Dutchmen, Irishmen, Africans, and at least one Englishman (Master Andrew of Bristol, a gunner) filled out Magellan's crews. A number of priests also accompanied the ships to serve as chaplains and convert any heathen encountered.

In accordance with the custom of the day, Magellan received a royal standard at a solemn mass. He swore allegiance to King Charles. The officers of the fleet, including any conspirators among them, took an oath of fealty to Magellan. The ships then dropped down the Guadalquivir River to the port of Sanlúcar de

---

*Subsequent events indicate that a serious plot against Magellan did exist. Although time has obscured the details of the conspiracy, it seems likely that the plotters (Spanish officers of the fleet) planned to allow Magellan to organize the voyage and to find the passage to the South Sea. They would then seize control of the venture and take it to the Spice Islands. In this way, the conspirators may have reasoned, Spain could take advantage of Magellan's navigation skills and of the secret knowledge he had gleaned from Portuguese charts, while ensuring that only loyal Spaniards would live to claim the Spice Islands. No evidence exists that King Charles knew of the plot, and if Magellan knew of it, he kept his own counsel.

Barrameda, where they took on last-minute stores. Here Magellan wrote his will, making provisions for his wife (who was again pregnant) and son, as well as other members of his family. He also provided for the freedom of his slave, Enrique.

On September 20, 1519, the armada headed for the open sea.

3

PASSAGE TO GLORY

One of those who embarked with Magellan, a thirty-year-old Italian nobleman named Antonio Pigafetta, kept a journal of the expedition.* Pigafetta, who describes himself as "a Patrician of Venice," came to Spain with the court of the papal nuncio in 1519. He tells how "desirous of seeing the wonderful things of the ocean" and "to gain some renown for later posterity," he wangled a place in Magellan's armada through the favor of the new Emperor Charles. In his narrative Pigafetta reports that from the outset he detected ill will toward Magellan: "The captains of the other ships did not love him. Of this I know not the reason, except by cause of his being Portuguese, while they were Spaniards or Castilians."

Pigafetta says that after completing the first stage of the voyage, to the Canary Islands, Magellan chose an unorthodox course. Instead of following the trade winds southwest across the

---

*Three other supposedly firsthand accounts of the voyage exist. One, by an anonymous Portuguese participant in the voyage, is no more than a brief sketch. A second is the logbook of the *Trinidad*'s pilot, Albo, and contains little more than nautical observations. The third, called the "Genoese Pilot's Account," contains more detail but is suspect because no Genoese pilot actually accompanied the fleet and the manuscript itself seems too polished for the work of a seaman. In any case, Pigafetta's lively and colorful journal not only sets forth a generally reliable chronology of the events of the journey but also provides marvelous descriptions of the wonder, adventure, and suffering that Magellan's men experienced.

Atlantic, he continued down the African coast almost to the equator and then struck out across the ocean. In this way, apparently, he hoped to evade Portuguese warships supposedly waiting to intercept him in the Atlantic north of the line. By taking this eccentric route, however, Magellan's ships had to fight through the doldrums—an area off Africa notorious for its dead air. The crossing from Africa became a nightmare. The ships drifted through maddening lulls that were broken only by drenching gales. Pigafetta describes what this part of the journey was like: "As we could not advance (because of squalls), and in order that the ships might not be wrecked, all the sails were struck; and in this manner did we wander hither and yon on the sea, waiting for the tempest to cease, for it was very furious. When it rained there was no wind. When the sun shone, it was calm."

At one point, Juan de Cartagena, the captain of the *San Antonio*, regarded by many of the Spaniards as Magellan's equal, openly challenged Magellan's authority at a conference of captains aboard the flagship, *Trinidad*. Cartagena, who had already questioned the captain general's orders on several occasions, now sneered that it was Magellan's poor navigation that had led the fleet into the belt of equatorial calms and that he no longer deserved obedience. Magellan suddenly threw himself on the startled Cartagena and wrestled him down. Pinned to the deck, Cartagena called for his fellow Spanish captains, Luis de Mendoza and Gaspar de Quesada, to attack Magellan "according to plan." But they sat still. Magellan then had a brace of loyal sailors hustle Cartagena below, where he was clapped into stocks. Antonio de Coca, another Spaniard, was named to replace Cartagena as captain of the *San Antonio*. A semblance of peace was reestablished among the officers.*

Eventually the ships arrived at the bay of Rio de Janeiro on the coast of Brazil on December 13, 1519. Although this was Portuguese territory, the empire builders of King Manuel had not yet turned Rio into a colony, and a Spanish fleet could still put into the bay without fear.

Magellan gave his men two weeks of rest in this lovely place. Friendly natives appeared. The men traded trinkets, mirrors, nails, and fishhooks for game and fresh fish. Native women frat-

---

*At some point later in the voyage Cartagena was freed and allowed to return to his ship, though not officially restored to his command.

ernized freely with the mariners, engaging in nightly revels ashore.

Pigafetta says that the natives valued the iron nails of the Europeans more than gold, and he backs up this assertion by telling how a beautiful girl stole one of these nails from the master's cabin of the *Trinidad*: "Picking it up with great skill and gallantry, she thrust it between the lips of her vagina and, bending low, departed, the Captain General and I having witnessed this."

On December 26, 1519, aware that the Southern Hemisphere's long, warm days of December and January would soon grow shorter and cooler, Magellan gave orders to begin the search for a strait that the armada could follow to the South Sea. For the next three weeks the fleet made its way southward along the coast, covering more than a thousand miles, and investigating a number of promising inlets. All proved dead ends. One of them was the uncommonly great river today called the Rio de la Plata. Magellan named it the Río de Solís after the explorer murdered on its banks four years earlier.*

The ships went on, past a wild coast of grassy brown hills, whipped by dust-laden cold winds. February wore into March. The days grew shorter, and storms more frequent. The temperature fell. The armada had now almost reached latitude 50 degrees south, and still there was no sign of a strait.

On March 31, 1520, as the southern winter closed in, the ships came to a sheltered harbor that Magellan named Port San Julián. Reluctantly concluding that he had no choice but to suspend the southward search for the winter, Magellan ordered the fleet to anchor. In this bleak place the expedition would lay over for the cold months.

On the very day of the armada's arrival at Port San Julián, delegations from all five ships came to Magellan and implored him to return to Spain. The king, they said, had not ordered them to suffer and die in pursuit of a strait that did not exist.

Magellan replied that he would rather perish than give up the search for the strait. He pointed out that Port San Julián offered plenty of fish, and the fleet still had enough bread and

---

*It was Sebastian Cabot who named it the Rio de la Plata a decade later because of the silver worn by the natives. The river measures 138 miles across at its mouth where it separates modern Uruguay and Argentina.

wine from Spain to meet its needs. He would not dishonor himself, or them, by turning back from the quest. He made it clear that there was no alternative to his orders. The fleet must spend the cold months in this strange, sterile land, where gray skies lowered and the wind blew sharp as a knife's edge. But the time would pass. Once through the strait, which they would certainly find with the return of good weather, he promised to lead them to paradisical lands—and to girls even kinder and more beautiful than those of Rio. Finally Magellan exhorted his Spaniards to exhibit the famed valor of Castilians. His listeners, shamed into silence, returned to their duty. But now the conspirators among the officers decided the time had come to challenge Magellan's control of the fleet.

Magellan soon perceived signs that unrest still persisted. The first indication came on the day following the arrival of the fleet at Port San Julián and only twenty-four hours after Magellan had refused his crews' request to return to Spain. It was Palm Sunday, April 1, 1520, and Magellan had invited his captains to share a meal aboard the flagship after hearing mass ashore. But two of his captains, Mendoza of the *Victoria* and Quesada of the *Concepción*, refused to attend.

That night, after first making sure of their control of the *Victoria* and *Concepción*, where anti-Magellan partisans already constituted the a majority, the rebels struck. Boarding the *San Antonio*, largest ship, a party of mutineers took control of the vessel, wounding some of her crew in a brief skirmish. Magellan loyalists aboard were imprisoned below. The *Concepción*'s captain, Quesada then took command of the *San Antonio*. By morning the mutineers had possession of three of the five ships in the armada and outgunned Magellan by a wide margin.*

In spite of the precarious situation, Magellan betrayed no concern. Instead he made sure that the men of his own ship, *Trinidad,* and of the little *Santiago* were still loyal. Having satisfied

---

*For some reason Juan de Cartagena, though once commander of the big *San Antonio,* did not resume his command. Instead he replaced Quesada as captain of the *Concepción.* Probably there was a considerable amount of confusion and self-interest among the conspirators. They also virtually ignored the little *Santiago* captained by João Serrão, a Portuguese, and brother of Magellan's dear kinsman Francisco Serrão and thus a man that Magellan could trust. The conspirators may have felt confident that the little *Santiago* could not affect the outcome of the rebellion. Oddly, Pigafetta hardly mentions the mutiny in his narrative. The details come from later reports.

himself on this score, Magellan accepted a letter from the leaders of the mutiny. Sent by a ship's longboat, the message informed Magellan that while the rebels would no longer recognize him as captain general, they would allow him to remain as senior captain if he agreed to pilot them back to Spain. They then tried to justify the mutiny by claiming that Magellan had exceeded his authority by leading them farther south than envisioned in the king's orders.

Magellan reacted by seizing the messenger boat from the rebels. He then sent his reply to the mutineers. He called on them to present their grievances personally aboard the flagship. They declined.

Magellan reluctantly decided he had no choice but to suppress the rebellion by force. He did not think it possible to continue the voyage with the *Trinidad* and *Santiago* alone, and to return to Seville, having failed to locate the strait, was unthinkable. First he dressed fifteen of his loyal sailors in the clothing of the mutineers seized earlier with their longboat. Manning the captured longboat with these tough crewmen, he waited for nightfall.

Under a bright, nearly full moon, Magellan now sent one of his bravest officers, the fleet quartermaster constable Gonzalo Gómez de Espinosa, in his own gig to the *Victoria*, where he reckoned he still had supporters among the crew. Espinosa carried a specific order from Magellan directing the mutinous officers of the *Victoria* to surrender and report to him aboard the flagship. Clemency was offered to *Victoria*'s crewmen if they would abandon the mutiny.

As Espinosa approached the *Victoria* to present Magellan's directive, the longboat taken earlier from the rebels, now filled with Magellan's loyal sailors, drifted after him, unnoticed despite the moonlight. The *Victoria*'s mutinous Captain Mendoza gave Espinosa permission to come aboard to parley. By the wan light of the *Victoria*'s lanterns, the quartermaster and a single aide climbed to the ship's deck. The longboat full of Magellan's sailors moved closer.

Without ceremony the quartermaster handed Magellan's written order to Mendoza. The rebellious captain, with his officers and crew looking on, read Magellan's missive with a contemptuous smile. He refused to obey, whereupon the courageous quartermaster carried out his part in Magellan's plan. He threw himself on Captain Mendoza and in one stroke cut the rebel's throat. At this Magellan's masquerading sailors in the longboat poured over the side of the *Victoria*, weapons at the ready and screaming threats. The mutineers on the *Victoria*, stunned by the swift death of one of their leaders and suddenly surrounded by armed men, threw down their weapons.

Quartermaster Espinosa signaled his success to the flagship. Now the *Trinidad*, ghostly in the moonlight, floated over to the recaptured *Victoria*, cannon prepared to fire in case of treachery. Assured, Magellan boarded the *Victoria*. He appointed his old companion Duarte Barbosa her new captain. He then had Mendoza's corpse "hung up by the feet, that they might see him from the other ships."

With the retaking of the *Victoria*, Magellan had three ships, and the rebels only two: *San Antonio* and *Concepción*. Magellan also outgunned his adversaries, a fact not lost on the remaining mutineers, who could see Mendoza's corpse hanging above the stern lanterns of the *Victoria*.

With his three ships, Magellan took up a position at the harbor's mouth, blocking any escape from Port San Julián. The rebels had only two choices: They could capitulate or they could try to fight their way past Magellan's guns.

Several hours passed. The ships lay motionless on the moonlit water of the bay. The mutineers seemed uncertain of their course. Magellan waited, artillery primed.

Shortly after midnight lookouts on Magellan's ships spotted the *San Antonio*, commanded by Gaspar de Quesada, apparently under way. In fact, she was adrift because secret adherents of Magellan in her crew had cut her cables. But aboard Magellan's loyal ships, it looked as if the *San Antonio* might be attempting to slip away to the open sea. The *Trinidad*'s gunners fired across her bow and into her rigging. Longboats from both the *Trinidad* and the *Victoria* made for the vessel. Magellan loyalists boarded her. Her mutinous captain tried to rally resistance, but few crewmen sided with him. Quesada surrendered.

The last rebel leader, Cartagena, realized the game was up. He signaled that his ship, the *Concepción*, would surrender. Magellan had suppressed the mutiny—and with little bloodshed.*

*Details of the mutiny vary, depending on the account. For example, some identify the *Concepción* as the vessel "escaping" from the bay. But all agree on the general succession of events and on the fact that Magellan suppressed the mutiny with little loss of life.

With the restoration of his authority Magellan made an example of the mutiny's leaders. He ordered Mendoza's body brought ashore and drawn and quartered. The pieces of the body were then spiked on poles. Magellan executed Quesada by having that captain's own valet strike off his head. He also had Quesada's body drawn, quartered, and exhibited on a gibbet. The captain general sentenced Cartagena as well as a priest who had incited mutiny to be left behind when the fleet sailed from Port San Julián.

Magellan also condemned forty others to death as traitors. He commuted their sentences, however, merely assigning them the hardest labor while the fleet remained in Port San Julián. He spared the common sailors who had taken part in the mutiny, reasoning that bad counsel had led them astray. However, he required that they take a new oath of loyalty to him. With the insurrection quelled, Magellan and his crews settled down to get through the winter as best they could.

Magellan now put the men to work fishing, hunting, building shelters ashore, and careening the ships. The process of careening called for emptying the vessels and pulling them over on their sides to clean and repair the hulls and to treat the bottoms with pitch to ward off the wood-boring teredo worm. While this task was going on, Magellan's clerks inventoried the offloaded supplies. To their horror, they discovered that the ship chandlers of Seville, using a variety of swindles (and perhaps bribed by Portuguese agents), had furnished far less in the way of provisions than required for the journey. As a result, the expedition would have to ration biscuit, salt meat, wine, and other stores even more stringently than anticipated and would have to augment supplies with game and fish to a greater extent than Magellan had expected. Nevertheless, he remained confident that stores would suffice for the voyage.

As the southern winter hardened into a frigid windswept May at Port San Julián, Magellan decided to send his smallest ship, the *Santiago*, under the loyal Captain Serrão, on a twofold mission to the south: to obtain new stocks of fish and other game (primarily seals), and to make a last-minute search for the strait that Magellan believed could not lie very much farther down the coast. If the *Santiago* found the strait, the fleet might try a winter passage. In any case, discovery of the strait would certainly elevate the morale of the crews. The *Santiago* set out, despite the rough winter seas.

The effort miscarried when the ship was wrecked in a raging South Atlantic storm. Thirty-seven survivors had to camp ashore, with few supplies, in the bitter winter weather. Total disaster was averted, however, when two crew members struggled back to Magellan with word of their shipmates' peril. The captain general sent a relief party that eventually rescued the shipwrecked crew.

During these frigid weeks at Port San Julián the barren countryside produced an astonishing event. Pigafetta reports it: "One day, we suddenly saw a naked man of giant stature on the shore of the harbor, dancing, singing, and throwing dust on his head." The captain general, according to Pigafetta, received this amazing figure with friendly gestures and presents. Soon afterwards more natives, including women, appeared.

Although Pigafetta exaggerates their height, claiming they stood eight feet tall, he found these native people fascinating. He says they used only a single llama skin for clothing, despite the bitter weather. They also wore heavy wrappings of this skin around their feet and ankles, causing Magellan to dub them Patagonians, meaning "big feet." Pigafetta tells how the natives could push arrows halfway down their throats. He says they also relished unskinned rats as food.

At first, according to Pigafetta, the men of the fleet enjoyed generally friendly relations with these strange Patagonians. But matters deteriorated when Magellan agreed to take some of them captive in order to transport them back to Spain as curiosities. (This action says much about the contemporary European attitude toward native peoples. Most Europeans, including Magellan, seem to have regarded natives as somewhat less than human.)

Magellan's crewmen captured two male Patagonians by inducing the "giants" to try on iron leg manacles, which the Patagonians mistook for ornaments. Some of Magellan's men then made their way to a nearby native camp to seize some Patagonian women as well. As the Europeans started to drag away a pair of females, Patagonian warriors ran to the rescue. Attacking the would-be abductors with poisoned arrows, the Patagonians killed one of the men. The others fled, and the Patagonians rescued their women. (The two male Patagonians, however, remained prisoners. Both died on the subsequent journey.) After these incidents the Patagonians exhibited an understandable hostility whenever they encountered the Europeans.

It was now a wintry August, but Magellan decided to move farther south to a river (later called the Río Santa Cruz) that the lost *Santiago* had discovered and that abounded with shad. When the ships weighed anchor, the mutineer Juan de Cartagena was left behind, as was the seditious priest Pedro Sánchez de Reina. Ignoring the priest's plea for mercy, Magellan provided the marooned pair with guns, powder, wine, and bread and then sailed away.*

Anchored safely at the Río Santa Cruz, Magellan rejected another request by his men that he abandon the search for a westward strait and instead sail eastward to the Spice Isles via the Cape of Good Hope and the Indian Ocean. On October 20, 1520, with the weather moderating, the fleet, now reduced to four vessels, resumed its search southward.

Only three days after leaving the Río Santa Cruz the ships rounded a cape that Magellan named Cape of the Eleven Thousand Virgins. Ahead lay a waterway that seemed to lead to the west through a maze of mountains, cliffs, inlets, and rocky islets.

Magellan, sensing that he had found his passage at last, ordered two ships, the *Concepción*, now commanded by the faithful Serrão, and the *San Antonio*, commanded by another of his kinsmen, Alonso de Mesquita, to explore ahead, while the *Trinidad* and *Victoria* waited at the entrance for their report.

Nervous days passed before the ships returned, firing their cannon in jubilation and reporting that they had seen no end to the waterway ahead. Says Pigafetta: "Thanking God and the Virgin Mary we went to seek the strait further on."

The ships began to feel their way through the contorted passage. An eerie, seemingly empty, inhospitable land rose on both sides as the vessels inched forward. Snowcapped mountains towered over them. The strangeness increased when the men of the fleet sighted many nocturnal fires, apparently lit by unseen natives, on the shores of the rugged land that stretched away to the south.†

---

*The fate of the marooned men remains unknown. Given the hostility of the environment and the Patagonians, however, they had little chance of survival.
†Pigafetta does not report these fires. The first mention of them appears in an account of Magellan's voyage by Maximilian of Transylvania, Charles V's secretary, published several years later. The mysterious fires led to the naming of this region Tierra del Fuego (land of fire). Magellan did not stop to investigate them.

At some point in this phase of the passage Magellan called a council of captains and pilots. Making it clear that he himself had no doubts, he asked for opinions about going on with the voyage. All now expressed support for continuing, except Esteban Gómez, the pilot of the *San Antonio*, who urged that they return to Spain, report success, and equip a new fleet to follow up their pathfinding effort. Although this was a reasonable suggestion, Magellan rejected it, saying, according to Pigafetta: "If they had to eat the leather on the ship's yards, he would still go on, and discover what he had promised to the Emperor, and he trusted that God would aid them and give them good fortune."

When the ships arrived at a place where the strait seemed to diverge into similar channels, Magellan divided his fleet. The *Trinidad* and the *Victoria*, under his command, followed one channel, while the *San Antonio* and the *Concepción* tried another. After some time in his rocky channel, Magellan sent a ship's boat ahead to explore. Three days later it returned with a joyful report: The open sea lay ahead, beyond a cape. Pigafetta says Magellan wept at the news and "called that cape Cape Desired, for we had been desiring it for a long time."

Magellan put back to find the *Concepción* and the *San Antonio* and give them the good news. He soon encountered the *Concepción*, but the *San Antonio* had disappeared. Fearing the ship had been wrecked, Magellan searched back along the length of the strait—in vain.*

Eventually surmising that the *San Antonio* had deserted with her stores, Magellan commanded the officers of his three remaining ships to give him written opinions about continuing the voyage. He probably did this only because he wanted to avoid any charge that he tended to ignore the counsel of his subordinates. Even as he sought the opinions of his officers, however, he made it clear that he personally had no intention of giving up the struggle.

---

*The *San Antonio* had deserted the rest of the fleet. Her pilot, Gómez, who had earlier urged that the fleet return to Spain, had seized the ship from her loyal captain, Mesquita. Somehow persuading the crew to desert their comrades, pilot Gómez had turned the *San Antonio* for home, taking with her much of the fleet's precious supplies. The deserter Gómez apparently made no attempt to rescue Cartagena and the priest marooned at the Río Santa Cruz but beat for home as rapidly as possible. Reaching Seville after a passage of six months, Gomez spread calumnies about Magellan's "cruelty" and conduct of the fleet. Although the Spanish officials only half believed the lies Gómez told, Magellan's reputation suffered.

The fleet continued on, and at last, on November 28, 1520, after thirty-eight days in the 360-mile-long waterway, the ships emerged onto the vast, gleaming waters of the South Sea. Fourteen months had elapsed since the armada had set out from Spain.

Having reached the open sea, the ships fired a joyful salute. The crews chanted a Te Deum. Magellan gathered his officers together on the quarterdeck of the *Trinidad* and, according to Pigafetta, addressed them: "Gentlemen, we now are steering into waters where no ship has sailed before. May we always find them as peaceful as they are this morning. In this hope I shall name this sea the Mar Pacifica."

4

MAR PACIFICA

Free of the maze of the strait, and having named for all time the Pacific Ocean, Magellan found himself bucking westerly head winds. He thus became the first to discover what all later mariners would learn: No sailing ship could strike directly west into the Pacific after leaving the strait because of the blasts that blew out of the "roaring forties" latitudes.

Accordingly Magellan turned his bows north along the west coast of South America until approximately mid-December. Then, at about latitude 35 degrees south, the ships, picking up favorable winds, struck out into the ocean. Bearing west by northwest toward the equator, Magellan hoped to reach the Spice Islands in four or five weeks. Given this timetable, he believed that the fleet's provisions, though uncomfortably scanty because of the *San Antonio*'s defection and the peculations of the Seville ship chandlers, would still prove sufficient. (Of course, the Spice Islands lay almost eight thousand miles across an ocean vast beyond the experience of any European mariner of the time.)

Bravely Magellan's ships plowed into the empty sea.*

---

*Under the best of circumstances it was hard to predict the length of voyages. Columbus on his fourth expedition took twenty-one days to cover the three thousand miles from Grand Canary to Martinique, but he had excellent weather. The trip from Lisbon to Goa, crossing well-charted seas and utilizing favorable winds, averaged seven months. This unpredictability also made it difficult to gauge supplies needed on a voyage. Shortages of food and water were common in the age of sail.

51

December wore away. The new year of 1521 dawned. Day after day the sun blazed down from an empty blue sky. No storms disturbed the placid passage. It was truly a pacific ocean. The sea rolled, and the men of the armada saw not even a glimpse of land. Wind and a powerful sea current carried the ships deeper into what began to seem an endless expanse of water.

As January wore away, fear crept into some hearts. The empty days passed in a blur of sun, heat, and sky. Strange stars glittered in the night. Unanswerable questions began to haunt the men. How far had they come? Would they ever see land again? It seemed no wonder that no traveler had yet discovered the southern continent in this immense, infernal Pacific

Rations dwindled. In the heat the short supply of meat started to rot. The water began to go foul, turning the color of urine. The men ate the meat anyway and drank the water, holding their noses against its stench. The water was not the only thing that stank. The ships leaked, and the bilges, fouled with excrement, sloshed constantly, making the air belowdecks unbreathable. Rats swarmed. Lice bore into skin.

Because the ships provided no specific living quarters for the men, seamen sprawled everywhere. They ate ship biscuit that crumbled to powder at a touch and crawled with worms, which they swallowed. The foul water thickened to a soupy consistency, and they forced themselves to drink it. The men prayed for rain to relieve the agony of thirst. But day after day the skies remained empty.

On January 24, 1521—fifty-seven days after they had emerged from the strait—lookouts sighted an uninhabited desert atoll, probably Pukapuka, one of the Tuamotu group. Although there was no anchorage, the ravenous crewmen rowed ashore in boats. On the island they found and devoured numerous nesting seabirds. But they found no water, and Magellan had to resume the voyage.

On February 4 the fleet sighted another uninhabited, waterless island, probably Caroline Island. Again they could not anchor because of lack of holding ground. But the men caught and ate many sharks. Once more the need for water forced the armada to sail on.

The ships now lay some four thousand miles out in the vast Central Pacific. Their crews had not had sufficient fresh food and water for more than two months. Now the last supplies ran out. Famished sailors trapped shipboard rats and wolfed them down. Some made a business of catching rats and selling them to their fellows. Occasionally a man would manage to hook a fish, but the sea yielded far less than they needed. Scurvy began to torture the seamen.

The ships crossed the equator on February 13, 1521, and sailed on, still tending west and north.*

Magellan's crews consumed all the rats on their ships. All the wormy biscuit had long gone. The men turned to eating sawdust and even the leather straps and sail covers used in the rigging. The starving sailors first soaked the leather pieces in the sea for days, hoping to soften them. Then they broiled them on embers for a day or more.

Men began to die of the scurvy that had racked them for weeks. Says Pigafetta: "The worst misfortune was that the gums of our men grew so much that they could not eat, and many died." By a quirk only a few officers had come down with scurvy, probably because the officers' rations had included raisins and carrot preserves, containing small amounts of vitamin C. Although eaten by now, these rations had provided the officers sufficient amounts of the vitamin to stave off, for a while, the scurvy that now killed nineteen crewmen in rapid succession.

Still heading west and north, the ships crossed another twenty-four hundred miles of open Pacific. The men prayed for the mercy of rain. Then, on March 6, 1521, ninety-eight days from the strait, a group of luxuriantly green islands appeared on the horizon. Lookouts spied canoes on the beaches. Magellan's men rejoiced. At last they had found an inhabited land. Where men lived they would find water and food.

The suffering mariners wept. Magellan led a prayer of thanksgiving. Now numerous outrigger canoes, manned by well-muscled naked men, flocked from the beaches.

Chattering in their own tongue, the natives boldly climbed

*Why did Magellan continue to climb north of the equator when he knew that the Moluccas lay virtually under the line? Perhaps he chose this course because he hoped to find other islands to the north where he might rest his men, repair his ships, and make ready for the final approach to the Moluccas. Despite Serrão's assurances, he had no way of anticipating what he might find in the Moluccas—a Portuguese fleet, hostile natives, armed Muslim merchant ships—so he may have wanted to avoid arriving in the Spice Isles in a weakened condition. It has also been suggested that he meant to reach and claim the Philippines, having learned of their existence and general location during his previous service in Malaya with Albuquerque. Whatever his reasons, he held to his course with remarkable persistence in the face of horrendous conditions.

aboard Magellan's flagship, the *Trinidad.* Swarms of others, all armed with spears and bows, boarded the *Victoria* and *Concepción.* With avid curiosity, the fearless visitors went through the ships, exclaiming over this or that piece of equipment, fingering metal utensils and instruments, and crying out in wonderment.

The islanders also pilfered anything that struck their fancy, from nails to spoons. When Magellan's men, already mentally and physically enfeebled by weeks of deprivation, tried to stop the larceny, the natives appeared to turn surly. Magellan's men then became exasperated. It was as if these light-fingered primitives suddenly embodied all the anguish of the past months. All at once petty theft seemed an affront not to be borne. The anger of Magellan's men escalated to rage, and some of them fired their arquebuses. Several native warriors fell dead. Others were wounded. Terrified, the islanders fled the ships, making off with the *Trinidad*'s skiff, a valuable tool for operations in shallow water.

The next day Magellan went ashore with a party of armed men. He was intent not only on recovering the purloined boat but also on obtaining supplies from the local inhabitants. But as the ship's party came ashore, the people of the place fled in fear, to the renewed fury of the Europeans.

Hungry and sick, with nerves rubbed raw by suffering, Magellan and his men ran into a nearby village. They set huts on fire and discharged their guns at any villager they saw. Seven more native people died in this attack. The stunned survivors begged for mercy. They returned the skiff to placate these horrifying strangers. The islanders also proffered ample supplies of fresh meat, vegetables, and water.

After partaking of this forced hospitality, the fleet lingered only another day, and set sail again on March 9, 1521. Magellan named these islands the Ladrones ("islands of thieves"). In fact, they were probably Guam and Rota, part of the southern Marianas group, lying about seventeen hundred miles northeast of the Spice Islands.

Now Magellan changed course. Instead of continuing to the west and north, he turned west by *south.** According to Pigafetta,

---

*Again it has been suggested that Magellan changed course at this time with the secret intention of reaching the Philippines. It is more likely that he was merely looking for any nearby decent haven in which to refresh and refit further before going on to the Spice Isles.

Magellan was now sure that the fleet had endured the worst of the journey.

On March 15, 1521, less than a week after leaving the land of the thieves, Magellan's three ships reached the island of Samar in the archipelago that a later voyager would name the Philippines. Magellan called them the Isles of Lazarus because it was here that his men would "rise from the dead." The Spiceries— the object of the voyage—now lay less than a thousand miles to the south.

On Samar Magellan's crews rested. Quickly they regained their health, thanks to fresh food supplied by friendly, but wary, natives. On March 28 the ships moved farther into the archipelago, anchoring off the smaller island of Limasawa. Here Magellan discovered that his Malayan servant, Enrique, could make himself understood in the local language. From this point on relations with the people of the region advanced rapidly.

The inhabitants of these islands possessed a considerable veneer of civilization. One nearby chieftain, who called himself Rajah Colambu, not only welcomed the newcomers personally but also presented them with gifts of fish and porcelain containers of rice. In exchange Magellan gave this native prince Turkish cloth "and a fine red cap." He presented the rajah's servants and soldiers with "knives and mirrors." Magellan also offered assurances that he had come for trade, not war.

To impress his hosts, however, he ordered his gunners to fire some of the fleet's cannon. The huge noise first amazed and then delighted the islanders. Magellan also demonstrated the defensive superiority of armor by having some of his men engage in swordplay. He claimed that each European could easily overcome a hundred native warriors in a fight.

At some point during these days of initial contact, Colambu's brother, the ruler of another island, came to Limasawa to see for himself these new arrivals. While dining aboard Magellan's ship, this monarch greatly intrigued the Europeans by boasting of the gold he owned. Proudly he displayed both his weapons and his teeth, all shiny with golden inlays.

For approximately a week more Magellan and his men traded, rested, feasted, and baptized the people of Limasawa as word spread of their presence in the islands. In early April, with the health of his crews restored, Magellan, guided by Rajah Colambu himself, sailed on to the large island of Cebu, centrally located in the archipelago and one of its major powers. Here the Europeans encountered a sophisticated ruler who was accustomed to trading with ships from the Asian mainland and beyond. Magellan sent Enrique, with a delegation, to this sovereign, Rajah Humabon, to express the peaceful intentions of his fleet. The rajah, however, demanded that the Europeans pay tribute for the privilege of trading in his domain. Enrique explained that Magellan had come to Cebu on behalf of the king of Spain, the world's most powerful monarch, who paid tribute to no other ruler on earth. A Muslim trader present at this meeting confirmed the claim about the might of King Charles. The prudent Rajah Humabon, a fat little man with a shrewd mind, thereupon withdrew his demand for payment and offered his hospitality. He also asked that Magellan send him a drop of blood from his right arm as a sign of friendship, and said he would do the same.*

When Rajah Humabon and Magellan met, they pledged "perpetual peace." Soon after, the rajah and many of his subjects accepted baptism. Humabon marked this holy event with a gala that featured dancing girls who plied their art naked, much to the delight of the Europeans.

The men of Magellan's expedition now set up a market ashore in order to trade their goods for native gold, which the inhabitants of Cebu seemed to possess in abundance. Magellan's sailors soon began to accumulate considerable wealth. Magellan also concluded a treaty with Rajah Humabon giving the Spanish exclusive trading rights in Cebu.

During this period some of Magellan's officers complained that the captain general seemed obsessed with converting the islanders to Christianity, devoting so much time to this effort that he had forgotten his real mission to reach the Spice Islands. They urged him to weigh anchor for the Moluccas. But Magellan ignored their advice and pressed on with his Christianizing of the natives.

Possibly Magellan sought the conversion of the islanders as a means of gaining political control over them. But in light of Magellan's character, it is more likely that he felt a sincere compulsion to bring Christ to the heathen. Perhaps his epic voyage

---

*The blood brotherhood ceremony carried much significance in these islands. Magellan had earlier performed such a ritual on Limasawa with Rajah Colambu.

across the Pacific had awakened in him an awe of the Creator of the vast world and had turned his faith into a force that now led him to seek spiritual as well as worldly glory.

Whatever the case, after the baptism of Rajah Humabon Magellan sought to convert that ruler's subordinate chiefs as well. He proclaimed Humabon, baptized Rajah Charles, the overlord of a new Christian realm in the islands. He demanded that all subchiefs also submit to Christ, pay tribute to Spain, and abandon their ancient idols. Most of the region's rulers complied. But a chief of the little island of Mactan off the coast of Cebu defied Magellan by refusing to renounce his gods.

Magellan sent a detachment of his men to burn the main village on Mactan. He again ordered the ruler to pay homage to Humabon and tribute to the Spaniards. The chastened Mactan islanders grudgingly paid a part of the required tribute. Dissatisfied with this response, Magellan decided to crush the recalcitrant Mactan islanders as a lesson to any other stubborn natives.

Several of his officers advised Magellan against attacking Mactan. They pointed out that the island could muster many hundreds of warriors and that its ruler probably expected such an attack. But Magellan viewed the Mactan island affair as an opportunity to demonstrate the strength of the Christian God as well as the ability of the Europeans to enforce their will in the islands. Perhaps he also scorned the military prowess of native warriors, recalling how he and his fellow Portuguese had won victory after victory over lightly armed Muslims in India, Africa, and Malaya. In any case, he ordered an assault against Mactan.

With sixty Europeans under arms, plus auxiliaries supplied by Rajah Humabon, Magellan, in three boats, reached Mactan three hours before daybreak on April 27, 1521. Keeping his armed men in the boats at first, Magellan sent a messenger ashore. He called on the local ruler to submit. The Mactan chief replied with defiance. At dawn Magellan decided to act. He counted off eleven of his men to guard the boats. He also requested his native allies to remain in their boats and "watch the Spanish fight."

Although Magellan had ordered his ships to provide support offshore with their heavy cannon, the ships had not yet come up. Nevertheless, Magellan, with forty-eight of his men, including Pigafetta, now began wading toward the beach to engage the waiting natives. To facilitate their getting ashore, most of Magellan's fighters wore only breastplate armor and helmets.

As Magellan's band emerged from the shallows, fifteen hundred islanders, armed with clubs and spears as well as bows and arrows, assailed them. Managing to keep the attackers at bay, Magellan ordered a party of his men to burn some huts in a nearby village. At this many of the native warriors left off fighting and ran to defend their homes. They also caught and killed two of the Spaniards engaged in burning the houses. Their fury redoubled, they returned to the assault against the rest of Magellan's invasion party, which now included many of his Cebu auxiliaries. Pigafetta tells what ensued:

> So many of them charged down upon us that they shot the captain [Magellan] through the right leg with a poisoned arrow. On that account, he ordered us to retire slowly, but the men took to flight, except six or eight of us who remained with the captain.
>
> The natives shot only at our legs, for the latter were bare: and so many were the spears and stones that they hurled at us, that we could offer no resistance. The mortars in the boats could not aid us as they were too far away. So we continued to retire for more than a good crossbow flight from the shore always fighting up to our knees in the water.
>
> The natives continued to pursue us, and picking up the same spear four or six times, hurled it at us again and again. Recognizing the captain, so many turned upon him that they knocked his helmet off his head twice, but he always stood firmly like a good knight, together with some others.
>
> Thus did we fight for more than one hour, refusing to retire farther. An Indian hurled a bamboo spear into the captain's face, but the latter immediately killed him with his lance, which he left in the Indian's body. Then, trying to lay hand on sword, he could draw it but halfway, because he had been wounded in the arm with a bamboo spear.
>
> When the natives saw that, they all hurled themselves upon him. One of them wounded him on the left leg with a large cutlass, which resembles a scimitar, only being larger. That caused the captain to fall face down-

ward, when immediately they rushed upon him with iron and bamboo spears and with their cutlasses, until they killed our mirror, our light, our comfort and our true guide.

When they wounded him, he turned back many times to see whether we were all in the boats. Thereupon, beholding him dead, we, wounded, retreated as best we could to the boats, which were already pulling off.

Magellan's epic journey had come to an end. He had lived forty-one years. Only nineteen months had elapsed since he had sailed from Sanlúcar to find the Spice Islands.

Seven of his men and four baptized Cebu islanders died with Magellan. Most of the Europeans who managed to escape received severe wounds. The Mactan islanders refused to give up Magellan's body, attaching great value to the corpse of this potent enemy.

Pigafetta makes it clear that if Magellan's overconfidence had brought on the battle with the natives, his self-sacrificing heroism had redeemed the lives of many of his companions: "Had it not been for that unfortunate captain not a single one of us would have been saved in the boats, for while he was fighting the others retired to the boats. I hope . . . that the fame of so noble a captain will not become effaced in our times."

Without the leader they had come to rely upon, the dispirited Europeans made their way back to the presumed safety of Cebu. But they soon noted a hostile alteration in the attitude of the baptized Cebu islanders. The people of Cebu had seen that the Christians bled like other men. Why should they fear these strangers or their alien Christ?

The Europeans betrayed their own growing unease and distrust of Rajah Humabon by removing their trade goods from the town and taking refuge aboard the ships. Tension worsened when Humabon learned that the Mactan islanders, having vanquished Magellan, intended to attack *him* unless he joined them to drive out the remaining Europeans. Yet Humabon still feared the Europeans. He hesitated to assail them despite the threat from Mactan.

At this point Magellan's servant, Enrique, entered the

drama. Enrique, who had received a slight wound in the battle
at Mactan, had thereafter taken to his sleeping quarters, probably
more in sorrow at his master's death than in pain. Deaf to all
orders, Enrique pined away in his hammock. Magellan's immediate successor, Duarte Barbosa, showed little sympathy for the
servant's feelings. Enrique was the only member of the expedition who could interpret the mutterings now being heard in
Cebu. He was the only instrument available for Barbosa to parley
with the suddenly sullen Rajah Humabon. Intent on employing
Enrique's talents, Barbosa threatened to flog the servant if he
persisted in his mournful sulk. Barbosa also repudiated the
promise made in Magellan's will that Enrique would be a free
man upon Magellan's death, declaring that the Malayan would
remain a slave in the fleet as long as he was needed. Enrique
returned to duty, but with a hunger for vengeance now in his
heart.

At the first opportunity he went ashore and told a tale that
turned the clever Rajah Humabon irrevocably against the Europeans. Enrique whispered that the Europeans were preparing a
treacherous attack on his town. He advised the rajah to defend
himself by striking first. Humabon took Enrique's advice and,
probably with the active connivance of the interpreter, prepared
a trap for the white men.

Pretending continued friendship for Magellan's crews, Humabon invited them to leave the shelter of their ships and join
him ashore for a feast featuring dancing girls, palm wine, and
the promise of a gift of jewels for the king of Spain. Again Pigafetta tells the tale: "Twenty four of the men went ashore. . . .
I could not go because my face still was very swollen from the
wounds I had received [in the Mactan fight]." Later that night,
reports Pigafetta, two Spaniards left the feast and returned to the
ships, saying they "suspected some evil." Pigafetta continues:

> Scarcely had they spoken these words when we heard
> loud cries and lamentations. We immediately weighed
> anchor and discharging many mortars into the houses,
> drew in nearer to the shore. While thus discharging our
> pieces we saw Juan Serrão in his shirt, bound and
> wounded, crying to us not to fire anymore, for the na-
> tives would kill him. . . . We asked him whether all the
> others and the interpreter were dead. He said that they

were all dead except the interpreter. He begged us earnestly to redeem him with some of the merchandise; but Juan Carvalho, his boon companion, and others would not allow the boat to go ashore so that they might remain masters of the ships.

Serrão's captors thereupon hacked him to death in full view of his companions aboard the ships.

The Europeans later heard what had happened at the feast: The smiling Cebu islanders had fallen upon their unsuspecting guests in the midst of the festivities and had cut them all to pieces in a matter of minutes, with the exception of Enrique.*

After the disaster of the feast, Magellan's surviving men fled from Cebu in their three vessels and took shelter on Bohol Island, not far away. Here a council of officers chose Juan Carvalho as the new captain general.

There were only 115 men still alive out of the expedition's original complement of 260. The officers judged it impossible to handle all three ships with these reduced numbers. For this reason the survivors now set fire to the *Concepción*, which had begun leaking badly in any case. Her hands were then distributed between the remaining two vessels, the *Trinidad* and the *Victoria*. The ships then set out southward for the Spice Islands. It was mid-May 1521.

With Magellan's strong hand removed, discipline aboard the ships quickly deteriorated. The *Trinidad* and *Victoria*, reports Pigafetta, began a wandering journey over these island-studded seas. Often short of rations, the men engaged in piracy as well as trade. In one episode they took three harem women captive, and Pigafetta says that Captain General Carvalho, who was no ascetic Magellan, "disported shamefully" with them.

At last, in November 1521, the two battered vessels came in sight of their long-sought goal: the Spice Islands. On November 8, firing their guns with joy, they entered the harbor of Tidore, the most important of the Moluccas. There, finally among friendly, civilized people who understood trade and had knowledge of Europe, Magellan's remaining men took their ease and resupplied their vessels. The ruler of Tidore received them with

*One of those murdered at the banquet was Enrique's tormentor, Duarte Barbosa. As for Enrique himself, he apparently settled down on Cebu, free at last.

genuine hospitality. He also informed them that Magellan's cousin Francisco Serrão, whose letters had spurred the captain general's ambition to sail westward to the Spice Islands, had died months earlier on the nearby isle of Ternate, never knowing of Magellan's expedition. (Though he did not say it, the ruler of Tidore himself had had Serrão poisoned as an agent of the Portuguese, whom the Spice Islanders had come to regard as oppressors.)

For six weeks Magellan's men relaxed, bought provisions for their vessels, and traded for cloves. Though the Spanish officers in the expedition no longer possessed sufficient forces to seize the Spice Islands for Spain, they made a pact of friendship with the rajah of Tidore and other Spice Island rulers as well. The Spaniards pledged that King Charles would send additional forces to protect the islands against the unpopular Portuguese. As a sign of their good faith the Spaniards chose five volunteers to stay behind on Tidore when the ships sailed for home. The five would represent Spanish interests in the islands and establish a formal trade in spices.

At last, with the holds of both ships bulging with precious cloves, the Spanish officers decided the time had come to depart Tidore for home. On December 11, 1521, the *Victoria* stood out to sea. But aboard the *Trinidad*, captained by Carvalho, a disabling leak was found, and she could not weigh anchor. The *Victoria* then returned to Tidore, and the officers convened to reconsider their course of action.

The Spanish leaders worked out a new plan for both ships. The *Victoria*, under her new captain, Juan Sebastián de Elcano, a tough, bearded Basque who had played a major role in the mutiny against Magellan nineteen months earlier at Port San Julián, would make for Spain by sailing westward across the Indian Ocean and around the Cape of Good Hope. Meanwhile, the *Trinidad* would undergo repairs at Tidore. She would then try to recross the Pacific eastward to Panama. There her men would convey her cargo of cloves across the isthmus and find transport to Spain. The Spanish officers apparently believed that by taking two separate routes, they would double their chances of getting back to Spain.

The *Victoria* sailed again from Tidore on December 21, 1521. She carried forty-seven men of Magellan's original crews, among them Pigafetta and thirteen natives. "With tears and embraces," says Pigafetta, "we departed." The *Trinidad*, with fifty-three of Magellan's men, was to sail in the new year after completion of repairs to her hull.

The men aboard the *Victoria* knew that to reach home, they would have to run a gauntlet of Portuguese warships that regularly plied the Indian Ocean. They would also have to avoid towns and islands in Portuguese possession because the Portuguese would certainly capture the *Victoria* and confiscate her valuable cargo if they sighted a Spanish vessel. The odds for success were, therefore, greatly against the *Victoria*'s getting home safely. Still, her crew had little choice but to trust in God and Captain de Elcano.

For two months the *Victoria* crept toward the Cape of Good Hope. The water went foul. Provisions gave out. For weeks the men subsisted on moldy rice and rats. The suffering recalled the worst of Magellan's Pacific crossing. Twenty-five men died.

At last the *Victoria* rounded the Cape of Good Hope. So far her luck had held in one respect: She had not encountered any Portuguese men-of-war. Now monsoon rains near the cape provided supplies of fresh water, relieving some of the agony aboard. But the storms also seriously damaged one of the *Victoria*'s masts, greatly slowing her progress. She crept on.

As the *Victoria* slowly made her way home, the *Trinidad* departed the Spice Isles on April 6, 1522, according to plan. She sailed under a new captain: Gonzalo Gomez de Espinosa, once Magellan's doughty quartermaster. Juan Carvalho, originally designated captain, had died. As previously agreed, Espinosa left behind five men to represent Spain in the Moluccas. He then sailed the *Trinidad* east into the Pacific. But headwinds and easterly currents made progress impossible. He had to return to the Spice Isles. In the interim a squadron of Portuguese warships, searching for Magellan, had put into Tidore, captured the five Spaniards left there, and forced the rajah to renounce his treaty with Spain. When the *Trinidad* limped back to Tidore, Espinosa surrendered to the Portuguese, who took her cargo and imprisoned her surviving crew. Only four of the *Trinidad*'s men ever saw Spain again. The *Trinidad* herself, worn and battered, eventually broke up in a storm.

Meanwhile, the *Victoria* pressed on. In July 1522, after six months at sea, she reached the Portuguese-ruled Cape Verde Islands off the west coast of Africa. There, desperate for food supplies, Captain Elcano decided to risk contact with the Portuguese.

The *Victoria* anchored in an island harbor. Elcano told Portuguese port officials that his ship had been en route to Spain from America when she had been blown off course. He now needed food, water, and time to repair his vessel. The Portuguese believed him. Furthermore, as long as the *Victoria* had not trespassed in forbidden waters, they were willing to provide the supplies requested. It did not occur to the Portuguese to doubt the story. They could never have guessed that the battered *Victoria* had just sailed fifteen thousand miles from the Spice Isles through the very heart of Portugal's heavily guarded trade routes. But after a few days in port the Portuguese authorities did become suspicious, perhaps because Elcano traded some of his cloves for supplies. America did not produce cloves. The Portuguese seized some of the *Victoria*'s crewmen for questioning about their voyage.

Elcano realized that he had better get away from the Cape Verdes before the Portuguese impounded his ship. Having managed to obtain sufficient provisions and having repaired the worst of the *Victoria*'s damage, he ordered the ship away, deserting the thirteen members of his crew who had been ashore.*

On September 6, 1522, almost three years after setting out with Magellan, the *Victoria* straggled into the harbor of Sanlúcar. Leaking badly, her sails stained and rent, her surviving crew members gaunt and exhausted, the *Victoria* had completed an epic journey, and with a cargo of spices still intact in her belly. Eighteen Christians and three "Indians" were aboard her.

The men of the *Victoria* had done what Columbus had meant to do: They had reached the East by sailing west. And they had done more. They had continued on to their starting point, accomplishing what no men had ever done before them. They had circled the globe.

The survivors of the *Victoria* thanked God for their deliverance and were heaped with praise and rewards for their feat. *Victoria*'s captain, Juan Sebastián de Elcano, reaped especially high honors. King Charles ennobled the Basque mariner, granting him a coat of arms that bore a representation of the globe and the proud motto: "You were the first around me." Elcano

---

*Unlike the stranded men of the *Trinidad*, most of these men eventually made it home after protracted negotiations between Portuguese and Spanish diplomats.

was also awarded a yearly pension of five hundred ducats.*

No one gave any credit to Magellan. The Portuguese captain's reputation lay in ruins as a result of calumnies heaped upon him by the Spanish officers of the *San Antonio*, the ship that had deserted the expedition in the strait. Even though some Spanish officials doubted the charges against Magellan, much of the mud had stuck, and by the time the *Victoria* returned, many Spaniards had come to regard Magellan as self-seeking, cruel, impious, and a secret conspirer against Spanish interests.

In this time of the *Victoria*'s triumphal return, Magellan had no defenders. His young wife, Doña Beatriz, had died, as had Magellan's sons. Officials in Seville had recorded their deaths as caused by plague. Even Doña Beatriz's father, whose son, Duarte, had also sailed with Magellan and perished, failed to speak out. Magellan's men forgot how much they owed their fallen leader. Even the estimable Pigafetta held his tongue, although he was resolved to give Magellan his proper due when the sensation of the world's first circumnavigation subsided.†

With the passage of a few months the excitement did diminish. The survivors took up the threads of their lives. Some went back to the sea. The *Victoria* returned to service in the Atlantic trade. She later sank in a storm, with all hands.

As the commotion over the voyage cooled, a more solid reality emerged in the afterglow. The *Victoria*'s circumnavigation had disclosed a world vast beyond all expectation. It had revealed the undeniable shape of the globe and the imperious fact of the Pacific Ocean. Now men wondered at this new huge ocean, speculated about it, coveted its potential riches. One of those who thought most often about Mar Pacifica was Charles, King of Spain and Holy Roman Emperor.

---

*One reason for Charles' generosity lay in the fact that the *Victoria*'s skipper had brought home a cargo that sold for forty-one thousand ducats, double the cost of the entire expedition resulting in a tidy profit for the financially pressed king. Although in the three years between Magellan's departure in 1519 and the *Victoria*'s return in 1522 Cortés had conquered the Aztecs, the gold of Mexico had not yet begun to arrive in Spain. The *Victoria*'s triumph meant an especially welcome windfall for Charles.

†Pigafetta was as good as his word. In future years he traveled from court to court defending Magellan and presenting extracts from his journal of the voyage. The first edition of his narrative, in French, came out in Paris in 1525. Through this, several Italian editions prior to 1540, and the English translation in 1555, knowledge of Magellan's leadership of the voyage became well disseminated. Pigafetta himself also became famous. Made a member of the religious and military order of the Knights of Rhodes, Pigafetta met his own heroic death defending Malta against the Turks in 1536.

5

IN THE WAKE OF MAGELLAN

Twenty-two years old when the *Victoria* returned from her epic voyage, Charles V had changed little in the five years since he had listened enthralled while Magellan explained his plan to find a strait through America. Except for a new growth of reddish beard that did little to disguise his low-slung Hapsburg jaw, the sovereign was as pale, stooped, and awkward as ever. He maintained an almost reflexive gravity in the conduct of business. He still spoke seldom, preferring to hear what others had to say rather than reveal his own thoughts. His watery blue eyes bulged, and he still stammered slightly when he talked. He pursued a conventional private life. Unlike his French rival, Francis I, he expended little energy on royal mistresses, finding pleasure instead in music and hunting. He also enjoyed the delights of the table, and had a particular fondness for pickled eel.

Yet if he appeared unchanged personally, his political position in the world had altered remarkably since Magellan had sailed to his destiny. Charles had become one of the world's most powerful monarchs. His power, however, derived less from the extensive lands he controlled than from his resolve to buy and use ruthlessly whatever military force was required to gain his ends.

His mercenary troops had already smashed all challenges to his authority in Spain. For the past year his armies had been engaged in a bloody war with Francis I of France, whose ambition was to thwart Charles in Europe and to control Italy. Since his accession Charles had also used the threat of military action to hold the Turks at bay on the southeastern borders of Europe.

It was this reliance on might to gain his objectives, together with the strategic advantages conferred by his extensive domains, that had changed the young emperor in European eyes from an uncertain youth to the dominant figure on the political scene. Yet, for all his trust in military strength, Charles understood that a policy of power was not appropriate in every case. In his German lands, for example, he tried to follow a course of moderation and persuasion to halt the spread of the Lutheran heresy. Still, for the most part, Charles relied on his armies to enforce his will.

In this new age of costly artillery and mercenary soldiers, the maintenance of an effective military force, however, was extremely expensive. Charles, committed to a policy of might and already deeply in debt as a result of the bribes he had distributed to secure his throne as emperor, had to go on borrowing heavily from the bankers in order to pay for his armies. Regularly negotiating new loans at high interest rates, he had mortgaged his empire well into the future.

When the *Victoria* returned in 1522 with her highly profitable load of spices, the young emperor saw it as evidence that the spice trade could furnish him with much-needed revenues. He approved a new expedition to follow in Magellan's wake. At the same time he resorted to diplomacy to keep the Portuguese from taking possession of the Moluccas before the Spaniards could do so. He proposed to the new Portuguese king, John III, that Spain and Portugal agree formally to continue the Tordesillas line around the world and use it to define the limits of their respective territories. He also suggested that Portugal recognize a Spanish claim to the Moluccas based on their geographic position. This latter proposition was immediately rejected by the Portuguese. In the end it was decided that a conclave of experts would determine ownership of the Moluccas.

As this tentative attempt at a diplomatic solution to the Moluccas question went forward, Charles suffered an unexpected blow to his treasury. In the summer of 1523 a fleet of six French privateers operating off Portugal captured two of three treasure-laden caravels that Hernán Cortés had dispatched from Mexico with the first shipments of Aztec plunder. The French corsairs made off with 680 pounds of Aztec pearls, 500 pounds of gold dust, three cases of gold ingots, numerous boxes filled with silver ingots, and coffers of jewels. Charles lost his share of a vast treasure—wealth he had counted on to shore up his shaky finances.* Galled beyond measure by the depredations of the French privateers, Charles could only console himself with the knowledge that in time, Cortés would make up the loss with additional shipments of New World treasure. Meanwhile, the deprivation of the Mexican plunder, even if temporary, made it more important than ever that Spain establish its claim to the Spice Isles as soon as possible.

Unfortunately for Charles, having committed himself to a diplomatic resolution of the Moluccas controversy, he had to wait another year, until the spring of 1524, before negotiations got under way on the matter. Although experts from Spain and Portugal met over several weeks to try to settle the dispute, the effort failed because with no accepted way to determine longitude, the participants could not agree on the position of the Moluccas in relation to the Tordesillas demarcation. The conference broke up with both countries continuing to claim the islands.

Charles now ordered his maritime officials to press on with Spain's second Pacific expedition. He had recently established as formal bodies the Council of the Indies and the Casa de Contratación. He had given the Council power to oversee government in Spain's New World (under his direction) while the Casa (until now an ad hoc board of trade) had been made the official organ for all commercial matters, including the actual preparation of voyages and the keeping of records, maps, and charts. Under the goad of these two powerful tribunals, the second Spanish armada to the Pacific quickly began to take shape in the port of La Coruña.

For Spanish geographers, mariners, and trade officials, this new Pacific voyage not only offered the wealth of the spice trade but also promised to answer some of the questions raised by the first crossing of the Pacific: Did Tierra del Fuego, sighted during

---

*King Francis, of course, delighted in the wealth stolen from Charles. He had never recognized the Spanish claim to absolute dominion over the New World, and when the Spaniards had complained of French incursions beyond the Tordesillas line, the French king had proclaimed: "The sun shines for me as for the Spaniard." The struggle between Charles and Francis for the dominant place in Europe was to be the central theme in the continent's politics for decades.

Magellan's voyage through the strait, mark the outcroppings of the much-desired southern continent? Did other islands of gold and silver, perhaps richer than the Spice Isles, lie out in the mysterious ocean that Magellan had named? Could men sail from Spanish America across this Pacific and back again, thus linking the as-yet-unknown lands of this great ocean to the growing Spanish Empire of the New World? Could Spain exploit and colonize the archipelago that Magellan had named the Isles of Lazarus?

Adding to the ferment was the knowledge that France, too, was intent on finding its way to the Pacific. It was widely known that for many years French fishermen had frequented the Grand Banks of Newfoundland, bringing back tales of a coast broken by many deep bays and potential northern straits through America. To investigate these reports, France had already sent a Florentine navigator, Giovanni da Verrazano, across the Atlantic. The French expedition, unable to challenge the powerful Spaniards in the southern reaches of the Atlantic, had been ordered to search in the northern latitudes for a "northwest passage" to Magellan's ocean.*

Command of the new Spanish armada went to Francisco García Jofre de Loaysa, a distinguished soldier and brother of the president of the new Council of the Indies. Although Loaysa lacked experience at sea, Charles and his advisers were unworried. They reasoned that the expedition would include many skilled mariners to oversee the day-to-day operations of the fleet. To make certain that this would be the case, the Casa de Contratación now offered the post of second-in-command and chief pilot of the fleet to the heroic old circumnavigator himself: Juan Sebastián de Elcano.

For Elcano, who had reaped the glory of the first voyage around the world, the luster of the achievement had faded badly by 1525, when the Casa offered him a berth with the new armada. Despite the honors Elcano had received from King Charles, life ashore had proven onerous. He had spent the money that the king had granted him, splurging on drink, women, and bright new clothing befitting a freshly made aristocrat. He had acquired

---

*Verrazano was to discover New York Bay, the Hudson River, and Narragansett Bay, but no northwest passage.

two beautiful mistresses: one at Valladolid and the other in the
town of San Sebastián. When the relatives of one of these ladies
discovered his duplicity, they threatened him with bodily harm.
Elcano had to retain a bodyguard to protect his person.

The landlubber's existence bored him. Without occupation
he drank wine and complained, becoming a querulous pest to
all who knew him. He grumbled that the honors and cash he
had received from Charles did not properly compensate him for
his glorious deeds. He had petitioned the king to make him captain general of the next expedition to the Spice Islands. He had
begged Charles for financial allowances for several poor relatives.
He had even had the temerity to ask the king to invest him with
the Order of Santiago, an honor that Magellan had received before *his* voyage. But Charles, no doubt fed up with Elcano's unceasing demands, refused these requests. The Basque had
languished on the beach, yearning for the sea.

Thus, when asked to join the second Pacific expedition as
second-in-command to the soldier Loaysa, Elcano accepted with
alacrity. He certainly realized that he would have de facto command of the fleet under sail. Further, as the only officer of the
fleet with experience of the Pacific, he would bear the chief responsibility for preparing the expedition for sea. He flung himself happily into the labor of readying the armada.*

The fleet being prepared at La Coruña consisted of seven
vessels: *Santa María de la Victoria*, 300 tons; *Sancti Spiritus*, 200
tons; *Anunciada*, 170 tons; *San Gabriel*, 130 tons; *Santa María del
Parral*, a caravel of 80 tons; *Santo Lesmes*, a caravel of 80 tons; and
Santiago, a pinnace of 70 tons. The Casa hired a total of 450 men
to crew these seven ships, three of which were bigger than any
of Magellan's vessels.

The armada's mission was fourfold. First it was to seize the
Spice Isles for Spain. Loaysa was to establish a trading fort in the
Moluccas and to station his three smallest vessels in Moluccan
waters as a permanent force. He was also to load his big ships
with spices before returning home.

---

*About this same time a group of Seville merchants, inspired by Charles's promise of
"privileges" to subjects who would undertake private voyages to the Moluccas, began
planning for still another expedition to the Spice Isles. These merchants hired the well-
known explorer Sebastian Cabot to pilot their fleet. Thus two efforts were now preparing,
and Spain bubbled with excitement at the prospect of purloining the spice trade from
Lisbon.

The three additional aims of the fleet were to further the tenuous Spanish claim to the islands discovered by Magellan, to establish a reliable sailing route across the Pacific from America and back, and to annex any new lands encountered in the Pacific, especially Terra Australis Incognita. But these last objectives paled in comparison with the establishment of Spanish power in the Spice Isles.

By July 1525 Spain's second expedition to the Pacific was ready. With flags flying and music playing, the seven ships headed out of La Coruña into the Atlantic, bound for Magellan's strait.

At the beginning of the voyage all went well. The ships crossed the Atlantic with little trouble beyond the usual storms and calms. The provisions held up. Morale was high, and scurvy no worse than usual. Guided by Elcano, the fleet arrived at the southern reaches of Patagonia in December 1525—high summer. From this point onward, however, according to a record kept by a seventeen-year-old page to Elcano, Andrés de Urdaneta, one disaster after another assailed the expedition.

According to Urdaneta, Chief Pilot Elcano could not even find the entrance to Magellan's strait at first, and by the time the armada finally entered the waterway in late January 1526, after a month's searching, the flagship, with Loaysa aboard, and two other vessels had become separated from the main body. Moreover, once in the strait, the fleet had to endure a daily struggle against brutal weather.

Although, miraculously, Loaysa and the other missing ships managed to rejoin Elcano in the strait, it was the last good luck the armada was to experience. After this, according to Urdaneta, one calamity after another, all brought on by vicious storms, wreaked havoc on the expedition. The armada's second-largest vessel, the 200-ton *Sancti Spiritus*, was smashed to pieces on a stormy beach. The surviving ships were constantly scattered by gales and even forced back into the Atlantic in one instance. The flagship ran aground and was refloated only by the desperate efforts of her crew. One vessel, the *San Gabriel*, battered beyond endurance, fled the strait and deserted the armada, only to sink later off Brazil. Another ship, the *Anunciada*, also went down with all hands after a storm threw her back into the Atlantic.

However, the fleet persisted, and on May 26, 1526, four surviving vessels (the flagship, the two eighty-ton caravels, and the little pinnace) reached the Pacific. It had taken them four months to struggle through the 360-mile strait that Magellan had negotiated in thirty-eight days. Nor were the armada's troubles over yet.

According to Urdaneta, a huge Pacific gale now scattered the fleet across the open sea so that the ships "never saw each other again." When this latest storm passed, the flagship—*Santa María*—found herself alone on the open ocean.*

The flagship now carried approximately 120 men (including Elcano and his page, Urdaneta). With so many mouths to feed, Loaysa and Elcano knew the ship's provisions would run low before she reached the Moluccas. Nevertheless, Captain General Loaysa, determined to seize the Moluccas in accordance with his king's orders despite his diminished forces, instructed Elcano to set a course northwestward into the Pacific and to ration supplies as needed.

For five weeks the overcrowded *Santa María* sailed into the Pacific. Scurvy began to afflict the men. On July 30, 1526, the ship had reached latitude 15 degrees north in the Central Pacific. Here Loaysa died, probably of scurvy. A week later Elcano also died. A pilot, Martin Carquisano, was elected the new captain general of an expedition that now consisted of a badly leaking vessel and 116 men, most of them, according to Urdaneta, "so worn out from much work at the pumps, the violence of the sea, the insufficiency of food, and illness, that some died every day."

Still the ship limped on. Reaching Guam, the mariners found lifesaving supplies of fresh food. They also found one of Magellan's old crewmen who had deserted there five years earlier during the *Trinidad*'s ill-fated attempt to return from the Spice Islands to Mexico. Much refreshed at Guam, the men of the *Santa María* took heart. After another stop, in the Philippines, they made for the Spice Islands. "We were 105 people," Urdaneta reported in his chronicle.

Against all odds they had crossed the Pacific in the wake of Magellan.

---

*Two of the three missing vessels survived. Although one caravel, *Santa Lesmes*, simply disappeared in the storm, the other, *Santa Maria de Parral*, went on to cross the Pacific alone, eventually fetching up at the Philippines. The pinnace, *Santiago*, sailed in the opposite direction toward the west coast of Mexico, and arrived there on July 20, 1526. Her starving crew received hospitality from local Indians—and survived to tell their stories to Cortés in Mexico City.

Now, as the paradisical Moluccas appeared on the horizon, they steeled themselves to carry out the mission their sovereign had given them. Whatever the cost, they intended to conquer the Spice Isles for their king.

In November 1526 the *Santa María* anchored off the coast of Halmahera, one of the largest islands of the Moluccas, which contained the rich state of Jilolo. It was sixteen months since she had left home. When the Spaniards went ashore on this lush island, they learned from a Portuguese beachcomber that the Portuguese now dominated the Spice Islands to a greater degree than expected. Though based primarily in the neighboring island of Ternate, the Portuguese regularly patrolled all the islands.

Nevertheless, the Spaniards presented themselves to the ruler of Jilolo who welcomed them warmly. The *Santa María*'s formidable bronze guns, it seems, greatly impressed this monarch.

For several weeks the Spaniards rested at Jilolo. One day a messenger arrived with a warning from the Portuguese commander in Ternate: The *Santa María* must leave the Moluccas immediately or face destruction by a Portuguese fleet. The elected Spanish chief, Carquisano, replied with defiance.

As if to emphasize their willingness to fight, the Spaniards sailed the *Santa María* on toward Tidore, one of the most important of the Spice Islands. Though the Portuguese often visited Tidore, they had not yet established a permanent presence there, and the Spaniards were able to approach the island unopposed.

Reaching Tidore on December 29, 1526, the *Santa María* anchored, and the Spaniards went ashore. Again they received a warm welcome from the gentle native people who had come to hate the Portuguese. Soon after the *Santa María*'s arrival at Tidore, a Portuguese patrol (probably stationed in nearby Ternate) came over to investigate the Spanish ship. The Portuguese boats quickly departed, however, when their commander saw the powerful armament of the *Santa María*.

Two weeks later, on January 12, 1527, as the Spanish amused themselves ashore at Tidore, another Portuguese fleet—now including several big warships—entered the harbor. This time the Portuguese attacked. The men of the *Santa María* manned their guns. Blasting away at the Portuguese flotilla, the disciplined

Spaniards defended themselves effectively. For several days the
Portuguese continued a long-range cannonade. The Spaniards
answered with their own long cannon. Though unable to silence,
the *Santa María*'s fire, the Portuguese inflicted serious damage
on her hull and rigging. But the Spaniards also badly damaged
the Portuguese ships, which finally withdrew, leaving the *Santa
María* the apparent victor.

The Spanish leaders, however, soon realized that their ship,
torn and battered, was finished as a fighting vessel. They ordered
most of her guns and other gear removed and fortified batteries
set up ashore. Only a skeleton crew was left aboard to guard her.

Now the Portuguese, suspecting the *Santa María*'s damaged
condition, returned to the attack. Driving the *Santa María*'s remaining crew to seek refuge ashore, the Portuguese boarded the
Spanish interloper. They stripped the big ship clean and left her
a hulk in the harbor at Tidore. Once again they sailed away,
clearly intending to wait until the stranded Spaniards saw the
hopelessness of their position and surrendered. But the determined Spaniards burned the wreckage of the *Santa María* to the
waterline and then dug in on Tidore, swearing to hold the island
for Charles.

Soon a vicious little war began. It pitted the Spaniards, allied
with Tidore and Jilolo, against the Portuguese and their allies on
Ternate and other smaller Spice Islands. The Spaniards also had
a new commander: Fernando Torre, formerly chief of the *Santa
María*'s marines. (Torre's predecessor, Carquisano, had died of
poisoned wine given him by a Portuguese captain who had, supposedly, come to negotiate a truce with the Spaniards.)

As the adversaries skirmished, the Portuguese soon recognized that overcoming Torre would prove difficult, even though
the fierce Spaniards were outnumbered and outgunned. Still,
they resolved to eradicate the Spanish invaders whatever the cost.
They saw clearly, as did the Spaniards, that in spite of its minia-
ture dimensions, this struggle in the Moluccas could very well
decide the ownership of the world's richest islands and the fate
of empires.

Meanwhile, in far-off Mexico Cortés was preparing a new
Pacific expedition. According to instructions he had received
from Seville, he was to send additional ships across the Pacific to
aid the Loaysa-Elcano armada, which presumably had arrived in
the Moluccas by now. (News of the two men's deaths had not,

of course, reached either Mexico or Spain, nor did Cortés have any inkling of the armed struggle in the Spice Isles between the Spanish and the Portuguese.)

Cortés built three ships on the west coast of Mexico: a pinnace, *Santiago*; a twenty-eight-ton *bergantina* named *Espiritu Santo*; and a caravel, *Florida*, which carried a crew of twelve and an armed force of thirty-eight. To command this flotilla, Cortés chose his cousin Álvaro de Saavedra Cerón.

Saavedra—more soldier than mariner—departed Mexico on October 31, 1527. For five weeks his little squadron ran before the trades just north of the equator. Then, on December 4, a great storm sank two of his three ships. The flagship, *Florida*, sprang a serious leak. Frantically her crew jettisoned precious provisions, lightening her just enough to keep her afloat.

Despite the water in her holds, the *Florida* survived the storm. Not one to admit defeat, Saavedra put his men on the pumps day and night. The *Florida*, leaking badly, pressed on across the Pacific. Bypassing Guam she reached a small island off Mindanao on February 2, 1528. Here Saavedra paused to caulk her seams and take on fresh water before going on to the Spice Isles.

One day, while the *Florida* was anchored just offshore, a ragged, bearded figure appeared out of the jungle. He called to the astonished Spaniards in their own tongue, begging for help. Taken aboard, *Florida*, the man sobbed out his story: He had been a member of the Loaysa-Elcano expedition, serving as an ordinary seaman aboard the eighty-ton caravel, *Santa María de Parral*. When the fleet had exited the Strait of Magellan almost two years earlier, the ships had been scattered by a huge storm. The *Parral*, alone and unaware of the fate of the flotilla, had continued on to the west, hoping to rendezvous with the rest of the armada. Instead she had been wrecked on this island off Mindanao. Although many of her crew had managed to get ashore, most of them had since perished of fever or at the hands of hostile natives. There were, however, two other survivors of the *Parral* on the island. They were being held captive by the local people.

Guided by the emaciated castaway, Saavedra and his men located the other Spanish captives and ransomed them from their captors. Marveling at the miracle that had allowed them to deliver their comrades, the men of the *Florida* finished the repairs to their ship and set sail with high hearts for the Spice Islands to the south, hoping to be united with still more of Loaysa's men.

Ten days later, with her Spanish standards aloft, the *Florida*, crept cautiously toward the Moluccas. While still some distance from land, she was approached by a small boat full of armed men. The men in the boat spoke Spanish and identified themselves as guerrillas operating on and about the islands. At first suspecting a Portuguese ruse, the men in the boat erupted in joy when they were finally convinced that Saavedra had come to help them. Praising God, the Spanish guerrillas led the *Florida* on to Tidore, where the Spanish commander, Torre, received Saavedra and his men. Expressing his gratitude for the reinforcements and the munitions that the *Florida* had brought from Mexico, Torre told Saavedra about the war with the Portuguese. Saavedra pledged to help all he could.

With the aid of the arrivals from Mexico, Torre's Spaniards, according to Urdaneta, began to prosecute their war against the Portuguese "with much greater heat." Saavedra soon realized that the Spanish forces did not really require his help to survive. Torre's men, though few, were in excellent condition, both physically and militarily. They had plenty of native support. Food supplies were readily available in the highly civilized islands. The guerrillas had constructed an oared galley from the timbers of the *Santa María*, and with it they had captured a similar Portuguese vessel. Thus they had two shallow-draft warships, both of more value in these island waters than the deep-sea *Florida*. With the additional ordnance and powder that the *Florida* had furnished, Saavedra reckoned that Torre could continue the war indefinitely, in this manner keeping alive the Spanish claim to the Spice Islands.

Saavedra concluded that he could best serve the cause by returning to Mexico, where he would report the situation and secure sufficient new forces to ensure a Spanish conquest of the Moluccas. After loading the *Florida* with cloves and taking aboard a few Portuguese prisoners, Saavedra put out from the Spice Isles on June 12, 1528, intending to sail eastward across the Pacific back to Mexico. But like Magellan's old ship *Trinidad*, the *Florida* immediately encountered powerful northeast winds that impeded progress. Though Saavedra tried to escape these head winds by sailing to the south, the wind remained contrary, now blowing from the *south*east. At last Saavedra turned back, and he reached Tidore once again on November 18, 1528.*

Still determined to get back to Mexico, Saavedra tried again in May 1529. This time he steered even farther to the south, until he was skirting the northern coast of New Guinea. Portuguese mariners had sighted this rugged coastline three years earlier but had not made a landing. Now Saavedra went ashore for water and supplies and became the first European to make contact with the inhabitants. He described them as "black people with frizzled hair, who are cannibals, and the Devil walks with them."

From New Guinea Saavedra, desperately seeking a favorable wind to take him eastward, turned farther north again. He managed to reach a number of islands in the Admiralty and Marshall groups. But adverse winds continued to thwart all his attempts to sail east. Then the stubborn Saavedra fell ill. Within days he died. His successor, dispirited by the long fight against the Pacific headwinds, gave up the attempt to cross the Pacific. The *Florida* again returned to the Moluccas, arriving in December 1529 after six months at sea.

Defeated by the Pacific, the survivors of the *Florida* joined their compatriots in Tidore who continued to fight for their king's "right" to a handful of islands located halfway around the earth from their homeland. Worn beyond repair, the *Florida* disintegrated on the beach at Jilolo. Now, with no deep-sea ship to sail, the Spanish guerrillas in the Spice Islands could not return to their homes or to Mexico even had they chosen to do so. Truly stranded, they fought on for king and country as the decade of the 1530s dawned.

But in fact, the Spaniards' struggle for the Moluccas no longer had any meaning. Completely unaware of the bitter war being fought on his behalf in the Pacific, Charles had sold his claim to the Moluccas.

---

*He could not return to Spain westward via the Cape of Good Hope, as the *Victoria* had done. The Portuguese, more numerous now in those waters and more alert for interlopers, would almost certainly have intercepted the *Florida* and her precious cargo.

6
RIVALS IN DEFEAT

In 1530, as his loyalists fought to win him the Spice Isles, King-Emperor Charles was just emerging from a five-year period of wildly fluctuating fortune. In July 1525, as the Loaysa-Elcano armada departed for the Pacific, Charles had seemed triumphant. His mercenaries had defeated the French in Italy, ending four years of bitter war. More important, Charles's implacable foe, Francis I of France, had been captured and brought to Madrid. For more than a year Charles had held the French king prisoner. He had released him only when Francis agreed to a humiliating peace whose terms included the surrender of his two sons as hostages to Charles.

With this humbling of Francis, it had seemed to Charles that he had finally destroyed the ability of France to thwart his ambitions, and that Hapsburg hegemony over Europe was assured. But within months of his release Francis repudiated his treaty with Charles, and the infuriated emperor found himself again at war, this time against a coalition of France, England, and the pope.

Although Charles's expensive German mercenaries again gained military victories—including, in 1527, a brutal sack of Rome that shocked all Christendom—the Holy Roman Emperor eventually realized that the war was gaining him little politically while costing him more in treasure and lives than he could afford. He also saw that years of unceasing warfare were sapping his ability to stem the spread of Lutheranism in his German lands. As the end of the 1520s approached, whole provinces of Germany had gone over to the Protestant heresy. To complicate matters, the Turks were growing daily more menacing on the empire's southeastern borders.

Worst of all, however, was the indisputable fact that war had all but emptied Charles's treasury. Although Aztec loot was now pouring into Seville from Mexico, even this bounty fell short of the king's requirements. Nor could he envision much likelihood of further augmenting his wealth in the near term. He had already mortgaged his revenues far into the future. His program to take the Moluccas had apparently miscarried.

The expedition of Sebastian Cabot had also failed to gain its objective. Instead of following to the Pacific in Loaysa's wake, Cabot had sailed up the Río de Solís, which Magellan had already disproved as a passage to the Pacific, and had brought back nothing of value, except tales about great silver deposits.

Even Charles's marriage, entered into in 1526 with his cousin Princess Isabella of Portugal, had yielded only half of the million ducats promised as the lady's dowry.

In view of the financial and political problems that plagued him, Charles decided, in 1529, to salvage what he could from the chaos. He made peace with France and the pope, allowing Francis to ransom his hostage sons for much-needed cash. Charles had also made an agreement with the king of Portugal in which he renounced his claim to the Spice Islands in favor of Portugal for the not inconsiderable sum of 350,000 ducats of gold.*

As it turned out, these European accords came just in time for Charles. In that same summer of 1529 the Turks laid siege to Vienna, and Charles had to mount another expensive military effort to turn them back again.

Thus, in 1530, as his guerrillas fought on in the Moluccas, Charles was far more focused on European and American affairs than on the far-off Pacific. Although Spain continued to claim the great ocean and any lands it might contain, including the southern continent and the Isles of Lazarus discovered by Ma-

---

*This agreement, known as the Treaty of Saragossa, did provide, however, that Spain could reclaim the islands at some later date if they proved beyond doubt to be in Spain's "half" of the world.

gellan, knowledgeable Spaniards realized that to make such claims valid, Spanish ships would have to sail regularly across the Pacific in *both* directions. That day seemed far off indeed.

The Spaniards in the Spice Isles fought on for several years, until word of the Saragossa Treaty reached them. Eventually they surrendered to the occupying Portuguese. But only eight of them ever reached home to tell the tale. As for the Spice Islands, they soon fell completely under Portuguese domination. Moreover, Spanish attention was soon further diverted from the Pacific by a sensational new American conquest.

In 1532 Francisco Pizarro, an illiterate sixty-one-year-old veteran conquistador, toppled the Inca Empire with 167 men, 62 horses, and matchless audacity, and started a new river of gold flowing from the New World to the Old. Soon Spanish settlers, drawn by dreams of Inca wealth, began making their way south from Panama and Mexico to the newly conquered territory of Peru.

To handle all this traffic, Pizarro in 1535 set up a new capital city on the coastal plain of Peru. He named it Lima. As its port he built the town of Callao on the nearby Pacific. The commerce to and from Lima-Callao—whether trade goods, would-be colonists, or Inca treasure—had to follow a tortuous route. To reach Peru, goods and people first had to travel by pack-train from the Caribbean, over the jungle mountains of the Isthmus of Panama to the Pacific shore of Mexico. Then ships built in Mexico had to fight their way southward to Lima-Callao against adverse winds and currents. Depending on the season, the trip could take months. The return journey was just as difficult and time-consuming.

Some Spanish officials thought it might be possible to speed up this process by establishing an all-water route between the Caribbean and Peru by way of the Strait of Magellan. Though much longer in terms of distance than the transisthmus pathway, such a water passage might actually prove shorter in terms of time. But was the southern path feasible? Only two expeditions had ever passed through the strait: that of Magellan himself and the later armada led by Loaysa and Elcano. Both had encountered horrible conditions. Was the strait too tempestuous, then, to be used by regular merchant vessels? The only way to answer this question was to send ships to test it.

Accordingly, in 1534 and again in 1539, almost before the dust had settled on Pizarro's conquest, Spanish expeditions were dispatched to probe the southern waterway to the Pacific. Both attempts, defeated by cold, ceaseless gales, contrary winds, shortages of supplies, and, in one case, mutinous crewmen, ended in dismal failure. Of the five vessels sent forth on these missions, only one managed to reach the Pacific, and then only after months of exhausting struggle.

Spanish maritime officials were forced to conclude that the strait was too difficult for use by trading vessels carrying valuable cargo. The transisthmus pathway remained the preferred route for trade between the Caribbean and the Spanish Pacific coast.

Meanwhile, France was once again actively seeking its own route to the Pacific in the far northern latitudes of the globe. Although an earlier French effort led by the Italian navigator Verrazano had been unsuccessful, France had never abandoned hope that its mariners might yet discover a northern equivalent to Magellan's strait. Nor had France ever acknowledged Spain's exclusive claim to America and the Pacific.

Despite France's refusal to recognize a Spanish right to the New World, it was careful to respect the power that Spain wielded from Florida to the Strait of Magellan. For all the boastful bluster of its king, France customarily confined its maritime activity to those northern latitudes of the Atlantic where Spanish ships seldom ventured.

But if most of the Atlantic was out of bounds for French ships, the Pacific was another matter. Although Spain ruled the Pacific offshore waters from Mexico to the Strait of Magellan, it could not assert supremacy over the vast ocean itself. The opportunity still existed for France to stake its own claims in the Pacific. In fact, France might yet seize the richest Pacific prize of all: the southern continent.

For French mariners, even more than for Spaniards or Portuguese, Terra Australis Incognita exerted a powerful appeal. This fascination stemmed from a storied voyage made from 1503 to 1505 by a French navigator named Binot Paulmyer de Gonneville.

According to his own sworn account, Gonneville, with sixty companions and a 120-ton ship, the *Espoir*, set sail from Normandy for the South Atlantic in June 1503, before Spain had established its dominance in those waters.

Bound on a combination trading and exploratory mission, Gonneville proceeded toward the Cape of Good Hope, but violent storms drove his ship far off course. For weeks the vessel floundered until, in January 1504, she raised a mysterious land inhabited by hospitable natives who welcomed the Frenchmen.

For months Gonneville and his men lay over in this pleasant land repairing the *Espoir* and assembling new stores and cargo. At last Gonneville set out for home and reached the Azores in March 1505. Continuing on toward his home port of Honfleur, Gonneville was captured by a pirate vessel in the English Channel, losing not only the goods he had brought back from his strange southern land but the records of his voyage as well. In the end Gonneville and twenty-five of his men made it back to France to tell their tale. Most believed Gonneville's account of his voyage. However, without the ship's records, no one, least of all the voyagers themselves, had any clear idea of the new land's true location.*

Because Gonneville's backers, who had lost heavily on his voyage, were unwilling to finance a new venture, no French navigator followed up the journey. But there was much speculation that Gonneville's discovery was part of the southern continent that geographers said stretched around the bottom of the globe.

As a result of Gonneville's adventure, many French mariners had since concluded that a Gonneville Land certainly lay somewhere in the Southern Hemisphere and probably stretched high into the Pacific. To claim this mysterious Terra Australis, however, French mariners knew they would have to find their own secure route to the great ocean. Moreover, considering the strength of Spain in the South Atlantic and the Portuguese in the Indian Ocean, the route would have to be found in the northern latitudes.

Although Verrazano had already failed to locate such a northern seaway, French mariners were all but certain that a passage existed. Fishermen who frequented North American water spoke of deep "passes" along those rugged North Atlantic coasts. Accordingly, in 1534, France launched a new attempt to find its own way to the Pacific and its Gonneville Land.

---

*One of the survivors of the voyage was a native of this southern land. Named Essomeric, this man had voluntarily accompanied Gonneville back to France as living proof of the new discovery. But Essomeric, no sailor, could not find his way home either, and he settled down to live happily in France.

The man chosen to lead the French search was Jacques Cartier, a tough forty-three-year-old corsair who operated out of the port of Saint-Malo in Brittany. With two ships and sixty-one men, Cartier initiated his search for a northwest passage by conducting a reconnaissance of the rocky coast of Canada during the summer of 1534. He returned to report that natives of the area confirmed the existence of a large waterway in the North American interior.

In the following year Cartier, now furnished with three vessels and 110 men, went back. This time he ascended the St. Lawrence River in small boats until rapids barred the way. After enduring a cruel winter at what is now Quebec, Cartier again returned to France, taking with him captive natives who told encouraging stories of westward-flowing rivers in the interior of the country, rivers that, Cartier surmised, led to the Pacific.

Because open war had once more broken out between France and Spain in 1536, Cartier had to wait before returning to America for a third time. At last, in the summer of 1541, with a tenuous peace again restored between King Francis and Charles, Cartier once more sailed for the New World.

The Spaniards viewed this latest French initiative as incompatible with the recently-declared peace. They protested, calling Cartier's venture a bald affront to Spanish "rights" in the Pacific. The English ambassador to Paris saw it that way, too, reporting home that the purpose of Cartier's voyage was "to seek the trade of spicery by a shorter way than the Portugals use."

France ignored the Spanish objections. This third voyage was intended to be Cartier's most ambitious yet. In addition to searching for a northern strait, Cartier was to prepare the way for a French colony in North America, to be planted by the nobleman Jean François la Rocque de Roberval. Once more Cartier pushed up the St. Lawrence, often dawdling to search for gold. With the coming of winter he and his men camped to wait for spring and the expected arrival of the French colonists.

Bivouacked in the cold, Cartier's men dug up considerable quantities of what they took to be gold and diamonds. They also engaged in frequent hostilities with the local people. With the spring thaw, Cartier decided that instead of waiting for the colonists to arrive, he would sail for home immediately with his cargo of rich metals and gems, thus winning the praise of his sovereign and backing for a new, more powerful expedition. To his chagrin, however, when he put in at Newfoundland for supplies, Cartier encountered the nobleman Roberval and his colonists.

Roberval, who outranked Cartier, was outraged that the mariner had deserted his post on the St. Lawrence. He ordered Cartier to return with him upriver. But Cartier slipped away to sea and back to France with his precious cargo. At home, however, instead of praise, Cartier reaped only derision and censure, for his "gold and diamonds" turned out to be worthless metal and glass.

To the French, Cartier's failure was a galling disappointment, compounded further when, in 1543, Roberval and his colonists, unable to cope with the harshness of America, returned to France. More than half a century passed before France followed up Cartier's three voyages. As for Cartier, he was ennobled but received no new commissions and died in 1557.

Although Cartier had achieved virtually nothing in his search for the Northwest Passage to the Pacific, his voyages managed to galvanize the Spaniards into making a major new attempt of their own to conquer the vast ocean. The Spaniards had never entirely abandoned the Pacific, even when preoccupied with Europe, Peru, and the Strait of Magellan. In the mid-1530s, for example, Cortés, by then viceroy of Mexico, had sent two ships into the ocean to search for islands rumored to abound in gold. The ships, commanded by one Juan de Grijalva, a nephew of Cortés's, had dutifully plowed westward. Grijalva had sighted a number of islands, but none that abounded in gold. With provisions running short, Grijalva's men mutinied and murdered their commander. Soon after, one of the two ships of the expedition sank in a storm. The surviving vessel continued on, unable to return to Mexico against the prevailing winds. This ship finally smashed up in the vicinity of New Guinea. Seven men survived the wreck, only to fall into the hands of natives who kept them as slaves until, after several years, the Portuguese governor of the Moluccas had ransomed them.

In 1539, ignoring the miscarriage of the Grijalva effort, the governor of Guatemala, Pedro de Alvarado, had obtained a license from King Charles authorizing him to mount still another search for "islands in the Southern Sea toward the westward." In preparation for this voyage, Governor Alvarado had had ten ships carried in sections across the Isthmus of Panama to the Pacific coast and then reassembled by local shipwrights. But when the governor was killed in an Indian uprising, the contemplated journey fizzled.

Despite such failures, Spanish officials decided in 1541 to thrust once more into the Pacific, this time in force. Specifically, Spain aimed to take possession of the archipelago claimed for Charles almost twenty years earlier by Magellan.

By the reckoning of virtually all geographers these Isles of Lazarus, northwest of the Moluccas, lay in the Portuguese half of the world. Yet the Portuguese had done little to promote their sovereignty there. Although their warships visited the islands from time to time and their merchants conducted a desultory trade, Portuguese forces did not dominate the island chain as they did the Spice Islands. Moreover, when Charles had sold his stake in the Moluccas to the Portuguese, he had continued his claim to Magellan's isles. The reason for this was twofold. First, Spanish maritime officials reckoned that if Spain could someday gain effective control of this little-known island chain, it could more readily assert its claim to the entire Pacific and the still-undiscovered southern continent. Second, Spain would gain a base for trade with the rich and powerful Chinese Empire.

With these purposes in mind, Viceroy Antonio de Mendoza of Mexico (Cortés's successor) organized a powerful armada of six ships and 370 men under the command of his brother-in-law Ruy López de Villalobos. The fleet sailed from Mexico on November 1, 1542.

For three months the six heavily armed ships ran easily westward under the lash of the prevailing trade winds. They arrived at Mindanao at the end of January 1543. Anchored off Magellan's Isles of Lazarus, Villalobos now gave them a new name, the one that has endured to this day. He called them the Philippines, "after our most fortunate Prince, Philip," the sixteen-year-old heir to Charles.

Villalobos then set about his task of seizing the Philippines. With his cannon and his armed men he easily cowed the natives. Like Magellan, he planted his king's banners ashore and urged baptism on the native people. He built a small fortress and a chapel. But the Spanish commander's early success was misleading.

A thousand miles to the south, in the Spice Islands, the Portuguese learned of the Spanish presence. Though busily engaged in exploiting the Moluccas, the Portuguese also coveted the Philippines. Like the Spaniards, they saw the archipelago as a future base for trade with China. But even if they had not had designs on the islands, the Portuguese could only regard the arrival of a Spanish fleet as a threat. Accordingly a Portuguese fleet sailed northward to eliminate the Spanish intruders. Catching Villalobos and his forces by surprise, the Portuguese demanded the surrender of the Spanish interlopers.

Villalobos refused. The Portuguese bombarded Spanish ships and shore installations. The Spaniards resisted as best they could. But outnumbered and outgunned, Villalobos concluded that he could not hold the Philippines by force. After embarking his men, he took refuge at sea. Despite dwindling supplies, he maintained his fleet in Philippine waters and managed to evade the Portuguese for months. Eventually, however, he had no recourse but to admit defeat. With his men near starvation, he made his way to the island of Tidore in the Moluccas and surrendered.

One of his ships, however, the *San Juan de Letrán,* twice tried to escape internment by sailing back to Mexico, eastward across the Pacific. The *San Juan* got as far as Iwo Jima on her first attempt and as far as New Guinea on her second. But as always, the fierce headwinds of the Pacific turned her back. She then gave up to the Portuguese as well.

In time the Portuguese repatriated the survivors of the Villalobos expedition. Villalobos himself, however, was not among the freed prisoners. He died of fever at Amboina in 1546. For Spanish mariners, it seemed, attempts to conquer the Pacific invariably resulted in defeat and death. Two more decades were to pass before Spanish mariners returned to the Pacific and the Philippines.

7
WINDS OF WRATH

For the dynasts of Europe there seemed to be no respite—ever—from the hostilities that roiled the continent. As Spain pressed the conquest of America throughout the 1540s, Charles continually grappled with the French monarchy, the Protestants of Germany and the Netherlands, and the Turks. He fought still another war with France and engaged in a bloody civil struggle with the Protestants of his German domains. Both ended in apparent victories for him. Meanwhile, he continued to mortgage his New World revenues far into the future in order to pay the bills for war and religious suppression.

The 1540s also marked the passing of Charles's fiercest antagonists. Martin Luther, whose teachings had rent Europe for a generation, died in 1546. Francis I of France died in 1547, as did Henry VIII of England. Of all the great figures who had shaped the era, Charles alone remained in power at the beginning of the 1550s. Charles at last seemed to have gained some of his political aims. If he had failed to achieve the universal monarchy he had once sought (and now denied seeking), he had at least cowed France and suppressed religious strife in Germany.

Then, in a series of rapid blows, the tenuous nature of Charles's triumphant situation was revealed. In 1551 a new religious war broke out in Germany, with Protestant armies winning a series of major military victories over Charles's forces. In 1552,

Henry II of France, successor and son of old King Francis, in alliance with German Protestants, launched himself against the emperor. By 1555 Charles found himself beleaguered as never before. He was mentally and physically weary. Now fifty-five, he had reigned over Spain for thirty-eight years and over the Holy Roman Empire for thirty-six. He suffered from gout, arthritis, ulcers, and asthma. He yearned for some rest. Thus, tacitly acknowledging the failure of policies that he had pursued for almost forty years, Charles, in 1956, abdicated the throne of Spain to his son Philip and retired to a monastery in Spain.*

At twenty-nine, Philip II became the first ruler of a united Spain, the first man ever recognized as true king by all Spaniards from Aragón to Granada.

Born at Valladolid in 1527, the year his father's mercenaries shocked the world by pillaging Rome, Philip had never had a real childhood but had grown up with priests and pious women as his companions. Thus he had learned to regard the Catholic Church as the font of all morality. His mother, Isabella of Portugal, had surrounded him with dank piety and joyless ceremony. She had required everyone to treat her prince with grave respect.

At his father's insistence, however, Philip had received an excellent education from a host of private tutors. Although he did well in science, art, and history, he never became easy with language, and he shied away from oral communication, preferring to make his thoughts known in written memorandums.

Entering early upon the business of the realm, Philip had become governor of Milan at thirteen and regent of Spain at sixteen. In that same year, 1543, Philip had married a cousin, Princess Maria of Portugal. She died two years later after bearing him a son, Don Carlos. Philip had then formed a morganatic union with a beautiful commoner, Isabella de Osorio, whom he loved passionately and by whom he had several children.

Although he was only one quarter Spanish by blood, the young Philip was a Spaniard in heart and soul, steeped in Spanish culture and thought. Yet with his blue eyes and light hair and beard, he looked more Flemish than Spanish. His coloring tes-

---

*Charles had earlier turned over the government of the Netherlands to Philip. Charles still held the imperial title, however. In 1557 he resigned this title to his brother, Ferdinand, thus permanently separating the empire of Spain from the Holy Roman Empire. Charles died in 1558.

tified to his Hapsburg heritage, as did his protruding jaw and underlip. Contemporary writers described the youthful Philip as of less-than-medium stature, small-boned, and finely proportioned, a delicate young man who detested exercise.

In 1554, at the age of twenty-seven, Philip annulled his marriage with his commoner wife, and married England's devout Catholic Queen, Mary Tudor. The purpose was to produce a Hapsburg heir to the English throne who would not only keep England Catholic but also maintain ties with Spain and its empire. The daughter of Henry VIII and Catherine of Aragón, Mary, called Bloody Mary by English Protestants, had succeeded to the throne upon the death of her young half brother, Edward VI, in 1553. Plain, often ill, and eleven years older than Philip, Mary loved her Hapsburg husband. She did not become pregnant, however, although Philip remained with her in England for several months until called to serve as his father's vicar in the Netherlands in 1555.*

Philip's empire seemed to possess limitless riches despite its burden of debt. Cargoes of gold and silver flowed to Seville from America, thanks to the discovery in 1545 of a mountain of silver at Potosí in what is now Bolivia, and to new deposits of gold found in Chile. As a result of this influx of precious metals, Spain's revenues were ten times those of England when Philip became king.

In addition to Spain and its American possessions, Philip controlled a vast European territory that included Roussillon, Franche-Comté, the duchy of Milan, the kingdom of Naples, Sicily, Sardinia, and the Netherlands. In alliance with his uncle, Ferdinand (soon to be Holy Roman Emperor) Philip exercised de facto control over much of Italy. He also maintained possessions in North Africa and claimed all the Pacific, including the Philippine Islands. Moreover, backed by a splendid, if costly, army of fifty thousand veteran infantrymen and a navy of 140 armed vessels, Philip exercised absolute authority over his domain. Yet for all his power the new king of Spain faced the same vexations that had tormented his father.

In 1556, Protestantism was flourishing as never before, especially in the northern provinces of the Netherlands. Spain's finances were, as always, in disarray as a result of Charles's huge debt. Inflation was rampant. The latest war with France, begun while Charles still reigned, continued to lacerate the realm even

*Mary died in 1558, and was succeeded by her half-sister, Elizabeth.

after Philip came to the throne. It was this conflict, fought most bitterly at sea, that posed the most immediate threat.

In 1553 and 1554 French privateers had blockaded the coast of Spain, taking twenty-five Spanish transatlantic ships. French privateers had also raided Spanish settlements in the New World. In 1555 a corsair who went by the name Pegleg had pillaged the ports of Hispaniola and Puerto Rico. In 1556, the year of Philip's accession, a French privateer named Jacques de Sores despoiled the city of Havana. As a consequence of these French depredations, delivery of much-needed precious metal from American mines was being interrupted.

To counter the French marauders and to safeguard Philip's treasure ships, Spanish colonial officials tried once more to establish the Strait of Magellan as a reliable route for shipping New World metals from the Pacific to the Atlantic and then directly on to Seville, thus confounding French pirates lurking in the Caribbean. To implement this strategy, Spanish navigators first had to map the strait and chart its tides and winds. As early as 1553, some three years before Philip's accession, the governor-general of Chile had sent two vessels to carry out such a mission from the Pacific side of the passage. But this undertaking had miscarried when the commander of the venture, after getting safely into the waterway, had turned back, blaming his failure on "the bad state" of his vessels, "scarcity of provisions," and "hostility of the natives."

Late in 1557 the Spaniards tried the strait again from the Pacific side. This time they sent forth three vessels and sixty men under a veteran captain, Juan Fernández de Ladrillero, who had already made ten round-trip voyages between Spain and the New World.

Although the intrepid Ladrillero lost contact with two of his three ships before reaching the strait, he pressed on and succeeded in carrying out a remarkable reconnaissance of Magellan's waterway. He and his small crew not only traversed the strait from west to east and back again, but also mapped it and charted most of its natural features. Returning to Chile in 1559, Ladrillero wrote a guide to sailing the passage and stated his conviction that treasure ships from the Pacific coast could certainly pass safely to the Atlantic via the waterway.

By the time of his success, however, the strait had once more lost its attractiveness, for Philip had made a favorable peace with

France, relieving the pressure to find a sea route safe from French rovers.

In addition, the Casa de Contratación had instituted regulations requiring Spanish merchant vessels to sail in formidable, efficient, and regularly scheduled convoys under the protection of Spain's new man-of-war, the galleon, a powerful ship of five hundred tons or more. As a result, privateer activity had greatly diminished in the Caribbean and Atlantic, and the impetus to make use of the Strait of Magellan disappeared.* Spanish interest in the Pacific began to flame anew, however, as Philip, laboring under his load of debt and seeking new wealth to ease the strain on his purse, turned to the part of his empire that had produced the least so far but promised the most.

With his passion for details, Philip was certainly familiar with Spain's futile efforts in the Pacific after Magellan. No doubt he recognized that as a result of Spain's failures in the Pacific, the southern continent—the golden utopia that now appeared as fact on all maps—still lay open to conquest by Portugal, or France, or even the English, who had recently sailed through Arctic seas as far as Muscovy, seeking a North*east* Passage to Asia. The Philippines also lay out in Magellan's still-untamed Pacific, awaiting the bold Spaniard who would seize that island chain once and for all.

If Philip knew the details, he also understood the cause of Spain's forty years of futility: No navigator had yet figured out how to sail from Asia back to America against the Pacific winds and currents. Until Spanish mariners discovered how to traverse the ocean in both directions, Spain's claim to the Pacific would remain hollow.

With the conclusion of the French war, Philip, driven by need and by pride, resolved to send an armed fleet to the Philippines. This new armada would have orders to conquer the islands and then find a way to send vessels back to America. With the Philippines under control and a transpacific route established, Spain would not only reap the benefit of trade with China, but also be in position to discover and claim the southern continent.

Philip ordered Luis de Velasco, the viceroy of Mexico, to pre-

---

*Convoys were not new, of course. Spanish merchants and treasure ships had been sailing in company for decades, but until the late 1550s the system had worked haphazardly at best. In time convoys consisting of as many as 100 vessels would become the norm.

pare the new expedition. The king also wrote personally to a fifty-two-year-old missionary in Mexico asking him to pilot the fleet. The obscure friar was Andrés de Urdaneta, once page to the old circumnavigator himself, Juan Sebastián de Elcano. If any man could solve the riddle of the Pacific winds, it was Brother Andrés.

In the year 1560, Andrés de Urdaneta could look back on a life filled with both physical and spiritual adventure. He had taken holy orders eight years earlier in order to devote himself to the salvation of "Indian souls". Before donning the habit of an Augustinian friar, however, Urdaneta had endured enough hazard and toil for several ordinary lifetimes. He had battled his sovereign's enemies. He had voyaged far and had written valuable accounts of his journeys. His honesty and simplicity had won him the esteem of all. Most especially, in the course of his life, Brother Andrés had come to know the Pacific Ocean better than any man of his time.

He had first crossed the Pacific in 1525 when, at the age of seventeen, he had served as page to Elcano during the muddled journey in which more than 350 men perished, including both Elcano and the expedition's commander, Loaysa. Urdaneta had seen with his own eyes that, under sail, no amount of courage can compensate for poor seamanship.

In the course of that doomed voyage Urdaneta, in spite of his youth, had frequently been entrusted with the most difficult tasks in the fleet. As the armada struggled through the Strait of Magellan, Urdaneta had often been placed in command of the boats sent to reconnoiter ahead of the big ships. On other occasions he had been given responsibility for obtaining supplies ashore. Invariably, he had performed well and had won respect beyond his years.

Urdaneta had kept a journal noting the events of the journey and observations of winds and currents. It was the beginning of a lifelong habit. It was also their initial step in assembling what was to become his encyclopedic store of data on the Pacific.

By the time the 105 survivors of the Loaysa-Elcano debacle reached the Moluccas in the single remaining vessel, Urdaneta had advanced from a page to a chieftain in the company. In the guerrilla war that the Spaniards subsequently waged against the Portuguese for possession of the Spice Isles, Urdaneta had played a leading role and had been a member of the council of officers who set the strategy for the Spanish fighters.

When Emperor Charles put an end to the Spice Island war by selling the Portuguese his claim to the islands, Urdaneta, still only in his early twenties, had remained in the Moluccas. Knocking around the western Pacific, and keeping his eyes and ears open for information, Urdaneta had picked up valuable lore about Pacific winds and currents.

In 1536, when he was nearing thirty, Urdaneta had made his way home to Spain after almost thirteen years in the Pacific. On September 4, 1536, he appeared before the Royal Council to give a report on his activities, and greatly impressed that body with his knowledge of the ocean. Charles also received him and rewarded him with fifty gold ducats in recognition of his services. But Spain must have seemed tame to Urdaneta, and he made his way back across the Atlantic to Mexico.

There, in April 1539, he joined the expedition of Pedro de Alvarado, the unfortunate governor of Guatemala who had had ten ships carried across the Isthmus of Panama and then reassembled with the idea of sailing westward into the Pacific. When Alvarado died in an Indian insurrection, his cross-Pacific enterprise had gone into limbo, and so, apparently, had Urdaneta.

In 1542, when the Villalobos armada sailed from Mexico to claim the islands that Magellan had found and that Villalobos named the Philippines, Urdaneta, despite his reputation, did not sail with the fleet. By remaining in Mexico, Urdaneta avoided the Portuguese captivity that was the fate of the Villalobos survivors.

Urdaneta served as an official in the viceroyalty of Mexico for several years after this until he joined the Augustinians in 1552. He then pursued the peaceful life of the monastery until, in 1560, he received King Philip's personal entreaty.

Brother Andrés was not a man to shrink from a task, but he thought it his duty to inform Philip that he was no longer the man he had been in his youth. He wrote the king a simple, dignified letter, setting forth an honest appraisal of his personal circumstances: "I am now over fifty-two, and in poor health, and owing to the hard labors of my earlier years, the rest of my life was to have been spent in retirement." Despite his misgivings, Urdaneta ultimately acceded to his king's wishes and presented himself to the viceroy to help organize the new Philippines expedition.

It is likely that Urdaneta soon began looking forward to the voyage as an opportunity to test his own strategy for mastering the easterly headwinds of the Pacific, for he had already formulated a general theory of the Pacific's winds and currents. In the Northern Hemisphere, he postulated, the ocean's air and water flowed in a clockwise fashion, sweeping in a huge whirl from the high latitudes toward the equator and then back north again in a vast endless round. In the Southern Hemisphere, he thought, the huge whirl flowed *counter*clockwise. This would explain why the winds in the vicinity of the equator came incessantly out of the east, creating insurmountable head winds for any ship that tried to sail back to America through the Central Pacific. It also argued that in order to pick up westerlies favorable for a return to America, a ship would have to travel to the high latitudes, north or south, where the circling winds and currents reversed themselves.

But how *far* to the north or south would a ship have to sail in order to pick up the westerlies needed to drive it back to America? To Brother Andrés that was the question to be decided by the voyage to come.

8
SOLVING THE WIND

If Brother Andrés knew the Pacific, he also knew how to organize a fleet, so the viceroy placed the whole enterprise in the monk's hands. Urdaneta was even given the task of choosing the venture's captain general. Since, as a cleric, Urdaneta was excluded from filling that post himself, he selected a brave and dignified nobleman, Miguel López de Legaspi, to lead the armada.

Approximately fifty years old at this time, Legaspi had served as a Spanish official in Mexico for many years and was well known to Urdaneta, who regarded him as a wise and generous man. Legaspi showed his enthusiasm for the command by selling much of his own property in order to meet the costs of fitting out the fleet.

With Legaspi's money and Urdaneta's expertise, the new armada was ready by December 1563. But then, because of the illness of the viceroy and bureaucratic delays, it languished for months. Finally, on November 21, 1564, the fleet sailed from El Navidad, on the west coast of Mexico. It consisted of six vessels: *San Pedro*, five hundred tons; *San Pablo*, three hundred tons; three pinnaces; and a small tender. The ships carried 350 men, including a contingent of tough infantry. They also carried a greater weight of ordnance than had the Villalobos fleet twenty years earlier.

For the first ten days at sea the armada proceeded westward in good order. Then, on a calm night, one of Legaspi's captains, Alonso de Arellano, skipper of the pinnace *San Lucas*, slipped his vessel out of formation and set off on his own.

Arellano apparently hoped in this way to gain the glory of the voyage for himself. Perhaps he also intended to steal a march on the plundering of the Philippines. In any event Arellano's defection was noted in the logs without comment. The other ships did not pause to conduct a search. Apparently most of them assumed, correctly, that their comrade had deserted. The squadron sailed on as before.

The *San Lucas*, under Arellano's impatient lash, ran far ahead of her former companions and reached the Philippines long before Legaspi and Urdaneta. But Arellano, fearing the arrival of the rest of the fleet, spent little time in the islands. Instead he filled his holds with a cargo of cinnamon and then hauled anchor. Familiar with Urdaneta's theories about picking up westerly winds in the high latitudes, he pointed the *San Lucas* northward.*

Sailing parallel to the China coast, the *San Lucas* crept into the Northern Pacific. Then, just as Urdaneta had predicted, the wheeling winds began to blow from the west. Exultant, Arellano tacked for home.

For twelve weeks the *San Lucas* ran before these spanking westerlies. No land appeared until, after months of endless rolling ocean, the misty coast of California came into view. Jubilant, Arellano tacked southward and coasted the *San Lucas* home to Mexico. The rogue master of the *San Lucas* had become the first mariner ever to cross the Pacific from west to east.

Realizing that his sudden appearance in Mexico would arouse suspicion, Arellano concocted some acceptable story to cover his desertion of his companions. In any case Mexican authorities did not question him very closely. Perhaps they were more interested in *how* he had recrossed the Pacific than in *why*. Arellano soon traveled on to Spain to report on his triumphant voyage.

In the meantime, the five remaining ships of Legaspi's armada had reached Guam in late January of 1565. On February

---

*The general outline of Arellano's desertion and subsequent voyage comes from his own later account.

13 they sighted Samar in the Philippines. On April 27, carefully navigating through the archipelago under Urdaneta's guidance, the ships reached Cebu, the geographic heart of the islands. It was here that Magellan had established his headquarters some forty years earlier and had converted Rajah Humabon and his people to Christianity. Here, too, many of Magellan's crew had been massacred at a native feast.

Cebu was also the place where both Spaniards and Portuguese had always encountered the fiercest native opposition. Like any good military man, therefore, Legaspi aimed to eradicate any native resistance on Cebu as the first step in his conquest of the islands. Anchoring just offshore, he sent a company of infantry to the beach. The landing party was met by howling throngs of warriors, who attacked with spears and knives. The Spanish soldiers quickly withdrew to the ships.

Now Legaspi, determined to take Cebu, ordered his big ships to fire into the town. The fleet's cannon soon convinced the islanders to surrender and invite the invaders ashore.

Despite their initial hostility, Legaspi was bent on establishing good relations with the people of Cebu. He knew he needed a secure base in order to achieve total subjugation of the archipelago. He assured the natives that he intended them no harm. He pardoned them for their resistance to his landing and for killing Magellan and his men in 1521. Then, in a formal ceremony, he took possession of Cebu for Philip. Meanwhile, Urdaneta built a church in the village, and the priests of the expedition set about the reconversion of the natives. Within weeks the Spanish had established effective sovereignty over Cebu.

Now Legaspi and Urdaneta decided to wait no longer to test the monk's proposed northern sailing route across the Pacific from the Philippines. Both were aware that the defector Arellano might have already succeeded in returning to Mexico. On June 1, 1565, Urdaneta departed for home aboard the three-hundred ton *San Pablo*. He had promised Legaspi that once back in Mexico, he would urge the viceroy to send immediate reinforcements to the Philippines.

Under the purely nominal command of Legaspi's seventeen-year-old grandson, Felipe, the *San Pablo* plowed into the North Pacific, searching for Urdaneta's westerlies. If Brother Andrés experienced any doubts during this northward journey, he kept them to himself. At last, somewhere above latitude 35 degrees north, the *San Pablo* picked up the hoped-for westerly winds. It must have been a moment of deep satisfaction for Urdaneta.

For the next three months Urdaneta, like Arellano before him, sailed on before the powerful winds of the North Pacific, sighting no land of any kind. Then, on September 18, 1565, the coast of California came into view. The *San Pablo* had arrived somewhere in the vicinity of the Santa Barbara Channel. The ship sailed on southward to the port of Acapulco, which it reached in October, after having traveled more than eleven thousand miles. Brother Andrés had demonstrated beyond doubt that ships could journey to and from the Philippines following his route.

After giving an account of Legaspi's situation on Cebu and securing the viceroy's agreement to send relief galleons, Urdaneta went on to Spain to report further. There, to his great satisfaction, he encountered the deserter Arellano.

Arellano, enjoying the acclaim, had taken credit for solving the Pacific puzzle, even though it was well known that Brother Andrés had first suggested the pattern of the ocean's winds and currents. To sort out the conflicting claims of Arellano and Urdaneta, Spanish maritime officials convened a panel of experts. Urdaneta's calm good sense and expertise quickly convinced all concerned that he—and Legaspi—deserved the honor for developing the Pacific route. The friar was hailed as a hero, while Arellano was ordered back to Mexico in disgrace. Soon thereafter Urdaneta also returned to Mexico. But now, at sixty, Brother Andrés reached the end of his strength. He would make no more voyages. He died on June 3, 1568, honored by all Spanish mariners as the man who had solved the Pacific puzzle.

Meanwhile, in the Philippines Legaspi had been methodically expanding the Spanish presence, although hampered by recurring insubordination among his officers. He followed a strategy of invading neighboring islands to broaden Spanish control in the archipelago. Despite these conquests, however, his circumstances began to grow precarious. Supplies of powder and shot were running low. Spanish forces, spread thin, were growing weary. Legaspi desperately needed reinforcements.

As the months passed, Legaspi also worried that the Portuguese would soon appear in force to retake the islands. Muslim traders carried news that a powerful Portuguese armada was being prepared in the Moluccas for just that purpose.

Then, on August 30, 1568, Legaspi's scouts sighted two big ships approaching from the east. They were heavily armed galleons from Acapulco. They carried soldiers, powder, food supplies, cannon, and ammunition. Their arrival more than doubled Spanish strength in the islands. The joyful Legaspi now felt confident that unlike Villalobos, he could hold the Philippines against any force that challenged him.

As it turned out, the Acapulco galleons arrived just in time. In September the long-rumored Portuguese squadron from the Moluccas appeared and blockaded the harbor at Cebu. Their ships' big cannon blasted the villages of natives who had allied themselves with the Spaniards. The newly reinforced Spaniards counterattacked. Their three five-hundred-ton galleons mauled the smaller, if more numerous, Portuguese vessels. The Portuguese withdrew, never to return.

With the Portuguese threat ended, Legaspi resumed his step-by-step subjugation of the Philippines. Even more important than the conquest of the islands, however, was the shining fact that thanks to Urdaneta, a sea link had now been established between America and the Philippines. Spanish galleons following Brother Andrés's path would soon be crossing the Pacific regularly.

Now Spanish mariners could devote themselves to that other mystery of the Pacific: Terra Australis Incognita. Most felt sure that since they had learned how to sail the Pacific, it was only a matter of time before their galleons would sight the shores of that golden continent.

For Philip of Spain the invasion of the Philippines and the solving of the Pacific winds represented two more triumphs in a reign that seemed to promise ever-increasing glory and success. By 1568, as the first galleons made their way to and from the Philippines, the king of Spain, now forty, could look back with satisfaction on the first twelve years of his reign. He had maintained peace with a France that was already stumbling into civil war between Huguenots and Catholics. The Turks—after the death of their sultan Suleiman the Magnificent—were quiet. England, under its Protestant queen, Elizabeth, was recovering from the upheavals of Mary's reign. Philip had even achieved some semblance of financial stability by restructuring his debt to Europe's bankers. He had, in fact, calmed much of the political turmoil bequeathed to him by his father. He had also stamped his own peculiar style on his government.

Closeted within his austere working chambers, the most powerful ruler in the world wrote long memorandums, setting forth with exactitude his thoughts on virtually every aspect of his realm. The bureaucratic Philip was intent on controlling every facet of the state. As a result, the machinery of government often choked to a standstill while the sovereign dealt with minutiae.

Philip, who reveled in the title His Most Catholic Majesty, remained inflexible on the two precepts that guided all his decisions: first, that God had anointed him to rule over his subjects for their own good, and second, that the Catholic Church was the repository of all religious truth.

From Philip's point of view there was but one dark cloud on his political horizon, and that lay over his Netherlands dominions, where heresy continued to make inroads. The Spanish Netherlands—one of Philip's richest domains thanks to a thriving cloth and fishing industry as well as an excellent merchant marine—consisted of a complex of states and towns, loosely gathered into seventeen provinces. The seven northern provinces—equivalent to the modern Dutch nation—had long had a sizable Protestant minority. The ten southern provinces— roughly equivalent to modern Belgium—remained overwhelmingly Catholic. Traditionally the Netherlands had always exercised a great deal of political and religious autonomy. Philip, however, was trying to change that by imposing Spanish systems and the Catholic religion, including the Inquisition, on the Netherlanders.

As a result, the Protestants of the Netherlands had initiated resistance to Spanish rule. In August 1566, fired by anti-Catholic sermons, Protestant mobs had rioted in Antwerp, Ghent, Amsterdam, and other towns, attacking Catholic churches, convents, and homes. Though outraged, Philip had first tried to conciliate his Protestant subjects by making a series of minor concessions. But turmoil had continued. Philip had then decided to quell what might become an open rebellion against his authority. He had ordered his best military commander, the duke of Alva, to march his Spanish troopers from their base in Italy to keep order in the Netherlands.

Tall, thin, dark, austere, Alva—a figure out of an El Greco

painting—had no qualms about using force to subdue the enemies of his sovereign. Moreover, he regarded the Netherlanders with contempt. "I have fought men of iron," he sneered. "Should I fear men of butter?"

In the spring of 1567 the duke, with ten thousand superb Spanish infantry, reached the Netherlands. By then, however, the worst of the disturbances had ceased. Many Protestants had fled the country. The duke settled down to "pacify" the land, making it known that he meant to crush any opposition to Philip's will.

Philip recognized from the start that however successful, Alva's operations in the Netherlands would be costly, putting renewed pressures on the kingdom's hard-won financial stability. For this reason the Spanish king and his colonial officials were more avid than ever to search out new sources of wealth in Spain's empire.*

With the Pacific winds solved at last, and the Philippines rapidly falling under Spanish domination, that search would now focus as never before on the still-unclaimed southern continent. By now, Terra Australis Incognita had become an unquestioned reality. The continent's outline appeared on all depictions of the world. Depending upon the globe, Terra Australis might stretch from the Indian Ocean to South America or from the East Indies to the South Pole. So vast a land, all agreed, *must* contain marvels and wonders and vast material wealth.

In fact, as Alva sought to "pacify" the rebels of the Netherlands and Legaspi toiled to subdue the Philippines, a young colonial official had already sailed off to claim the prize for Philip.

---

*Inflation had also begun seriously straining Philip's purse. In 1567 the city of Barcelona, for example, raised the wages of all officials, since "every article of human need is incomparably more expensive than it ever has been." Clearly the inflation that had plagued Spain since the mid-1540s had worsened in the 1560s.

9
INCA VISIONS

Despite their small size, the city of Lima and its port of Callao were thriving centers of commerce and government in the late 1560s. Lima, founded by Pizarro, was the capital of the viceroyalty of Peru. In its warehouses were stored the treasures of the Potosí silver mines, awaiting shipment to Seville. In its taverns, lusty sailors drank the sour local wines. In its whitewashed churches, which rang with bells imported from Spain, black-robed priests intoned the mass to sullen natives often converted by force to the true faith. The city exemplified life in Spain's New World.

Among the many minor officials who labored at the viceregal business in Lima at the time was a dark-eyed, fiery man in his mid-thirties named Pedro Sarmiento de Gamboa. Born in Galicia in 1532—the year that Pizarro overthrew the Incas—Sarmiento had managed to gain considerable education in his youth, including a knowledge of Latin and mathematics. He served in the Spanish Army as a very young man. Sometime around his twenty-first year, however, he had struck out for the New World in search of wealth and adventure.

Settling in Lima, where men with even a little learning were in demand, Sarmiento won a post in the viceregal administration. For the next few years he led the life of a minor government official. But Sarmiento was no ordinary man. Fascinated by the night sky of the Southern Hemisphere, he began studying astronomy. He then taught himself navigation and produced a number of works on cosmography. He also dabbled in magic, as did many scholars of the day. The Inquisition regarded him with suspicion, but he was never prosecuted for his interest in the occult. At some point he began a study of Inca legends and history and soon made himself the leading authority in the field.

In September 1564, Sarmiento's life was altered forever. A governor-general arrived from Spain to conduct the affairs of Peru after the death of the viceroy, the count of Nieves. The new governor-general, Lopé García de Castro, a man of good sense and honesty, was to rule pending appointment of a permanent viceroy.

Castro came to depend heavily on local officials for help in carrying out his complex duties. Sarmiento made himself useful to the governor and soon found himself well placed to propose a venture that he had long been contemplating: a *scientific* search for the southern continent. Like all Spanish officials, Sarmiento dreamed of Terra Australis Incognita. Unlike other officials, however, he was certain he knew where to find it.

His confidence was based on his knowledge of the Incas. He knew that they were not indigenous to the Andean plateau but had originated elsewhere and had conquered a native people. He speculated that the Incas, in some dim time now long forgotten, had come to Peru from a land across the sea. Surely, Sarmiento theorized, so powerful and sophisticated a people must have originated in an extensive, well-favored land, a continent. Furthermore, he had come across numerous hints in Inca legends and history of past ties with mysterious lands to the west.

Sarmiento suspected that underlying the Inca stories was a foundation of fact. Islands mentioned in many legends, he thought, were probably the outlying portals to the southern continent. He also thought it likely that these islands lay only a relatively short distance over the western horizon since the Incas had never possessed vessels capable of extended ocean voyages.

As for the continent itself, Sarmiento imagined that it lay no more than two thousand miles from Peru, a huge mass of mountainous land that stretched from Tierra del Fuego toward the northwest. He also thought he understood why no Pacific navigator had yet sighted the continent. Following prevailing winds and currents, previous Spanish voyagers had sailed too far north.

He theorized that the continent lay near the Tropic of Capricorn, far *south* of the equator.

With Urdaneta's successful return from the Philippines, Sarmiento apparently judged the time ripe to propose a voyage into the Pacific aimed at locating Terra Australis. He put the project before Governor Castro and quickly won his approval.

Although Sarmiento expected to be put in charge of the voyage that was, after all, his brainchild, command of the venture went to twenty-five-year-old Álvaro de Mendaña, the gentlemanly nephew of the governor, who was neither a seaman nor a scholar. Sarmiento swallowed his fury, however, and agreed to go on the journey as Mendaña's subordinate.

Two ships were readied for the voyage at the port of Callao: the 250-ton *Los Reyes* and the 107-ton *Todos Santos*. The ships carried 150 men. But only 70 of the complement were mariners or soldiers. The rest were "Indian" slaves impressed to do the heavy labor once the expedition reached Terra Australis. Four Franciscan friars were also aboard the ships to convert the infidels of the southern continent. Mendaña's orders were to sail into the ocean until he reached the shores of the southern continent. After establishing a colony, he was to send back his ships for additional colonists and reinforcements.

Young Captain General Mendaña was handsome, amiable, brave, and well meaning. He looked upon the voyage ahead as a splendid adventure. An optimist by nature—and as naíve about men as he was ignorant of the sea—he anticipated few difficulties during the journey. After all, according to Sarmiento, the ships should strike the coastline of Terra Australis somewhere between the Tropic of Capricorn and the equator in three weeks or less. And if, against all odds, problems *should* arise during the passage, Mendaña expected to rely on the sage counsel of the expedition's chief pilot, Hernán Gallego.

Gallego, fifty years old, had spent many years navigating Pacific waters from the Strait of Magellan to California. He was by far the most experienced mariner in the company. He must have realized that in order to sail the course Sarmiento proposed, Mendaña's two ships would have to make their way across the ocean without the aid of the strong easterly winds that blew near the equator. Thus the enterprise might find itself becalmed in mid-ocean. Yet Gallego apparently offered no objection to Sarmiento's plan. Possibly he felt it necessary to defer to the strong-willed scholar. Perhaps he reasoned that if the southern continent really lay only two thousand miles away, as Sarmiento insisted, the prize would be worth a few weeks of light air. In any event, Gallego set the course west by southwest as instructed, and the expedition set out from Callao on November 19, 1567, with flags and trumpets signaling the high hopes of those aboard. The *Los Reyes* and the *Todos Santos* each carried provisions for a voyage of no more than two thousand miles in accordance with Sarmiento's ideas.

As the two ships edged into the Pacific, time passed in a steady, monotonous procession. The vast placid ocean spread away on all sides. Day after day lookouts spied no land at all: not an island, not a sandbar, much less a continent.

After twenty-six days of light winds and empty ocean, the pilot, Gallego, reckoned that the ships had reached a point approximately a thousand miles south of the equator and more than twenty-five hundred miles west of Peru. According to Sarmiento's theory, they should already have sighted the continent in these waters. Still, there was nothing visible but the endless, heaving Pacific.

One of the officers, Gómez Catoira, kept a record of the journey. According to Catoira, the men now began to grumble, wondering whether they had embarked on a fool's errand. To make matters worse, according to Catoira, the winds diminished until the ships were barely making any headway at all.

In this situation the old Pacific hand, Gallego, advised Mendaña to alter his course slightly to the north in order to pick up more wind and take advantage of an ocean current in this region. Sarmiento flew into a rage at Gallego's suggestion. Any deviation from their agreed-upon course, he argued to Mendaña, would defeat the very purpose of the venture. A turn to the north would merely take them over previously explored ocean and would deny them the chance to find the continent that probably lay near at hand.

Mendaña was torn. He wanted to believe Sarmiento. But he could not ignore Gallego's experienced advice. Finally, acutely aware of the dissension building in the crews, he accepted Gallego's suggestion and altered course to the northwest. Furious, Sarmiento predicted their mission would fail.

Another two weeks passed, and still the ships sighted no land.* It was now the new year of 1568. The ships had been at sea for six weeks. Water and food were growing short. Many of the men were now openly advocating abandonment of the voyage. Gallego calmed matters by promising that they would find land before the month of January was out.

Now, having sailed northwest to latitude 6 degrees south, the ships picked up a westward-flowing current and turned due west. They sailed for fifteen hundred miles more without a sight of land. By mid-January the expedition had been at sea for sixty-two days. The drinking water had gone foul. The food was almost gone. Friction between Sarmiento and Gallego was mounting every day as the two men disagreed over the ship's course, the set of sails, and even rations. Mendaña tried to keep peace with all and succeeded only in irritating everyone.

On January 15 lookouts spotted a tiny atoll ahead. Naming this speck of earth Isle of Jesus, Mendaña decided to anchor and let the crews search ashore for food and water. He instructed Gallego to find an anchorage. But Gallego, convinced that the atoll was uninhabited and thus lacking food and water, ignored Mendaña's order.

Carried by the strong westward current, the ships continued past the island. Mendaña, apparently distracted by other business, did not notice Gallego's disobedience until numerous native canoes suddenly materialized, a certain sign that the island indeed offered food and water. Again Mendaña ordered Gallego to anchor. But it was too late. The ships had drifted past the atoll and could not fight their way back against the strong current. When the famished, crewmen realized that Gallego had cost them a chance to anchor and resupply, they exploded in wrath. The expedition was on the verge of mutiny. A contrite Gallego again managed to calm the storm by promising they would find a far richer island just ahead.

The ships sailed on. But no land appeared. The grumbling grew worse, and when the ships nearly went aground on a line of coral reefs, the men threatened to seize the vessels from the pilot. At last, on February 7, 1568, having been driven southwest again by a storm, Gallego himself spied what seemed to be an

---

*Incredibly they had sailed between the Tuamotus and the Marquesas without sighting any of those lush islands.

expanse of land. He ordered a mariner to climb the mainmast to confirm what his own eyes were telling him. Catoira wrote, "The sailor reported land, and presently it was visible to us. And we hoisted a flag, and received the news with great joy." It was the eighty-first day of the voyage. The *Los Reyes* and *Todos Santos* had traveled more than six thousand miles from Peru.

It took two more days for the ships to reach the land so long sought. Seen from the sea, the country looked very much like the coastline of a continent. Green-covered mountains reached to the clouds and stretched away to the horizon. All aboard were certain they had reached the southern continent. The ill will engendered during the voyage was now forgotten. After skirting dangerous coral reefs, the ships anchored safely in a palm-fringed bay.

Now an armada of dugout canoes swarmed out from the beaches. Black, frizzy-haired warriors, with fierce filed teeth and armed with bows, arrows, and lances, paddled about the Spanish ships with remarkable agility. Offering gifts of bells and beads, the Spaniards tried to persuade the skittish canoeists to come aboard. In time greed overcame fear, and the natives clambered onto the ships. Awed, they exclaimed at the wonders they found. Then they began to steal anything that caught their fancy, until the sailors locked away anything loose.

After this initial exchange the Spaniards, led by the friars, went ashore and planted a cross on the beach. All agreed to name this new land Santa Ysabel, after the patron saint who had guided them on their long voyage from Peru.

Almost immediately after the raising of the cross, the Spaniards began felling trees for construction of a brigantine, a small vessel that would be used to explore the shallow waters and rivers nearby. Satisfied with the start made in this new land, Mendaña established a camp ashore, although many of the men continued to dwell aboard ship.

On the day after their arrival at Santa Ysabel, the Spaniards were visited by a resplendent local chief named Bilebanara who wore a fearsome painted face and an intimidating headdress of long white and multicolored plumes. The chief, accompanied by a number of his people, agreed to provide the hungry newcomers with fresh food and water in exchange for trade goods.

Despite his pledge, however, two days went by with no sign of the hoped-for supplies. Though the famished Spaniards picked coconuts from trees along the shore, they found little nourishment in the sweet meat. Accordingly, Mendaña sent an armed party under one of his officers, Pedro de Ortega, into the nearby jungle to find Chief Bilebanara and inquire about the promised supplies. Received peacefully, Ortega learned only that there would be no provisions forthcoming despite the earlier promises. Puzzled but unable to obtain any further explanation, Ortega returned to Mendaña with the unhappy news.

Given the deteriorating condition of his men and the odd recalcitrance of the natives, Mendaña concluded that he had no choice but to seize food, if possible. With this in mind he dispatched another party into the jungle under Sarmiento's command. Mendaña emphasized that Sarmiento was to use force only if needed.

Sarmiento soon encountered Chief Bilebanara and one of the chief's uncles, named Havi. Like Ortega, Sarmiento was told only that no food could be spared for the Spaniards. Deciding to search further for supplies, Sarmiento took Chief Bilebanara and Uncle Havi with him as more or less willing guides and set out for a ridge that lay some miles inland. There, according to the natives, Sarmiento might find villages willing to trade for food. But night fell before the Spaniards could reach the ridge. It began to rain. The Spaniards made camp in the jungle.

During the night the jumpy Spaniards heard warriors moving about and shouting in the dark. The nervous soldiers periodically fired their guns into the shadows, hoping to frighten their visitors away.

At dawn Sarmiento, fearing an attack by the natives still hiding in the jungles, thought it prudent to return to the ships. He made it clear that Chief Bilebanara and Uncle Havi were now hostages, and the Europeans started back through the forest, trailed by skulking warriors. At some point Bilebanara managed to slip away. Suddenly, as if the chief's escape were a signal, the natives attacked. The Spaniards fired, wounding several blacks. Sarmiento himself cut down one warrior with his sword. With Uncle Havi still a captive, the Spaniards fought their way to the safety of the ships.

Mendaña heard Sarmiento's report with fury. He blamed the resentful Sarmiento for precipitating the conflict with the black warriors. Mendaña returned Uncle Havi to his people. Sometime later the natives repaid this gesture of goodwill by leaving a small amount of food on the beach for the newcomers.

For another month, while building their brigantine, the Spaniards eked out an existence along the shoreline of Santa Ysabel. Early in March 1568 Mendaña sent his camp master, Ortega, with sixty men to try again to scale the inland ridge.

Although by now Bilebanara's tribe was cautiously tolerant of the Europeans, the inland people attacked the Spaniards as they climbed the ridge. Nevertheless, Ortega and his band pressed on until they reached the top of the rise and there made a disheartening discovery.

Instead of the rolling plains of a great continent, they saw the blue of the sea beyond. Santa Ysabel was an island, not the southern continent.

10

KING SOLOMON'S
ISLANDS

Though the Spanish were disappointed to find that Santa
Ysabel was not, after all, Terra Australis, there was a general feeling that the island was an outpost of the continent.

Mendaña's men therefore pushed hard to finish the brigantine taking shape on the beach. Only when the boat was ready
could they begin reconnoitering the coral-studded waters around
Santa Ysabel and its environs. Moreover, the brigantine, unlike
the clumsy big ships, would allow the Spaniards to range farther
along the shores after much-needed provisions.

Meanwhile, an uneasy peace prevailed between the local
people and the newcomers. Mendaña sent out no more scouting
parties, and the islanders provided sufficient food for the Spaniards to get along. It was during this relatively tranquil time, however, that an event convinced most of the Spaniards that the
islanders were "black devils" and perhaps not altogether human.

One day a number of native canoes suddenly appeared in
the bay where the Spanish ships rode at anchor. The blacks, making signs of peace, paddled toward the vessels. They indicated
that as a gesture of goodwill they had brought a gift of meat for
the white strangers. One of the islanders then proudly displayed
this bounty. Gazing down from their ships, the hungry Spaniards
beheld a bloody arm and shoulder recently severed from the
body of a child.

"We were all struck with great wonder and pity to see so much cruelty," reports the chronicler Catoira. One of Mendaña's Indian slaves was sent to receive the proffered meat. According to Catoira, the limb was then buried with many exclamations of disgust on the part of the Spaniards. The natives, he says, paddled away to a nearby island where they enjoyed the rest of their cannibal dinner.*

Finally, after eight weeks of labor, the five-ton brigantine, christened the *Santiago*, was finished. On April 7, 1568, the undecked vessel, which would hold about thirty men, departed on a scouting mission under Chief Pilot Gallego's command. The party soon sighted other islands in the vicinity, all of them very similar to Santa Ysabel. They named the largest islands Malaita and Guadalcanal. When the Spaniards tried to land on Guadalcanal, they were attacked by islanders, who refused to retreat until fired upon.

After returning to Santa Ysabel, Gallego reported to Mendaña that none of the nearby islands seemed to offer much in the way of provisions. Nor was there evidence of a continental landmass in the vicinity.

In spite of this disappointment, Gallego went on a second reconnaissance in the brigantine. It only confirmed his first bleak impression of the island chain. But Mendaña, still hoping that the southern continent did not lie very far off, refused to be discouraged. He was determined to maintain a Spanish base in these islands. If Santa Ysabel could not furnish sufficient food supplies, perhaps they would have better luck on another island. On May 12, 1568, three months after their landing on Santa Ysabel, the Spaniards moved southeast to Guadalcanal.

It proved no more hospitable than Santa Ysabel. Food supplies had to be coerced from the natives. There was fever among the Europeans. Bloody clashes between Spaniards and islanders were virtually incessant. On one occasion native warriors ambushed a Spanish watering party and hacked nine men to pieces. They then danced away with their severed limbs—presumably to a cannibal feast. Inevitably the Spaniards wreaked a terrible ven-

*Cannibals or not, the Spaniards continued to seek the goodwill of the natives, even, in one instance, helping Chief Bilebanara's people achieve victory in a battle with a neighboring tribe.

geance, burning villages, murdering captives, and quartering the bodies of fallen warriors.

Sarmiento was in the forefront of these bloody operations. Scorning Mendaña as "soft" because he continued to urge mild treatment for the "black devils," Sarmiento and his many adherents called for a policy of terror to cow the "savages and cannibals." Mendaña refused. The fighting went on unabated. Friction worsened among the Spaniards.

In the end the Spaniards abandoned Guadalcanal even though they had found indications of gold deposits in its jungle streams. On Mendaña's orders the ships moved to another island, which Mendaña named San Cristobal. Smaller than Guadalcanal and Santa Ysabel, this island also had a population of hostile natives unwilling to part with the food supplies that the Spanish still needed desperately. Once again there were clashes and murdered Spaniards, followed by reprisals, burned villages, and provisions forcibly removed from storehouses.

It was now mid-July 1568. The Spanish ships were much in need of repair and cleaning. Thus, despite the presence of hostile natives all around, the company decided to careen the vessels at San Cristobal. The crews disembarked and camped onshore. The *Los Reyes* and the *Todos Santos* were pulled up onto the beach. For three weeks the crews scraped and scrubbed their bottoms, repairing leaks and applying pitch. All this time the Spaniards had to defend a perimeter around their camp, which was under almost constant attack. In early August, with the ships once again floating safely off the beach, Mendaña convened a meeting of the company to consider the expedition's future.

Speaking first, he reminded his listeners that their orders were to find the southern continent and create a settlement there. Though so far unsuccessful, he declared, he himself was still anxious to continue the search. But suppose they did *not* find the continent, Mendaña asked. Would any of the officers and men be willing to settle on one of the islands already discovered?

The question stunned the audience. The marine officers among them pointed out that both their ships were much worn despite the recent careening. Moreover, many of the crewmen were sick. The soldiers noted that the enmity of the blacks showed no signs of abating, while Spanish firearms were wearing out and ammunition was running low. When the guns fell silent, they said, any settlers on these islands would be easy prey for the "cannibals."

In the end it was clear that the majority of Mendaña's men wanted only to return to Peru. Some told the commander that considering the state of the ships even *that* voyage might be beyond their strength.*

Despite the overwhelming sentiment for going home, Sarmiento argued against it. He was still convinced that Terra Australis lay nearby and that these benighted islands could be used as a staging area to reach it if only Mendaña would permit him to bring the "Indians" to heel.

After listening to all these points of view, Mendaña seemed to hesitate. He was apparently unwilling to admit the failure of his venture. Then the pilot, Gallego, weighed in with his opinion. The deterioration of the ships, he said, dictated that they return to Peru, and that was that. Mendaña gave in.

The Spaniards prepared to depart. For the return journey the troublesome Sarmiento was given command of the *Todos Santos*, probably to avoid further friction with Mendaña and Gallego, both of whom remained aboard the larger the *Los Reyes*. The Spaniards filled their casks with fresh water from the streams of San Cristobal. They celebrated a mass and weighed anchor. It was August 11, 1568. They had been away from home almost nine months.

Dissension was soon rampant aboard the ships as Sarmiento, Mendaña, and Gallego wrangled over the course to be followed back to Peru. Sarmiento, still confident that the southern continent had to lie to the south and west, insisted they should sail that way, at least for a time. Immediately overruled, he took refuge in a sullen silence.

Mendaña argued that the ships should steer south*east*. He was now convinced that Terra Australis lay in *that* direction. The patient Gallego, familiar with the contrary winds near the equator, urged that they sail north, across the equator into the high Pacific. There, he said, they would be able to pick up westerlies and follow Urdaneta's recently discovered route back to America.

---

*A few brave souls opposed giving up, saying they wanted to remain and search for more of the gold previously found in Guadalcanal's streams.

With his irresolute nature shining forth as never before, Mendaña tried to compromise between his own and Gallego's point of view. The ships, he said, would sail according to the wind. When it favored the course proposed by Gallego, the ships would go north. Otherwise they would try to head southeast, as Mendaña wished. As a result, the ships wandered aimlessly for days, until the mariners raised a protest against their meandering. "The landsman reasons and the seaman navigates," the crew declared to Mendaña, according to Catoira's account.

Finally Mendaña adopted Gallego's course. The ships kept on northward. Within a week they crossed the equator, passing the Gilbert Islands without sighting them. On September 17 they sighted Namu in the Marshall Islands. To their consternation, however, the Spaniards could locate no water on the island.

The ships continued on. About October 1, 1568, they came to a speck of land crowded with seabirds. But once again they found no water. After naming the place San Francisco Island, they resumed the voyage.*

Every day *Los Reyes*, the bigger of the two vessels, ran far ahead of the *Todos Santos*, captained by Sarmiento. According to the standing orders, however, the *Los Reyes* shortened sail each evening to allow the smaller ship to rendezvous for the night. Following this system, the vessels plowed northward. Daily the men prayed for the westerly winds to appear so the ships could turn for home. Their prayers went unanswered. Rations dwindled to a pint of water and less than a pound of bread a day for each man.

Sometime in mid-October the *Todos Santos*—and Sarmiento—failed to keep the usual evening rendezvous with the *Los Reyes*. Mendaña and Gallego concluded that Sarmiento had deserted the expedition. Furious, they sailed onward with the dawning of the new day.

Soon after this a huge cyclone whirled down on the *Los Reyes*. Now the ship, already in poor shape, had to struggle against gigantic, wind-whipped seas. At one point a massive wave struck her broadside, and she rolled over on her beam end. As she lay helpless, the sea poured in through a dozen open seams in her decks. She was soon in peril of sinking, but even as the storm continued to rage, Gallego and his sailors sawed away at the

*The speck is now known as Wake Island.

ship's mainmast and rigging in a desperate effort to right her once more. At last, though pounded by waves, the men managed to free the ship from the dead weight of her mast and rigging, which they hurled into the sea. Slowly the *Los Reyes* rolled upright again. The mariners rigged a foresail from a blanket and scraps of canvas in order to keep some way on their embattled vessel. For another day and night the *Los Reyes* fought the storm. When the tempest finally moderated, the *Los Reyes* was a near wreck. She had lost her mainmast, her boat, and even her sterncastle. Seawater sloshed belowdecks. Still, she limped northward.

Now thirst and hunger became a torment. The drinking water had turned foul as urine. There was no rain. The little ship biscuit still available was wormy. The crewmen were inert with thirst and despair. Then, as if God had taken pity on them, the men felt the first westerly breezes. The *Los Reyes* turned eastward.

Still, though the wind now blew ceaselessly, there was no rain. Thirst and hunger tortured all aboard. Scurvy appeared. Every day men died. Weeks passed. The suffering men began to mutter of mutiny, as if by killing their leaders they could relieve their agony. There was even some mad proposal to reverse course and try to sail back to the Philippines, now thousands of miles astern.

In this crisis Mendaña exhibited leadership qualities not often visible in the past. Addressing the men with passionate words, he put matters to them plainly: To reverse course, after they had come so far with so much pain, would be to doom all. Mutiny would not bring rain or food. They had to hold on, he argued. They would soon reach land if only they held on. His words stayed the would-be mutineers.

Only a few days later signs appeared to support Mendaña's hopeful words. A pine log was found floating in the sea. Since it was clean of barnacles, it must have come from some nearby shore. Then it began to rain. The men caught the life-giving water in barrels. At last they were able to quench their thirst fully.

A week later, on December 19, after four months of suffering, the *Los Reyes* sighted the coast of Baja California. The horrendous journey had ended. Thirty men had died on the return voyage.

The *Los Reyes* limped into the harbor of Colima, where Mendaña and his men gave thanks to God. At last they could rest, care for their sick, and repair their ship.

A week or two later, to the astonishment of all, the lost *Todos Santos* also struggled into the harbor. Battered, her rigging in shreds, but with Sarmiento still in command, the *Todos Santos* dropped anchor, a near derelict.

Sarmiento refused to explain how or why he had lost contact with the flagship. He did report that the *Todos Santos* had also suffered through the appalling cyclone that had almost sunk the *Los Reyes* and that many of his men had suffered the tortures of scurvy. Though amazed at the survival of the *Todos Santos* and delighted at the safe return of so many men thought lost, Mendaña, as commander of the expedition, ordered local officials to arrest Sarmiento, probably on charges of insubordination and desertion.

The *Los Reyes* and the *Todos Santos* spent many weeks in Colima undergoing repairs. The two ships finally returned to Callao on September 11, 1569, almost two years after their departure. The imprisoned Sarmiento remained behind.

Back in Peru, Mendaña received little praise for his voyage. Nor did he find much support for a return to the far reaches of the South Pacific. Although it was generally acknowledged that the young commander had completed a remarkable journey, officials in Lima pointed out that he had not, after all, discovered Terra Australis. As for the islands he did find, they seemed to hold little promise. One administrator in the viceregal government, writing to King Philip, delivered this negative verdict on Mendaña's discovery: "In my opinion . . . the islands they discovered were of little importance, although they say they heard of better lands; for in the course of these discoveries they found no specimens of spices, nor of gold and silver, nor of merchandise, nor of any other source of profit, and all the people were naked savages."

This Spanish official then gave Mendaña's islands the name they have borne ever since: the Solomon Islands. Perhaps he came up with the name because like many contemporaries, he speculated that King Solomon's secret, inexhaustible gold mines lay somewhere out in the Pacific. On the other hand, he might have meant the name as sarcasm. Whatever the case, the fanciful name stuck.

In November 1569, six weeks after Mendaña's return to an indifferent Callao, a new viceroy arrived in Peru to take over the reins of government from Mendaña's uncle. The new viceroy,

Francisco de Toledo, an abstemious fifty-three-year-old career official, was more interested in developing Peru than in exploring the Pacific. Mendaña, therefore, decided to return to Spain with his uncle, the former governor-general. Perhaps, he thought, officials in Seville would see the potential value of his Solomon Islands.

Sarmiento, released from his arrest, returned to Lima and again found a place in the government. As an experienced administrator, a talented mathematician, and a scholar of Inca history he had much to offer. Within a short time he became a trusted adviser to Viceroy Toledo, his dream of Pacific glory deferred.

Mendaña, meanwhile, found only more disappointment. Back in Spain, he pleaded for a new voyage to the Pacific, arguing that if the islands of Solomon were not themselves Terra Australis, the long-sought continent had to lie within some reasonable distance of them.

King Philip's councillors for the Indies encouraged Mendaña to hope that when more pressing matters ameliorated, he might obtain the backing he sought. However, they pointed out, given the political situation in Spain, he might have to wait for a long time. Most of Spain's military and economic strength was reserved for the Netherlands, where Philip was now engaged in suppressing a full-scale rebellion.

As the 1570s began the northern, Protestant provinces of the Netherlands were aflame. Despite his use of torture and overwhelming force, the duke of Alva not only had failed to "pacify" the Netherlands as promised but had precipitated a revolt that defied all attempts to stamp it out. Under the banner of one of their grandest nobles, William, prince of Orange, the Netherlanders were standing up to the ruthless Alva on land and at sea. Though often beaten in battle, the rebels confounded Alva time and again by finding more armies and more ships with which to resist. The "men of butter," as Alva had once scornfully called the Netherlanders, were showing themselves to be extremely tough. Yet Philip remained as determined as ever to restore Spanish dominion over the lowland provinces, whatever the cost in Spanish blood and Spanish treasure.

Although virtually all European nations, like jackals circling a beleaguered lion, watched for opportunities to gain from

Spain's preoccupation with the lowland revolt, one country had already profited greatly from the rebellion: Protestant England. Under the Virgin Queen, England regularly furnished clandestine support to the Dutch rebels while its sea rovers, always operating without Elizabeth's official sanction, raided Spain's Atlantic and Caribbean empire. So far England had played this dangerous game with great skill, managing to fill the queen's treasury, damage Spain, and help its coreligionists all, without provoking Philip to war.

Then, in 1572, as the lowland rebellion raged on, a young English aristocrat conceived a scheme that, if approved by the queen, would dramatically raise the stakes in the perilous game that England was playing.

11

ENGLISH SCHEMES AND SPANISH GOLD

Sir Richard Grenville, scion of a well-connected Cornish family, was thirty-one years old in 1572. Yet he had already won a reputation as a brave soldier and a canny politician. A member of Parliament, the handsome Grenville was a loyal retainer of Queen Elizabeth's. For three generations his family had supported the crown. Grenville's grandfather had served Elizabeth's father, Henry VIII, as marshal of Calais. Grenville's father had been commander of the *Mary Rose* in 1545 and had lost his life when that vessel sank. As heir to a distinguished line young Grenville was a man of influence and often welcomed at Elizabeth's court.

Like most of the English aristocracy, Grenville harbored a deep hatred for Catholic Spain. He viewed Philip II as an enemy bent on the eventual destruction of Protestant England. As a Cornishman and shipowner Grenville was acutely aware of the undeclared war raging on the seas between English corsairs and Spain. For almost a decade English marauders had been raiding the Spanish New World—often with the surreptitious support of the queen—while Spain, with the lowland rebellion on its hands, had been retaliating by "arresting" English "pirates" and turning them over to the Inquisition for punishment. Hundreds of Englishmen, Grenville knew, were rotting in Spanish prisons or laboring at the oars of Spanish galleys.

Publicly Grenville supported Elizabeth's "neutrality" toward Spain, but in private he hoped Elizabeth would alter her policy to give overt military aid to the Protestant rebels in the Netherlands. Many of the queen's closest councillors shared his hope. This faction, strongly sympathetic to the rebel cause, argued that by helping the Netherlands Protestants with military force, Elizabeth could ensure creation of a new, powerful ally to stand with England against Spain throughout the world.

Although Elizabeth always listened to these firebrands among her councillors, she refused to commit herself to their policies. Instead she vacillated, temporized, and spoke of peace while turning a blind eye to English piracies and a deaf ear to Spanish protests. Only by keeping Philip off-balance, she seemed to imply, could she preserve a precarious peace. She was supported in her caution by her chief minister, Lord Burghley, who saw only calamity for England in an open struggle with the enormous Spanish Empire.

Thus, like many other Englishmen of the time, Sir Richard Grenville was casting about for ways to damage Spain and enrich himself but without embroiling Elizabeth in war. In 1572 he hit upon a scheme that seemed perfect. The idea called for a flotilla of English ships to sail through the Strait of Magellan into the Pacific. The English expedition would claim "any lands, islands, and countries southwards beyond the equinoctial, where the Pole antarctic hath any elevation above the horizon". If brief, these first Englishmen into the Pacific would find and claim the southern continent for England, denying the prize to Philip. They would then make their way up to the high latitudes in search of the Northwest Passage that supposedly linked the Pacific and the Atlantic in the north, and come home. If successful, this Pacific voyage would give England an empire and its own route to it. It would also be undertaken without the queen's official sanction, thus allowing her to disavow it should anything go amiss.*

One of those who fervently supported Grenville's idea was Dr. John Dee, a renowned astronomer and mathematician, who also enjoyed the confidence of Queen Elizabeth. Though a Renaissance scholar who espoused the new scientific knowledge and practices of the day, Dee could not quite let go of his belief in

---

*It was understood, though not stated, that the English expedition would also take any Spanish prizes that came its way.

magic and the occult. Like Sarmiento in far-off Peru, Dee made astrological charts as he formulated astronomical tables. He practiced alchemy along with the physical sciences. He was half genius and half crackpot, but his influence was enormous. He knew most of the leading intellectuals of Europe and was a personal friend of the great mapmaker Gerardus Mercator.

A pioneer in "mathematical navigation," Dee believed implicitly in the existence of Terra Australis, which appeared not only on Mercator's maps but also in the atlas published in 1570 by Abraham Ortelius of Antwerp. This atlas, widely circulated in England, showed the southern land as the largest continent of all. Although no mariner had yet visited Terra Australis, Ortelius depicted it as a huge mass covering all the Antarctic Circle and stretching northwest in the Pacific from the Strait of Magellan almost to the Tropic of Capricorn.

Dee promised to support Grenville's scheme to find the continent when the young man approached the queen for her approval. Grenville was delighted. He knew that Dee's opinion carried great weight with Elizabeth, who often relied upon the scientist for advice. (Among other things, Elizabeth had asked Dee to name the most propitious day for her coronation.)

When the time came, Dee argued forcefully in favor of the Pacific voyage. All the world knew that the Spaniards were bent on finding the southern continent. Further, the Spaniards had now succeeded in bringing the Philippines firmly under their control. This success in the Pacific was due not only to the fact that Spanish pilots had discovered the secret of the Pacific winds and currents but also to the qualities of the new Spanish galleons. These vessels, operating as men-of-war as well as merchantmen, were 125 feet in length and approximately 35 feet in the beam. With their sleek lines the galleons, even at five hundred tons, could sail relatively close to the wind and could attain a speed of eight knots. Some of them could carry as many as sixty cannon.*

With such ships the Spaniards had already initiated a steady traffic with the Philippines. They had also opened a lucrative trade with China. Each year a galleon loaded with the silver that was often more prized in Asia than gold, sailed west from Aca-

---

*Few Pacific galleons bothered with heavy ordnance, however, since Spain no longer had formidable enemies in the great ocean. Most Pacific galleons carried only a few cannon in case of native hostility.

pulco. Following the regular galleon routes, it ran before the easterly trades, crossing the Central Pacific a few degrees to the north of the equator. Reaching Manila, it anchored for trade with junks from China, exchanging Potosí silver for spices, silks, velvets, ivory, and porcelain—all goods greatly desired in Europe. For the return trip, this Manila Galleon (as it was called) would sail to approximately 35 degrees north latitude. There it caught the westerlies to California and then ran down to Acapulco.

To Dee and other geographers, it seemed only a question of time before a Spanish galleon happened upon Terra Australis. Unless England acted expeditiously, Spain might soon claim the southern continent as it had claimed the Americas: by default.

Elizabeth approved Grenville's proposal. Sometime in the summer of 1573, Grenville began assembling his expedition. It was at this moment that Francis Drake returned from one of the most successful privateering raids ever mounted by one of Elizabeth's sea dogs.

It was Sunday, August 9, 1573, when Drake sailed into his home port of Plymouth. Most of the populace was at church. News of his arrival raced through the town. When the word reached the church, the service ceased. The congregation ran down to the harbor to greet the thirty-three-year-old hero. They soon heard a marvelous tale of audacity and good fortune.

In the previous months, operating on the Spanish Main and the Isthmus of Panama, Drake had made off with huge amounts of Spanish treasure. In one brilliant stroke he had even captured the main Spanish silver port of Nombre de Dios. He had not carried off all the silver that lay in the town because of a bad wound and bad weather, but his incursion had so shaken the Spanish that they had moved their silver port to Portobelo.

Drake had also plundered the Caribbean towns of Cartagena, capital of the Spanish colonial empire, and Santa Marta. In another exploit, he and a party of his men, together with approximately twenty black ex-slaves who cooperated with the English, marched across the Isthmus of Panama in January 1573 and captured a Spanish mule train loaded with silver. Later, in alliance with a French privateer, Drake had waylaid still another treasure train, capturing even more rich booty.

At one point, while operating on the isthmus, Drake had climbed a tall tree and had glimpsed the great Pacific lying before him. Awed, he had prayed that God would one day "allow him to sail on that ocean in an English ship."

If Drake was acclaimed a hero upon his return to England, however, he was denounced as a pirate by the enraged Spanish. As the news spread of Drake's reappearance in England, Philip's diplomats howled their outrage to Elizabeth. The queen of England blandly fended off their wrath. She deplored Drake's lawless actions but claimed she could do nothing, for Drake's had been a private venture that violated no English laws. Elizabeth did see to it, however, that the politically embarrassing Drake was removed from the scene until Spanish fury abated. Drake was sent to join the English forces in Ireland.*

Elizabeth also decided that with the wound of Drake's voyage still so fresh, Grenville's planned thrust into the Pacific would constitute an impossible provocation of Philip of Spain. Much to the disappointment of Grenville, Dee, and their advocates, she withdrew her support for the voyage to Terra Australis.

Still, the notion of an English challenge to Spanish domination of the Pacific was now planted. In fact, the idea had become deeply rooted in the restless and rapacious mind of Francis Drake himself.

A portrait of Francis Drake, probably painted in the 1580s at the height of his later fame, shows a man with direct blue eyes, a neat brown beard, a compact, powerful figure. It pictures a man who liked fine clothes, especially the crisp, ruffed collars fashionable in his time and the brocaded waistcoats that proclaimed a gentleman of substance. But the portrait also sets forth something of the man's spirit. It shows a man of supreme confidence, a man whose coolness, imagination, and ability caused lesser men to follow him gladly.

Born near Plymouth about 1540, Francis Drake grew up in a fervently Protestant household, the eldest of twelve sons. His father, Edmund, was a poor farmer. Driven from his small holding by religious rioting, Edmund Drake moved his family to Kent, where he apparently supported himself by acting as a sort of chaplain to the seamen who frequented the king's dockyards on the Medway River.

By an almost natural process, the boy Francis absorbed

*It's likely that the queen praised Drake privately—and shared in his profits as well.

knowledge of ships and the sea as he grew up. At fourteen he signed aboard a small coastal vessel and rose to become her master when he was not yet twenty. Young Drake was soon taking part in slave-trading voyages to the West Indies, sponsored by his kinsman John Hawkins. In 1568, still in his twenties and now captain of a fifty-ton vessel, the *Judith*, Drake sailed to Spanish America as part of a six-vessel trading flotilla under the command of Hawkins. The voyage proved a turning point in his life.

As Hawkins's squadron engaged in peaceful trading at the Mexican port of San Juan de Ulúa, a Spanish fleet bearing a new viceroy arrived at the harbor. The viceroy was furious to find Spanish subjects flouting King Philip's long-standing command against trading with the Protestant English. Yet the English vessels were well armed, and the viceroy had no wish to initiate a fight. To put the English off their guard, the viceroy sent word to Hawkins that he would not interfere with the Englishmen if they would let him enter the harbor peacefully. Hawkins, preferring trade to battle, agreed. But once safely inside the harbor, the viceroy's fleet launched a sudden attack on the six English ships. The English were overwhelmed and tried to flee the harbor. Only the ships captained by Hawkins and by Drake managed to get away to the open sea.

Following his escape from San Juan de Ulúa, Drake swore that as long as he lived, he would do all he could to "synge the beard" of King Philip. Beginning in 1570, he returned to the Spanish Main on three separate privateering missions, including the foray of 1572–73 that made his name feared from the Bay of Biscay to the Gulf of Mexico. In 1574 and 1575, while lying out of sight in Ireland, Drake talked of an expedition through the Strait of Magellan, to singe Philip's beard in the Pacific.*

Meanwhile, Philip floundered still deeper into the quagmire of the Netherlands rebellion. In 1576 Spanish soldiers stationed in the rebellious provinces rose in mutiny after they had gone months without pay. The troops sacked Antwerp with barbaric fury. As a result, many hitherto passive Netherlanders joined the rebels, and the revolt took on a bloody new life. In this same

---

*Not all English marauders experienced Drake's success against Spain. In 1574 an English corsair named John Noble attacked Spanish treasure ships off Nombre de Dios. He was jumped by Spanish warships, and twenty-eight of his men were killed. Noble himself was captured along with two of his men and two ship's boys. The boys were sentenced to the galleys. Noble was hanged along with his two surviving crewmen.

year Philip, overwhelmed by the costs of suppressing the rebellion, restructured his huge debt by deferring payments on loans, in effect declaring a state bankruptcy. Still, despite debt and military failure, Philip remained convinced that he was doing God's will in the Netherlands and continued to pour Spain's resources into the effort to put down the Protestant rebels.*

As Philip's woes mounted, Elizabeth began listening with a sympathetic ear to those urging decisive action against Spain. Drake, recalled from Ireland and supported by a number of the queen's councillors, was now allowed to lay his Pacific scheme before Elizabeth. In the process of explaining his ideas he no doubt made it clear that while the enterprise would include keeping a sharp eye out for Terra Australis and the Northwest Passage, the emphasis would be on profitable privateering. Elizabeth gave her tacit approval.

Drake was now to make the voyage that Sir Richard Grenville had conceived some five years earlier. In the summer of 1577 he began to assemble a fleet at Plymouth. Publicly he claimed that he was mounting a trading journey to the Levant. English merchants, probably knowing better, gladly subscribed a sum of more than four thousand pounds for the voyage. The queen also invested privately, insisting that Drake keep her involvement a secret even from her ministers.

Grenville, who had first broached the idea of a Pacific voyage, played no part in Drake's preparation. Though Drake officially was headed for the Levant, Grenville certainly suspected his true destination, for he made it clear within his own circle that he thought Drake a usurper of his enterprise. But Drake was England's darling, and Grenville's resentment was ignored.

The squadron finally mustered by Drake consisted of five vessels: the flagship, *Pelican* (renamed *Golden Hind* during the voyage), of 120 tons; *Elizabeth*, 80 tons; *Marygold*, 30 tons; *Swan*, a supply ship of 50 tons; and a pinnace, *Christopher*, of 15 tons. Another pinnace, the 12-ton *Benedict*, was carried in pieces in the hold of the flagship to be put together when needed.

Drake's flagship carried eighteen long guns on two decks. Described as a swift and powerful vessel, the *Pelican* was crewed

---

*Philip's original military commander, the duke of Alva, had gone into retirement in 1573 after failing to control the revolt. The rebels were also developing an ever-stronger national sense under the leadership of William of Orange.

by 80 men. The second-largest ship, *Elizabeth,* carried sixteen guns, as did the bark *Marygold.* Drake's forces were more than sufficient to overpower most trading vessels. The fleet was manned by approximately 160 officers, sailors, and soldiers. All were English or Irish, except for a black named Diego.

Most of the hands who signed up had no reason to doubt the official story that they were bound for the Levant. At the same time they anticipated that any voyage with Drake would also aim at the capture of prizes. Since, according to custom, all members of the enterprise, including ordinary mariners, shared in any loot, the men of the forecastles were content with their prospects.

In addition to the ordinary sailors and soldiers, however, Drake had signed aboard a dozen or more "gentlemen volunteers." Many of these were the sons of old and wealthy families. They could not help thinking of themselves as Drake's equals. Many of them had also put money into the voyage and expected to have a voice in decision making. Though none of these gentry would have dreamed of disputing Drake's authority over the ordinary seamen and soldiers, they did not understand that Drake, as commander, was to have authority over the expedition's upper class as well. In time this misunderstanding was to imperil the entire enterprise. For the time being, however, few saw anything but glory and riches ahead.*

As the expedition neared readiness, Drake received final and secret orders, making it plain that assault and pillage were his prime objectives. Specifically he was told that after passing through the Strait of Magellan, he was to turn north and raid the harbors and shipping of Spanish settlements along the coasts of Peru and Mexico. If he found Terra Australis and a northern route home, well and good. But the discovery of the southern continent and the Northwest Passage was to be of secondary importance.

---

*Unlike the mariners and the public, the gentlemen certainly knew Drake's destination— at least in general terms.

12

SIR PIRATE

Drake set sail on November 15, 1577, but almost immediately a fierce storm battered the fleet, forcing the ships back to Plymouth for repairs. He departed again on December 13. This time the weather continued fair as the ships stood away south toward the Cape Verde Isles on the first leg of the long passage to the Pacific. Expectations were high for the success of the voyage. Drake himself seemed confident that he would achieve his ambition to be the first Englishman to sail upon the broad Pacific.*

En route to the Cape Verdes, Drake told his mariners their true destination. No objections were recorded.

It was early February 1578 when the fleet departed the Cape Verdes for the South Atlantic. Now ensued a nightmare passage,

---

*In fact another Englishman had already claimed this honor. He was John Oxenham who had served with Drake himself in Drake's earlier privateering expedition to Panama. Some time late in 1575 Oxenham had fitted out a ship of 140 tons, scrambled together seventy men, and had sailed for Panama. He had then crossed the Isthmus of Panama in 1576. After building a forty-five-foot pinnace, he and about fifty of his surviving men had operated for a month in the Gulf of Panama, capturing a number of Spanish ships. Thus he became the first Englishman to lead an expedition into the Pacific. But Oxenham and his men were captured by Spaniards when they tried to retreat with their booty back across the Isthmus. Most of Oxenham's men were hanged, but he and two others were taken to Lima where they were jailed by the Inquisition. It is probable that Drake knew that Oxenham had departed for the Spanish Main in 1575. But he probably did not know that Oxenham meant to cross the Isthmus—and he certainly did *not* know of the fate that had overtaken the expedition.

reminiscent of Magellan's voyage almost sixty years before. For fifty-four days the English ships struggled across the ocean, fighting storms and enduring calms all the way, until, on April 5, 1578, they reached the coast of Brazil. They turned south to seek Magellan's strait. The autumn days grew shorter and colder; the sea angrier. But dissension was worrying Drake even more than the wretched weather.

Since the start of the journey the gentlemen in the fleet had groused about Drake's assumption of authority over them. Unlike the common seafarers, the inexperienced gentry did not understand the rigorous law of the sea: that there can be but one hand on the tiller lest the enterprise flounder into disaster. To the gentlemen Drake seemed a tyrant, and they murmured against him among themselves, spreading fear and division within the fleet, even down to the ordinary sailors.

The chief culprit in this subtle form of mutiny was one of Drake's good friends, the young courtier Thomas Doughty. Well connected with many of England's leading men, Doughty was also a disciple of Dr. John Dee's. Under Dee's tutelage he had studied navigation as well as the subjects of magic and alchemy.

Doughty had met Drake in Ireland, where he often traveled as a courier between the earl of Essex, then trying to pacify that land, and the government of England. At the time Drake was trying to obtain the backing of Elizabeth for his projected Pacific voyage, and Doughty had helped bring Drake's idea before the influential men of England. He had also taken an active role in organizing the venture. When he decided to accompany the fleet, Doughty had expected his position at sea to be the equal of Drake's. Disabused of that notion after several clashes with Drake over relatively minor matters, Doughty had resorted to sowing discord belowdecks, placing Drake in a situation that he would have to rectify or see his enterprise dissolve into anarchy. For the moment, however, as April turned into a cold and stormy May, Drake could do little, for he was caught up in the daily battle to make way south toward the strait, along the bleak Patagonian coast.*

*During this time the Englishmen had their first encounter with the natives of Patagonia. Despite earlier Spanish descriptions of these nearly naked people as "giants," Drake's men saw them as simple savages of no unusual height. The Englishmen, however, were repelled by the native diet of raw rats, and they marveled that the natives seemed able to endure the cold with no discomfort, though clad only in strips of skin and foot wrappings.

With the coming of June, however, and the bitter southern winter, Drake decided to make for Magellan's old anchorage of Port San Julián. Here he intended to give his men a respite from their labors and to clear the air with Thomas Doughty and the gentry.

Entering the bay of Port San Julián on June 20, 1578, the Englishmen were astonished to discover gibbets standing on the barren shore like weathered bones. These were the execution trees used by Magellan almost sixty years earlier, when the Portuguese mariner had had to quell a mutiny against *his* authority in this very place. The cold, dry air of Port San Julián had preserved these grim artifacts of mutiny, and Drake could have looked upon them as signposts for his own actions.

Before Drake could implement his next step in the matter of Thomas Doughty, however, he and his men had a bloody confrontation with local natives, who attacked an English shore party and killed an English gunner. Drake himself shot down the Indian who killed the gunner, and the others fled.

Despite this clash and the continuing hostility of the local people, Drake was determined to remain at Port San Julián until matters were settled with Doughty and the gentry. He issued orders for Doughty's arrest, charging his erstwhile friend with conspiracy to undermine the common enterprise. A court of officers and gentlemen, forty in all, met on an island in the bay to hear the case. Witnesses testified that Doughty not only had intrigued "to overthrow" their venture but also had sought to depose Drake. The assembled officers reached a verdict of guilty and agreed that Doughty "deserved death." He was given his choice of three methods of punishment. He could be marooned in Port San Julián, sent to England to answer for his deeds, or be executed immediately. Doughty chose the last alternative, requesting only that he might die "a gentleman's death."

Doughty and Drake shared a final meal, begged each other's forgiveness, and drank a toast to old friendship. Then Doughty went to the block. A swordsman struck his head from his body. Doughty was buried under Magellan's gibbet, the grave marked by a broken old grindstone.

Now Drake gave orders that in spite of the Antarctic winter, the fleet should be readied to go on to the strait, only three or four days' sail to the south. He also set forth in no uncertain terms the rules that would govern the journey still ahead. All would share equally in the hardships of the voyage. There would be no special privileges for gentlemen. As commander he would have the first and final word on all matters. The essence of his talk was contained in a single famous line: "I must have the gentleman to haul and draw with the mariner and the mariner with the gentleman."

The fleet set sail again on August 17, 1578. There were now three ships in the squadron—the *Pelican, Elizabeth,* and *Marygold*—as well as the two pinnaces. (Drake had earlier abandoned the fourth large vessel, the *Swan,* when she had become unseaworthy.) Arriving three days later at the entrance to Magellan's strait, Drake changed the name of his flagship from the *Pelican* to the *Golden Hind.* He probably rechristened his vessel to mark a new beginning after the unhappy travail of the past. He chose the name *Golden Hind* because this animal was the chief figure in the coat of arms of Sir Christopher Hatton, who had been one of the principal backers of the voyage at the court of Queen Elizabeth. On August 21, 1578, Drake and his men entered the Strait of Magellan.

Though, like all others before them, the Englishmen encountered strong head winds and swells, they made good progress through the maze of the strait.* On September 6, 1578, the rocky steeps of the strait suddenly opened up, revealing, beyond the bows, the waters that Magellan had called Mar Pacifica. It had taken Drake only sixteen days to make the 363-mile passage, a remarkable feat. Magellan had taken thirty-eight days. Elcano and Loaysa had needed four months. Drake's were the first non-Spanish European ships to sail onto the wide Pacific. But the Englishmen found an ocean that was far from peaceful. As the ships left the strait, a tremendous offshore wind suddenly rose and carried them far out into the deep. Then a full-scale Pacific storm engulfed them with screaming blasts of wind and mountainous seas, and English sailors got their first taste of weather at the bottom of the world.

For an incredible seven weeks the gales raged, virtually without letup. The ships fought to stay together. The furious Pacific drove the vessels farther and farther south. At one point Drake judged that he had been blown a hundred miles or more south

---

*They also encountered friendly, primitive people as well as a strange seafowl that they caught, salted away as provisions, and gave the name penguin.

of the strait. Yet all about him there was only the furious sea. This circumstance indicated that Tierra del Fuego, which the Spaniards thought a part of Terra Australis, was in reality a scattering of islands at the tip of South America with only the open sea beyond.

One night, as the fleet fought the weather, the *Marygold*, sank, "swallowed up," according to Drake's chronicler, "by the mountains of the sea." Twenty-nine men went down with her. They were heard crying for help in the darkness.

As the surviving vessels struggled on, a second ship, the *Elizabeth*, disappeared. There were no signs that she had foundered, however—no flotsam, no boats, no reports of men calling for help in the night—and so Drake continued to hope that she was still afloat and had merely been separated from her companions by the storm. If so, she would meet the *Golden Hind* again at a previously designated rendezvous point at 30 degrees south latitude. But first the ships would have to survive the infernal Pacific weather.

At last, toward the end of October, the weather improved. The *Golden Hind* and her accompanying pinnaces were able to gain a respite at some coastal islands. With the skies suddenly fair, Drake set off north to look for the *Elizabeth*. It was November 1, 1578. Almost a year had passed since the fleet had left Plymouth. Within a week Drake reached the thirtieth parallel and began searching for the *Elizabeth*. She did not appear, however, and Drake decided to tarry no longer, though he hoped she was still afloat somewhere in these waters.*

The English marauders now fell on the unsuspecting Spaniards at the newly established little Chilean port of Valparaiso. They then began a remarkable four-month reign of terror along the Spanish Pacific coast. Moving steadily north, Drake and his men successfully attacked ships and harbors along the way, including the viceregal port of Callao itself. The *Golden Hind*'s

---

*In fact, the *Elizabeth* was still afloat. Separated from the flagship by storms, her master, John Winter, had returned to the shelter of Magellan's strait instead of to the agreed-upon rendezvous point. Anchored in the strait, Winter had lighted signal fires at night, hoping that Drake, if still afloat, would reenter the strait. Thus, while Drake was making his way north, hoping to rendezvous again with the *Elizabeth*, the object of his search was anchored far to the south. Eventually Captain Winter's crew insisted that he set sail for England. The *Elizabeth* arrived home in June 1579. Winter had very little good to say about Drake. Captain Winter has often been excoriated for desertion of the *Golden Hind*, but many have judged his actions as merely prudent in view of the horrible weather.

holds filled with such loot as silver, silks, and wine.

Yet the English corsairs did not go entirely unscathed. At the very start of the campaign two of Drake's men were killed at the Isle of Mocha when Indians, mistaking the Englishmen for the hated Spaniards, ambushed a watering party. Some of Drake's crew suffered serious wounds in subsequent actions as well. In addition, after his profitable raid on Callao, Drake was forced to abandon a valuable prize and a number of captives in order to escape Spanish pursuers.* For the most part, however, the Spaniards proved easy prey.

By the end of February 1579 Drake lay in waters well to the north of Peru. By this time two well-armed Spanish warships were hunting him all along the coast. But, Drake worried very little about these vessels, for his attention was now fixed on overtaking a great prize: the *Nuestra Señora de la Concepción*, bound for Panama with a huge load of silver.

Drake had learned of this treasure vessel while interviewing prisoners during the looting of Callao. He had also found out that she had departed on her voyage before word had come of Drake's presence in the Pacific. Thus her unsuspecting captain could not know that "El Draque" intended to run her down on the open sea.

Because the *Nuestra Señora de la Concepción* was one of the few Spanish vessels in these hitherto peaceful Pacific waters to carry any large cannon, Spanish mariners had nicknamed her "Cacafuego." Although the name has often been translated as "Spitfire," it is more accurately, if less decorously, rendered as "Shitfire," a term that reflects the rough humor of sailors everywhere and at all times. Despite the *Cacafuego*'s lead and her heavy ordnance, Drake and his men were confident not only that the *Golden Hind* could catch the Spaniard, but that she could outfight her as well.

On March 1, 1579, the *Golden Hind* sighted the Spanish ship eight or nine miles dead ahead. The *Cacafuego*, moving sedately north toward Panama, had sighted the *Golden Hind* as well. But there was no alarm aboard the Spanish treasure ship. Though her master, Juan de Antón, was surprised to see another

*One of the commanders of the pursuit at Callao was the redoubtable Pedro Sarmiento de Ganboa, the same man who had helped Mendaña discover the Solomon Islands a decade earlier. Now an important figure in the viceregal government, Sarmiento was infuriated by the English raiders, especially after it became known that their chief was "El Draque" who had previously despoiled the Spanish Main.

vessel suddenly astern of him, he had no reason to fear her, for these waters had been so long the province of Spanish galleons and coastal shipping that it was impossible to imagine an enemy ship in the Spanish Pacific.

Captain Antón, however, was curious about the newcomer. It also appears that, weary of the long coastal voyage to Panama, the officers and men of the *Cacafuego* viewed the oncoming *Golden Hind* as a potential companion on the journey north. Captain Antón may have speculated as well that the strange vessel was bringing him an important message.

In any case, the *Cacafuego* put about and waited for the *Golden Hind.* Showing no sign of his real intentions, Drake slowly came alongside the Spaniard. Then, with the suddenness of thunder, a trumpet sounded aboard the *Golden Hind.* Drake's men shouted, "We're English! Strike!" Another trumpet sounded. Drake's arquebusiers fired a volley. Aboard the *Cacafuego* there was consternation. All at once English cannon spoke with chain shot. The *Cacafuego*'s mizzenmast came crashing down. An English boarding party swarmed over the *Cacafuego*'s side. It was all over. The Spaniards surrendered.

His English captors now brought Captain Antón to Drake aboard the *Golden Hind.* Antón, who had lived in England and spoke English well, later reported that Drake welcomed him aboard with courtesy and even commiserated with him about the loss of his ship, saying, "Have patience, such is the usage of war."

It took four days for Drake's men to transfer the *Cacafuego*'s magnificent cargo to the holds of the *Golden Hind.* In the end the booty totaled thirteen chests of silver coin, approximately twenty-six tons of silver bars, eighty pounds of gold, and coffers of pearls and gems. Having relieved Captain Antón of these goods, Drake, with characteristic courtesy, returned the *Cacafuego* to the Spaniard with gifts and a receipt, detailing the treasure taken from the *Cacafuego*'s holds. He did this to protect the Spanish captain from any suspicion by his own government that he might have colluded in the stripping of his ship. He also gave the Spanish captain a letter of safe conduct, in case he should encounter the *Elizabeth,* which, for all Drake knew, might still be operating somewhere in the Pacific.*

---

*The *Elizabeth,* of course, was on her return voyage to England. One amusing incident occurred during the looting of the *Cacafuego.* A Spanish cabin boy, watching the stripping

Now having gained a treasure beyond imagining, Drake vacated these waters. He knew that astern of him to the south the Spaniards were in full cry. The *Golden Hind*, heavily laden as she was, pressed on northward.

Pausing for the occasional prize and foray ashore, as well as necessary repairs, Drake drove past Mexico and far up the coast of California. He was searching for a northern equivalent of Magellan's strait, a passage that would permit the *Golden Hind* to make a relatively short return to the Atlantic and home. But though he sailed past the mouth of Columbia River and as far north as the frozen forty-eighth parallel, no strait appeared, and he turned south again. In the vicinity of what is now San Francisco, he put in to rest and repair the *Golden Hind's* leaking hull.

Here the Englishmen spent a month in peaceful traffic with the local people. Drake reported many signs that the California country contained gold. He also saw some similarity between the cliffs of northern California and the white cliffs of Dover and because of this he gave the region the name New Albion.*

It was now July 1579. Having failed to locate a northern strait home and too prudent to risk a return voyage via the south, where the Spaniards lay in wait, Drake saw only one course open to him: He would have to cross the Pacific to the Spice Isles and from there cross the Indian Ocean, round the Cape of Good Hope, and head north to England. Though this course would entail a gigantic journey through unknown seas, it was the safest way to bring home his enormously valuable cargo.

As the hot July sun beat down, the *Golden Hind* departed New Albion. Striking out into the Pacific, she first headed southwest, toward the middle latitudes, and then swung due west. For more than two months, the *Golden Hind* sailed the Pacific without any sight of land. Following charts captured earlier from Spanish prizes, Drake kept the kindly trade winds in his sails, and the *Golden Hind* made excellent time. Unlike Magellan, whose men had suffered terribly on the first Pacific voyage sixty years earlier, Drake's crew enjoyed a comparatively easy crossing. Where Ma-

---

of his ship remarked to the English sailors that, instead of the *Cacafuego*, his ship should now be called the *Cacaplata*—in other words *Shit Silver*. The remark delighted the English.
*Drake also conceived the idea that this region of northern California, which the Spaniards had not yet made their own, might become an English colony. He, therefore, "annexed" the land for England and upon his departure set up a brass plate setting forth the English claim to the territory.

gellan's men had had to swill foul, greenish water, Drake's crew had plenty of fresh water, thanks to rainsqualls. Where Magellan's men had had to eat the leather straps of their rigging, Drake's mariners had ample provisions.

On September 30, 1579, having come almost six thousand miles across the Pacific, the Englishmen reached the Caroline Islands, where they were greeted by swarms of native canoes that followed the big ship for four days until driven off by musket fire.

Continuing to the west, the *Golden Hind* reached the Moluccas, where Drake added six tons of cloves to his already immensely rich cargo. Then, on January 9, 1580, after her skein of good fortune, the *Golden Hind* ran into ill luck while sailing southwest from the Moluccas: The heavily laden ship suddenly ran aground on a coral reef in the island-dotted seas east of the Celebes. With her belly grinding on the sharp coral, the *Golden Hind*, survivor of innumerable adventures was suddenly in mortal peril.

Drake, ever the realist, ordered his men to jettison the least valuable cargo and the cannon, hoping to lighten the ship enough to float her off the reef. For eighteen hours the men worked to dislodge the ship. As one crewman described it. "We lightened our ship upon the rocks of three tons of cloves, 8 pieces of ordinance, and certain meal and beans, and then the wind (as it were in a moment by the special grace of God) changing from the starboard to the larboard of the ship, we hoisted our sails and the happy gale drove our ship off the rock into the sea again to the no little comfort of all our hearts." Still whole and sound, the *Golden Hind* resumed her voyage.

As if protected by some special providence, she went on westward, driven by the prevailing northeast winds and almost always under fair skies. She traversed the Indian Ocean twice as fast as the *Victoria* had under Elcano. She covered the thirty-five hundred miles in fifty-six days. Although head winds held her up for a month at the Cape of Good Hope, once into the South Atlantic she made good time north past the Cape Verde Islands and the Canaries.

On September 26, 1580, almost three years after departing, the *Golden Hind* entered Plymouth Harbor. Drake had circumnavigated the world, a feat heretofore accomplished only by Elcano.

Drake was hailed as a hero. All marveled that he had returned with more than half his crew still alive. Even more marvelous was the enormous treasure that the *Golden Hind* carried in her holds. Queen Elizabeth herself, no longer disguising her support for her corsairs, boarded the ship at Plymouth. On the deck of the ship, now famous throughout England, Francis Drake knelt while the sovereign dubbed her pirate Sir Francis. Spanish fury at Drake's epic voyage, and the queen of England's approval of it, knew no bounds.

Sir Francis Drake had proved the Spanish Empire vulnerable everywhere—and the Pacific Ocean open to men of daring and enterprise.

13

AT THE BOTTOM
OF THE WORLD

After Drake's assault on the Spanish Empire, the firebrands among Queen Elizabeth's councillors pressed even harder for England to assist the Protestant rebels in the Netherlands by making an open declaration of war against Spain. Although the queen continued to resist this pressure, she did increase English aid to the rebels, and she let it be known that she would support privateering ventures against Spain, including new enterprises into the Pacific.*

Drake's incursion also affected Spanish policy. It demonstrated again to Philip and his advisers the peril of permitting England's already considerable sea power to grow unchecked. The Spanish king began contemplating an invasion of England to topple Elizabeth from her throne and to restore a Catholic monarchy. From a Spanish perspective, the justification for such an action already existed. Not only did Elizabeth countenance "piracy," but in the Spanish view, she was not even the legitimate heir to the English throne. As the daughter of Henry VIII and

---

*Drake's voyage, while a roaring success as a privateering effort, was largely a failure from the perspective of the hopeful geographers of the day. He had not, after all, found the southern continent. He had not even looked for it. Nor had Drake found the Northwest Passage, although he had made a serious effort. Moreover, it soon became clear, after Drake had returned with his magnificent haul of booty, that commerce raiding would be the object of any new English incursions into the Pacific. Searches for the southern continent and the northwest strait would be secondary goals from now on.

Anne Boleyn, whom the Catholic Church refused to recognize
as the legitimate wife of an illegally divorced Henry, Elizabeth
was a "bastard" outside the royal line of succession. Pope Pius
V, in 1570, had already excommunicated her on these grounds.
By his own standards, Philip had reason enough to invade England even if Elizabeth had not countenanced "piracy."

Nevertheless, Philip was not yet prepared to undertake so
great a venture as the invasion of England. As 1581 opened,
Philip still had the Protestant rebellion to quell in the Netherlands. Moreover, he had a new and delicate problem in Portugal.

The Portuguese ruler had died in 1580, leaving no heirs.
Through his mother, the Portuguese princess Isabela, Philip
claimed the Portuguese throne, and in 1581 he enforced his
rights by sending an army to Portugal. In effect, Philip annexed
Portugal, thereby greatly augmenting Spain's military and commercial power. Still, because the situation remained unsettled in
Portugal, Philip postponed the "enterprise of England" until a
more propitious time.

In the interim, he approved a measure designed to block
any further English attempts to break into the Pacific. This was
a proposal made to the Spanish sovereign by Pedro Sarmiento
de Gamboa.

Sarmiento had gone back to Spain after his futile pursuit of
"El Draque" along the South American coast, arriving home
even before Drake made his triumphal return to England. Sarmiento gave a full report of Drake's "piracies" in the Pacific,
and then, with the royal wrath high, he recommended to Philip
that Spain establish colonies and fortresses in the Strait of Magellan. In this manner, he declared, Spain could finally tame the
strait for regular Spanish traffic while closing it to all unauthor-
ized vessels. If English privateers could not get into the Pacific,
Sarmiento pointed out, they could do no harm to Manila galleons, Peruvian mines, or Chilean towns. Nor could England claim
Terra Australis. By colonizing and fortifying the waterway, Spain
would be closing the Pacific to the English.*

Philip approved Sarmiento's plan and named him "gover-

*The annexation of Portugal's eastern empire would also do much to deny English pri-
vateers access to the Pacific. The route around Africa and across Indian waters would
now also be closed to Englishmen.

nor" of the strait. Sarmiento set to work recruiting colonists, artisans, and soldiers to establish his fortresses at the bottom of the world. On September 25, 1581, a year and a day after Drake's return to England, Sarmiento embarked several hundred people, including at least thirty women and twenty-six children, and set sail for Magellan's strait in sixteen chartered merchant ships, guarded by eight men-of-war.

From the beginning the enterprise was buffeted by one setback after another. Ships and lives were lost to storms. Worn vessels were badly battered by heavy seas. Disease depleted the ranks of the colonists. Perverse winds caused a series of delays. In Rio, where the fleet lay over after the Atlantic crossing, dishonest supply officers secretly sold the colonists' stores to local merchants. There, too, the commander of the naval contingent deserted the venture, leaving Sarmiento only five decrepit ships.*

Despite all these handicaps, Sarmiento and his people persisted, and they entered the strait in February 1584. Struggling to overcome weather, short supplies, and native hostility, Sarmiento managed to plant two settlements. One, located near the entrance to the strait, he named Nombre de Jesus. The other, about halfway through the passage, he called Rey Don Felipe. About three hundred people constituted the total population of the two colonies.

In spite of rationing and heroic efforts to fish and farm, the settlers were soon so short of food that Sarmiento sailed back to Brazil to obtain additional stores. Then weather, shipwreck, and even mutiny twice thwarted his efforts to return to his stranded settlers with supplies. Finally, in June 1586, intent on organizing a full-scale relief force for his people, he embarked for Spain.

Much had occurred in Sarmiento's absence from Europe. Open war had finally broken out in 1585 between England and Spain. An English army, under the earl of Leicester, had gone to the Netherlands to support the Protestant rebels. The Dutch Protestants of the northern part of the Netherlands had begun

---

*The deserter was Don Diego Flores de Valdes, a high-ranking nobleman who was nominally Sarmiento's superior but had no faith in Sarmiento's program. After deserting Sarmiento in Rio, Don Diego encountered five French vessels, interlopers, that were illegally loading logwood in northern Brazil. He sank all five, a feat that made him a hero in Madrid and disposed Spanish officials to disregard Sarmiento's later complaints against him. In later years Don Diego commanded a flotilla in the Great Armada.

calling the territory under their control the United Provinces. To show their solidarity with their English allies, they had named Leicester governor-general.*

Now Sarmiento fell victim to the war. In August 1586, as he was on his way back to Spain, his ship was intercepted by marauders in the employ of Sir Walter Raleigh. Taken to England, along with his captured vessel, Sarmiento found himself in an oddly hospitable custody. He met Raleigh and had a chance to converse with the queen herself. He was set free after three months of captivity. But again misfortune struck. While traveling through France, he was captured by French Protestants who were then engaged in a civil war with the Catholic majority. Imprisoned with little hope of release this time, Sarmiento could only lament the fate of his colonists.†

Meanwhile, a young Englishman, scorning talk of Spanish fortresses in the Strait of Magellan, led a squadron of heavily armed ships back to the Pacific. Twenty-six-year-old Thomas Cavendish had originally trained to become a lawyer and, despite his youth, had already been twice elected to the House of Commons. While serving in the House, Cavendish had become friendly with Sir Walter Raleigh and had voyaged to Raleigh's Virginia colony in 1584–85. The experience had lit in him a fire for adventure and glory at sea.

Early in 1586 Cavendish, described as "short of stature" and looking even younger than his years, began organizing his own privateering venture to the Spanish Pacific, where he intended to seize as many prizes as possible and then return to England by continuing around the world, as Drake had done.

Cavendish left Plymouth on July 21, 1586. His company consisted of his flagship, *Desire*, 120 tons, and two smaller vessels, the *Content*, 60 tons, and the *Hugh Gallant*, 40 tons. The crews of all three ships totaled 123 men and boys.

After a relatively easy Atlantic crossing Cavendish's squadron

---

*The former Protestant leader, the great William of Orange, had been assassinated in 1584.

†In the three years that had now passed since Sarmiento departed the strait, most of the colonists had died, leaving a handful of survivors. Sarmiento spent three more years in his French prison until Philip II finally ransomed him in 1589. Once back in Spain, Sarmiento pleaded with royal officials to send rescuers to his colonists, to no avail. Sarmiento's own end is unclear. Some stories say he found his way to the Philippines, where he died sometime around 1610. Another has him drowning at sea in 1592. A third version has him living to a ripe old age in Seville. Whatever the case, he never managed to bring help to his colonists.

entered the strait on January 6, 1587. Only a day later the English interlopers encountered a party of starving refugees from Sarmiento's now-abandoned colony of Nombre de Jesús, near the strait's entrance. After first offering succor to these pitiful people, fifteen men and three women, Cavendish sailed away to the west, abandoning the Spaniards to a lingering death. It was a heartless act that no chronicler of the journey ever explained.

Moving farther into the strait, Cavendish's ships anchored off Sarmiento's other settlement, Rey Don Felipe. Here the Englishmen discovered twenty-one men and two women still alive. According to Cavendish's chronicler, Francis Pretty, the Spaniards had "dyed like dogges in their houses and their clothes" and had lain unburied because the survivors were too weak to dig the necessary graves. As a result, the colony was "wonderfully taynted with the smell and the savour of the dead." Despite their condition, Pretty writes, Sarmiento's colonists refused when Cavendish proposed to take them aboard his ships. Pretty says they were determined to make their way to the Río de la Plata. "Our Generall named this town Port Famine," writes Pretty laconically.*

With nearly twenty-four hours of summer sun each day to light the way and his weather luck holding, Cavendish took only seven weeks to make the passage through the strait, entering the Pacific on February 24, 1587. Unlike Drake a decade earlier, Cavendish reached the Pacific during a lull in the usually horrendous weather.

Once out on the ocean, Cavendish turned his bows north toward Chile. Within a few days of leaving the strait, he and his men began a rampage along Spain's Pacific coast. Like Drake, Cavendish sacked and burned towns. He captured vessel after vessel. His holds filled with loot. With the redoubtable Sarmiento now removed from the scene, it seems that the Spanish marine officials of Chile, Peru, and Mexico were even less able to cope with Cavendish than they had been with Drake. Never during Cavendish's murderous cruise along the Pacific coast did Spanish ships seriously threaten the English marauders. Then, proceeding north toward California, Cavendish looked for one big prize comparable to Drake's *Cacafuego*.

*In January 1590 a ship from Bristol found only one man still alive at "Port Famine." He was taken on board but did not survive. It would thus appear that every one of Sarmiento's colonists eventually perished.

He soon found his target. She was the six-hundred-ton galleon *Santa Ana*. Cavendish had learned from prisoners that she was due to arrive in Mexico from Manila with a cargo of riches from China. Cavendish, now operating with only two big ships, the *Desire* and the *Content*—having previously abandoned the *Gallant* and a Spanish prize—waited off Baja California to intercept the galleon. On November 4, 1587, she came into view, and the English attacked.

The big galleon, with no idea that English privateers were operating again in the Pacific, had stored most of her long guns in her hold for ballast and to make room for additional valuable cargo. Nevertheless, the Spaniards resisted bravely. Using rocks and light weapons, they repulsed the first English attempt to board. Cavendish then ordered the *Desire* and the *Content* to stand off and hammer the galleon with their heavy ordnance. For five or six hours the *Santa Ana*, helpless to reply in kind, took the pounding. Finally her captain ran up a white flag.

After putting the galleon's 190 crew and passengers ashore, Cavendish and his men looted her of some fifty tons of luxury goods, including silks, gold, and pearls. With this treasure stowed aboard his flagship, Cavendish set fire to the *Santa Ana* and then set out to cross the Pacific.*

Although her consort the *Content* was lost during the Pacific crossing, the *Desire* made a swift passage to Guam and then went raiding into the Philippines, arousing fury among the Spaniards of the archipelago. Cavendish even looted the villa of a bishop who later complained of "an English youth" who had damaged his house and then had gone away "laughing."

With his Philippine business concluded, Cavendish pointed the *Desire* homeward. His remarkable luck continued. The *Desire* crossed the Indian Ocean unscathed, rounded the Cape into the Atlantic, and reached Plymouth on September 9, 1588, two years and one month after setting out.

After sailing on to London, Cavendish showed off his loot in the capital. He fitted his men with gold chains and clothing of silk. He even decorated the *Desire* with sails of blue damask. Queen Eliz-

---

*The English privateer apparently did a poor job of burning the *Santa Ana*, for the Spaniards, whom Cavendish had put on the beach, managed to get out to her and extinguish the flames. They were then able to get her safely to Acapulco, where they told their story to outraged Spanish officials.

abeth, openly proud of her privateer, was pleased to accept an invitation to dine aboard her, as she lay anchored in the Thames.

Cavendish's return was a jubilant cap to the major defeats that England had inflicted on Spain in recent months. In 1587, when the savagery of the Netherlands rebellion had entered its twentieth year, Sir Francis Drake had led a devastating assault on Cádiz. It was then that Philip, still convinced after two decades of pitiless conflict that he possessed God's mandate to crush heresy, had concluded that the time was ripe for the invasion of England. In July 1588, Philip's Invincible Armada had sailed, only to meet disaster at the hands of English sea dogs and Atlantic weather. English independence and the Protestant revolt in the Netherlands were saved.

Despite the defeat of his Armada, however, Philip clung to the anti-Protestant policies that had been draining Spain's wealth and military strength throughout his long reign. Well over sixty years of age when Cavendish returned from the Pacific, Philip, like some malevolent spider, continued to spin his webs everywhere, fomenting rebellion in Ireland and intervening in the religious civil wars in France. At one point he even sent an army to raise a siege of Paris on behalf of the Catholic faction in France.

Because of such policies, Philip's empire was now stretched to the breaking point. Spain's armies no longer ran roughshod over the battlefields of Europe. Spanish ships could no longer keep English and Dutch vessels from roaming the Atlantic. Spain was in economic turmoil, too. Prices had doubled since the time of the old emperor Charles. Production of goods and food was static. No longer could the empire provide sufficient silver to pay Philip's debts. As the 1590s unfolded, Spain, for all its seeming greatness, was a nation in crisis.

For England, on the other hand, the defeat of the Invincible Armada was an enormous encouragement. After the Armada, England not only fought the Spanish armies in the United Provinces but also renewed exploration and colonization along the coast of North America in defiance of Spanish claims to the whole of the New World. But it was at sea that England most effectively confronted its enemy. English warships attacked Spanish shipping and installations throughout Philip's hard-pressed empire. Although English privateers concentrated primarily in the Caribbean, the Atlantic, and Spanish home waters, the failure of Sarmiento's scheme to close the Strait of Magellan also beckoned English corsairs to the Pacific.

Thus, in August 1591, Thomas Cavendish, still only thirty-one years old, again set sail for the Pacific. This time the objective was not only to plunder but also to open to trade with China. Cavendish's fleet consisted of five formidable vessels: the flagship, *Leicester*, of 400 tons; the *Roebuck*, 240 tons; the *Desire*, Cavendish's former flagship, 120 tons; the *Dainty*, a bark of 60 tons; and a large pinnace of perhaps 30 tons. A total of 350 men manned these ships. Among the voyagers was John Davis, a skilled navigator who, at forty-one, had already spent a number of years exploring Arctic waters in a search for the Northwest Passage to China. Davis, who had made extensive northern journeys in 1586 and again in 1587, was captain of the bark *Dainty*.

The remarkable luck Cavendish had enjoyed on his first voyage now deserted him. The Atlantic crossing, plagued by both calms and gales, took three months. On the journey south along the Patagonian coast, Cavendish's ships were scattered by a series of storms. By the time the fleet came together again and entered the strait, it was April, and freezing autumn tempests forced the battered ships to take shelter. But as if the ghosts of Sarmiento's colonists were getting vengeance, the weather only worsened. Cavendish's men were soon sick, starving, and clamoring to retreat from the strait. Finally, Cavendish agreed to return to Brazil for a time, to refresh his crews and repair the ships. As he prepared to get under way, Cavendish once again demonstrated the hardness of his heart by setting ashore eight sick men from his flagship.

Back in the Atlantic, the young privateer's bad luck continued. Assailed by a "most monstrous storm," Cavendish on the *Leicester* lost touch with the *Roebuck*, Davis's *Dainty*, and the pinnace.*

Eventually Cavendish was reunited with the much-damaged *Roebuck* off the coast of Brazil, and the two ships set out to raid the Portuguese-held island of St. Helena, two thousand miles to the east in the South Atlantic, where the hungry English hoped to obtain provisions and repair their ships. Somehow, however,

---

*The fifth vessel of the fleet, Cavendish's old flagship *Desire*, had apparently been abandoned or lost at an earlier date.

Cavendish missed St. Helena's. The ships then made for Ascension Island, an equally isolated dot of land some twelve hundred miles to the north and west of St. Helena's. But they could not find Ascension either.

With his ships now rotting under him and his men mutinous, Cavendish seems to have despaired of the whole enterprise. He wrote his will and dictated a report on the voyage. Then he died. Like so many others aboard the *Leicester* and the *Roebuck*, he was buried at sea. He was only thirty-two. With the death of Cavendish, the *Leicester* and the *Roebuck* made their separate ways back to England, where the survivors told their wretched story.

Meanwhile, Captain Davis aboard the *Dainty* had once again made his way to the strait, hoping to reunite with Cavendish. Unable to locate Cavendish and prevented by weather from debouching onto the Pacific, the intrepid Davis, too, turned homeward. His voyage soon deteriorated into horror. As the *Dainty* plowed across the Atlantic, her overused sails and tackle rotted. Men died from exhaustion. Others shook with fever. Maggots, bred from salted penguin meat that had gone putrid in the storage casks, infested every inch of the ship. On June 11, 1593, with only himself and four men still strong enough to work the sails, and only a dozen others still alive, Davis reached Bantry Bay, Ireland. There, his own strength running out, he ran the ship aground.*

Even as Davis was running aground in Ireland, still another English sea dog, Sir Richard Hawkins, the son of the famed privateer John Hawkins, was making for the Pacific in another *Dainty*, accompanied by two other vessels. Unaware of Cavendish's fate, Hawkins, too, meant to plunder the Spanish Pacific and return by circumnavigating the world.

After touching on what are now the Falkland Islands, Hawkins made it through the strait in good time. Then, although his two smaller vessels had been lost, Hawkins and the *Dainty* set to work, capturing and burning four Spanish vessels at the port of Valparaiso. The Spaniards, however, were now much better prepared to meet privateers off their Pacific coast, and Hawkins ran

---

*Davis went on to make many other voyages, most of them far more fortunate than this one. In 1596–97 he sailed with Raleigh to Cádiz and the Azores. In 1598–1600 he accompanied a Dutch expedition to the East Indies, and still later he piloted the East India Company's 1601 voyage to the Indian Ocean. In December 1605 he met his death at the hands of Japanese pirates near Sumatra.

into two waiting Spanish ships north of Paita on June 22, 1594. After a fight that lasted three days, Hawkins was wounded and forced to surrender. He was taken as a prisoner to Lima.*

After the Hawkins debacle the English seemed to conclude that further challenges to the Spanish in the Pacific were not worth the cost. Spain's sea power on the Pacific coast was growing, and no English flotilla was likely to be strong enough to overcome this local superiority. England redirected its efforts, concentrating on the creation of colonies in North America. For England the Pacific had become a Spanish sea.

In the mid-1590s, as England withdrew from the Pacific, the Spanish Empire, still in the firm grip of the aging Philip, continued to struggle against a rising tide of debt and Protestant power. In 1595 Spain had to expend some 4.6 million ducats yearly just to pay the interest on its debts. Yet Philip refused to abandon his struggle against Protestantism in the Netherlands and France. In this pass, Spanish maritime officials once more entertained the idea of an expedition into the Pacific to find Terra Australis.

The leader of this new venture would be a man who had endured twenty-five years of neglect, mistreatment, and ridicule. He was Álvaro de Mendaña, who had commanded the ill-fated Spanish voyage to the Solomon Islands a quarter of a century earlier.

---

*Hawkins remained in a local jail until 1597, when he was removed to Spain. Ransomed, finally, in 1602, Hawkins led a full and vigorous life upon his return to England, serving as mayor and member of Parliament for Plymouth. One of the most interesting aspects of Hawkins's career is the fact that he was one of the first mariners to mention the use of oranges and lime juice as a remedy and preventive for scurvy. This knowledge of the efficacy of citrus juice as a cure for scurvy continually passed in and out of sea lore. Yet it was centuries before it became generally accepted.

14

SIREN SONG

Mendaña was fifty-three years old in 1595. He had never relinquished his dream of returning to the islands that he had discovered in 1568 and that a Spanish official, in a sardonic comment on the scarcity of wealth found there, had named the Isles of Solomon.

Despite bureaucratic foot-dragging and wild swings of personal fortune, Mendaña had clung tenaciously over the years to his conviction that the Solomon Islands were worth colonizing not only for their own sake but also because they could serve as staging areas for Spain to claim richer lands that lay nearby in the South Pacific. One of those might even be the much-desired southern continent. Mendaña had begun advancing this argument some twenty-five years earlier, when he had returned to Spain after his first voyage, hoping to win approval for a new journey to the Solomons.*

*Since Mendaña's voyage further "proof" had come to the fore that the elusive continent lay out in the South Pacific, ripe for the taking. A respected pilot, Juan Fernández, who was engaged in the coastal trade between Callao and Chile, had reported that several years earlier while searching for a usable wind to take him southward, he had sailed out into the ocean at about latitude 40 degrees. After about a month sailing west and southwest, he later declared, he happened upon a "very fertile and agreeable continent, inhabited by a white and well-proportioned people, of our own height, well clad." Fernández and his men had returned to Chile, determined to go back someday to their "continent" when "properly fitted." Until then Fernández refused to divulge to anyone the exact location of his discovery, though knowledge of it became widely disseminated.

147

Although his proposal for a new Solomons venture had been refused at first in Madrid, Mendaña had persisted. In 1575, after five years of effort, he had won royal assent for his project. In the following year he had sailed again for the New World to begin organizing the enterprise. But he had encountered a series of obstacles that would have daunted a less obsessed man. First, after arriving in Panama en route to Peru, which was to be the jumping-off place for his voyage, Mendaña had been unjustly imprisoned for several months by political enemies of his family. In time he had won his freedom and had gone on to Peru, only to experience more frustration when the viceroy—perhaps on the advice of Mendaña's old enemy Sarmiento—had withheld his support for the venture.

The viceroy had had reasonable grounds for barring the voyage. Drake was just then operating in the Pacific, and the viceroy had suspected that other English marauders might soon be making their way through the Strait of Magellan to raid the Pacific coast.* The viceroy and his trusted counselor Sarmiento had been focused on fortifying the strait against interlopers. They had also been preoccupied with attempts to strengthen the local defenses of Spain's Pacific coast.

Discouraged but still not defeated, Mendaña had settled down in Peru to await a better day. He persisted in the planning of his project, however. Years passed, and so did the threat of English pirates. At last, in 1595, a new generation of Peruvian officials, desperate to find sources of revenue for the crown, gave Mendaña permission to proceed with his voyage. After years of disappointment Mendaña suddenly found himself in charge of a full-scale mission to reclaim the islands that he had stumbled upon almost three decades earlier. He had outlasted all his enemies, including his old nemesis Sarmiento.

Bubbling with enthusiasm, Mendaña assembled a fleet at Callao: a large flagship, the *San Jerónimo*; a second large vessel, the *Santa Ysabel*; and two smaller vessels, the *Santa Catalina*, a frigate, and the *San Felipe*, a galleylike vessel that could be propelled by oars as well as sails. A total of 378 people made up the

---

Mendaña must have known of the claims of the pilot. In any event, Juan Fernández never got the opportunity to rediscover his continent. Nor is there any evidence that he ever seriously sought to do so. He continued in the coastal trade, discovered the Chilean islands that bear his name, and died at a great age in 1604.
*In reality it was some years before Cavendish followed in Drake's wake.

armada's complement. They included sailors, soldiers, missionary priests, and a motley crowd of would-be colonists, together with their wives and children. The potential settlers also numbered in their ranks a goodly proportion of criminals, prostitutes, and adventurers who hoped only for profit.

It was soon clear that Mendaña had learned little of the art of command since his first ill-fated voyage. In addition to permitting felons and fortune seekers to join his enterprise, he allowed his young and proud wife, Doña Ysabel, to bully him into permitting her to go along on the journey. Nagging, nervous, and cruelly imperious, Doña Ysabel insisted on participating in decisions beyond her competence. In addition to Doña Ysabel, three of her brothers, each of whom had invested in Mendaña's undertaking, held positions of authority in the venture. One of them, Lorenzo Barreto, actually commanded the flagship.* As if Doña Ysabel and her brothers did not represent enough potential dissension within the fleet, Mendaña also enlisted dozens of undisciplined, quarrelsome soldiers, most of whom hated the ships and distrusted him.

Fortunately he recruited an excellent navigator as his chief pilot. This was thirty-year-old Pedro Fernandez de Quirós, a Portuguese who had become a subject of King Philip's when Spain annexed Portugal in 1580. Brought up in the slums of Lisbon, Quirós went to sea as a lad. He married a Spanish woman by whom he had a son and a daughter. For some years now Quirós had been living in Peru, where he had gained a reputation as a steady man with first-class navigational skills. Nevertheless, he was regarded with scorn by many Spaniards in Mendaña's fleet because of his "low" birth and his Portuguese origins.

After departing Callao on April 9, 1595, the expedition spent some time visiting other ports on the South American coast in order to gather additional stores. At one point during this period Mendaña's crews, acting more like pirates than explorers, captured a vessel that they thought more seaworthy than their own *Santa Ysabel.* This ship, almost as large as the flagship itself, was forcibly exchanged for Mendaña's older vessel. She was rechristened *Santa Ysabel.* During this time, too, Mendaña apparently became belatedly aware of the bad character of many of his colonists and set at least some of them ashore. Finally, on June

*A sister of Doña Ysabel's was also aboard the flagship to keep the lady company.

16, 1595, the four ships of Mendaña's fleet departed from the port of Paita.

It soon became apparent that over the years Mendaña had allowed a golden haze of dream to cloud his recollection of the Solomons. He had assured his company that the islands lay some four thousand miles to the west of Peru.* Yet when lookouts sighted a group of lovely palm-fringed islands on July 21, 1595— after only five weeks at sea and a cruise of only about two thousand miles—Mendaña declared that the ships had reached their destination.

As the ships neared the sighted islands, however, and natives appeared, Mendaña conceded his error. These islanders differed considerably from the dark-skinned, frizzy-haired natives who inhabited the Solomons. These people were much lighter in color, and they bore distinctive blue tattoos.

The fleet anchored in the shelter of these islands. Many Spaniards went ashore. The ships were visited by the local people. Mendaña named this group of islands Las Marquesas de Mendoza in honor of the current Peruvian viceroy.†

In a later report the pilot, Quirós, described the golden-skinned Marquesans as well muscled and attractive. The women, he declared, were "very fine", and many among the Spaniards thought them "as beautiful as those of Lima, but whiter and not so rosy." Despite their friendliness and beauty, however, the Spaniards—at least the arrogant and brutal soldiers among them—treated the islanders with contemptuous cruelty, looting their possessions and demanding their obedience. Soon, as had happened so often in previous Spanish encounters with "Indian" cultures, the natives turned hostile and tried to drive the Spaniards away from their shores. The Spaniards retaliated with murderous gunfire. According to Quirós, the soldiers often shot down the islanders merely for "sport." Mendaña showed himself incapable of controlling his soldiers. Thus, for two weeks, while the fleet replenished supplies and rested, Spanish soldiers butchered any "treacherous savages" they came across. Quirós estimated that two hundred islanders perished at the hands of their visitors.

---

*The Solomons lay some eight thousand miles out in the Pacific.
†The islands are still known as the Marquesas, and the natives are, of course, Polynesians, while those of the Solomons are Melanesians.

Leaving the Marquesas the armada continued westward, searching for the Solomons. Food rations and water supplies dwindled. Though several islands were sighted, the Spaniards could not land because of surf and dangerous reefs. As the hot days dragged on, the soldiers squabbled among themselves and with the sailors. Quirós was blamed for poor navigation. Mendaña was accused of having misled the company about the distance to the Solomons.

Then, on September 7, more than a month after departing the Marquesas, the armada found itself among a group of high volcanic islands that reminded the eager Mendaña of his long-lost Solomons. The ships approached cautiously. Mendaña was virtually sure he had reached his goal.

That night, under a blanket of thick fog, the armada's second-largest ship, the *Santa Ysabel*, disappeared. Since it was unclear whether she had foundered or merely lost her way, Mendaña decided to anchor as soon as possible in order to search for her and to refresh his people.

Now, as the expedition sought a safe harbor, natives with black skins and frizzy hair—very much like Mendaña's Solomon Islanders—came out in canoes to meet the Spanish ships. But Mendaña soon found that these warriors did not understand when he spoke to them in the tongue of the Solomons. Disappointed, he realized that he had not yet reached his hoped-for destination.*

Mendaña continued seeking an anchorage. After two days— and a murderous clash between Spanish soldiers and native canoeists, who seemed to the military men to be threatening the ships—the fleet moored in a sheltered bay where there were a number of villages and a river that emptied into the sea. The local people seemed friendly. They came aboard the Spanish vessels with smiles. Happily they received the gifts the Spaniards offered them: bells, beads, feathers, cloth, and other trinkets. One of those who visited the ships was an older man with skin "the color of wheat." He gave his name as Malope and said he was chief of a nearby settlement.

For four days the goodwill continued. But then a party of

---

*Mendaña had drifted southward and was now among a group of islands today called the Santa Cruz Islands. Just north of the New Hebrides, they lie approximately eight hundred miles south of the equator and three hundred miles east of the Solomons.

Spanish soldiers, ashore to fill water casks, were ambushed by a band of armed natives who wounded three of them. Mendaña, now suffering from malaria, sent a detail of soldiers ashore to retaliate. The soldiers attacked Malope's village. They burned down huts, killed any islanders found in the town, and stole their pigs. The following day, as if to prove his "toughness" to his men, Mendaña ordered still another assault. That afternoon, shouting from the beach, Chief Malope protested that it was not *his* folk who had ambushed the Spanish but another clan from the other side of the bay.

Although Mendaña accepted Malope's explanation, he apparently also concluded that the strain between the Spaniards and Malope's people had grown too great for the expedition to remain in the region. Accordingly, when Mendaña's brother-in-law Lorenzo came back from an unsuccessful search for the still-missing *Santa Ysabel* and reported that he had found another good bay with many small islands in it, he ordered his ships to move to this new port, which lay within easy sailing distance.

When the ships dropped their hooks at their new anchorage, however, there were more hostilities and more bloodshed. The Spanish soldiers disembarked and ravaged the many hamlets in the area, shooting down any natives who resisted. When Mendaña and his brother-in-law Lorenzo tried to restrain the worst excesses of the soldiers, the military men left the ships and began building their own camp settlement ashore in defiance of Mendaña, who had designated a different locality for a camp. As the soldiers' bivouac took shape, however, Mendaña decided not to insist on his own site. Instead he admonished the soldiers—now that they were residents of the island—to treat the natives and their property with respect. The soldiers reacted to this warning by resorting to new violence to force supplies from the islanders. Soon cowed natives from nearby villages were carrying food both to the soldiers and to the anchored ships in the bay, where most of the expedition was still housed.

Although Mendaña knew he had not rediscovered his Isles of Solomon, he also knew that he lay somewhere in the general vicinity of those islands. Therefore, it seemed prudent to establish an initial colony on this island, where, in any case, the soldiers and others in the expedition appeared determined to settle. Once his colonist families were firmly rooted here, he thought, he could search further for the Solomons and the southern continent. Mendaña now gave the island a name: Santa Cruz.*

Santa Cruz seemed to offer good prospects for a permanent settlement. The ground appeared fertile. There was excellent anchorage in the bay, which the Spaniards called Graciosa. There was good water. The beaches were clean white sand. Moreover, the natives, terrified of Spanish guns, were now inclined to accept the newcomers. Mendaña was content to begin the work of Pacific colonization in this place.

But now the fickle soldiers changed their minds. They demanded that Mendaña abandon Santa Cruz and take them to a "better" land—or to the Solomons. Mendaña, having committed himself to Santa Cruz and still anxious to locate his missing ship, *Santa Ysabel*, was reluctant to leave and said so. Upon this the soldiers, apparently to provoke a permanent warfare that would make it impossible for the Spaniards to stay at Santa Cruz, began attacking the natives with even greater ferocity than before.

Soon, with hostility everywhere, many of Mendaña's colonists and mariners joined the soldiers in petitioning to leave. Mendaña, laid up with fever aboard the flagship, tried to placate everyone. Quirós also tried to smooth matters. All lands, he argued, had their rough beginnings. The Spaniards had been on Santa Cruz for only a month. If they forsook their colony now, he declared, they would be acting against both God and king, to say nothing of their own honor. But Quirós's words fell on deaf ears. Some of his listeners even threatened to kill him, and they whined that at this point they would be satisfied only if the fleet went on all the way to Manila, "where Christians lived."

Mendaña's imperious wife, Doña Ysabel, who was often more resolute than her husband, entered the controversy. Convinced that the root cause of the expedition's dissension was the lack of discipline among the soldiers, she urged her husband to execute the military commander. It was the only way, she argued, to bring the soldiers to heel and avert civil war among the Spaniards. Her three brothers backed Doña Ysabel's point of view. Mendaña, shivering with malaria, agreed, promising to act quickly.

Meanwhile, as these discontents boiled among the Spaniards, the estimable Quirós departed on a brief foraging trip. This excursion included a visit to Chief Malope, who—despite past wrongs—furnished Quirós with much-needed food supplies.

*It was the island of Ndeni in the group still called the Santa Cruz Islands.

When he returned to the Spanish camp, Quirós learned of a plot by the soldiers to assassinate Chief Malope in order to incite new native attacks that might furnish the final excuse to depart Santa Cruz. A party of soldiers, Quirós was told, had already left to carry out the bloody deed.

Horrified, Quirós immediately sent a messenger after the soldiers with an explicit order forbidding them to harm Malope. He then boarded the flagship to report this new outrage to Mendaña. From his sickbed Mendaña told Quirós that on the following morning he meant to go ashore and "do justice" to the chief of the soldiers. It appears that Quirós made little effort to dissuade his commander.

With the next dawn the feverish Mendaña went to the beach with Doña Ysabel's brothers and some trusted men. Encountering a squad of soldiers, he inquired where they were bound. They replied that they were off to Malope's village "to obtain supplies." Mendaña admonished them to do no harm to Malope. They only laughed in reply.

Mendaña and his grim company then approached the soldiers' camp. The commander came out, unarmed, to meet them. Then he appeared to sense what was afoot. He shouted for his weapons. But it was too late. Mendaña's men fell on him, stabbed him to death, and stripped his corpse. A friend of the dead man was also stabbed to death. Now Mendaña's men, with bloody swords still drawn, began shouting, "Long live the king! Death to traitors!"

Mendaña ordered his men to behead the two corpses in the camp. The heads were set up on posts as a grisly caution against further disobedience by the soldiers. Then the expedition's priest, accompanied by Doña Ysabel and others, came ashore to join Mendaña and his victorious assassins. With bloodstains still fresh on the ground, Mendaña gathered the shocked colony to hear mass. In his sermon the priest urged obedience on all and claimed that the killing of the camp master and his companion was ordained by heaven.

There was, however, still more madness to come. That afternoon a soldier returned from Malope's village, reporting that his companions had murdered the chief while they were taking a meal in his house. They had done this, the messenger said, because they were convinced that Malope intended "treachery." When the rest of the soldiers came back, the one who had inflicted the fatal wound on Malope was put in stocks. "He is well dead!" protested the murderer. The young officer who had apparently been in charge of the murderous soldiers was beheaded, despite his wife's pleas for mercy. His head, too, was impaled on a post.

After this latest bloodletting the turmoil finally subsided. It was decided that the perpetrators of the crime against Malope, even his admitted murderer, would be kept as prisoners and not killed out of hand. Quirós suggested that to assuage the just anger of the natives, the three executed Spaniards be shown to the islanders. But in no case, he said, should the Spaniards put to death any more of their own, for this would only deprive them of much-needed hands in the days ahead.*

Malope's people were anguished by his death. Though the Spaniards went so far as to present them with the head of the young officer in payment for the life of their chief, the islanders were not satisfied. Gathering in the jungles, where they were safe from Spanish guns, they attacked the settlers relentlessly. To make matters worse, fever, like a judgment from heaven, became rampant among the Spaniards. Many began to die. Mendaña, who had already been ill for some weeks, grew more feeble every day. He made his will. He named Doña Ysabel governess of the expedition and her brother Lorenzo, captain general.

On October 18, 1595, as furious natives bombarded the Spanish camp with stones and lances from the jungle, he died. And though Mendaña's long voyage had come to an end, the chaos and agony in the camp of the Spaniards were not done yet.

---

*Though he escaped execution, Malope's murderer found himself the focus of much ill will from his companions. He died, supposedly of "melancholy," a few days after his imprisonment.

15

VOYAGE IN HELL

Mendaña was not the last to die of the fever epidemic that now raged through the ranks of the Europeans. Every day Spaniards succumbed. And every day the natives, still enraged over the murder of their chieftain, Malope, kept up their pressure, shooting arrows from the trees into the Spanish stockade. Finally the Spaniards sent soldiers to attack Malope's village again. The soldiers, invincible when in the open, burned the cluster of huts and forced the inhabitants to furnish them with food.

But now virtually all the settlers had lost heart. Even most of Mendaña's loyalists began imploring the new governess, Doña Ysabel, and her brother Captain General Lorenzo Barreto to abandon the island.

Quirós was one of the few who opposed leaving. He blamed the sickness in the camp on poor diet and on the need to sleep on the chilly ground. Doña Ysabel, comfortable enough in her well-appointed cabin aboard the flagship, hesitated about relinquishing the settlement. Then Captain-General Lorenzo took an arrow in the leg. The wound festered. He died on November 2— All Souls' Day—only fifteen days after Mendaña. Quirós assumed responsibility for day-to-day operations, but Doña Ysabel insisted that she alone would make the big decisions. To ensure that she would retain the power to do so, she kept possession of the keys to the ships' stores.

For another two weeks the colonists struggled on against worsening conditions until even Quirós had to admit that Santa Cruz had become untenable. Accordingly, on November 18, 1595, having dug up Mendaña's body for later reburial, the ships weighed anchor, leaving behind a bitter legacy of death and destruction. They also left behind a number of discarded pet dogs that ran barking along the beach as the ships sailed away.

Doña Ysabel ordered Quirós to try once more to locate the Solomons, suggesting that the fleet's missing ship, the *Santa Ysabel*, might have found her way there. If the search for the Solomons proved fruitless or the *Santa Ysabel* was not there, she declared, the expedition would then make its way to Manila and organize a second try at settling the Solomons. Quirós acceded to her wishes but advised that it would be more efficient, in view of the reduced numbers in the fleet, to scuttle the two smaller ships, the frigate *San Felipe* and the galleylike *Santa Catalina*. Both vessels, Quirós pointed out, were near wrecks. Moreover, it took thirty men to sail them. These men could be put to much better use aboard the shorthanded flagship, the *San Jerónimo*. Despite the logic of Quirós's argument, Doña Ysabel refused to abandon the *San Felipe* and the *Santa Catalina*.

The battered fleet set out, ostensibly to seek the Solomons and the long-lost *Santa Ysabel*. After sailing vaguely to the west for two days, Quirós turned northwest toward the Philippines. Doña Ysabel made no objection.

With his vessels rotting and his crews weak from hunger, Quirós drove his ships toward the equator. By December 10, 1595, after three weeks at sea, they lay just south of the line, on an empty sea that seemed to burn under a pitiless sun. Rations for most members of the expedition had been cut to half a pint of foul water and a little flour each day. Many were nearly mad with thirst. Doña Ysabel, however, kept a supply of freshwater on board for herself, her family, and her servants, declining to share it. She also had her own sources of fresh meat: live pigs and a calf. Two of her pigs were pets.

The ships plowed on, and the misery increased. One of the vessels, the *Santa Catalina*, disappeared without a trace. Now even the flagship, the *San Jerónimo*, was leaking badly and hardly making way in the light air. Every day the dead—children, women, and men—were jettisoned into the sea. Still, Doña Ysabel would not part with any of her supplies. She washed her clothes with freshwater while mothers watched their children endure agonies of thirst. When Quirós remonstrated, she snapped that she had a right to do what she pleased with her own property. If the people complained, she suggested, Quirós should have two of them hanged as an example to the others to hold their tongues. He pressed no further. Some weird sense of duty and loyalty apparently impeded him from deposing this vile creature, or perhaps he simply lacked the power to confront Doña Ysabel's armed servants.

By December 19, the *San Jerónimo*, accompanied by the badly leaking frigate *San Felipe*, lay 250 miles north of the equator. The men in the frigate, exhausted by privation and by incessant pumping, implored Quirós to allow them to transfer to the flagship and let the frigate sink. Though he approved, Doña Ysabel again refused her permission. Soon afterward the frigate disappeared in the night, and it was presumed that her weary crew had finally lost their battle to keep her afloat.

The *San Jerónimo* continued on—alone. Then, on New Year's Day 1596, she arrived off the coast of Guam, approximately twelve hundred miles west of the Philippines. But hope for relief was thwarted: The ship's tackle was so rotted that the crews could not lower a boat to get ashore for water, and the ship itself could not approach the shallows. The *San Jerónimo* now turned due west, making for the Philippines. With favorable winds the ship made good time. But at last the desperate survivors of the *San Jerónimo* had had enough of Doña Ysabel. They threatened mutiny unless she shared her private provisions. Frightened, she handed over the last fresh meat on board: her calf. Even now she hid away her pet pigs, and the famished sufferers had to make do with bits of veal shared out among themselves.

On January 12, 1596, lookouts sighted the Philippine coast. As the *San Jerónimo* approached, natives came out to the ship and sold the Spaniards food in exchange for silver, knives, and beads. The starving survivors of the *San Jerónimo* gorged themselves, a number of them, constitutions weakened by privation, died of too much food and water. As the ship neared the port of Manila, she was met by a small boat carrying four Spaniards who seemed to Quirós as beautiful "as four thousand angels." The *San Jerónimo* finally anchored on February 11, 1596.

Now back in civilized society, Doña Ysabel complained loudly to local officials about the disrespect shown her by the survivors of the *San Jerónimo*. The magistrates, however, took no action. Having reburied Mendaña, Doña Ysabel then married one of his relatives, Fernando de Castro. Despite the hardships of their recently concluded voyage, she and her new husband ordered Quirós to prepare the *San Jerónimo* for a return journey to Mexico.

As Quirós set about refitting the big vessel, word came that, battered but still afloat, the *Santa Catalina*, the small vessel thought lost weeks earlier at sea, had arrived at Mindanao. The frigate, however, lost more recently, was never heard of again.

On August 10, 1596, the *San Jerónimo* set out to recross the Pacific. Following the by-now-standard route across the North Pacific, Quirós brought her back to America, arriving at Acapulco on December 11, 1596. The long, hideous journey to find the Solomons and Terra Australis had ended at last. Quirós alone had completed it with honor.

The terrible months of his voyage in hell with Mendaña and the monstrous Doña Ysabel had forged Pedro Fernandez de Quirós into a man with a mission. He burned with a new and holy craving. Having experienced horror where he had expected to find heaven, Quirós now longed to bring God to the great Pacific—especially to Terra Australis Incognita. Back in Peru and united with his own family after the awful journey, Quirós made a proposal to the new viceroy, Luis de Velasco.*

Quirós proposed to Viceroy Velasco that he sail once again to the South Pacific. He told the viceroy that he was now convinced that the Solomons and Mendaña's recently discovered island of Santa Cruz were in close proximity to the southern continent. He felt certain that once permanently established on one of these high islands south of Capricorn, he could find Terra Australis and convert its inhabitants to the true faith, expanding the Spanish Empire beyond anything Columbus had ever imagined.

The viceroy apparently listened politely. But he could spare no

---

*Velasco was the successor to Viceroy Mendoza, Sarmiento's mentor, who had blocked Mendaña's voyage for so long. The new viceroy was also the son of a previous viceroy by the same name, he who had sent Legaspi and the monk Andrés Urdaneta on their successful journey to the Philippines.

funds for another expensive voyage into the Pacific unless ordered to do so by Madrid. His reluctance may have had a bit of
Spanish snobbery about it as well; after all, Quirós was a lowborn,
half-educated Portuguese. In any case Velasco suggested that
Quirós travel to Spain to seek support. If Madrid ordered new
efforts in the Pacific, the viceroy would do what he could to ensure its success. Quirós, undaunted, prepared to take his case to
Spain.

His departure, however, was long delayed. He had to obtain
money for his passage. He had to prepare his proposals. He had
to write officials for an audience. It was not until February 1600
that Quirós managed to make his way to Spain. He found his
adopted nation in a state of confused transition.*

Philip II had died two years earlier at the age of seventy-one
after a reign of forty-two years. Two years before his death he
had again suspended repayment of his loans to the bankers, thus
forcing a restructuring of his debts; he died owing 68 million
ducats. Almost half of Spain's yearly budget of 9.7 million ducats
was earmarked to service obligations to creditors.

In addition, Philip had left a country beleaguered by enemies. War with England and the Dutch rebels, who had now
declared themselves an independent nation, continued unabated. Spain had also fought an expensive, fruitless war with
France from 1596 to 1598.

In addition to the twin burdens of debt and war, Philip had
bequeathed to Spain a weak successor. His son, the frivolous
Philip III, was more interested in gaming and amusement than
in governing. Instead of spending long hours attending to the
details of administration, Philip III left government to others,
notably to the duke of Lerma.

Lerma was determined to preserve the Spanish Empire despite diminishing resources. Unlike the old king, he did not try
to fight Spain's enemies and support its friends everywhere at all
times. Instead his policy was to concentrate Spain's still-
formidable power against England, where the aging Queen Elizabeth continued to govern, and against the self-proclaimed
Dutch Republic of the United Provinces, whose merchant fleets

---

*As usual, there is little in the record about Quirós's personal life, but it appears that he
left his wife and children in Peru when he went to Spain.

were already trading in the East in defiance of Spanish and Portuguese edicts.*

Despite the government's transitional state, Quirós managed to wangle an audience with the new king and, more important, with Lerma. Quirós spoke passionately of his plan to find and convert the southern continent. But he received no encouragement and concluded that he could not hope to find in Madrid the support he needed.

He then resolved to take his ideas to Pope Clement VIII. He reasoned that if he could secure the Holy Father's blessing on his enterprise, the Spanish government, however reluctant, would be obliged to provide him with whatever he needed to find another New World out in the Pacific. So Quirós, with the fortitude of a man who believes himself in the service of God, donned the plain brown dress of the saint whom he admired most, Francis, and journeyed to the Eternal City.

---

*Lerma's policies were aided by the fact that France was growing less inimical to Spain. The French king, Henry IV, now nominally a Catholic, had granted religious freedom to heretics in the Edict of Nantes. The religious civil wars that had tortured the country for almost two generations were soon to subside.

16

SAILOR OF GOD

Quirós reached Rome in 1601. His first act was to present himself to the Spanish ambassador to the Papal States, Don Antonio de Cardona y Cordova, the duke of Sesa. This grandee, impressed by Quirós's credentials and his ardor, called together a panel of mathematicians and geographers to hear his plan and advise on its feasibility.

It is easy to imagine how he appeared to his interrogators: a Portuguese zealot in his simple brown habit, face and hands burned dark from his years in the sun and looking much older than his thirty-nine years. In the end he answered his questioners with such impressive clarity and certainty that these learned men agreed that the Portuguese pilot should be allowed an audience with the pope.

Soon after, Quirós put his case to His Holiness, emphasizing the souls to be saved in Terra Australis. The pontiff gave his blessing to Quirós's enterprise, and wrote letters endorsing the search for and conversion of Terra Australis. To aid Quirós in this work, Clement presented the Portuguese pilot with a precious splinter said to be from the cross of Christ.

Triumphant, Quirós returned to the Spanish court more certain than ever that God had chosen him for His holy work. But he found that the grandees of Madrid still hesitated to recommend his program to the king. Some of those at court even questioned the value to Spain of exploring the world further. As

Quirós later recalled it, "Some [declared] that sufficient lands had been discovered for His Majesty and that what signified was to settle them, rather than go in search of those [that] were new."

But Quirós would not be denied. He pestered and clamored for two more years. Finally, he won over the Council of State, although the Council of the Indies still refused to sanction his venture. Nevertheless, one council's support proved sufficient. A letter of instruction was drawn up for Quirós to present to the viceroy of Peru.* Signed by Philip III, the letter commanded the viceroy to give all aid to Quirós's mission "to win souls to heaven and kingdoms to the crown of Spain." The viceroy was also to outfit two ships from the royal revenues, to enlist friars for the conversion of the heathen, and to grant Quirós "full authority" over the enterprise.

Armed with his letter, Quirós embarked for America. His journey was anything but easy. Shipwrecked, thwarted by colonial officials in Venezuela, and embarrassed by a lack of money, Quirós needed almost a year to make his way to Peru. In Lima, after presenting his royal missive, he was received with honor by the viceroy, who declared himself much moved by Quirós's fervor and dedication.

At this critical moment the monstrous Doña Ysabe' reappeared to threaten the project. Still living in Peru and dreaming of a dukedom in the far Pacific for her second husband, Mendaña's widow complained that Quirós's proposed voyage would usurp her "right" as heiress of the discoverer of the Solomons to reap the supposed wealth of those islands. The viceroy weighed the objections of the lady against the instructions of his king and rebuffed the complaint.

At last Quirós began assembling his armada at Callao. Although the king had talked of two ships, three vessels were actually readied, one of them a small pinnace, essential for reconnoitering the reef-strewn waters around Pacific islands. In its final form the expedition included Quirós's flagship, the *San Pedro y Paulo*, of 150 tons; the *San Pedrico*, of 120 tons; and the pinnace that bore the name *Los Tres Reyes*. A talented Spanish navigator, Luis Vaez de Torres, commanded the *San Pedrico*. The

*This was still another viceroy, Gaspar de Zuñiga y Azevedo, the duke of Monterey, who had succeeded Velasco.

captain of the *Los Tres Reyes* was Bernal Cermeno, an experienced mariner. Unfortunately for Quirós the viceroy pressed one of his favorites on the fleet as chief pilot. This was Juan Ochoa de Bilboa, whom Quirós disliked immensely from the start. Another important figure in the fleet was a proud soldier, Diego de Prado y Tovar.

Quirós's three vessels carried three hundred soldiers and sailors, six Franciscans, and four friars of St. John. Unlike Mendaña's ill-fated squadron of ten years earlier, this one included no women. Quirós did not intend to repeat Mendaña's mistakes. His men would plant their colony and convert their natives before bringing women and children to their New World.

In addition to ship biscuit, salt meat, and other stores sufficient for a year's voyage, the ships were supplied with fresh water stored in hundreds of earthen jars in an attempt to avoid the spoilage so often caused by wooden water barrels. Because Quirós intended to colonize the lands to be discovered, his holds were also stocked with domestic animals, farm implements, seedlings, fruit trees, and trinkets for bartering with the natives.

The ships departed the harbor of Callao on December 21, 1605. Because of the underlying spiritual character of the expedition, Quirós insisted that all his officers wear the habits of friars for the occasion. He dedicated his fleet to Our Lady of Loretto, the patroness of the Franciscans. With cheers ringing in the ears of the crews, the ships sailed out past the island of San Lorenzo to the south of Callao. "We sailed with good will to serve God and spread our Holy Faith, and to bring credit to the King our Lord; all seemed easy to us," wrote one pilot.*

Quirós, having considered the problem of Terra Australis for some eight years now, had concluded that Mendaña and others who had searched for it had failed to strike its shores because, by sailing a more or less straight course, they had failed to cover sufficient area of the vast ocean and thus might have missed the

*There are four more or less detailed accounts of the voyage. The pilot, Gonzalez de Leza, quoted here, wrote a record that is most useful. It is full of notations of positions, sightings, and other information that a pilot would want to remember. A Franciscan friar, Juan de Torquemada, who did not accompany the voyagers, wrote an account pieced together at a later time from conversations and testimony of those who had gone on the voyage. Torres, captain of the *San Pedrico*, wrote a brief but interesting report that focuses on the later segments of the journey. But the most complete and interesting account was composed by Quirós himself and dictated to his faithful young secretary, Belmonte Bermúdez, who accompanied Quirós on the voyage. Bermúdez became a poet of some note in his later years.

great land by the narrowest of margins. Quirós, on the other hand, proposed to follow a route designed to carry him through many more degrees of latitude in the South Pacific than any of his predecessors. Although he planned, generally, to tend toward the southwest, his purpose was to cover large areas of ocean, rather than just keep to the west. Accordingly, he had worked out a zigzag course. He intended first to sail southwesterly to latitude 30 degrees. Then, if no land appeared, he would turn *north*west to latitude 10 degrees. If no land appeared during this leg of the voyage, he would turn southwest to 20 degrees. Then, still assuming that he found no land, he would once more make northwest to 10 degrees and sail along that parallel to Santa Cruz, the island where Mendaña had died. It would serve as a base for further probes.

As the fleet headed out into the Pacific, Quirós issued detailed orders covering his men's conduct. True to the religious nature of his enterprise, he prohibited swearing and "blasphemy" aboard his ships. He also forbade his men to gamble and ordered his officers to throw overboard any gaming tables found on their vessels. (Backgammon was allowed.) He insisted that his men attend daily mass. He also admonished his officers to treat any natives encountered "as fathers to their children." Needless to say, Quirós's rough-and-ready crewmen resented the ban on swearing and gambling—two vices considered essential pastimes at sea. It was the beginning of the voyage, however, and spirits were high. The men offered no open objections to Quirós's unusual strictures.

With the weather fine at first, the fleet made good way and, after a month at sea, reached a point almost three thousand miles out on the ocean, at latitude 26 degrees south. This was much farther to the south than any previous expedition had ever ventured. Yet no sign of the southern continent appeared.

At this point squalls and swells began buffeting the ships. Soon the men began to murmur among themselves, griping at Quirós's moral prohibitions and at the apparent futility of his meandering search for Terra Australis. To complicate matters, the supply of good water started to dwindle despite the care taken to preserve it in earthen jars.*

---

*Quirós did have aboard his ships a device for distilling water. It apparently worked well

As the seas grew rougher in these southerly latitudes and as water grew scarcer, Quirós gave in to pressure from some of his officers and changed course to the west-northwest—that is, back toward Central Pacific waters already traversed by Mendaña ten years earlier. By making this change, Quirós hoped to locate islands with fresh water. He knew he was compromising his own program for finding the southern continent, but he thought it prudent to make the course change.

On their new heading the ships sailed deeper into the Pacific. The weather continued stormy, and water and fuel rations had to be cut. Although in these latitudes the armada came upon numerous islands, most were waterless and uninhabited. Others were surrounded by dangerous reefs and surf that made landing impossible. Still others were peopled by hostile natives. But even those few accessible islands whose inhabitants welcomed the Spaniards offered inadequate supplies for the fleet's needs.

By mid-February 1606 the ships had been at sea for almost two months, and there was still no sign of the southern continent. Moreover, egged on by the chief pilot, the viceroy's friend Bilboa, the men were grumbling more than ever. Many were wondering aloud when, if ever, they would reach this so-called southern continent with its supposed riches. The chief pilot reported that the sailors were exhausted, implying they were justified in their complaints. A later account quotes a sailor as saying he was "tired of being always tired, that he would rather die once than many times, and that they might as well shut their eyes and let the ship go to the bottom."

At this moment, as if matters were not bad enough, Quirós fell ill. Weak with fever and concerned about both the physical and mental condition of his querulous crewmen, he decided to make still another course change. The fleet would turn due west and make directly for Mendaña's island of Santa Cruz. There, Quirós knew, the expedition would find a good anchorage and plenty of water. There, too, he told himself, the men would be able to rest and recover their physical and moral strength. After

---

enough—at least in the beginning. According to later reports, the device managed to distill "50 jars" of potable water. It needed fuel to be operated, however, and apparently fuel was short. It is also likely, though not certain, that the quality of the water distilled by the device left much to be desired. In any case, "50 jars" were clearly not sufficient for the needs of the fleet.

that there would be time enough to resume the search for the southern continent.

Despite the course change, the island of Santa Cruz did not appear. Many days passed. The muttering among the crews worsened. Aboard the flagship quarrels erupted daily as some men argued that the ships should give up and make for Manila, while others, equally adamant, resisted any idea of abandoning their mission.

February faded into March. The armada had now been nearly ten weeks at sea. As before, there were more landfalls on inhospitable islands, clashes with native people, chronic shortages of food and water, and always the resumption of the search westward. Quirós, becoming sicker each day, stubbornly clung to the westward course, insisting that the fleet must soon reach Santa Cruz.*

As the ships plowed on through the empty, ocean, the feverish Quirós called a conference of officers in an attempt to determine their exact position. At the conference the chief pilot, Bilboa, got into a petulant disagreement with Quirós about the distance they had traveled from Peru. The argument escalated until Quirós, accusing Bilboa of trying to sabotage the voyage, had the chief pilot arrested and put in irons aboard the flagship's consort, the *San Pedrico*. Gonzalez de Leza was appointed chief pilot in Bilboa's place. The fleet went on. Although, according to Quirós's own later account, Bilboa's adherents within the ships were distressed by his arrest, "the ship was [at last] without those . . . disturbances which had been going on. . . ."

Now, incredibly, no land at all appeared for three weeks. Food supplies dwindled to the vanishing point. Luckily, sufficient rain fell to relieve the thirst of the crews.

Finally, on April 7, 1606—107 days out from Peru—the fleet came upon an inhabited island.† The Spaniards anchored, went ashore, and with their terrifying muskets intimidated the islanders into supplying provisions. The chief of the island then met with Quirós aboard the flagship and told him, by signs, that a

---

*Santa Cruz actually lay more than twenty-five hundred miles farther west in Mid-March.
† This was the isle of Tuamaco in what are now called the Duff Islands. The ship still was some five hundred miles east of the Solomons.

"large island" with an active volcano lay only a five-days sail to the west. Quirós was sure that this was Santa Cruz at last. He also learned from the chief that numerous other islands lay in that area. The most important information, however, was that a "huge land" lay to the south. Joyfully Quirós concluded that this must be the southern continent itself. With his heart glad after so many weeks of struggle, Quirós sent the chief away with gifts.

For two weeks the Spaniards rested and refreshed themselves at the chief's pleasant little island, and for once relations with the native people were generally amicable. On April 18 the Spaniards resumed their voyage.*

Now Quirós again changed course. Having learned of the "huge" landmass to the south, he saw no reason to continue searching westward for Santa Cruz. He ordered the ships to turn southeast and the mariners to keep a sharp eye out for the great land supposed to be there. With favorable winds the ships swung to the south and east for four days. They visited still another pleasant island and encountered more friendly natives.

Then, on April 22, the weather closed in, and the ships cautiously hove to in those reef-strewn waters. When clear skies returned, Quirós ordered a resumption of the voyage, but now he told his pilots to "put the ships' heads where they like, for God will guide them as may be right." After an outcry against this quixotic command, Quirós agreed to continue south.

On April 29, 1606, having visited several more islands, the ships sighted what certainly seemed to be a landmass. As they neared the verdant land, it appeared to broaden and fill the horizon. On May 1, the flotilla entered a wide bay, "big enough," according to Captain Torres of the *San Pedrico*, "for all the fleets in the world." Land rose on every side. Trees crowded hills that climbed gently into the sky. Quirós sent his most competent officer, Torres, to scout ahead while the other ships remained offshore. Torres returned to report that this land was a most beautiful place, watered by a broad river. He declared that rolling plains, forests, and land suitable for farming lay beyond the bay.

---

*At the last moment the Spaniards spoiled the amity with the local people by kidnapping four of them upon departure. Apparently they intended to use these hostages as "guides and linguists" during the voyage ahead. Three of the four hostages, however, escaped within a few days by jumping overboard and swimming to nearby islands. The fourth, who had been a prisoner of the islanders, preferred Spanish captivity to imprisonment on the island. He remained aboard and presumably helped guide the Spanish ships.

On a less optimistic note, he said that the region was inhabited and that the natives had not seemed friendly. Quirós felt sure that he had, at last, found the southern continent. Nor was he the only one to conclude that the expedition had discovered Terra Australis. His new chief pilot, Gonzalez de Leza, also thought so, for in his journal he noted that the land in sight seemed "very extensive" and "very high" and did not appear to be "less than continental."

On May 3, 1606, having received Torres's glowing report of the land ahead, Quirós ordered the ships to anchor. They did so with joy and with "many thanks to God."*

Anchored off the coast of what he *knew* was Terra Australis, Quirós prepared to claim this new New World for Spain, to establish upon it the kingdom of God, and to save its heathen inhabitants from the agonies of hell.

---

*The fleet had discovered the extensive island group later named the New Hebrides, several hundred miles south and east of the Solomons and some hundreds of miles south of Mendaña's Santa Cruz. The large islands, many of them grouped close together, gave the appearance of a continental mass when viewed from the armada's perspective.

17

CAPTAIN QUIXOTE

For the first week or so the Spaniards explored inland and along the coasts. They found grassy plains suitable for the establishment of great cities. They found uplands that would make magnificent pastures for their animals. They discovered a broad and gentle river nearby. Flowing from the uplands, it emptied into the great bay itself. Quirós called it the Jordan. Search parties returned from their initial forays into the interior reporting that they found the country fertile, overflowing with fruits, grains, and roots such as yams. The region was also fat with pigs and fowl. If the land was bountiful and welcoming, however, the natives were anything but.

The later chronicler of the voyage, the Mexican friar Torquemada, who based his account on eyewitness interviews, quotes one of Quirós's men describing one of the first encounters between the Spaniards and the native people:

> The boats having arrived at the shore the next day, the natives with their King came to the beach, very anxious about our arrival, and trying to induce us to return [to the ships] by presents of fruit. But our people, jumping on shore, succeeded in making peace with them. The native King, making a line along the ground with his bow, said that no one was to pass beyond it. Luis Vaez

[de Torres], considering that it would be cowardly not to do so, crossed the line. Scarcely had he done so, when the barbarians quickly shot off a flight of arrows. In payment for this audacity and evil intention, our people killed some of them, including the King. The rest fled to the mountains. At this time, while the ships were at anchor, the Spaniards made several expeditions into the interior in search of provisions, of which they were in want, as well as to treat for peace with the people. But the natives are of such bad disposition that they never would come to any agreement. On the contrary, they watched and guarded the way many times, but were never able to do any harm. The trees and leaves impeded the flight of arrows, always catching them among the leaves, but with bullets the branches make little difference. In this way and in this dangerous state of affairs the days passed. . . . *

Clearly, though Quirós had desired to bring the peace of God to his new land, his Spaniards had already aroused the native population to furious enmity. To deal with the islanders' antagonism, Quirós appointed what he called a Ministry of War and Marine for the security of his people. He named Torres camp master with responsibility for shore operations. He appointed Bernal Cermeño, captain of *Los Tres Reyes*, admiral of the marine forces.

Then Quirós, who was still very ill and perhaps just a bit mad by now, gathered the entire company aboard the flagship and conducted a solemn, and to later eyes a somewhat pathetic, ceremony. He inducted his men into a religious order that he had invented: The Knights of the Holy Ghost. Quirós explained that his knights would devote themselves to the ideals of chivalry and to spreading the word of God in the New Land. He presented each man of the company with a cross, made of blue taffeta, to be worn on his breast at all times. Despite the skepticism of some, the Knights of the Holy Ghost seemed to suit most of the men and there was a general celebration aboard the ships

---

*The good friar's cold recital of mayhem, murder, and machismo is virtually a summary of the half-righteous, half-fearful, always contemptuous attitude that the Spaniards—and most other Europeans as well—brought to their contacts with the native peoples not only in the Pacific but in all the Americas.

soon after Quirós had completed his ritual. The festivities included music, dancing, and the firing of guns. In a peculiar counterpoint to the Spaniards' fiesta, the natives ashore began shouting and singing their own chants. But perhaps they were merely calling on their own gods to protect them from these fearsome strangers.

At the following dawn Torres, as campmaster, went ashore and began building a structure to serve as both a fort and a church. Quirós then led the rest of his forces to the beach. Drawing them up on the strand, their blue crosses fluttering in the breeze, Quirós conducted still another lofty rite. This time he took formal possession of the new land for Spain. Kneeling and kissing the ground, he cried out: "Oh, land, sought for so long, intended to be found by many, and so desired by me!" He named his newly claimed continent Austrialia del Espiritu Santo.*

Having annexed his southern continent for King Philip, Quirós proclaimed that the land's first settlement would be called New Jerusalem. He also confirmed that the nearby river was to be called Jordan. Then, after mass and more celebrations, he appointed magistrates and municipal officers for his New Jerusalem. This day was, for Quirós, the climax of years of struggle.

The day-to-day problems of the colony, however, could not be solved by ceremonies, proclamations, or appointments. Perhaps the most pressing difficulty was the chronic food shortage, which the Spaniards tried to alleviate by raiding native villages, precipitating numerous clashes with the islanders. Soon, despite Quirós's orders to treat the indigenous people gently, the Spanish soldiers were inflicting death and destruction on the natives as casually as they might have shot game at home.

One day, for example, a party of foraging soldiers entered a native village where they seized fourteen pigs and, as if for sport, three small boys who had not managed to flee in time. The natives then rallied to attack the Christians as they retreated back to the shore with their booty. The Spaniards, however, drove off the attackers by "force of bullets." The friar Torquemada, telling the story, reports that the Spanish raiders, having not lost a man, embarked on their boats with pigs and boys in-

---

*The spelling is correct. Although most of Quirós's contemporaries referred to the unknown southern continent by its Latin name, Terra Australis, Quirós named *his* continent in honor of King Philip III, who was, of course, a Hapsburg of Austria. Hence, Austrialia.

tact, "joyful and contented at the good success of that day."

Despite such incidents, most of the Spaniards seemed to believe that their enterprise was flourishing. But not all Quirós's people were pleased with the state of his colony. Many privately ridiculed him and were contemptuous of his piety and his interminable speeches. To these cynics he seemed more a madman than a saint. His New Jerusalem appeared to be an illusion, and his precious heathen merely black savages "who had the Devil in their souls." For such skeptical spirits, Espiritu Santo (as Quirós's land was now familiarly called) seemed far from a paradise. Furthermore, it had occurred to some by now that the land might not be a continent after all but only another island—larger than many others, perhaps, but certainly not a new America. With the glory of discovery still bright around Quirós, however, his detractors expressed such doubts only to each other for the moment.*

As if to confirm the mocking judgment of his secret critics, Quirós began to exhibit behavior that even his loyalists recognized as bizarre. It began only three weeks after the expedition's arrival at Espiritu Santo, when Quirós suddenly announced that because of native hostility, the fleet would up anchor and explore the seas farther to the west.†

Quirós then delayed departure for a day to allow his men to catch supplies of fresh fish for the journey. Many of the mariners applied themselves to the nets, and the crews feasted on the catch. Unfortunately the fish were poisonous, and many men, including Quirós, became desperately ill. Nevertheless, Quirós ordered the ships to get under way on the next day, May 28. He then reversed himself when the poisoned men proved too sick to work. Finally he decided to allow the flotilla to lie at anchor for a week while the crews recovered.

During this time armed natives came down to the beach, seeking the return of the three boys whom the Spaniards had kidnapped earlier and were still holding aboard the flagship. The natives offered to exchange pigs for the return of their children.

---

*The former chief pilot, Bilboa, who had now been replaced, was given his liberty at Espiritu Santo. However, though Bilboa begged for pardon, Quirós refused to forgive his earlier disloyalty or to return him to a position of responsibility within the fleet.

†Perhaps Quirós wished to explore again because he, too, had begun to suspect that his "continent" was an island. To many in the expedition, however, his abrupt abandonment of New Jerusalem seemed evidence of mental instability.

The Spaniards, apparently valuing the youngsters as hostages, refused, although they did bring the boys ashore to display them to the islanders as proof that they were still alive and well. When one of the children cried out to be reunited with his people, Quirós admonished the boy: "Silence, child! You know not what you ask. Greater good awaits you than the sight of heathen parents and friends and their communion!" When the importuning natives seemed to become threatening, the Spaniards fired on them, and they fled.

On June 8 Quirós, now holding forth on his "need" to get a near view of a "great and high chain of mountains" that appeared to lie to the west, led his fleet from the bay. Once outside the sheltered waters, however, the ships could make no way against strong head winds, and again Quirós changed his mind. The fleet, he ordered, must return to New Jerusalem. He declared that the men would spend the southern winter there, "building a strong house, sowing the land, getting a better knowledge of the season, and building a brigantine" to explore the coast.

Obediently the armada turned back to the bay. The *San Pedrico* and the *Los Tres Reyes*, more agile than Quirós's lumbering flagship, the *San Pedro y Paulo*, reached the anchorage before dusk. The flagship, however, continued to struggle. When night fell, a dangerous onshore wind rose, threatening to drive her aground. Says the later account by Friar Torquemada: "So, for this and other reasons, they beat out under the sprit-sail to the entrance of the bay, where they hove to for the rest of the night, waiting for the morning, to see if they could reach the port. But this was found to be impossible, for the force of the wind obliged them to drift from the mouth [of the bay] until they were outside...." For days the *San Pedro y Paulo* now fought against unceasing head winds. But she was unable to hold her position, much less reenter the bay where the other two ships lay waiting.

The men of the anchored vessels apparently observed the flagship's struggles with no undue concern, for Peruvian-built ships like the *San Pedro y Paulo* were notoriously poor sailors under such conditions. No doubt the talented Captain Torres and the other experienced pilots of the smaller vessels anticipated that the flagship would eventually make its way into the bay to join them. In the meantime, there was nothing to be done but wait.

Aboard the flagship, however, matters looked far more threatening. With each passing hour the *San Pedro y Paulo* fell farther to leeward. Nor was there any sign of a slackening in the wind. It began to seem that it would be impossible for the big ship to sail back to the bay. Quirós now made still another peculiar but far-reaching decision: The flagship would make for Mendaña's island of Santa Cruz, the rendezvous point agreed upon at the start of the voyage, should any of the ships lose contact.* Accordingly, the *San Pedro y Paulo* came about one night and began running to the west before the wind, disappearing from the view of the anchored ships in the bay.

For another week the flagship sought to find Santa Cruz. The island did not appear. Quirós changed course, this time to the north. Friar Torquemada tells what happened next:

> The Captain [Quirós] reflected on the little chance there was either of proceeding or going back. He felt that the voyage was long, while the provisions were running short, and resolved to take the opinions of all as to what should be done: either shape a course for China, or follow the route for Mexico, now that Heaven had permitted that they should lose their consort. All those who understood the case gave their opinions, judging, for evident reasons, that it would be best to make the voyage to Mexico. The opinions were taken down in writing, and signed. Then, with great regret at their failure, they made sail for Mexico, a course very different from their original intention.

Quirós blamed himself for the failure of his enterprise, calling himself unworthy because of his "many great sins."

The long, sad voyage to Mexico, following the galleon route across the North Pacific, took four more months. Despite storms, sickness, and short supplies, it was a lucky voyage. Rain fell often enough to replenish the drinking water. For once the crews were

---

*After completing the passage of the Pacific, the fleet had abandoned this notion of making rendezvous at Santa Cruz. It seems obvious that Quirós was no longer thinking clearly. Otherwise he would have realized that if the flagship should change course, the Spaniards left behind at New Jerusalem would have no way of knowing that she was still afloat, much less that she was trying to make her way to Santa Cruz. Why didn't he just send a boat to the other vessels telling them what he intended? No one will ever know.

able to use their nets effectively, taking aboard more than enough fish to feed all the men. Though battered and weather-stained, the *San Pedro y Paulo* arrived back in Acapulco on November 23, 1606. Only one man, an elderly friar, had died on the passage.

Meanwhile, far across the vast Pacific the other two ships of Quirós's expedition were embarked on a much different voyage.

When the *San Pedrico* and the far smaller *Los Tres Reyes* anchored again off New Jerusalem after Quirós's decision to spend the winter months at Espiritu Santo, their crews had expected that the flagship would eventually overcome head winds and join them. Thus, when the men of the *San Pedrico* and the *Los Tres Reyes* woke on the morning of June 12, 1606, to find that Quirós's ship had disappeared, they thought at first that the flagship's crew had mutinied and forced the commander away or that his vessel had been wrecked. The two smaller vessels set out to search for their commander. Unfortunately they had no way of knowing what course the flagship might have taken, and the truth—namely, that Quirós had set sail for Santa Cruz—never occurred to anyone.

Searching along the coast of Quirós's "continent," the two smaller vessels found no sign of the flagship. They did, however, confirm the fact that Espiritu Santo was an island. Then, conceding that their search for Quirós was in vain, the commanders of the two remaining vessels opened sealed instructions that they had received from the viceroy of Peru in case Quirós died or in case the ships of the fleet became separated. These secret orders directed the surviving Spaniards to look for land as far south as twelve hundred miles below the equator. If they failed to find land, they were to return to Spain via the Philippines, the Spice Islands, and the Cape of Good Hope.

In view of the perilous situation, it was now agreed that Captain Torres of the *San Pedrico* should take charge of what was left of the expedition. He was an excellent navigator and a fine seaman. Under his leadership the *San Pedrico* and the *Los Tres Reyes* departed Espirito Santo and sailed down to latitude twenty-one degrees south, more than fulfilling the dictates of the viceroy. They found no land. They did, however, experience some unexpectedly cold weather. Torres then turned his bows northwest, until the ships reached the eastern tip of New Guinea, which an earlier Spanish mariner, Inigo Ortiz de Retes, had claimed for Spain in 1545.

Still unexplored and unmapped, New Guinea was a mystery. Was it an island or part of a greater landmass? Torres tried to round its eastern cape in order to sail along its northern coast, through waters already familiar to Europeans. Head winds thwarted his effort. He decided that he had no choice but to attempt to try the *south* coast of New Guinea, if there was navigable water there. With this purpose in mind, in mid-July 1606, he guided his two small ships into the shallows that lapped the southern reaches of this mountainous country.*

Keeping as close to the shore as he dared, Torres felt his way through a shark-infested, reef-strewn passage until his ships found deep water. Unknown to the Spaniards, the northern shore of what is now Australia lay just to the south, at one point less than a hundred miles away. For two months, after gaining open water, Torres made his way west along New Guinea's southern coast, charting his route and noting landmarks and bays where it was possible to anchor. He also described the inhabitants of New Guinea as "wild and unfriendly."

At the end of September 1606 the two vessels reached the western tip of New Guinea, proving that this unknown land was a great island, not part of a landmass. Here Torres and his men encountered armed Muslims, who, he reported later, "go conquering the people who are called Papuas and preach to them the Sect of Mahomed." The Muslims sold the Spaniards provisions and confirmed that the Spice Isles lay only some two hundred miles farther to the west. Torres now sailed on to Ternate, where he and his men were accorded a warm welcome.†

After spending some time in the Spice Isles, during which he and his men helped quell a rebellion, Torres took the *San Pedrico* on to the Philippines, leaving the *Los Tres Reyes* behind in the Moluccas. The *San Pedrico* reached the capital city on May 22, 1607.

---

*What is known of Torres's voyage comes from his own brief report, written later.
†Since Philip II's annexation of Portugal in 1581, the Spice Isles, indeed the whole of the Portuguese trading empire in the East, had been incorporated into the Spanish Empire. Though the islands were still administered by Portuguese, Spaniards were no longer at risk in Moluccan waters, a far cry from Elcano's time.

*   *   *

Meanwhile, in far-off Peru Quirós, having returned safely from the Pacific was bombarding Spanish officials with reports of his new "continent" and with proposals that he be allowed to return to it. But the viceregal officials had neither the power nor the inclination to grant his request. Quirós again determined to travel to Spain to make his case before the royal court.

After arriving in Madrid in October 1607, Quirós initiated a remarkably persistent, perhaps half-mad, campaign to win the royal favor. In one lengthy "memorial" after another to the king and his counselors he insisted that he had found a continent. In these retrospective memorandums Quirós recalled his discovery as a true paradise. In one of his petitions, for example, he wrote: "I can show to a company of mathematicians, that this land will presently accommodate and sustain 200,000 Spaniards. None of our men fell sick from overwork, or sweating, or getting wet. Fish and flesh kept sound for two or more days. I saw neither sandy ground, nor thistles, nor prickly trees, nor mangrovy swamps, nor snow on the mountains, nor crocodiles in the rivers, nor ants in the dust, nor mosquitos in the night." Quirós's Espiritu Santo had no hostile "Indians" or poisonous fish either—at least in the discoverer's memory.

Despite his unending pleas, Quirós got nowhere. Nor did it help his cause when Torres wrote a report from Manila on *his* voyage, criticizing his former commander as irresolute. An old enemy, Fernando de Castro, the second husband of Doña Ysabel, also wrote to Madrid, urging the rejection of any proposals by Quirós. Still another who wrote to ridicule the Portuguese navigator was his former fleet accountant, Juan de Iturbe, who had been one of the most mutinous of the Spaniards on the voyage out to Espiritu Santo.

These dim assessments of Quirós, together with his own un-relenting hyperbole, inclined Spanish officials to regard him with skepticism. This negative attitude was expressed in a report by one of the grandees who advised Philip III: "The Cardinal of Toledo [one of the king's counselors who had often heard Qui-rós's petitions] considers time spent on this matter time lost, for Your Majesty has neither the resources to keep even his present possessions, let alone new enterprises as remote and uncertain . . . but that, if Your Majesty should later decide to undertake it, then it should be entrusted to a person possessing the character, prudence, and reliability called for by such a project. . . . "

Still, Quirós persisted. Then, suddenly, against all odds, it seemed that the Portuguese navigator would achieve his purpose after all. Toward the end of 1609 he was told he might proceed to Peru, where the viceroy would furnish him with all he needed to sail again to the Pacific. But now—Quixote-like—Quirós balked, demanding that his authority over any new Pacific enterprise be made explicit in a royal order to the viceroy. This was too much. The project hung fire. Once more Quirós's memorials flowed. Once more Spanish officials shuttled Quirós from one official body to another.

Finally, in October 1614, Quirós was told he had permission to accompany still another new viceroy who was on his way to assume his new office in Peru. This nobleman, Quirós was told, had been given explicit instructions to provide everything he needed to make his long-delayed voyage. In truth, however, the viceroy had been ordered to humor Quirós, to keep him busy in Lima, but to avoid spending any of the royal substance on his Pacific enterprise.

After all these years of frustration Quirós clearly despaired of ever achieving the full authority he believed he needed and deserved. He decided to accompany the new viceroy to Peru and hope for the best. On the voyage out, however, he died. He was only fifty, but he was already an old man, worn out by his travels and his travails.*

Quirós may have dreamed of a new Spanish Empire, but in reality Spain's glory had begun to fade long before he met his end. Although Spanish treasure fleets still plied the Caribbean and the stormy Atlantic, and galleons still crossed the Pacific, by the first decade of the seventeenth century Spain had already started the long decline that would leave it a second-rate power at the end of the century. In fact, even before Quirós had set out upon his journey to his New Jerusalem, an unlikely European power was challenging Spain's preeminence on the sea lanes of the world and had already fought its way into the great Pacific. This new power was the rebellious Spanish province of the Netherlands.

---

*The indomitable navigator, Torres, had also faded into obscurity, but the strait he discovered, which separates New Guinea and Australia was named after him.

18

THE REBELS SET SAIL

The Dutch ascent to maritime supremacy was set in motion by a fateful edict issued by Philip II, King of Spain. Designed to curtail the then-modest sea power of the rebellious Netherlanders, the decree produced an effect directly opposite the one intended.

Following his seizure of the Portuguese throne in 1581, Philip forbade Lisbon merchants to trade with the Netherlands. For decades prior to this Dutch merchants had been purchasing vast quantities of spices in Lisbon and carrying them to northern Europe for resale. By abolishing this commerce, Philip hoped to cripple the economy of the Dutch insurgents and force an end to the revolt. But instead of withering away as a result of Philip's embargo on spices, Dutch traders began to employ their ships in smuggling, privateering, and carrying the goods of other nations. The rebel fleets continued to grow both in number and in competence. In addition, the Netherlanders began to dream of sending their own vessels to the East to seize the spice trade for themselves.

In the meantime, however, the Netherlanders had to focus their efforts on the struggle against Spain, which was as bloody and bitter as ever. In 1581 the seven northern provinces of the Netherlands—already joined together in a political union under the name United Provinces—formally repudiated past allegiance to Spain. This was the equivalent of a declaration of independence, and from that time forward the United Provinces considered themselves a sovereign nation, governed by their own head of state, Prince William of Orange, titled Stadtholder, and by their own legislative body, the States-General.*

In 1585 English troops arrived to fight alongside the rebels of the United Provinces. The Dutch freedom movement gained even more momentum when the English fleet destroyed the Spanish Armada in 1588. As a result of that defeat, Spain could no longer spare sufficient ships to supply and support its armies in the Netherlands, and Dutch privateers—the Sea Beggars, as they styled themselves—were able to take control of the waters off the low-lying shores of the United Provinces. Slowly the rebel armies gained the upper hand on land as well. Thus, as the decade of the 1590s opened, the United Provinces were, in fact as well as in name, an independent state. Philip of Spain, however, refused to acknowledge that reality. He insisted on continuing the armed struggle to reconquer the United Provinces. Soon Spain found itself stretched militarily and economically as never before, for Philip, already at war with England as well, now also sent troops to France in order to support Catholic forces there in a civil conflict between Huguenots and the traditional Catholic majority.

As a consequence of these policies, the Spanish economy, always handicapped by the royal debt, tottered on the edge of catastrophe. Although the flow of precious metals into Seville from the empire had increased sevenfold since the days of the old emperor, Charles, the amount was not nearly enough to finance Philip's armies and service his debts at the same time. The state's budget deficit soared, as did inflation.†

Yet in spite of all these troubles, the Spanish Empire still possessed formidable military and naval strength as the 1590s began. Spanish colonial officials had greatly strengthened the

---

*The largely Catholic southern half of the Spanish Netherlands, roughly equivalent to modern Belgium, remained under the Spanish crown and was, on the whole, loyal to Philip even though some of the most atrocious events of the revolt had taken place on southern soil.

†It is estimated that the worth of silver and gold imported into Spain in the 1590s averaged 7 million ducats annually. In the 1540s the average had been 1.1 million ducats. The wealth of the empire accounted for 25 percent of Philip's revenues, but it was a more or less reliable source that could be, and was, used as collateral for enormous loans. To make matters worse, prices in Spain had more than doubled since the time of the old emperor.

defenses of the Indies both on land and at sea. Local naval forces had been augmented, and formidable fortresses had been built at such strategic points as Havana, Puerto Rico, and Santo Domingo, making many of Spain's New World ports virtually impregnable. This fact was made manifest in 1595, when Drake and Hawkins led a privateer fleet to the Caribbean and achieved only limited success.

On the other hand, Spain's naval strength in Europe was much diminished, as a joint English and Dutch fleet showed when it successfully attacked the port of Cádiz in July 1596, capturing a Spanish treasure fleet in the process.

But if Spain still wielded considerable power in the 1590s, at least in the Americas and the Philippines, its satellite Portugal had declined sharply under Philip's rule, especially in sea power. In 1590, Portugal possessed only about three hundred ships and seven thousand mariners to defend its Eastern empire. In contrast, the fleet of the rebel United Provinces—forced to expand thanks to Philip's ill-considered decree against the Dutch spice trade—possessed at least three thousand vessels of between a hundred and four hundred tons, most of them capable of long deep-sea voyages. The Dutch were also building as many as a thousand vessels each year. Moreover, the United Provinces could count on more than a hundred thousand mariners to crew superbly crafted vessels built from efficient new designs.

By the 1590s, formidable Dutch fleets were trading regularly in the Baltic and prowling the Arctic ice in a (vain) effort to find a Northeast Passage to China. Dutch merchantmen had passed through the Strait of Gibraltar and had opened trade with Italy, Constantinople, and the Levant. In 1593 Dutch ships even reached the Guinea coast of Africa.

By 1595 the Dutch state—the United Provinces—was ready to challenge for control of the spice trade, as first contemplated more than a decade earlier.* In that year, nine Dutch merchants formed. The Company of the Far Lands and sent a fleet of four big-bellied ships, manned by 248 mariners, to find their way to the Portuguese-dominated East.

---

*The European appetite for spices was as ravenous as ever in this era. The largest consumers were still in the Baltic countries, Germany, Russia, Poland, and Scandinavia. It appears, however, that the Mediterranean hunger for spices had begun to decline. Nevertheless, the market was still enormous in northern and eastern Europe. Luther had once complained that, in Germany, there was more spice than grain.

Still unwilling to challenge the Spaniards by sailing the Strait of Magellan, the Dutch ships—under the command of an experienced master, Cornelis de Houtman—made their way around the Cape of Good Hope, across the Indian Ocean, and east toward the Spice Isles. While Quirós, Doña Ysabel, and the other survivors of Mendaña's ill-fated expedition were struggling to reach the safety of the Philippines after their star-crossed voyage from Santa Cruz, these Dutch ships, despite fevers and scurvy, managed to make their way to the spice marts of the East. The Dutch found the Easterners eager to break the Portuguese stranglehold on their economy by trading with the newcomers. Houtman and his men quickly filled their holds with pepper. In August 1597 Houtman returned with three of his four ships still intact, carrying eighty-nine survivors of the journey and a fortune in spices.

In the following year, 1598, Dutch merchants, overjoyed by the success of their first voyage, sent thirteen ships eastward via the well-charted and relatively safe Cape of Good Hope route.* Two other expeditions also set out that year, and these were far more problematic, for they aimed to reach the Portuguese East by sailing through the Strait of Magellan and across the Pacific. Thus, for the first time Dutch seamen and ships would go forth to confront Spanish sea power far from home, in what were really Spanish home waters.

The initial Pacific-bound flotilla consisted of five ships from Amsterdam: the *Hope*, 250 tons; the *Charity*, 160 tons; the *Faith*, 160 tons; the *Fidelity*, 100 tons; and the *Good News*, 75 tons. Piloted by an Englishman, these ships managed to get safely through the strait though badly battered by weather. After reaching the Pacific side of the strait, however, the fleet commander, Sebold De Weert, decided not to risk a Pacific voyage after all. The ships turned back for home.

Meanwhile, the second Dutch Pacific enterprise, consisting of four armed trading vessels—the *Maurice*, the *Henry Frederick*, the *Concord*, and the *Hope*—and 248 men, had already departed for the strait. This squadron was under the command of Oliver Van Noort, a tough old sailor who was part merchant, part pirate, and all business. Some years earlier Van Noort—after many years

---

*Of the thirteen ships that took the Cape route, eight returned safely with magnificent cargoes.

aboard trading vessels and privateers—had abandoned life at sea and had opened a Rotterdam inn. But when Dutch ships had begun to return from the East with their rich cargoes of spices, Van Noort, at fifty, had found himself itching for a share of that new wealth. The innkeeper became a mariner again.

With the backing of a consortium of Rotterdam merchants and the enthusiastic support of Dutch authorities, Van Noort had set sail for the strait in July 1598, making it clear that in addition to trading in the Spice Isles, he intended to take any Spanish or Portuguese prizes that came his way and to raid ashore if the opportunity offered.

After a skirmish with Portuguese warships off Africa, during which his English pilot was killed, Van Noort crossed the Atlantic, reaching Brazil on February 5, 1599. After detouring to raid Ascension Island for provisions, burning an unseaworthy ship, the *Concord,* and marooning two of his sailors for infractions of discipline, he led his squadron south to Port Desire on the Patagonian coast. There, in September 1599, Van Noort careened his three remaining ships and took supplies aboard. There, too, three of his sailors were killed in a fight with giant "savages" who were "painted unto terror."

By late November 1599 the Dutch were in the strait, struggling toward the Pacific, fighting both tempests and hostile natives. At one point in the strait Van Noort encountered the fleet of his countryman De Weert, as it made its way back toward the Atlantic after its brief incursion into the Spanish Pacific. Despite De Weert's retreat, Van Noort pressed on against the tempests that blew incessantly from the west. He also suppressed a mutiny among his crews, sentencing one unnamed officer to marooning on the wild shores of the strait.

At last, in February 1600, after two months of struggle, Van Noort reached the Pacific, where he offered "thanks to the Almighty for [this] happy success." With his company now reduced to 147 men, Van Noort, following the example set by Cavendish and Drake, raided the Pacific coast of Spanish America. Unlike Drake and Cavendish, however, the Dutchman won no great prizes, for the major ports of the Spanish Pacific were now bristling with defenses too strong for the small Dutch force. Further, at that season, there were no galleons due in Spanish American waters.

Thus, in May 1600 Van Noort struck out west to cross the

Pacific. He now had only two ships, his flagship *Maurice* and a smaller vessel, apparently a Spanish prize. Reaching the Philippines without incident, he began a new campaign of piracy. Again, rich prizes proved elusive although Spanish fighting ships were not. One day, December 14, 1600, as the *Maurice* and her smaller consort were cruising off Manila, the inevitable occurred: Two Spanish galleons gained the "weather gauge" on the Dutch ships and closed in for the kill. Not only did the Spanish outgun the Dutch vessels, but Van Noort's eighty surviving crewmen were outnumbered three to one.

Soon one of the Spanish warships overtook the *Maurice* and Spanish soldiers swarmed aboard, overwhelming the Dutch mariners, who fled below, where they cowered in the near blackness. Meanwhile, the other Dutch vessel, thinking the *Maurice* taken, fled the scene, the second Spaniard in pursuit.

With the Spaniards in possession of his deck, and his crewmen hunkered down below, Van Noort exploded in fury, shouting down to the men hiding in the hold. "Up you go after them," he boomed, "or I'll set fire to the powder, and we'll all go up together!"

Van Noort's men feared the fury of their commander more than the guns of the Spaniards. They flung themselves back up on deck. Slashing furiously and firing wildly, the Dutch hurled the surprised Spanish into the sea. The Dutch cannon also fired, pouring shot into the galleon's belly at point-blank range. The galleon shuddered and sank, leaving dozens of Spaniards bobbing in the sea. Van Noort was not finished with the hated Spanish enemy, however. He ordered his men into the ship's boats, and the Dutch, stabbing with knives and pikes, dispatched as many of the swimming Spaniards as they could reach. Meanwhile, Van Noort's companion vessel was captured and her crew made prisoners.*

Alone after the battle and with only a few dozen men left, Van Noort decided to make for home. Though he had relatively little booty in his holds, he recognized that with his diminished strength he had little chance of gaining more. Moreover, unfavorable monsoon winds were making it impossible to reach the Spice Isles for trade, even if in his weakened state he dared confront the Portuguese in those waters.

---

*These Dutch captives were eventually hanged by the Spaniards in retaliation for Van Noort's cruel treatment of the helpless Spaniards in the sea.

Following the route blazed by Elcano, Drake, and Cavendish before him, Van Noort crossed the Indian Ocean, rounded the Cape of Good Hope, and reached Amsterdam on August 26, 1601, thirty-seven months after departing. He was the first Dutch navigator to circumnavigate the world, and the fourth ever to have made such a voyage.

While Van Noort's great journey had resulted in little profit, it *had* shown that ships from the United Provinces could attack the Spanish Empire in the Pacific, cross the great ocean, and maintain themselves in those far distant waters. The Dutch were now more determined than ever to seize the East for themselves. Moreover, the task became less daunting when the implacable enemy, Philip II, sole monarch of the Spanish Empire for more than forty years and architect of both its glory and its decline, died in 1598, at the age of seventy-one, after a last terrible illness.

The old king's son, the frivolous Philip III, left the direction of the government of Spain to the duke of Lerma, who was financially corrupt and given to playing favorites. While the duke meant to continue the seemingly interminable struggle with England and the United Provinces, Spain's policy was no longer to deplete its strength by retaliating against every enemy thrust. Lerma understood that incessant war was a losing proposition for Spain, draining its treasure faster than it could come from America. But with the Dutch demanding an independence that Spain regarded as impossible, war was inescapable. The duke's solution was to try to limit the *level* of hostilities.* By the time Van Noort's battered little ship limped home in 1601, Lerma's government was already well embarked on its new course, one that seemed to herald a weaker, less tenacious Spain, whose Pacific empire could be plucked by daring Dutch mariners.

The English, too, were determined to grab a share of the Eastern trade, even though English sea power, since its triumph

---

*The duke of Lerma, Francisco Gómez de Sandoval y Rojas—to give him his full name—while a venal administrator who amassed a fortune said to be more than forty million ducats from government service, ruled Spain for almost twenty years. Inevitably, given his administrative style and international strategy, Spain declined considerably under his stewardship. But considering the fact that Philip had left behind a debt of sixty-eight million ducats, requiring half of Spain's yearly budget just to pay interest, it is unlikely that any administrator could have rescued Spain from its decline. It was while Lerma governed that Cervantes wrote *Don Quixote.*

over the Armada, had ebbed considerably relative to that of the United Provinces. English merchants had already made at least two unsuccessful attempts during the 1590s to send ships around the Cape of Good Hope to trade for spices. In 1591 three small vessels had departed England on such a journey. Only one of these vessels made it to India, and she did little business except for some minor piracy. Eventually this ship was abandoned in the Atlantic, and a French ship rescued her crewmen and carried them back to England. Following this first fiasco, a second English fleet had departed for the East in 1596, and was never heard from again.

Despite these disasters, however, London merchants remained confident that English mariners could successfully take part in the Eastern trade with their more numerous Dutch allies. They based this optimism—at least in part—on the fact that a number of English navigators had been engaged to guide the first Dutch flotillas eastward. If Englishmen like John Davis could pilot Dutch traders, they could steer English ships as well. Thus London merchants, organized by royal charter in 1600 into the English East India Company, sent still a third English fleet east in April 1601. The squadron of four ships, under the command of Captain James Lancaster,* in June 1602 reached Sumatra. There Lancaster loaded his ships with spices. He then returned to England with a rich cargo that turned a magnificent profit for his backers. In this manner was the "John Company" launched.

But English efforts were minor compared to the Dutch stampede eastward. In 1601, the year of Van Noort's circumnavigation, a total of sixty-five Dutch vessels, in *fourteen* separate flotillas, set out for Eastern waters and the Pacific. Most of them made successful voyages, returning with cargoes of spices and other goods that brought their owners wealth beyond avarice.

As if paralyzed by the suddenness of the irruption, the Spanish and Portuguese reacted slowly to the presence of Dutch and English interlopers in Eastern waters and in the Pacific. In Europe, however, the Spaniards struck back against England by landing forces on the Isle of Wight in 1601. A year later a Spanish fleet put three thousand fighting men ashore in Ireland to aid Catholic rebels there. While these measures discomfited an En-

*Captain Lancaster had been the leader of the first, ill-fated English voyage of 1591.

gland that had grown somewhat tentative under the aging queen, Elizabeth, they did nothing to deter the exuberant Dutch.

As the Dutch fleets went eastward, the canny governing body of the United Provinces, the States-General, recognized that if its country was to succeed in creating a permanent trading empire in the East, a coordinated national program was needed. Voyages undertaken by independent operators, each competing with the other—no matter how successful—could be only temporary triumphs. What was required was an agency to channel Dutch maritime energies in the national interest. Thus, in 1602, the States-General formed the Dutch East India Company, a joint-stock company with investment open to all. Managed by a board of seventeen directors, the company was charged primarily with coordinating the effort to gain control of the spice trade for the United Provinces.

Under its charter, the company received a monopoly over all activities in the Indies. It could make treaties, establish ports, appoint governors, dispense justice, and issue licenses to ship-owners to do business in the Indies. It was also granted the right to wage war against Spain and Portugal. It could maintain its own armed forces. It could coin money, appoint its own officers, and enact laws under which native peoples would have to live. The company was granted ''sovereignty'' over the Strait of Magellan and the Cape of Good Hope. In effect, the Dutch East India Company was to be the Dutch government abroad.

19
THE COMPANY

In the opening years of the seventeenth century the Dutch East India Company launched a full-scale armed invasion of the Pacific and Indian oceans as scores of ships it owned or licensed began searching out new markets and aggressively wresting old ones from Portugal and Spain. The Dutch newcomers enjoyed a number of advantages over their antagonists. Not only were their ships better armed and easier to work, but their captains were usually better navigators, and their charts and instruments were more reliable than those of the Spanish and Portuguese.

The Dutch also possessed less tangible advantages over their enemies. Unlike the proselytizing Catholic powers, these Protestant burghers had no interest in imposing their religious beliefs on the native peoples with whom they came in contact. Trade, not salvation, was their purpose. For this reason they seemed less threatening to native cultures than did the Catholic imperialists, with their black-robed priests and insistent rituals. And unlike the Spaniards and the Portuguese, who demanded that native rulers acknowledge the sovereignty of far-off European kings, the agents of the Dutch East India Company gave the impression that they were content to let local inhabitants govern themselves—as long as they cooperated in business. Thus, in these early days of the Dutch incursion, native potentates, most of whom hated the oppressive Spaniards and Portuguese, often welcomed the Dutch and even aided them to drive their Catholic rivals from their strongholds.

For example, when Dutch ships visited Ternate in the Moluccas at the beginning of the seventeenth century, the island's sultan offered the company a monopoly in spices in exchange for an alliance against the Spaniards and Portuguese and Dutch recognition of his rule over the entire archipelago. The Dutch agreed and then, with native allies, launched seaborne assaults on enemy outposts throughout the Moluccas. In 1605 the Dutch captured the Portuguese trading center of Amboina, and the Portuguese began a fighting retreat entirely from the Moluccas.*

Nor were the Moluccas the only targets of the company. Dutch ships also attacked at numerous points along the Spanish-Portuguese sailing routes. In 1606, for example, Dutch fleets bombarded such widely separated Portuguese-held ports as Mozambique in Africa and Malacca in Malaya. Though the Dutch failed to capture either place, they inflicted much damage and seriously disrupted trade. The company also made it a practice to intercept Portuguese and Spanish vessels on the high seas. At the same time it established fortified trading posts wherever feasible, from India to the Persian Gulf.

Despite all its offensive energy, the company occasionally stumbled. Dutch attempts to trade at Canton in 1604 and 1607 were blocked by Portuguese forces stationed at Macao. The Portuguese also managed to cling to their major installations in Malaya, India, and East Africa despite Dutch onslaughts. In 1606 a Spanish force from the Philippines even counterattacked in the Moluccas, recapturing some territory previously lost to the Dutch. Despite such occasional hard lessons, however, the Dutch were resolved to pay whatever price was required to dominate Eastern seas.†

In Europe, meanwhile, the Dutch war against Spain contin-

---

*Dutch indifference to the form of local government did not last. Within a decade or two the Dutch would be dictating laws to the sultans and deciding what spices could be grown on what islands. The immediate effect of the company action in the Moluccas, however, was to make the ruler of Ternate dominant—for a while—in the islands, a circumstance that aided the company when the grateful sultan filled Dutch cargo holds with spices.
†Although the Dutch were almost fanatically intent on crushing any opposition from Portuguese or Spanish interests, they never succeeded in driving either the Portuguese or the Spanish entirely out of Asia. Portugal held on at Macao, Goa, and other enclaves until the twentieth century. The Spanish clung to the Philippines almost as long.

ued unabated. In 1606 a Dutch war fleet blockaded the Tagus River, Lisbon's link to the commerce that was its lifeblood. In the following year a squadron of Dutch warships pounced on a Spanish fleet off Gibraltar and destroyed it completely. These actions, together with the Dutch East India Company's aggression in the East, proved that the United Provinces could now wage war on a global scale. Moreover, they showed that the Dutch could achieve their aims without the aid of England, which had signed a separate peace with Spain in 1604.

The cessation of the conflict between England and the Spanish enemy had come rapidly after the death of Queen Elizabeth, in 1603, at the age of seventy. The queen had ruled for forty-five years and had carried on open war with Spain for the last eighteen years of her reign. Her Stuart successor, James, however, possessed little of Elizabeth's Protestant zeal. Nor did he esteem the Dutch, whom he saw as "provocative, proud, and grasping." Even less did he harbor malice toward a beleaguered Spain that, under the new government of the duke of Lerma, was disposed to make peace. Moreover, English merchants, especially the East India Company, yearned for an end to war in order to develop their Eastern commerce unhindered by hostilities.

The result was that Spain and England signed the Peace of London in 1604 without reference to the United Provinces. Few in England fretted about deserting their Dutch ally, for it seemed certain that the United Provinces would gain political recognition without their help. Moreover, many Englishmen, alarmed by Dutch power in Europe and by the Dutch success beyond the Cape of Good Hope, had come to view their former partners more as rivals than allies.

The Dutch at first displayed little resentment at England's defection. But beneath their placid exterior they privately took exception to a clause in the Anglo-Spanish peace treaty that granted English merchants the right to trade freely with the Spanish Empire, a provision that could result in enormous profit for the English East India Company. The merchants of the Dutch East India Company also bristled when English traders began stepping up their commercial efforts in the East after the peace with Spain. For the time being, however, the Dutch swallowed their displeasure and went on with the task of seizing the Spanish and Portuguese Empire.

*   *   *

As the Dutch expanded ever further into Pacific waters, Dutch mariners, like all who had sailed the ocean before them, felt the pull of the southern continent. Although the spice trade remained their main business, the captains of company ships always kept a weather eye out for Terra Australis. In fact, from the first days of the company's Pacific invasion, Dutch shipmasters had been reporting glimpses of a low-lying territory south of the mountainous land called New Guinea. Could this be the continent?*

The Dutch had also heard rumors that New Guinea itself might be overflowing with gold and spices. Thus in 1605 the company decided to investigate New Guinea and any nearby lands. One of the company's intrepid captains, Willem Jansz in his pinnace *Duyfken (little dove)*, was sent out from Bantam, company trading post on Java, to explore New Guinea. Although the Dutch already suspected, probably from native sources, that New Guinea might be an island, they did not know what this still-unknown region might offer.

After reaching the southern shore of New Guinea, Jansz guided his *Duyfken* along the mountainous coast, thick with green forest and vivid in the tropical sun. For weeks the *Duyfken* followed the shoreline eastward for almost nine hundred miles. To Jansz the wild land seemed savage and devoid of wealth.

At last, having satisfied himself that New Guinea held little that the company wanted, Jansz turned away from the coast and made his way to the south. He soon sighted land again.† To Jansz who had not followed the New Guinea coastline far enough east to discover the strait that separates the great island from what is now Australia, the barren country before him seemed only an unpromising arm of the New Guinea landmass. Scouts sent ashore to find water and to investigate the terrain reported that the land was a desert inhabited by "wild, cruel, black savages." At some point, it appears, a band of these aborigines murdered a Dutch landing party. Unable to obtain sufficient water or food and convinced that neither New Guinea nor this wild region to the south of it was worth further exploration, Jansz turned about. Reaching Bantam in June 1606, Jansz gave a negative account of

---

*It was, of course, the northern coast of Australia.
†This was the northernmost point of Australia, now called Cape York Peninsula.

New Guinea and its environs. He made it clear that in his opinion, Terra Australis did not lie in those waters.*

In Europe, meanwhile, a weary Spain once more declared bankruptcy, and the duke of Lerma sent out peace feelers to the United Provinces, indicating that Spain would now be satisfied with retaining for itself the southern half of the Netherlands, thus admitting the existence of the Dutch state. Spanish and Dutch diplomats began meeting. The Spaniards still could not bring themselves to grant Dutch independence, but in 1609, after two years of wrangling, the ministers cobbled together an armistice that suspended hostilities for a twelve-year period. In reality the truce was a tacit acknowledgment by Spain of the independence of the United Provinces of the Netherlands. Dutch and Spanish guns fell silent in Europe. The Treaty did not apply in the rest of the world, however, and the Dutch, free of the need to guard their shores in Europe, expanded their imperial ambitions throughout the globe. In 1610 the Dutch established settlements in Guiana and the Amazon region—in the heart of Spanish America. They set up a colony on the Guinea coast of Africa. Henry Hudson, under contract to the Dutch East India Company, explored the far north, looking for the Northwest Passage. Dutch fur traders were active in the Hudson Valley. The Dutch seemed to be everywhere.

But it was in the East and the Pacific that the Dutch tide ran strongest.† In 1607 the Dutch East India Company had made Bantam, in Java, its central headquarters. Soon new streams of Dutch merchant fleets were sailing between Amsterdam and Bantam and then on to newly built Dutch trading posts at Amboina in the Moluccas, the Malabar Coast of India, and even Formosa and Japan.

In 1611 one of the Dutch captains, Hendrik Brouwer, discovered a new route to Java, a sailing pattern that greatly cut the travel time from Europe. Previous to this the Dutch had followed the Portuguese method to the East: Rounding the Cape of Good

---

*It was two months *later* that the Spanish navigator Torres, after being separated from the quixotic Quirós, also sailed along the southern coast of New Guinea. Though Torres reported the open-water passage to the south of New Guinea, this information remained a closely guarded Spanish secret until the late eighteenth century.
†One of the provisions of the truce of 1609 was that Spain and Portugal pledged not to interfere with Dutch trade in the Pacific.

Hope, they sailed north along the East African coast until they picked up monsoon winds that blew them across the Indian Ocean and on to Java.

Like all his colleagues, Brouwer knew that in the higher latitudes south of the Cape of Good Hope, the winds blew unceasingly from west to east. On one of his voyages from Holland, he decided to try to take advantage of this fact. Instead of turning north at the Cape of Good Hope and waiting for the seasonal monsoon, he turned due east—and was driven before the prevailing westerlies for four thousand miles. He then turned the bow of his ship northward and picked up winds and currents that carried his vessel north to Java. His sailing time was half that of the usual route.

Typically, company officials at Bantam decided to test Brouwer's idea before adopting it for all their ships. They carried out an experiment with three vessels that left the United Provinces for Java at the same time. Two of the craft took the old Portuguese way, and one vessel sailed the new route. The ship that followed Brouwer's charts reached Bantam ten months before either of its companions. Thereupon the company ordered all its ships to sail the new course.

Kept secret, Brouwer's route added greatly to Dutch power by enabling company vessels to come and go in the East with a frequency that no other nation could match. In effect Brouwer's discovery more than doubled the number of armed Dutch merchants operating at any one time in the Indian Ocean and on the edge of the Pacific.

The new track, however, was not without its hazards. Under the goad of the prevailing westerlies, some Dutch ships overran their northward turning point and came dangerously close to a low-lying sandy region studded with perilous shoals and sandbars. The Dutch soon began to wonder about the nature of this patch of ocean. Was there land beyond these shallows?*

But any formal exploration of this unknown area was now deferred indefinitely as the Dutch East India Company embarked on a remarkable new program to extend Dutch influence over the entire Pacific. At the western edge of the ocean this objective was to be achieved by expansion of Dutch settlements through the island-dotted seas from Java to New Guinea. In this manner,

---

*There *was* land beyond, of course: the western coast of Australia.

it was thought, the Dutch would become so powerful in those waters that no other nation, including England, would be able to traffic in the Pacific with impunity. Eventually, even the long-established Spanish and Portuguese enclaves would wither and die. At the eastern side of the Pacific, the Dutch planned to take control of the Strait of Magellan, cutting off access to the Pacific to all shipping but their own. They also planned to drive the Spanish from the Pacific coast of South America, turning that region, too, into a Dutch fiefdom.

To justify this imperious new policy, the directors of the Dutch East India Company cited Article 34 of the company charter, issued by the government of the United Provinces, which declared that only ships of the Dutch East India Company or vessels it licensed were allowed to sail east of the Cape of Good Hope or west through the Strait of Magellan. All others would be subject to attack and confiscation. While the article was originally intended to apply only to Dutch interlopers, now, with the huge increase of Dutch power on the sea-lanes of the world, the lords of the Dutch East India Company decided to extend Article 34 to cover the shipping of all nations.

Since the Dutch already dominated the Cape of Good Hope approaches to the Pacific, most Spanish and Portuguese ships entered the Pacific through Magellan's waterway. Thus control of the strait was the key to extending Dutch hegemony over the entire Pacific. Some within the company hierarchy also proposed establishing land fortifications in the strait to guarantee Dutch ascendancy there. This idea was rejected as premature. In the early stages of its program the company would rely on Dutch warships.

Nor would the current truce between Spain and the United Provinces deter the company. The treaty between Spain and the Dutch republic applied only in Europe. In the far regions of the world hostilities were the rule whenever Dutch and Spanish forces met.

To initiate the company's new strategy, Admiral Joris Van Spilbergen sailed from Zeeland on August 8, 1614, with six men-of-war, bound across the Atlantic for the Strait of Magellan. Van Spilbergen's fleet, supremely confident, sailed through the strait in April 1615 despite the Antarctic winter closing in. Reaching the Pacific unopposed, Van Spilbergen sacked Spanish coastal towns and took prizes. Then, having forcefully demonstrated the ability of the United Provinces to project their power to the strait and the Pacific, Van Spilbergen struck out into the ocean, making for the Spice Islands and the company post at Amboina.*

The Van Spilbergen raid made it clear to the world that the Dutch East India Company possessed both the will and the power to turn the Pacific into a Dutch sea from Tierra del Fuego to the Philippines. Then an enterprising Dutch merchant turned this dream to nonsense because of something that Francis Drake had reported nearly forty years earlier.

*He eventually returned home to Zeeland in July 1617 with two ships, having circumnavigated the world.

20
AROUND THE HORN

Isaac Le Maire, a merchant of Amsterdam, was past fifty in 1614, but he still possessed a lively imagination that often led him to concoct schemes that were as impossible as they were ingenious. At one time Le Maire had served on the executive committee of the Dutch East India Company. He had withdrawn from the company in 1605, when it rejected some of his grandiose proposals. Among other things, he had been one of the first to suggest that the company establish forts at the Strait of Magellan in order to block Spanish traffic to and from the Pacific. He had also called for conquest of the Spanish Pacific coast.

Although these ideas later became strategic goals of the company, they had been beyond its power to carry out when Le Maire first put them forward. Le Maire had persisted. Control of the Pacific was the key to the future, he had argued. What the company needed was boldness—not prudence.

After his withdrawal from the company, Le Maire had poured a stream of criticism on its policy with regard to the Strait of Magellan and the Pacific, pointing out that although the company claimed a monopoly over the strait, it had never sent a single vessel to the East via that waterway. At one point the acerbic Le Maire even proposed that the company turn over its Strait of Magellan "rights" to him so that he might send his own armed ships to establish Dutch power in it and in the Pacific. The company had politely refused.

Although the company at last adopted Le Maire's aggressive strategy by dispatching Admiral Van Spilbergen to the Pacific via the Strait, Le Maire received no credit for the policy change. To the company he remained an unwelcome outsider.

Yet Le Maire yearned with all his merchant's heart to partake of the profits being earned in the East by other Dutch traders. He especially longed to send his own ships across the Pacific. Unfortunately he required a license from the Dutch East India Company to carry out such a project, and he was too proud to apply for the necessary permit even if the company would grant it. He fumed in frustration until his ingenious mind hit on a possible solution to his dilemma: Why not circumvent the company by finding a new way to enter the Pacific?

Although it was generally believed that the Strait of Magellan was the only waterway connecting the Atlantic and the Pacific and that a coast of the southern continent formed the south side of the strait, Le Maire had his doubts. He recalled that when Francis Drake had passed through the strait into the Pacific almost forty years earlier, vicious head winds had forced the English ships back into a broad sea south of Tierra del Fuego. Drake, of course, had overcome the contrary winds, but his experience had convinced him that Tierra del Fuego was a series of islands, not part of the southern continent. The chronicler of Drake's voyage had said as much: "The uttermost Cape or headland of all these islands stands near in 56 degrees, [beyond which] there is no main nor island to be seen to the southwards, but that the Atlantic Ocean and the South Sea [Pacific] meet in a most large and free scope."

To Le Maire's knowledge no mariner had ever followed up Drake's experience by trying to sail around Tierra del Fuego into the Pacific. Yet such a course might afford an easier passage than that of Magellan's tortuous strait. Moreover, independent traders, such as Le Maire himself, had every right to utilize this route, if it existed, since the Dutch East India Company held no title to it.

Le Maire took his idea to an experienced Dutch navigator, Willem Schouten, forty-seven, who had spent many years in the service of the company and had accumulated a great store of knowledge about the Pacific. Schouten agreed that Le Maire might have hit upon a clever notion. He undertook to pilot an expedition to test the theory.

Schouten was familiar with Quirós's Pacific voyage of 1605–6 and knew of the Portuguese navigator's claim to have touched upon Terra Australis. He suggested to Le Maire that in addition to searching for a new passage to the Pacific, the expedition should try to find the southern continent.

With Schouten now a partner in the enterprise, Le Maire and his thirty-year-old son, Jakob, who would actually sail with the venture as his father's representative, prepared their voyage.* In early June 1615, while Admiral Van Spilbergen was pounding the Spanish Pacific, the Le Maire expedition sailed. It consisted of two vessels: the 220-ton *Eendracht,* carrying a crew of sixty-five and armed with nineteen cannon and the 110-ton *Hoorn* with twenty-two crewmen and eight cannon. There were sufficient rations to provide each of the eighty-seven men aboard the two vessels with a half pint of beer per day and four pounds of ship biscuit. In addition, each man got a half pound of butter a week. Every sailor also received "five cheeses," which were expected to last the whole voyage. The younger Le Maire was in overall command of the ships. Schouten served as master of the *Eendracht,* and his brother, Jan, was captain of the *Hoorn.*

As the first step in their careful plan to find a new way into the Pacific, Le Maire and Schouten took their ships some twenty-five hundred miles southward to Senegal on the west coast of Africa. There they exchanged beads and knives for twenty-five thousand lemons, which they dried and stored aboard.†

From the African coast the *Eendracht* and *Hoorn* set out on a southwest course to cross the Atlantic Ocean. By October 1615 the ships were in mid-ocean. Now for the first time the crewmen

*Apparently the elder Le Maire did obtain some kind of permission from the Dutch government to trade in the Pacific. Later events make it clear, however, that he did not obtain a company license for the Strait of Magellan. It may be that by these maneuvers Le Maire was seeking a legal cloak for his daring enterprise.
†As a result of this purchase the men of the *Eendracht* and the *Hoorn* did not suffer much from scurvy—despite their diet of ship biscuit, beer, and fat—during the long voyage that lay ahead. No one knew exactly why. Dutch and English sea captains had often noticed that when men had citrus fruit available on long voyages, the worst ravages of scurvy could be avoided. Although it was many years before casks of lime juice became standard aboard sailing vessels, enlightened captains had always tried to obtain fresh fruit, and vegetables for their men whenever possible. The English privateer Hawkins had also taken aboard a load of African lemons on his voyage to the Pacific some twenty years before Schouten and Le Maire.

were told the true destination of the ships. Until this moment they had been kept in the dark. According to later accounts of the voyage, the crew rejoiced to find they were headed for the Pacific. Most of the men expected that the ships would obtain a rich cargo in the Spice Isles and that each crew member would profit proportionately.

After crossing the Atlantic, the two ships proceeded to Port Desire in Patagonia, approximately five hundred miles north of the forbidden Strait of Magellan. There, in December 1615, the ships were careened for cleaning. There, too, the expedition suffered a serious setback when the little *Hoorn* caught fire and was burned beyond repair. Luckily her fittings, including the guns and anchors, were salvaged and brought aboard the *Eendracht*, as was her crew. Undaunted by their loss, the Dutch weighed anchor again on January 13, 1616.

The *Eendracht* now pressed on alone, passing the Strait of Magellan on January 24, 1616. She continued southward, along the eastern coast of Tierra del Fuego, seeking open ocean. The Dutch sighted sandy beaches, clouds of sea birds, and "whales by the thousands." But they saw no passage through the cold and forbidding land that lay to their starboard. Had Drake been wrong after all? Was it possible that Tierra del Fuego was *not* an island or an archipelago? The *Eendracht* continued southward. Gradually, as the ship plunged through gray seas, an extensive land appeared off the port side as well.

Now, with land on both sides of the ship, Schouten and Le Maire wondered if they had blundered, if the southern continent indeed lay ahead, blocking passage to the Pacific. The *Eendracht* went on.

Eventually, to the joy of the Dutch, a heavy swell started running at them and the sea turned a dark blue. Both these were signs of deep ocean ahead and evidence that the land to larboard was not part of the southern continent after all but probably a very large island. Schouten and Le Maire had already given it the name Staten Land. The Dutch sailed on, grim land on both sides.*

Suddenly, around sunset of January 29, 1616, the land to the west, to starboard, ended in cliffs, and the rolling sea spread out ahead. The Dutch mariners exulted, certain now that they had

---

*They were in the passage now called Le Maire Strait.

reached the southernmost limit of the South American continent. The *Eendracht* turned westward, rounding a rocky headland which the Dutch named Cape Hoorn (the name of their lost ship as well as a town in Holland).

As Cape Hoorn fell behind, the *Eendracht* fought westward against heavy seas that came at her head-on. In these open seas, which Drake's chronicler had accurately described four decades earlier, the Dutch seamen spotted great soaring seabirds, "larger than swans, with wings stretching a fathom across [that] flew screaming around the ship." They were albatrosses.

Having turned Cape Hoorn, Schouten and Le Maire entered the Pacific, jubilant that they had found a new route to the great ocean, "a way," as they later put it, "that had until then been unknown to man." The *Eendracht* made for the Pacific coast of South America, fighting her way north through weather that had become stormy and bitterly cold. At the beginning of March she reached the island cluster of Juan Fernández. Landing parties went ashore for water. The men also caught fish to replenish their supplies.*

On March 3, 1616, after only two days at Juan Fernández, the *Eendracht* resumed her journey, heading northwest across the empty ocean. Less than a week after leaving Juan Fernández, Schouten's brother, Jan, died. For another month the *Eendracht* sailed to the north and west. No land appeared on the heaving face of the Pacific until April 10, 1616, when the Dutch sighted an island inhabited not by human beings, but "by three dogs."†

Soon the *Eendracht* found herself among the numerous islands in the Tuamotu group. As the ship neared one atoll, tattooed warriors paddled out in their canoes to view the strangers. Though wary of the newcomers, the islanders were also curious. But there was trouble when the Dutch sent a party ashore for water. A band of natives tried to seize the crewmen's muskets. The Dutch fired, killing several of their attackers and wounding others. The incident, reminiscent of so many other bloody first

---

*They also found the island overrun with wild pigs and goats originally brought there in 1563 by the island's discoverer, the Spanish pilot who had named the islands after himself and had tried and failed to establish a colony there. The domestic animals had been abandoned and had reverted to a wild state. Apparently they had flourished.

†The island was probably one of the Tuamotu group—Puka Puka—first seen by Magellan and often sighted by subsequent voyagers. The dogs had probably been abandoned by fishermen from nearby islands.

meetings between Europeans and the local peoples in these waters, spurred the Dutch to move on.

For the next month or so, the *Eendracht* picked her way through the Tuamotus until, by May 1616, she was once more on an empty ocean, sailing due west. Suddenly, to the great surprise of the Dutch who had not expected to come upon such a vessel on the open sea, lookouts sighted a sail-rigged double canoe. Aboard this large craft were people whom the Dutch later described as "red folk who smeared themselves with oil." The Dutch fired a shot across the bows of the canoe as a signal to halt. Not understanding the meaning of the cannon shot, the people in the canoe panicked and tried to flee. The Dutch sent a ship's boat to chase down the canoe and take her in tow.

In a classic example of miscommunication leading to unintended bloodshed, the frightened natives fought against the Dutch attempt to take control of their craft, and the nervous Dutch fired upon the islanders, killing some of them. In the end the Dutch crew gave up trying to take the big canoe. However, they did capture two long-haired men from the canoe. These they brought aboard the *Eendracht.* The warriors, clearly terrified, knelt on deck before their Dutch captors and kissed their hands and feet. The Dutch eventually convinced the pair that they meant them no harm. The two, bearing gifts of beads and knives, were returned to their canoe, which had remained in the vicinity.

On the following day, the *Eendracht,* now sailing in company with the big canoe, anchored at the home island of these people.* But there was more gunfire when a swarm of native craft surrounded the *Eendracht*'s boat and again when a chief led an attack on the ship. The *Eendracht* hauled anchor and moved to a nearby atoll, Schouten and Le Maire soon decided to resume the voyage.

After following a more northerly course for another few days, the *Eendracht* anchored again off a high volcanic island which, with a nearby island, appeared to be a pleasant site. A village of circular huts stood on the beach opposite the *Eendracht*'s anchorage. When the Dutch went ashore to obtain water from a river that flowed nearby, they found that despite a brief show of hostility, the villagers were friendly.†

*Probably the island was Tafahi in the Tonga group.
†The islands were Futuna and Alofi, today two of the Hoorn group, a thousand miles south of the equator, halfway between Samoa and Fiji.

The Dutch spent two weeks at this happy anchorage. Nightly the Europeans and islanders entertained each other with songs and dances. One evening, to astonish the natives, Le Maire even had the ship's gun fired. The Dutch also played on their drums and trumpets for the amusement of all. Meanwhile, the villagers feasted their visitors on roast pork and fruits, as well as coconuts harvested fresh from the numerous palm trees. The Dutch, however, refused the native liquor, *kava*.

Inevitably the time came for the Dutch to plan the next stage of the voyage. Jakob Le Maire, sure that the *Eendracht* now lay in the vicinity of the Solomon Islands and thus, according to the widespread supposition of the day, near the western reaches of the southern continent, suggested that the ship continue on westward to those seas where the Portuguese navigator Quirós had so confidently placed Terra Australis. But Schouten, by far the expedition's most experienced seaman, expressed concern about the seaworthiness of their vessel. Rather than search westward for the continent in what were essentially unknown waters, he said, the *Eendracht* should head to the northwest and coast the northern shore of New Guinea to the Moluccas. There they could safely repair their vessel and conduct their business with the Dutch East India Company. The younger Le Maire bowed to Schouten's judgment. On June 1, 1616, the *Eendracht* set off for the northwest.

On June 25 the ship arrived off a lush coast that the Dutch mariners took to be New Guinea. Suddenly swarms of black-skinned warriors paddled out in canoes and began hurling stones at the ship with primitive slings. The Dutch, describing their attackers as "coal black with rings in their noses," fired a few shots in their direction, and the stone-throwing blacks fled. But they returned to the assault on the next day. This time the Dutch fired in earnest, and a number of warriors were killed.

Continuing along this coast for the next few days, the expedition was able to replenish its water supply despite continuing hostility from the inhabitants.* Throughout July the *Eendracht* crept westward, at last arriving off the northern coast of the *real* New Guinea. The Dutch, following the shoreline to the west,

---

*The Dutch were off not New Guinea but the island that was later named New Ireland. The *Eendracht* was still some five hundred miles east and north of New Guinea. Nor were all the islanders hostile to the Dutch. A few showed themselves friendly and ready to trade.

passed numerous small islands and fought through a series of gales and calms.

Now, as the expedition began to run seriously short of supplies, the Dutch often landed and tried to trade with the populace: nails, knives, and beads for bananas and coconuts. Sometimes the landing parties were attacked. On other occasions they managed to establish friendly relations. August passed. The weather was often stormy. The *Eendracht* went on. At one point the Dutch sighted a large island off the New Guinea coast, which they named after Schouten's dead brother.

One day, to their joy, the men of the *Eendracht* encountered people who spoke the Malayan tongue, which one of the Dutch crewmen spoke fluently. From this point on the ship was among "civilized folk" who understood the principles of trade and reported the presence of many Dutch vessels in these seas. The men of the *Eendracht* knew now that, barring some last-minute disaster, they would soon be safe among their countrymen.

On September 17, 1616, the *Eendracht* dropped her hook at Ternate, which was now under Dutch control. The Dutch residents of Ternate welcomed the *Eendracht* warmly. When fifteen members of her crew asked to be discharged here so that they could join the forces of the Dutch East India Company, Schouten and Le Maire readily agreed. For a week the *Eendracht* lay at Ternate, resupplying and taking on a cargo of spices. She then set off toward Java, where the company headquarters was located.

On October 28, 1616, the *Eendracht* arrived at the company's port town of Jacatra in Java, where Schouten and Le Maire were received with unexpected hostility by company officials. They were then haled before a high-ranking company official, the soon-to-be-famous Jan Pieterszoon Coen, to explain "irregularities" in their voyage. Coen treated Schouten and Le Maire as if they had committed a criminal act. He refused to believe that the unlicensed *Eendracht* had not used the Strait of Magellan to reach the Pacific. He then confiscated the ship and her cargo.*

Since Admiral Van Spilbergen was then in Java, preparing to depart for home after his armed raid through the Strait of Magellan and on the Spanish Pacific coast, Coen decided to send Le Maire and Schouten home with him as virtual prisoners. Six-

*Coen, who was not yet thirty years old, held the post of president in the Dutch East India Company hierarchy. In a relatively brief time he reached the pinnacle as governor-general of the company and became one of its most effective leaders.

teen of the *Eendracht*'s crew were also sent home in this manner, the other surviving crewmen having previously volunteered for company service in the East. On the homeward journey the younger Le Maire died. He was only thirty-one years old.

When Van Spilbergen reached Amsterdam after his round-the-world voyage, Schouten told the full story of the *Eendracht*'s adventures. Old Isaac Le Maire resolved that he would have justice. He sued the Dutch East India Company. After two years of legal maneuvering, he won his case, thanks largely to the testimony of Willem Schouten. The elder Le Maire recovered both his ship and her cargo. The case also established the existence of the passage around Cape Hoorn, a fitting tribute in Le Maire's mind to the memory of his dead son.

Ironically, the Spanish provided the final proof of Le Maire and Schouten's claims about Cape Hoorn. Within a few years of the *Eendracht*'s initial voyage, a Spanish expedition passed from the Atlantic to the Pacific around Cape Hoorn and then returned from the west to the east through the Strait of Magellan, proving beyond doubt that Tierra del Fuego is an island.

Schouten and Le Maire's discovery of Cape Hoorn, and the open waters to its south, put an end to the Dutch plan to seal off the Pacific at the Strait of Magellan. With the Cape Hoorn route providing a wide path to the Pacific, no Dutch fleet, no matter how large or well armed, could ever hope to keep Spanish men-of-war (or any others for that matter) from entering the ocean. The Spanish sea route to the Pacific could not be cut.

The gentlemen of the Dutch East India Company could not own the ocean. They could still dominate it, however. They knew they could take a large step toward that end by discovering the rich southern continent. This now became one of the company's chief goals.

21

THE SHORES OF ENIGMA

In 1616, while Schouten and Le Maire's *Eendracht* was crossing the Pacific after opening a new route to the great ocean, another vessel, also called *Eendracht*, was completing a very different voyage. This second *Eendracht*, commanded by an experienced master named Dirk Hartog, had been following the new Dutch route to the East, letting the roaring forties drive her across the Indian Ocean for four thousand miles and then turning due north for Java.

Captain Hartog had sailed this course several times in the past with no difficulty. On this occasion, however, the *Eendracht* caught too much wind and drove two hundred miles past her usual turning point before he managed to get free of the roaring forties. Once properly headed north, however, the *Eendracht* plowed on sedately over deep open water, and Captain Hartog anticipated no further problems despite his ship's having run farther east than usual. Then, as his *Eendracht* made her way north under sunny skies, Hartog sighted land off his starboard beam where his charts indicated only open water and, perhaps, some of the half-hidden shoals previously reported in these waters.

Hartog decided to creep in closer to the low-lying land to starboard and saw that he had come upon a small island, useful perhaps as a way station on the long voyage to Java. He landed on the island, set up a pewter dish to mark his discovery, and christened the place after himself: Dirk Hartog's Island. Then Hartog made an astonishing find: Farther to the east of his isle he could make out a coastline stretching north and south as far as the eye could see. Could this be the coast of the much-sought-after southern continent? Hartog did not dare find out, fearing that if he ventured closer to this unknown land, he might be wrecked in the surging surf. He contented himself with noting the position of his discoveries and bestowing the name of his ship on the land beyond. He called it Eendrachtsland.

After sailing on to Bantam, Java, Hartog reported his find to officials, who were much intrigued. Was Hartog's Eendrachtsland part of that mysterious region that lay south of New Guinea and that company mapmakers had now named New Holland? If so, Hartog's discovery only added more mystery to the enigma that was New Holland. Questions begged for answers. Were New Guinea and New Holland one landmass? How far to the south did New Holland extend? Was Captain Hartog's Eendracht's Land the western coast of New Holland or a separate land?

Such questions now began to fascinate many, and there was soon a widespread sentiment that the company should underwrite a thorough exploration of New Holland's unknown shores. But just at this moment a political crisis claimed virtually all the company's attention. The trouble centered on the Dutch company's relations with its English counterpart.

Since its inception the English East India Company, like the Dutch, had followed a policy of sending armed merchant ships to the East and establishing fortified trading posts. Much fewer in number than the Dutch, the English had achieved only limited success in the Indies. Nevertheless, they were a factor in Eastern waters.*

The Dutch at first accepted the participation of their English coreligionists in the Eastern trade. Even when the English had signed a separate peace with Spain in 1604, the Dutch choked back a natural resentment. For their part, the English—despite the official Anglo-Spanish peace—often aided Dutch efforts to drive the Spanish and Portuguese from their enclaves.

---

*Unlike the Dutch, the English did not send their ships eastward on a regular, yearly basis, but only when sufficient cargo, crew, vessels, and investors had been assembled. According to the records, a total of eight English trading fleets sailed east between 1600 and 1611. Still, the English company was a growing presence.

As time passed, however, the Dutch grew increasingly indignant over what they saw as English inroads into their commercial empire. The ill feeling first surfaced around 1611, when the Dutch began to grumble that the English did not provide their fair share of naval forces against the Portuguese and Spanish but left the hardest fighting to the Dutch. The English countered with complaints that the Dutch restricted their freedom to trade.

Hotheads on both sides started issuing threats. To cool the tensions, representatives of the two trading companies met in London in 1613 and again in 1615. Though the meetings accomplished little of substance, they quieted matters for a while.

Then, in 1616—the year of Schouten and Le Maire's voyage and Hartog's intriguing sight of Eendrachtsland—the friction between the Dutch and the English flamed anew. There were new threats of violence from traders on both sides.

It was in this atmosphere of crisis that the Dutch East India Company decided to forgo temporarily any voyages to solve the puzzle of New Holland. And at this critical juncture the company turned to Jan Pieterszoon Coen for leadership. Though only thirty years old in 1617, Coen had a well-deserved reputation for ruthlessness, vision, and administrative genius.

Born at Hoorn in 1587, Coen came from a merchant family. At the age of twenty he had gone to the Indies, where he initially served as a company agent. He quickly rose to become the company's "president" at Bantam, and it was he who had sent Le Maire and Schouten home in disgrace.*

When Coen became governor-general of the Dutch East India Company in October 1617, during the "English crisis," he saw clearly that a new framework was required to govern relations between Dutch and English merchants in the East. Thus he arranged still another peace conference. Held in London in 1618, the meeting resulted in a "treaty of defense" that called for Dutch and English traders to maintain a joint fleet. Though many on both sides were skeptical, Coen hailed the treaty and had its terms proclaimed throughout the company's empire. Apparently he rea-

---

*Coen, however, a realist above all, soon came to acknowledge the reality of Schouten and Le Maire's passage of Cape Hoorn. More important, he was among the first to recognize that the existence of an open waterway to the south of Tierra del Fuego would doom any Dutch attempts to block off the eastern entrance to the Pacific. Schouten and Le Maire's cape eventually lost its Dutch spelling and became "Cape Horn," and ships began to go "around the Horn."

soned that if Dutch and English merchants were forced to work together to create a combined naval force, the ill will of recent years would dissolve in a new spirit of cooperation. For the next few years Coen employed all the power of his personality to implement the treaty of 1618. And relations between English and Dutch traders did seem to improve, despite some minor incidents.

During this period the young governor-general also set out to restructure the company itself. Having grown by haphazard response to opportunities, the company had developed into a sprawling jumble both administratively and militarily. Despite its formidable appearance, it was, in fact, a flimsy edifice, vulnerable to a determined enemy. To rectify this, Coen brought various administrative components of the company under central control. More important, he set out to impose direct company rule on strategic territories heretofore governed by native princes.

As a first step he led Dutch forces in 1619 against the important town of Jacatra on the western end of Java. Ruthlessly he destroyed the city and drove out its indigenous rulers. He then transferred the company headquarters there and gave it the name Batavia.* Coen made Batavia the new central point of the Dutch East, ordering that all company commerce be cleared through it.

With Batavia established, Coen continued his cold-blooded program to extend Dutch political control to additional islands in the Indies. He authorized the use of force whenever local resistance was encountered. At the nutmeg-growing island of Great Banda (Bandalontan), for example, he had twenty-five hundred inhabitants massacred and eight hundred more carried as prisoners to Batavia until the people acceded to company suzerainty. Coen also dictated the type and amount of spices to be cultivated on many of the islands that now came under company control. This was done to ensure that supplies would remain short, and demand high, in Europe.

Coen's harsh measures quickly paid off for the company. Profits soared. Batavia flourished. Coen was praised by all. But his efforts had worn him out. In 1622, after almost five years of toil, he resigned his post and returned to Holland.

With Coen's strong hand off the tiller, the "English problem" soon revived. Again the Dutch complained about the "reluctance" of the English to spill their blood in what the Dutch

*Today it is Djakarta, capital of Indonesia.

considered the common cause. In 1622 the aggressive Dutch had
sent a fleet to seize Macao, the Portuguese enclave on the mainland of China. Instead of the expected victory, they had been
repulsed with many casualties. Stung, the Dutch blamed the English for failing to provide the naval forces called for under their
treaty of defense. The English rejected the Dutch accusations. Ill
feeling mounted on both sides.

In 1623, a year after the Macao incident, the acrimony
turned deadly at Amboina, where the English kept a trading post
alongside the Dutch fortress that commanded the island. The
suspicious Dutch charged that their English colleagues were con-
spiring to seize the fortress and to throw them off the island. The
English protested their innocence. Nevertheless, the island's
Dutch governor, Herman Van Speult, had ten Englishmen and
nine Japanese residents of Amboina seized and horribly tortured
until they sobbed out confessions. All nineteen were then executed. This bloody event, known as the Amboina Massacre, ignited great fury among the English both in the Indies and in
London. But it also showed the nabobs of the English company
that they could neither protect their agents in the East nor expect the Dutch authorities to do so. For many English traders
the message of Amboina seemed to be: "Get out of the game,
or be bullied into getting out." The English began withdrawing
from competition with the Dutch in the East Indies. From now
on the English East India Company would concentrate on the
less lucrative Indian trade. Though the English vowed future vengeance for the Amboina Massacre, the Dutch regarded the threat
as no more than facesaving rhetoric. With the withdrawal of the
English, however, the company could turn its acquisitive eyes to
the enigma of New Holland.

Since Hartog's sighting of Eendrachtsland in 1616 and
throughout the years of the "English crisis," company officials
had continued to receive tantalizing accounts of land south of
New Guinea. In 1618, for example, the Dutch ship *Zeewulf* had reported finding a low-lying coast north of Eendrachtsland, where
the charts had previously shown only open ocean. Although no
one aboard the *Zeewulf* could be sure whether he had seen continuous land or a series of islands, the sighting was further indication
of an extensive New Holland. Other ships had also arrived at the
company's headquarters at Batavia with similar reports.

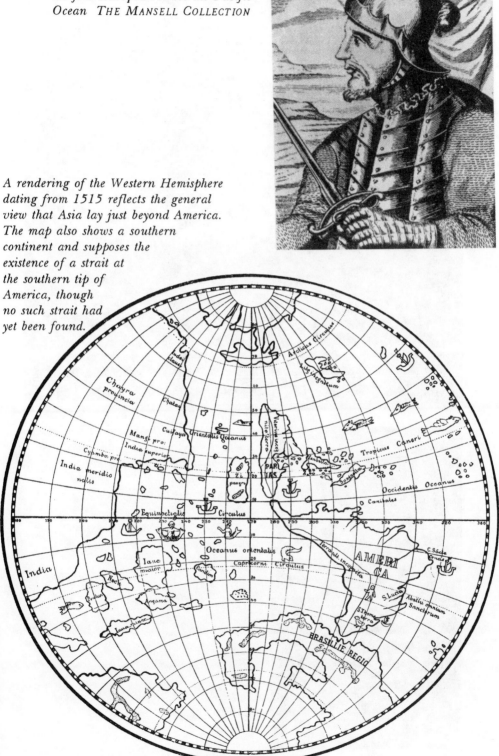

Vasco Nuñez de Balboa (1475-1519), the first European to see the Pacific Ocean THE MANSELL COLLECTION

A rendering of the Western Hemisphere dating from 1515 reflects the general view that Asia lay just beyond America. The map also shows a southern continent and supposes the existence of a strait at the southern tip of America, though no such strait had yet been found.

Ferdinand Magellan, portrayed by an unknown artist. This portrait, like others of Magellan, was not done from life but is based on descriptions of the Portuguese navigator. MARITIME MUSEUM, SEVILLE

Charles V, Holy Roman Emperor and King of Spain ART MUSEUM, MUNICH

King Francis I of France National Library, Paris

In 1545 Spaniards discovered a "mountain of silver" in what is now Bolivia. Even this enormously rich mine, depicted here in a drawing done at that time, could not produce the wealth to satisfy Spain's need, and thus many Spaniards turned to the Pacific in search of new riches. Hispanic Society of America

Spanish cruelty in the exploitation of native peoples in the New World was legendary, engendering anti-Spanish propaganda like these drawings. Spanish mariners often carried their practice of brutal treatment of natives to the Pacific peoples they encountered. NATIONAL LIBRARY, PARIS

A Spanish convoy in a
sixteenth-century engraving
NATIONAL LIBRARY, PARIS

By the late 1500s mapmakers
were depicting the undiscovered
southern continent as a gigantic
land mass stretching around the
globe and filling the South
Pacific. BRITISH MUSEUM,
LONDON

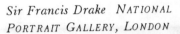
Sir Francis Drake NATIONAL
PORTRAIT GALLERY, LONDON

*Dr. John Dee, astrologer to
England's Queen Elizabeth, in 1572
urged the queen to send an expedition
to the Pacific to claim the southern
continent for England.* ASHMOLEAN
MUSEUM, OXFORD, ENGLAND

Drake's ship, the Golden Hind
*(foreground), is shown in this
sixteenth-century engraving
capturing the Spanish treasure
ship* Cacafuego *off Peru.*
BRITISH LIBRARY, LONDON

In the first half of the seventeenth century the Dutch East India Company, under such ruthless leaders as Jan Pieterszoon Coen, became the dominant force in the western Pacific, driving off the Spanish and Portuguese and establishing Dutch sovereignty over much of the East Indies. RIJKSMUSEUM, AMSTERDAM

Philip II, King of Spain, struggled against Dutch rebels, English privateers, and French heretics. His stubborn policies sapped Spain's strength and led to the rise of the Dutch republic as a maritime power. THE PRADO, MADRID

Dutch mariner Jakob Le Maire was the first to enter the Pacific by going "around the horn" instead of passing through the Strait of Magellan. RIJKSMUSEUM, AMSTERDAM

*To control East Indian trade the Dutch East India Company in 1619
built a fortified headquarters at the western end of the island of Java and
named it Batavia. Today it is Djakarta, the capital of Indonesia.*
RIJKSMUSEUM, AMSTERDAM

*Abel Janszoon Tasman, shown here with his wife and daughter, made two
voyages in the 1640s aimed at claiming the Pacific continent for the
Dutch republic.* NATIONAL LIBRARY OF AUSTRALIA, CANBERRA

Pirate and scholar, William Dampier voyaged widely in the Pacific in the late seventeenth and early eighteenth centuries. His colorful writings did much to revive European interest in the Pacific after it had begun to wane. NATIONAL PORTRAIT GALLERY, LONDON

In 1741, during the War of Jenkins's Ear, Commodore George Anson led a squadron of British warships into the Pacific to attack Spanish shipping. Anson's voyage laid bare many weaknesses of the fleet but it also ignited British resolve to beat its rival, France, to the Pacific continent. NATIONAL PORTRAIT GALLERY, LONDON

Scottish scholar Alexander Dalrymple argued forcefully during the 1760s that the Pacific continent, or the South Land as it was coming to be known, not only existed but that its discovery would be the key to future British greatness. NATIONAL MARITIME MUSEUM, GREENWICH, ENGLAND

As depicted in this eighteenth-century sketch, in June 1767 on a voyage designed to locate the South Land, Captain Samuel Wallis and his crew became the first Europeans to touch on Tahiti. BRITISH MUSEUM, LONDON

Louis Antoine de Bougainville was the most successful of the French Pacific navigators and the first Frenchman to circumnavigate the globe. NATIONAL MUSEUM, PARIS

Captain James Cook NATIONAL MARITIME MUSEUM, GREENWICH, ENGLAND

One of the most intriguing sightings had come from a highly regarded Dutch commander, Frederick Houtman, who in July 1619 happened upon a coast far to the *south* of Eendrachtsland. Although high seas and surf kept Houtman from risking a landing, he spent many days charting and sounding this shoreline as he made his way north. This proved to be dangerous work, for at one point he just managed to escape an area of dangerous shoals.* Upon completion of his run to Batavia, Houtman voiced his conviction that the land he had sighted was a continuation of New Holland's western coast. If so, then New Holland was continental in scope.

Three years later, in 1622, the ship *Leeuwin* sighted a cape even farther south of the region seen by Houtman. This headland appeared to mark the southern limit of New Holland's western shore.†

By the early 1620s the company charts of New Holland depicted a long, curving western shore and a northern seaboard, like the top and left-hand side of a rectangle. Was there a southern side to that rectangle? An eastern side? Or was New Holland perhaps a huge outcropping of the immense Pacific continent said to stretch from Tierra del Fuego to New Guinea? And what might lie within the vague lines drawn on the maps?

Such questions had nagged company officials even during the years of the English crisis. Governor-General Coen had authorized preliminary planning for an exploration to be undertaken when affairs permitted. But Coen had gone home, and the program languished until another high-ranking company official decided, late in 1622, to prepare his own mission to New Holland. He was Governor Van Speult, of Amboina, who later authorized the "massacre" on that island. Van Speult was particularly interested in learning if New Guinea and New Holland were connected. He also wanted to investigate any commercial possibilities in that area.

In January 1623, a month before the Amboina atrocity, Van Speult sent forth two ships, the *Arnhem* and the *Pera*, under the command of Jan Carstensz, a veteran company pilot. Carstensz first coasted the southern shore of New Guinea. Although the mountainous, jungle-clad land appeared inviting, he was unable

---

*These shallows were later named after Houtman.
†It is today called Cape Leeuwin, and it indeed stands at the southwest corner of Australia.

to learn much about the country because of the hostility of the natives. These, described as "naked savages" and "cannibals with bones in their noses," not only scorned any palaver but also attacked the Dutch fiercely.

After creeping along the south coast of New Guinea for weeks, Carstensz came upon shallow, reef-strewn waters ahead. To Carstensz this maze of coral seemed a perilous dead end. To escape, he came about and threaded his way back into deeper, safer water. By reversing his course in this manner, Carstensz, like Jansz before him, failed to discover the waterway separating New Guinea from the land to the south and leading to the ocean farther east. Instead he concluded that he was in the midst of a single landmass and that the water from which he had just retreated was a shallow bay.*

Tacking to investigate the land to the south and sailing past what is now the Cape York Peninsula of Australia, Carstensz entered the Gulf of Carpentaria. The land seemed flat, barren, and "worthless," inhabited by people whom Carstensz described as "the poorest creatures that I have ever seen." The Dutch kidnapped some of these aborigines, with the hope that they could be taught to speak Malay, permitting Carstensz to learn more of the country. The natives naturally resisted the Dutch attempts to take them prisoner, and soon Carstensz was noting in his log that "the blacks receive us as enemies everywhere."

It was now late April 1623. Carstensz, convinced of the uselessness of the country he had seen, decided to return to Amboina. Before he could issue the necessary orders, however, his consort, the *Arnhem*, deserted. Furious, Carstensz noted the defection in his log, and then made for Amboina, where he reported his discouraging news.†

After the bleak picture painted by Carstensz, there was no immediate follow-up on the part of company officials. Yet company captains continued to report intriguing glimpses of New Holland which seemed to belie Carstensz. In 1627, for example, the merchant vessel *Gulde Zeepaert* ("golden sea horse") was

---

*Carstensz named this waterway Shallow Bay. He had no knowledge of Torres's passage through these same waters two decades earlier.
†In the meantime, the *Arnhem*, too, had returned safely. According to her captain, she had been blown across the Gulf of Carpentaria and had discovered the land on its western side, which the ship's master named Arnhem Land. This territory, too, seemed barren and worthless. There is no indication that the *Arnhem*'s captain was punished for deserting Carstensz.

driven for more than a thousand miles along the southern coast of New Holland, past the looming cliffs of what is now called the Great Australian Bight. After naming the land Nuytsland in honor of an important passenger aboard his vessel, the *Gulde Zeepaert*'s master, Frans Thyssen, at last made his way to Batavia, where his report added a third side to the New Holland map.

In 1628 another ship, the *Vyanen*, driven ashore on the *northwest* shoulder of New Holland, sighted greenery inland from the infertile coast. Thus there were constant hints that New Holland's interior might prove richer than its arid shoreline. Yet the basic mystery remained, and it was clear that the enigma of New Holland could be resolved only through systematic exploration. For many in the company such an enterprise seemed inevitable, a natural consequence of the Dutch political, military, and cultural tide now reaching flood stage.

In Europe, as the 1630s began, the Dutch state, despite war and turmoil, was entering a golden age. Dutch national energy was surging in almost every field, from banking to science to the arts.

In 1621 the twelve-year truce between the United Provinces and Spain had expired. Even though Spain had already become entangled in the terrible Thirty Years' War that broke out in Germany in 1618 and that eventually involved most of Europe, it still refused to acknowledge the fact of Dutch independence. Thus the struggle between Spain and its Dutch "rebels" was joined once more. By 1630 the seaborne Dutch had won victory after victory. In 1623, for example, a Dutch war fleet rounded Cape Horn to assault the Spaniards in Chile and Peru.* In 1623 and 1624 Dutch ships attacked Spanish installations in Puerto Rico and on the west coast of Africa. They seized the Brazilian port of Bahia and then lost it again. In 1628 a Dutch squadron intercepted Spain's yearly silver fleet from America.

Nor had the Dutch success in these years been limited to

---

*This was the famed Nassau Fleet. The forebears of Holland's prince of Orange had come from the German duchy of Nassau, and Dutch ships and fleets were often named to honor that fact. Curiously, during the fleet's cruise, lookouts in one of the Dutch warships, the *Orange*, reported sighting the snow-covered mountains of a great continent in latitude fifty degrees south. At a later date the *Orange* reported a second sighting in forty-one degrees. Such sightings by experienced mariners seemed to many at the time clear evidence that the southern continent stretched for thousands of miles across the South Pacific.

war. The Dutch trading empire, already paramount in the East, began to make inroads in the western half of the world as well. In 1621 the Dutch founded a *West* India Company to exploit the Atlantic, the Caribbean, and Africa, and it established Caribbean colonies and the settlement of New Amsterdam in North America.

Even as the 1630s unrolled, the astonishing Dutch skein of success continued, apparently unstoppable. In 1630 the Dutch began the conquest of northeastern Brazil. In 1634 they captured the islands of St. Eustatius and St. Maarten, in the Caribbean, as well as Curaçao and Surinam. In 1638 Dutch forces took the Portuguese colony of Elmina on the Guinea coast of Africa. The conquest of Ceylon began.

In 1639 a Dutch squadron of eleven ships defeated a vastly superior Spanish fleet off Gravelines and then, before the year was out, defeated another Spanish fleet off the Downs, taking thirteen galleons in the process. A year later the Dutch routed a Portuguese fleet off northeastern Brazil and then, on the other side of the world, captured Malacca.

The little Dutch Republic was a global power, mistress of the seas. Every other European nation was eclipsed by its brilliance. Spain, perpetually at war in France and Germany, faced new revolts in Portugal and in the province of Catalonia. England was on the verge of civil war between monarch and Parliament. The northern states of Europe were aflame with the Thirty Years' War. France, governed by an aging Cardinal Richelieu, was still suffering from the religious chaos of the previous century.

It was the Dutch golden age. It was the age of Van Dyck, of Rembrandt, of Spinoza. It was an age of religious toleration and free inquiry. Amsterdam was the center of the world, enjoying a prosperity not dreamed of just two generations earlier. The Dutch trading empire stretched from New Amsterdam to Pernambuco in Brazil to Elmina in Africa and around the Cape to the Indies, where the Dutch East India Company fed on the energy of the mother country.

Standing at the apex of its national existence, the United Provinces, now often called Holland after its dominant province, lacked but one addition to guarantee its greatness for decades to come: the long-sought Pacific continent. With ownership of this rich prize—so often glimpsed and, apparently, so tantalizingly near—Holland would become unassailable in the world.

With Europe in disarray, and with the Dutch East India Company at its triumphant political and financial acme, no better opportunity would ever present itself for the Dutch to find and seize Terra Australis. Nor would there ever exist a better instrument to carry out such an enterprise than the Dutch East India Company. Moreover, an energetic and farsighted man had now assumed the chair once occupied by the redoubtable Coen. He was Anthony Van Diemen.

Van Diemen had come to the East Indies as a clerk. By dint of hard work and imagination, he had achieved the post of governor-general in 1636 at the age of forty-three.* Like his predecessor, Coen, Van Diemen was fascinated by New Holland and Terra Australis. Only three months after becoming governor-general of the company, Van Diemen dispatched an expedition under the veteran navigator Gerrit Thomasz Pool to investigate New Holland further. But Pool's effort failed when he was murdered by natives in New Guinea.

It was not until 1642 that Van Diemen felt ready to send out a follow-up to the Pool thrust. By then Van Diemen had in mind a much-expanded program, based on the ideas of a farsighted Dutch navigator named Frans Jacobszoon Visscher.

In a book with the resounding title *Memoir Concerning the Discovery of the Southland*, Visscher had asserted that any search for the southern continent had to begin by determining, once and for all, the extent of New Holland. This could best be accomplished, he declared, if an expedition were first to sail to 55 or 60 degrees south and then run eastward at those latitudes. If a southern landmass existed in the south Pacific, a voyage following this course would certainly find it. Such a voyage would also determine if New Holland was part of Terra Australis. Visscher's book was also full of ideas for rediscovering the Solomon Islands and determining if there was, in fact, a navigable waterway separating New Guinea and New Holland.

Governor-General Van Diemen was impressed by Visscher's writings and used them to develop his own plan for a grand exploration of the South Pacific. Essentially an expansion of Vis-

---

*After five years at home, Coen had returned to Batavia again in 1627 as governor-general. But he had no longer been the dynamo of five years earlier. Although as coolly efficient as ever, Coen never found time to implement the exploration program he had envisioned during his first term. Worn out by his responsibilities and by fever, he died in 1630 at the age of thirty-three.

scher's ideas, Van Diemen's scheme called for an expedition to sail *westward* at first across the Indian Ocean to the island of Mauritius, off the African coast. Only then would the explorers turn south, sailing down to latitude fifty-four. At that point, according to Van Diemen's plan, the ships would turn east once more, keeping to the fifty-fourth parallel. At this latitude they would sail east across the Pacific as far as possible. In this way, Van Diemen postulated, the expedition would certainly come across any large body of land that might lie under or beyond the Tropic of Capricorn.

In any case, Van Diemen thought, even if his ships failed to find Terra Australis, they would, by sailing east across the Pacific, establish a new trade route to Chile. They could also take the time to check out sailing conditions at Cape Hoorn and claim any undiscovered islands for the Dutch Republic. They could even determine, as Visscher had suggested, whether New Guinea and New Holland were part of the same landmass. It was a remarkably ambitious agenda, but as governor-general of the company Van Diemen possessed both the means and the will to carry it out.

Filled with enthusiasm for this elaborate project, Van Diemen ordered two ships—the *Heemskerck* and the *Zeehaen*—to be fitted out for the venture and provisioned for a year at sea. Van Diemen chose as pilot for the effort the theorist Visscher, whose book had prompted the expedition in the first place. He also picked a veteran captain to head the enterprise. He was Abel Janszoon Tasman, a man of thirty-nine, who had already spent a decade in the service of the Dutch East India Company.

Van Diemen had every hope that Tasman and Visscher would at last solve the Pacific's greatest mystery, the southern continent.

22

TASMAN

Tasman was a nearly perfect model of a Dutch ship captain: competent, obedient, ambitious, thrifty, and ruthless when necessary. But he was also uninspired, cautious to a fault, and prejudiced against all things non-Dutch—that is, all things that were not neat, clean, and readily comprehended.

Tasman's career was also typical. Born in Groningen in 1603, he came from a poor, but devout, family. After some early education he did what most Dutch youths did in his time: He went to sea. He soon proved himself a better than average mariner. Like many another young officer, he viewed the company's Eastern empire as the surest path to comfort and position. Given the opportunity, he joined the company, and by 1634, at the age of thirty-one he was in the East Indies as master of a small vessel.

Like most of the Dutch masters out East, Tasman participated in trading ventures and assisted in suppressing native rebels and smugglers. In 1636 he went home to Holland and got married. Two years later he returned to the Indies with his wife and with a contract that required him to serve in Eastern waters for ten years.

Soon after his return to the Indies, Tasman took part in a voyage that had been authorized by Governor-General Van Diemen himself: a search of the Pacific for "islands of gold and silver," rumored to lie in the waters east of Japan. Two ships were sent on this mission under the command of a senior Dutch captain, Mathias Quast. Tasman captained the second vessel.

Departing Batavia in June 1639, the two Dutch ships plowed about in bad weather through the North Pacific but found no islands of gold and silver, nor any other land worth exploiting. After a cruise of five months the ships returned to Batavia in November 1639. Of the expedition's original company of ninety men, forty-one died of scurvy or fevers.

Despite the failure of this voyage, Van Diemen liked Tasman, seeing in him a capable captain who would scrupulously carry out his orders in the search for the southern continent.

Van Diemen issued precise written instructions to Tasman. After first setting forth sailing routes and general rules of conduct, the governor-general cautioned Tasman that, should he find nations on a level with those of Europe, he was to make it plain that he had come for the sake of commerce, not conquest. He was also to display specimens of the goods that the Dutch had to trade. He also ordered Tasman to pretend that he had no interest in precious metals "so as to leave [the natives] ignorant of the value of same." Tasman was to pretend that the Dutch preferred copper, pewter, or lead to gold or silver. As for any "wild barbarians" encountered, Van Diemen urged his commander to "take due care that no injury be done them in their houses, gardens, vessels, or their property, their wives, etc." At the same time, Van Diemen declared, if any Pacific natives should wish to accompany the Dutch ships back to the Indies, Tasman was "at full liberty to bring them hither."

The governor-general also promised that he would "not be found ungrateful" should Tasman discover "any rich countries, or regions, islands, or passages profitable to the Company." In this sentence, Van Diemen expressed the basic purpose of Tasman's voyage—indeed, the fundamental goal of *all* Dutch exploration in the Pacific: profit.

On August 14, 1642, Tasman's two vessels—the *Heemskerck*, with sixty men aboard, and the *Zeehaen*, with fifty men—set out to find, in Van Diemen's ringing words, "the remaining unknown part of the terrestrial globe!"

In accordance with Van Diemen's plan, the expedition sailed first to Mauritius, approximately three thousand miles west of Java in the Indian Ocean.* Arriving there on September 5, 1642, after an uneventful passage, the two ships underwent extensive repairs and modifications. Then, on October 8, 1642, they set out southward. The goal was to get to latitude 54 degrees south and then to turn eastward to look for Terra Australis.

For a month the two ships struggled southward in heavy seas. Although it was the southern spring, it was also the season of icebergs, and the cold was numbing despite the time of year. Tasman's men, used to tropical climes, found it exhausting to work in the frigid weather. Day after day icy swells struck the ships head-on. Then, suddenly, thick fogs engulfed the ships. Danger was everywhere as the Dutch mariners had to dodge mountains of ice, some of them ten to twenty miles long, floating in the murk. Tasman complained in his log that under such conditions it would be difficult "to survey known shores, let alone to discover unknown land."

But the ships kept to the southward. Tasman tripled the number of lookouts, warning his sentinels to keep a sharp eye out for shoals, sunken rocks, and, above all, ice. Tasman believed that land, and perhaps treacherous shallows, might lie anywhere in these cold and dismal southern waters of the Indian Ocean. The lookouts had already sighted seaweed and pieces of trees floating in the sea. At night, the *Heemskerck* and the *Zeehaen* kept in touch by firing their guns. The ships pressed on, continually battered by the dreary, frigid sea.

When the *Heemskerck* and the *Zeehaen* reached a point between 49 and 50 degrees south, however, both Tasman and his chief navigator, Visscher, concluded that with the hammering the two vessels were now taking, it would be imprudent to persist in trying to reach the southward goal of 54 degrees. The ships simply could not endure more pounding. Accordingly, while still some four hundred miles short of his planned destination, Tasman came about. Now the ships made their way northeast to latitude 44 degrees south. There, with the weather less threatening, they turned due east for the Pacific. Though not precisely where they were supposed to be, Tasman's ships were far to the south of the usual trading routes.

Holding their position at 44 degrees, the ships flew for four thousand miles before the roaring wind until they reached the

---

*Tasman's voyage was very well documented in his own logs and profusely illustrated with careful sketches of what was seen on the journey.

waters south of what is now Australia. There, on November 24, 1642, lookouts sighted an extensive land ahead. Was this the continent at last? Skirting the coast, Tasman looked for towns or other signs of civilization. But he saw only mountains and woodlands. In accordance with the arrogant custom of the day, Tasman took possession of the land as "our lawful property," apparently by right of discovery. He gave it the name Van Diemen's Land in honor of his sponsor.*

Rushing past Van Diemen's Land, the *Heemskerck* and the *Zeehaen* forged into what is now called the Tasman Sea. On December 13, 1642, another rugged coast suddenly appeared. Magnificent mountains, snow-topped and covered with thick forest, rose toward the sky.

At first Tasman and Visscher speculated that they had reached the Solomon Islands. But as the voyagers swung northward along these shores, Tasman realized that he had come upon a country higher, larger, and more beautiful by far than the islands described by Mendãna. Tasman called his discovery New Zeeland.

Tasman now crept northward, keeping his ships near enough to shore so that his lookouts could spot any cities or signs of habitation. At the same time he stood off far enough to keep the *Heemskerck* and the *Zeehaen* safe from the dangers of shoals and a lee shore. During the slow passage northward, the Dutch saw neither cities nor signs of "civilized" beings. But one day a large double-hulled canoe was spotted coming from the shore. Paddled by half-naked heavily tattooed armed men, the garishly decorated canoe boldly approached the Dutch ships. Abruptly it halted. The warriors brandished their weapons and made threatening gestures at the Dutch vessels.

Using a number of dialects learned during previous voyaging, the Dutch tried to communicate with these hostile men, who answered in an unknown language. Displaying trinkets, the Dutch attempted to induce some of their visitors to come aboard. The wary warriors could not be persuaded, however, and rowed away. The Dutch anchored in a nearby bay. Tasman ordered a careful watch kept through the night.†

*It was the great wild island off the southeast coast of Australia, later to be named after Tasman himself: Tasmania.
†The fierce warriors who seemed to menace the Dutch were the Maoris, a Polynesian people who were storied fighters in their own world.

In the morning another canoe visited the ships. But its passengers only stared at the Europeans as if studying them. At some point after this, the Dutch vessels moved closer inshore and nearer to each other so that the officers of the *Zeehaen* could more easily come to a council called aboard Tasman's *Heemskerck*. Suddenly, as if in response to this change of position, seven more large canoes, all filled with armed men, came out from the beach and began drifting about, observing the Dutch. When two of the canoes appeared to make for the *Zeehaen*, her nervous captain, who was attending the conference on the flagship, sent a small boat back to his vessel with an order to permit only a few of the natives aboard. He did not want a crowd of "savages" on his deck. Who knew but that they might try to sieze the ship?

The messenger boat, with seven hearty men at the oars, delivered the captain's order and was on its way back to the *Heemskerck* when one of the drifting native canoes suddenly rammed it. The canoe's fighting men then flung themselves into the Dutch boat and began beating the astonished European sailors with clubs and pikes. Three Dutch mariners were killed outright, and another was mortally wounded in this attack. Three men leaped from the boat and managed to swim to the *Heemskerck*. The natives hauled one of the dead sailors into their canoe. Then all the native craft paddled away. The stunned Dutch fired after them from their ships but hit nothing.

In the aftermath of this bloody encounter Tasman named his unfortunate anchorage Murderers' Bay. He also decided that his best course was to weigh anchor and find a safer harbor. The Dutch vessels now made for the open sea. As they did so, however, another ten or twelve canoes, manned by howling natives, came after them, apparently intent on capture. Tasman ordered cannister fired in the direction of the pursuers. The noise of the cannon and the whistling bullets, sent the canoes fleeing.

Tasman's decision to retreat from Murderers' Bay illustrates his preference for prudence over vengeance. There is little doubt that with his ships' heavy ordnance, he could have bombarded the local villages and taken a fatal revenge for the killing of his men, justifying his action by a claim that he was merely protecting his crews from "savages." But Tasman would have regarded any such retaliation as bad business. To expend more lives, toil, time, and costly ammunition for no material gain would be a vain deed. It was one thing to massacre twenty-five hundred na-

tives on the isle of Great Banda, as Jan Coen had done, in order
to regulate the production of cloves. It was quite another, useless
act to kill natives to assuage wrath.

The Dutch, mourning their dead, resumed their voyage
northward along the grand shoreline. The extensiveness of the
land to his starboard caused Tasman to speculate that he was
now off the western coast of the southern continent and that the
mountainous land that rose on his right hand might actually
stretch away many thousands of miles. He wrote in his journal:
" . . . we deemed it quite possible that this land is part of the
great Staten Landt though this is not certain. This land seems to
be a very fine country, and we trust that this is the mainland
coast of the unknown south-land."

As Tasman followed the coast north, it suddenly curved
sharply to the east. Continuing to follow the coast, the Dutch
came to what seemed to them a very deep inlet, for more of the
rugged land was visible ahead to the north, thus indicating that
the ships were crossing the entrance of a large bay. Tasman
thought it wise to avoid this waterway, fearing that his two vessels
might become entrapped in its waters or driven ashore. The ever-
cautious Tasman continued on across the "bay" until he again
had a continuous shoreline to starboard.*

In early January 1643 the Dutch reached the northern limit
of their newly discovered land. Now much in need of water and
fresh vegetables, they tried to get landing parties ashore in order
to secure supplies, but contrary winds and heavy surf thwarted
them. Moreover, on at least one occasion would-be landing parties also spotted native warriors waiting ashore, "giant men," according to the Dutch, who "shouted threats and brandished
weapons."

The frustrated Tasman decided to forgo any further exploration of New Zeeland. Although, in his view, this lush land
might be part of the continent, confirmation would have to wait
until he replenished his stores. He therefore stood away and
struck out northeast into the open ocean, toward islands previously discovered by Schouten and Le Maire, where his crews
might rest and refresh themselves.

After a cruise of two weeks the *Heemskerck* and the *Zeehaen*

---

*It was not a bay, but a strait. Specifically it was the passage that separates the two great
islands that make up most of New Zealand.

came upon a group of islands inhabited by friendly Polynesian people.* The islanders welcomed the Dutch explorers with great hospitality. The Dutch went ashore and were entertained by the "king" of the island. They quickly obtained all the fresh water, meat, and fruit they wanted. With the unconscious arrogance that characterized so many actions of European explorers in the Pacific, the Dutch gave the individual islands of this group such names as Amsterdam, Rotterdam, and Middleburg. Though there was some thievery—of nails mostly—on the part of the local people, relations between them and the Dutch remained generally good. The natives went about unarmed, apparently aware that there was no point in trying to resist men who possessed cannon, muskets, and pistols. The islanders even went so far as to punish their own thieves when the Dutch complained of pilfering. In one example, cited by Tasman, a native youth accused of having stolen a Dutch pike was punished by having his head struck with a coconut until the fruit's hard shell shattered. Tasman considered the incident proof of native devotion to law.

On February 1, 1643, the Dutch moved on. Now Tasman set a course west by north where, it was thought, the Dutch might find Mendaña's long-lost Isles of Solomon.† Following this heading, the voyagers soon found themselves among dozens of islands not shown on their maps. Unknown to them, they had blundered into the reef-strewn Fiji Islands located at approximately 17 degrees south. They were the first Europeans to have reached the Fijis. But thick fog, shoal waters, and thunderous surf kept them from landing. Moreover, the Dutch had to sound continuously as they made their way through a network of perilous shallows. At one point the vessels escaped shipwreck only by a hair when they sailed over a reef that had just enough water covering it to allow the hulls to pass.

With no knowledge of these hazardous waters and fearing that the weather might grow worse before it got better, Tasman called a council of officers to consider the situation. It was decided that the best strategy would be the cautious one: to change course and sail due north to latitude 4 or 5 degrees south and then to turn west for Batavia by way of familiar waters north of

---

*These were islands of the Tonga group later named the Friendly Islands. Schouten and Le Maire had visited them a generation earlier.
†Tasman's direction was on target, but the Solomons were more than twenty-five hundred miles away across dangerous seas still uncharted by the Dutch.

New Guinea. In this manner they could escape to better weather and safer seas. Though Visscher would have preferred to investigate the southeastern region of New Guinea and, perhaps, even visit New Holland, he apparently did not press his view forcefully.

The ships began a creeping passage to the north. The weather continued to be abominable, with rain, fog, and rough seas. February turned into March. Tasman noted in his log that for weeks past the Dutch had endured "nothing but rain." Finally, about mid-March, the weather improved. The ships, now off New Guinea, turned at last toward home. At last enjoying good luck and favorable winds, the two vessels made excellent time, traversing well-known seas with little trouble.

The *Heemskerck* and the *Zeehaen* arrived at their home port of Batavia on June 15, 1643. On that date Tasman made his final entry in his log: " . . . at daybreak, I went to Batavia in the pinnace. God be praised and thanked for this happy voyage. Amen."

Measured by any objective standard, Tasman and Visscher had accomplished much in their ten-month voyage. They had discovered the land called Van Diemen's Land, which was eventually called Tasmania. They had shown that the southern continent did not extend into the high latitudes of the Indian Ocean. They had discovered, charted, and named the hitherto unknown land of New Zeeland, which might, after all, be the western coast of the continent. They had claimed the Fijis. And if Tasman and Visscher had made no attempt to approach New Holland from the Pacific side, they *had* shown where the company should seek both New Holland and Terra Australis in the future.

Governor Van Diemen, however, expressed disappointment with the results of the voyage. In addition, a council of the company decided that the voyagers had been "to some extent remiss in investigating . . . the lands and peoples discovered." The company regarded Tasman's voyage as a failure. He had not properly investigated the coastal areas that he took to be the southern continent. He had not continued *eastward* across the Pacific to determine, beyond doubt, the position and extent of the southern continent, if one assumed that New Zeeland was its western shore. It counted little that Tasman had lost only ten men during his journey. The sad fact was, the company pointed out, that Tasman had failed to answer conclusively *any* of the questions about Terra Australis or New Holland. Beyond his discovery of a few islands, he had really proved only that the vaguely outlined land of New Holland did not extend beyond 40 or 41 degrees south. He had not even determined whether New Guinea was or was not separated from New Holland by a navigable waterway. Worst of all, Tasman had found no new sources of trade or wealth.*

Nevertheless, the governor-general and the company council had to admit that Tasman's effort was in many respects "remarkable" for valor and toil. For this reason, they granted him and his officers a bonus of two months' pay, while the crewmen were awarded one month's salary. Moreover, it was soon decided that Tasman deserved a chance to redeem himself.

More important, it was clear that with so many questions about New Holland and the southern continent still unanswered, a second voyage was essential, and who was better qualified to lead it than Abel Janszoon Tasman?

---

*In retrospect the company realized that Tasman had circumnavigated New Holland without ever having seen it. It became clear that New Holland was separate from any great lush continent in the South Pacific.

23

WHERE IS TERRA AUSTRALIS?

On January 29, 1644, approximately six months after returning from his earlier voyage, Tasman sailed from Batavia once
more. This time he had three vessels: the *Limmen*, the *Veemeeuw*,
and a fishing vessel, the *Bracq*. Once more Visscher accompanied
him as pilot.

Tasman's overall mission this time was to establish beyond
doubt the relationship between New Guinea and New Holland
and then to determine, at last, the true size and shape of New
Holland itself. With these puzzles solved, the company would be
much better placed to answer the most tantalizing question of
all: Where lay Terra Australis Incognita?

Following instructions, Tasman sailed for the Arafura Sea
between New Guinea and New Holland and coasted along the
southern shore of New Guinea. Inevitably he reached the shallow, reef-strewn waters that separate New Guinea from Australia:
the Torres Strait. Like all his Dutch predecessors, however,
Tasman mistook this passage for a dangerous bay.

Fearing that he might run aground or be trapped by contrary winds, Tasman, with Visscher's concurrence, turned the
bows of his vessels south, away from the hazards of the supposed
bay before him. He was satisfied that no usable waterway separated New Guinea and New Holland.

After crossing to what is now Cape York Peninsula, Australia, Tasman began following the northern coast of New Holland back to the west, searching for one of his lesser objectives: a deepwater channel leading to the south. No such passage appeared, however, and Tasman continued to sail west, charting the coast and observing the land and its people.

Although much of this northern shore was jungle and swamp, in contrast with the barren coasts farther west, the land still seemed dismal and unpromising to the Dutch mariners. Of the natives, Tasman wrote:"The people are bad and wicked, shooting at the Dutch with arrows without provocation when they were coming on shore." He kept on sailing along the coast. Soon his ships reached the oft-sighted desert coast of the northwest and west of New Holland. Again Tasman remarked on the primitive character of the people, declaring that they were "savage and go naked. None can understand them."

There was a note of unmistakable discouragement in Tasman's logs now. Clearly he saw little of value in New Holland, and he was losing heart for the hard voyaging still ahead. He went on, however, proceeding south along the western coast of New Holland. By the time his ships reached 22 degrees south, it was the middle of the southern winter. Tasman and his men dreaded the prospect of plunging into the cold and stormy seas that lay farther to the south. Tasman also judged that he was ill provisioned for such a demanding journey. His men were weary, and his ships in need of repair. He decided to forgo any further exploration although he had fallen far short of his goals. He turned his bows homeward and arrived back at Batavia in August 1644, after a cruise of eight months.

He was again severely criticized by company officials for having "found nothing that could be turned to profit, but . . . only naked, beach-roving wretches, destitute even of rice, miserably poor, and in many places of very bad disposition." Governor-General Van Diemen was also disappointed by Tasman's voyage. Nevertheless, it had served a purpose. It had shown (if Tasman was correct) that New Holland and New Guinea *were* connected and that New Holland, arid and impoverished, was *not* a part of the southern continent and thus was not worth further exploration.

Tasman's voyages, though unprofitable, indicated that Terra Australis probably lay to the east of New Holland, somewhere under the Tropic of Capricorn. Was it possible, then, that Tasman's "New Zeeland" was, as he suspected, the coast of that much-desired but elusive paradise? To Van Diemen it seemed obvious that in spite of Tasman's poor results, the company had to continue to search for the continent for the sake of future profit and for the perpetuation of Dutch domination of the Pacific.

But when Van Diemen proposed still another expedition, company executives in far-off Amsterdam complained that so far his schemes had brought nothing but extraordinary expenditure. They informed him that instead of looking for new lands, the company preferred to exploit to the fullest what it already possessed. "[Your] plans . . . ," they wrote, "somewhat aim beyond our mark."

Given his prestige with the company, Van Diemen eventually might have persuaded Amsterdam to back still another voyage. But in 1645 he died. With him also died any prospect of further company exploration in the Pacific.

Tasman, still only forty-two, returned to more ordinary duty. Despite the criticism heaped upon him, the company elevated him to the rank of commander. He did no more exploring, but in 1647 he led a trading fleet to what is now Thailand. Some years later he fought against the Spaniards in the Philippines. He became wealthy. Visscher, too, returned to service with the company.*

As the years passed, it became clear that although the company reaped no profit from them, Tasman's voyages had great geographic value. He had discovered many new lands, including Tasmania, New Zealand, the Tonga Islands, and the Fijis. His journeys had filled in much of the empty space in the vast Pacific. He had also revealed much about New Holland. When Tasman died in 1659, he was revered for his endeavors. Nevertheless, he *had* left the great question unanswered.

In the years immediately after Tasman's two voyages the golden age of Holland seemed to glitter more brightly than ever. In 1648 Spain at last acknowledged Dutch independence by the

---

*Although he played a key role in both Tasman's voyages, Visscher seems to have been one of those unassertive, elusive characters, content to stay in the background and to do his job, a gray "company man" to the end.

Treaty of Münster. After eighty years of struggle, the seven United Provinces of the Netherlands were officially free of the Spanish crown.*

To many Europeans the Treaty of Münster was merely belated recognition of Dutch military and cultural superiority. In the 1640s the Dutch fleet numbered some ten thousand vessels and employed almost 170,000 seamen. The republic, through its East India Company, controlled the spice trade. The Dutch West India Company maintained profitable trading installations in Africa and in America.

People from all over Europe came to the United Provinces, seeking asylum, freedom of religion, and freedom to make money. Amsterdam was the financial capital of the world. The stolid burghers of the Dutch republic were rich enough to support the finest art of the day. No other country in the world possessed more wealth, power, and prestige.

The Dutch light shone all the more vividly because of the darkness that prevailed elsewhere. Spain, after the cruel Thirty Years' War, was more feeble than ever. France, with a boy king, Louis XIV, on the throne, was ruled by a regent, Cardinal Mazarin, who sought to control the nation's unruly nobility and to restore stability after decades of internal strife and foreign wars. The Hapsburg realms of Austria and the Holy Roman Empire were recovering from the Thirty Years' War—as was the new northern power, Sweden. Russia was just escaping from medieval darkness. In England civil war was in full cry. Only a year after Dutch independence King Charles I was beheaded, and an English commonwealth proclaimed under the leadership of Oliver Cromwell.

With the coming of the 1650s, Holland seemed to stand alone above Europe's travail. Then, barely visible in the glow of Dutch greatness, Holland's high tide began to ebb.

It started with the spice trade. By 1650 the ships of the Dutch East India Company had carried so many cargoes of pepper, cloves, nutmegs, and ginger to Europe that the market became glutted. No longer rare, spices began to lose their luster as the symbol of wealth and luxury. Slowly, but steadily, prices fell. In

---

*The ten southern provinces of the Netherlands—roughly modern Belgium—had remained loyal to Spain, or had been reconquered, and were still to be known for years as the Spanish Netherlands.

addition, European tastes were starting to change. The sugar of the Caribbean was becoming the luxury of choice for the wealthy. This trend away from spices accelerated rapidly.

Then, in 1651, England—a new mercantile Puritan England—began to pursue a more aggressive commercial policy. Proclaiming that national strength depended on trade and sea power, Cromwell's England adopted a series of laws called The Navigation Acts which, among other things, required that English goods be carried in English ships. This was a measure aimed specifically at the Dutch, whose ships were often the carriers for other nations. The assertive English, who had not forgotten the Amboina Massacre thirty years earlier, also returned to competition with Dutch merchants in Africa, America, and even the East Indies.

Inevitably, in 1652, a naval war, known as the First Anglo-Dutch War, broke out between England and the United Provinces. Even though the Dutch achieved regional victories in the East Indies and in the Mediterranean, the English won the decisive battles in the North Sea and were the clear, if surprising, victors, when the conflict ended in 1654.

Despite their defeat by the English, however, the Dutch *looked* as strong as ever in the far reaches of the globe during the 1650s. They were unable to hold off a Portuguese reconquest of northeastern Brazil, but they continued to swarm throughout the East. They seized control of the Cape of Good Hope and set up a new base at Cape Town. They forced the Spaniards completely out of the Moluccas. They took Malacca. They finished the conquest of coastal Ceylon. They conquered Malabar from the Portuguese in India. They established flourishing trade fortresses on the Guinea coast of Africa.

But the English, too, were expanding. In 1656 Cromwell, whose religious sensibilities seldom clouded his political acumen, joined with Catholic France in a highly profitable war against Spain. In this assault on a weakened Spain, Cromwell used his growing naval power to win the port of Dunkirk in the Spanish Netherlands. England also took a number of Spanish possessions in the Caribbean, including the rich sugar island of Jamaica. Nor did Cromwell's death and the subsequent restoration of the Stuart King Charles II in 1660 end English aggression at sea. Squadrons of English warships ranged Atlantic and African waters in the 1660s.

Soon a newly revived France also began seeking a place on the global stage. The young French king, Louis XIV, who took personal control of his government in 1662, was bent on making France the world's foremost power. Toward that end he began building a magnificent army and fleet.

Complicating the situation for the Dutch state was the fact that Louis XIV exercised considerable influence over the English Charles II. An alliance between Catholic France and Protestant England, inimical to the interests of the Protestant Dutch, appeared to be a possibility, one that the Dutch feared greatly, for despite its wealth, the Dutch republic, with a population of less than three million, would be at a disadvantage if it had to engage a France that numbered some eleven million people and an England with a population of five million.

Meanwhile, the rift between Holland and England, driven by commercial rivalry, continued to widen. When the Dutch forced the Portuguese to make concessions to them on the Malabar Coast of India, the English regarded it as a direct threat to their own interests in the Indian Ocean. When the Portuguese surrendered some of their African forts to the Dutch, the English, without declaring war, took some Dutch forts on the African coast and sent an armed force to occupy New Amsterdam in America. The result was the Second Anglo-Dutch War of 1664–67. This conflict culminated in a brazen Dutch raid on the Medway that forced King Charles II to sue for peace. The English, however, held on to most of their gains, including New Amsterdam, which they rechristened New York.

It was at this time that Louis XIV launched his nation into a series of wars, supposedly to achieve control of all French-speaking areas of Europe not yet under the French crown. In reality, however, Louis XIV sought supremacy on the European continent.

Suddenly it was clear to the Dutch that their days of absolute dominance were over. Holland's very existence as a nation was actually in jeopardy. France was a great power and an implacable enemy. England was a maritime rival to be feared and resisted. The Dutch republic could no longer stand alone. Dreading French designs, the Dutch allied themselves with their old antagonists, the historical enemies of France: Hapsburg Spain and Austria. As a result of this marriage of convenience, Europe's powers found themselves in what many considered an "unnatural" alignment: Catholic France versus Protestant Holland and Catholic Spain and Austria.

Further complicating this arrangement was the sometimes ambivalent policy of Protestant England under its Stuart monarch. Though, generally, England supported France and opposed its Dutch maritime rival, English diplomacy could flip-flop. For example, after the Second Anglo-Dutch War, England entered a short-lived alliance with the Dutch republic, even as it carried on a privateering war against Holland's ally Spain in the Caribbean. For the most part, however, Stuart England—despite its overwhelmingly Protestant population—lined up with Catholic France. Thus, in 1672, when Louis XIV at last carried out a long-standing threat to invade the Dutch republic, the English king, Charles, after receiving a large secret subsidy from the French, joined Louis against Holland. The result was the Third Anglo-Dutch War.

Beleaguered by the French army on land and the English fleet at sea, the Dutch fought back valiantly under a new young leader, William, prince of Orange. English Protestants admired the determined resistance put up by the Dutch. At the same time they distrusted France and resented Louis's influence on Charles. As the war went on, it became more and more unpopular in England—until the Protestant Parliament forced Charles to withdraw from the struggle, leaving Louis XIV and William of Orange to fight on.

Now the "unnatural" ties between England and France began to unravel. Despite three wars and a persistent commercial rivalry, England, impelled by a Parliament sympathetic to William of Orange, sought to reestablish old ties with the Dutch state. In 1677 William of Orange, regarded as a hero in England for his ongoing resistance to the French king, married Mary, of England, Charles's niece and a Protestant, bringing about what later became a fateful dynastic union.

A year later William, battered by the French, was forced to sue for peace with Louis XIV. Even so, he made it clear that Holland would continue to oppose French dominion in Europe. He also made it plain that he hoped to induce England to join in a European coalition against Louis. Despite pressure from Parliament and the population, however, Charles shied away from any open alliance against the powerful French. Nevertheless, immense forces had now been set in motion, and they were to transform Europe.

Louis XIV accelerated that transformation when he renewed his aggression as the critical decade of the 1680s opened. Resuming hostilities against the Dutch republic and its ally Spain, Louis XIV's armies invaded the Spanish Netherlands and pushed across the Rhine. In England Parliament, and most of the people, pressed Charles to join with William of Orange and with Spain against Louis. Charles refused.*

In 1685, having again invaded the Spanish Netherlands and having again been stalled by heroic Dutch resistance, Louis made a colossal political blunder. With a stroke of his pen, the French king revoked the Edict of Nantes, which had guaranteed freedom of religion to French Protestants. The Huguenots of France, terrified of renewed religious persecution, fled the country, taking with them much of their wealth and all their talent. Many of them made their way to Holland where they were warmly welcomed. More important, Louis's arrogant act fired up all European Protestants against him. In England it enraged Parliament and people alike and greatly energized those who sought to bring the kingdom into alliance with William of Orange against Louis.

In the same year Charles died, setting off still another political convulsion, one that began when his brother James succeeded to the throne of England. An avowed Catholic, James II was an unabashed supporter of Louis's and thus much mistrusted by the Parliament. When a son was born to James in 1687 and baptized a Catholic, English Protestants refused to accept what they termed "the Catholic succession."

In a series of complicated, swift political moves, Parliament invited William of Orange to take the throne of England. He accepted with alacrity. He was escorted to England by the powerful English fleet in 1688 and installed as King William III of England. James fled to France.†

---

*Such an alliance at this time would have had some odd ramifications, for English buccaneers in the Americas were openly engaged in hostilities with Holland's ally Spain despite the existence of an Anglo-Spanish treaty that supposedly outlawed buccaneering in the Caribbean. Had Charles joined the anti-French coalition, England would have been allied with Spain in Europe and at war with Spain in America.

†Sheltered and aided by Louis XIV, James, and his Stuart heirs, spent many years trying to regain the English throne. James himself was defeated by William of Orange in Ireland in 1690 at the famed Battle of the Boyne, ending forever his aspirations.

This Glorious Revolution, also called the Bloodless Revolution, not only united the leadership of England and Holland but also brought into existence the powerful anti-French alliance that William and the Protestants of Europe had sought for so long. The rivals in commerce had become allies in war. From now on England, with a fleet that had already become more formidable than any other, would be the enemy of royal France.

A new Europe was now emerging, a Europe that would see England and France wage a titanic struggle that would last well into eighteenth century. It was also a Europe in which the Dutch republic would play an ever-decreasing role.

With the tumultuous events in Europe, the Pacific, with its great unanswered questions, had become a backwater. The Dutch, clinging to their East Indian empire and fiercely defending themselves at home, had lost interest in the southern continent. More important, they had no ships, no men, and no money to spare for exploration.

At the same time England and France were too focused on internal matters to wonder where Terra Australis might lie. In Spain a weary government struggled just to keep its empire intact.

Thus only buccaneers and adventurers found the waters of the Pacific inviting in the late seventeenth century. But one of these buccaneers was destined to reignite the world's passion for the Pacific.

24
BUCCANEER WITH A PEN

Tall, angular, long-jawed William Dampier seemed always to look out upon the world through heavy-lidded, suspicious eyes. Even his few friends thought him a morose, prickly spirit, whose rasping manner revealed a man who felt superior to most of those with whom fate had cast him.

Dampier was born in rural Somersetshire in the southwest of England in 1651. There he attended school until his parents died when he was just sixteen. Young Dampier, seething with curiosity about the world, then went to sea. He made a voyage to Newfoundland and to the East Indies. In 1673 he served in the Royal Navy as a seaman during England's third naval war against the Dutch. He took part in two battles. When he fell sick, he was discharged.

In 1674, at twenty-three, Dampier drifted to the island of Jamaica, but he found little to interest him there and, after six months he shipped aboard a coasting vessel in the Caribbean. During the next few months, while cruising in these sunny waters, the highly intelligent youth began to fill his journals with detailed records of his adventures and with scientific observations, in the process revealing both a sharp mind and a nature that was more *in*quisitive than *ac*quisitive.

During this period Dampier also visited the Gulf of Campeche, on the Yucatán Peninsula. There he spent some time working among the log cutters who made a living by chopping down the enormous hardwood trees there and shipping them to Europe, where they were much in demand.

Most of the rugged loggers whom Dampier met in the Yucatán were also members of the buccaneering brotherhood of the Caribbean. They lived according to their own lights, devoted themselves to the pleasures of the moment, and, whenever they needed more money or excitement than they could obtain by cutting timber, would enlist aboard the numerous pirate ships operating in the area. The adventurous young Dampier, already describing himself in his notebooks as a man fascinated by "the various and wonderful works of God in different parts of the world," was greatly attracted to the buccaneering life.

In the mid-1670s the "buccaneer brotherhood" had already been in existence for more than fifty years. During that time it had not only grown into a formidable force of seagoing brigands but also had developed into a virtual outlaw nation with its own laws, bases, and governing councils. Strangely, this ferocious commonwealth of pirates had evolved from peaceful communities of peasants—English, Dutch, and French Protestants—who had settled on bleak, uninhabited Caribbean islands some three generations earlier in defiance of Spain's claim to exclusive ownership of the Americas. These Protestant settlers had eked out livings as herdsmen, farmers, and fishermen until early in the seventeenth century, when the Spaniards had begun a systematic campaign to drive them away by destroying "illegal" settlements and arresting their inhabitants. The buccaneers had then turned to piracy against Spanish shipping.

By the 1650s the buccaneers had become a bloody brotherhood, attracting to their ranks seagoing rogues who shared three common characteristics: the Protestant religion, a fierce hatred of Catholic Spain, and a hunger for loot.

Firmly ensconced in their bases on Tortuga and Jamaica, the buccaneers resisted all Spanish attempts to stamp them out. In the almost continuous wars that the European nations fought among themselves in the latter half of the seventeenth century, the buccaneers often acted as irregulars against Spain, and by the 1660s they had gained a worldwide reputation for both ferocity and military effectiveness.*

---

*The word "buccaneer" derives from the Indian word *boucan*, meaning a rack used for

Even during brief periods of European peace, the buccaneers continued their private war against Spain. In fact, one of the most famous buccaneers of the era—the Welshman Henry Morgan—sacked the proud Spanish city of Panama in 1671, just after England had agreed to suppress buccaneering in exchange for Spanish recognition of English rights to Jamaica as well as other Caribbean holdings.*

In 1680, when he was nearly thirty, Dampier joined the brotherhood of brigands, attaching himself first to a band of outlaws led by a certain Captain Sharp. In this cutthroat company Dampier crossed the Isthmus of Panama to raid the Pacific coast. After participating in a series of actions that resulted in more toil than profit, Dampier returned to the Caribbean and eventually made his way to Virginia. There he joined another buccaneering enterprise, that of Captain John Cook aboard the ship *Bachelor's Delight*. Sailing for Africa in August 1683, the *Bachelor's Delight* spent several months taking prey along the Guinea coast. She then made her way around Cape Horn, as it was now known, and into the Pacific, where the company pillaged the shores of South America. Sometime later, after a visit to the Galápagos, the *Bachelor's Delight* laid up in Mexico. There Captain Cook died, apparently of natural causes, and the crew chose the English buccaneer Edward Davis to succeed him.

The *Bachelor's Delight* was not the only buccaneering vessel in Mexican waters at the time. Another ship, the *Cygnet*, captained by a tough privateer named Charles Swan, was operating in the area. The *Cygnet* had left England in 1683, passed through the Strait of Magellan, and, like the *Bachelor's Delight*, had also raided northward along the South American coast. Now Captain Swan's *Cygnet* and Captain Davis's *Bachelor's Delight* met up with each other and joined forces. For several months in 1685 they cruised in tandem, hunting particularly for Spanish silver galle-

---

smoking meat. As herdsmen the Protestant settlers who later became pirates often smoked meat on their "boucans" and were therefore *boucaniers*. Oddly, even when their own countries fought one another, English, Dutch, and French buccaneers usually clung together against the hated Spaniards.

*Word of this treaty had not reached Morgan when he started on his raid into Panama. It might not have deterred him in any case. In the aftermath of his descent on Panama, Morgan was arrested by English authorities and taken to London for trial. Pointing out that his attack on the Spaniards in Panama was part of a local war declared by the English governor of Jamaica, Morgan denied any guilt. Treated by the English public more as a hero than a pirate, Morgan escaped punishment. Later he was knighted and became the lieutenant governor of Jamaica.

ons bound from Peru to Panama. From time to time additional pirate vessels, both English and French, joined in the venture.

Although successful together, the crews of the *Bachelor's Delight* and the *Cygnet* decided to part company. Dampier, restless as always, left Captain Davis and the *Bachelor's Delight* and instead sailed off with Captain Swan in the *Cygnet* to plunder Peruvian waters.

Some time later the two ships encountered each other again and once more cruised together for a while. During this interlude Captain Davis told Dampier that while the two ships had been apart, the *Bachelor's Delight* had sighted a large body of land some 450 miles west of Chile in latitude 27 degrees 20 minutes south and had given it the name Davisland. Unfortunately, said Davis, he had had no opportunity to explore his find, for he had just sacked a settlement in Nicaragua and was intent on getting away from the scene as fast as he could.

Dampier recorded Davis's find in his journals. He noted that the men of the *Bachelor's Delight* had described "Davisland" as "a long tract of pretty high land, tending away toward the northwest out of sight." Dampier appended his own guess about the nature of Davis' discovery: "This might probably be the coast of Terra Australis Incognita."*

Once again Captain Swan and the *Cygnet*, with William Dampier still aboard, parted company with the *Bachelor's Delight*. Heading north now, the *Cygnet* began operating along the coast of Mexico and California. In this cruise the *Cygnet* experienced what Dampier called "bad success."

Captain Swan suggested that the company cross the Pacific to the Philippines. In March 1686, the *Cygnet* set out due west from Mexico. For seven weeks she plowed the Central Pacific, making good time. Unfortunately her improvident buccaneer crew had failed to store sufficient supplies for a lengthy voyage, and rations ran out while the ship was far from her destination. With hunger gnawing at their bellies, the men decided to kill their officers—and eat them. First to go would be Swan himself, described by Dampier as "lusty and fleshy." At the last moment

---

*Dampier's speculation, as well as other later accounts of "Davisland," led many geographers to wonder, along with Dampier, if Davis had not blundered upon the eastern coast of the southern continent. Davis himself never followed up on his sighting since his business was plunder, not exploration.

the *Cygnet*'s captain was saved from the cookpot, when the island of Guam was sighted on May 20.

After revictualing at Guam, the *Cygnet* went on to the Philippines, where she turned into a tiger of the sea, attacking any prey that happened into her path. For six months the *Cygnet*'s crew engaged in an orgy of drunkenness, debauchery, and murder. Dampier claims in his journals that he was only a helpless and disapproving observer of these events and that he abhorred the excessive violence aboard ship.

Among buccaneers a captain was by no means the tyrannical monarch that he was on ships in "honest service." In fact, he could be deposed at any time by majority vote of his crew. Thus it was that at some point during this Philippine cruise the majority of the *Cygnet* company, repelled by endless violence, voted Captain Swan out of office and set him ashore along with thirty-six men who chose to remain with him.*

Dampier, who had apparently played a significant role in Swan's deposition, now accompanied the remaining *Cygnet* crew on a cruise of the Philippines, China, and the Spice Islands. In the midst of this meandering voyage, which seems to have produced little profit, the ship ran into an enormous circular storm which Dampier described in his logbook as a "typhoon."†

In January 1688 the *Cygnet* company fetched up on the northwest coast of the land that the Dutch called New Holland. There the pirates careened the *Cygnet*—in what is now called Cygnet Bay—to clean and repair her.

The bleak land around the bay seemed menacing to the superstitious buccaneers, who believed tales that it was inhabited by monsters. But Dampier, curious as always, took the opportunity to explore some of this odd land. While the company scraped the *Cygnet*'s bottom, mended rigging, and salted turtles and fish for provisions, Dampier tramped about, filling his journals with descriptions of plants, animals, and his encounters with natives. He cared little for the country, calling it "dusty and dead." Of the people, he says: "The inhabitants of this country

---

*Swan and his men apparently obtained another ship and later rejoined other privateers in the Spanish Pacific.

†The name was most likely derived from the Chinese *tai fung*, meaning "great wind." It may have also derived from the Hindustani word for a storm, *tufan*. In any case, Dampier's word "typhoon" eventually became the accepted European name for a Pacific hurricane.

are the miserablest people in the world. . . . They have no sort of clothes, but a piece of the rind of tree tied like a girdle about their waists. . . . They have no houses, but lie in the open air, without any covering, the earth being their bed, the heavens their canopy." He also wrote that New Holland was "a very large tract of land. It is not yet determined whether it is an island or a main continent, but I am certain that it joins neither to Asia, Africa, nor America."

When the refurbished *Cygnet* went to sea again, she headed for the Indian Ocean. Reaching the Nicobar Islands, lying between Ceylon and Malaya, the crew of the *Cygnet* marooned Dampier, together with two other Englishmen, a Portuguese, and some Malayans.*

Desperate to escape their island prison, Dampier and his companions obtained a native canoe and, enduring incredible hardships, managed to row it some two hundred miles to Sumatra. Several of Dampier's mates died on this journey. Dampier himself was near death when the canoe finally reached safety.

After recovering his strength, the indomitable Dampier bounced around the East Indies for several years, at one time even serving as chief gunner at the English East India Company fort at Benkulen in India. At last, in 1691, Dampier found his way back to England after an absence of twelve years, during which he had circumnavigated the world by fits and starts. Now forty years old, he had little to show for his dozen years of adventure except a tattooed Malayan "prince," whom he had bought from a slaver as a body servant.

To support himself, Dampier now exhibited the "prince" in London and at country fairs. In his advertisements Dampier referred to the Malayan as a "famous painted Prince" and "the just wonder of the age," concluding: "He is exposed to public view every day . . . at his lodgings [in London] . . . but if any persons of quality . . . do desire to see this noble person at their own houses, or any other convenient place . . . they are desired to send timely notice and he will be ready to wait upon them. . . . "

---

*Dampier later claimed that this was at his own request and that he hoped to establish a trade in ambergris on the islands. But it hardly seems credible that he would choose to exile himself on these dots of land in the middle of nowhere. More than likely the crew of the *Cygnet*, having enjoyed little recent success, had again quarreled among themselves, and the losing faction, including Dampier, had been marooned at the first convenient spot. Certainly Dampier, always scribbling in his logs, must have seemed a peculiar pirate to his shipmates.

Unfortunately the tattooed Malayan contracted smallpox and died at Oxford in 1692. Dampier, entering the fifth decade of his life, found himself without prospects. He could not even resume his old trade on the Spanish Main, for England no longer had any use for its buccaneers.

The Dutch Prince William of Orange, William III in England, had led England to join Holland and Spain (among others) in a new war against the French king, Louis XIV. Allied against their inclination with the hated dons, Dutch and English buccaneers found themselves at loose ends. Spanish shipping was no longer fair game. At the same time the French enemy offered few prizes worth the effort. Under these circumstances, the old buccaneering brotherhood of the Caribbean was in decline, although French buccaneers continued to find desultory employment in Louis's forces.*

The old buccaneering life was finished for Dampier. But he was nothing if not resourceful. Unable to be a pirate, he became a writer. Using the journals and logs of his travels, he put together a lively narrative entitled *A New Voyage Round the World*. The work won wide acclaim and earned Dampier sufficient funds to keep him in style. It also transformed the old pirate into a respected explorer. Powerful men began to listen when he spoke. They paid special attention when he urged that England take up the search for Terra Australis Incognita in the Pacific. Thus, when the war with France sputtered to an inconclusive end in 1698, the Admiralty decided to send a ship to the Pacific to search out the mysterious southern continent. Dampier, now the recognized authority on the Pacific, was given command of a 290-ton vessel, the *Roebuck*, and told to use her to claim Terra Australis for England.†

---

*However, the Jolly Roger piracy that became so familiar in the ensuing decades began to flourish as never before. Former buccaneers against Spain were now making their way to the Indian Ocean to attack the shipping of *all* nations. Soon Madagascar became a virtual pirate nation, a haven for pirates who attacked the English East India Company, the Dutch East India Company, and the great mogul himself. Oddly the *Cygnet*, Dampier's old ship, also made her way to Madagascar. Eventually she capsized after a piratical action in the Indian Ocean, drowning many of Dampier's old shipmates.

†Though, in the latter half of the seventeenth century, Europeans were more caught up in war than in exploration, there had been *some* exceptions. Sir John Narborough commanded a voyage of discovery in 1669 aboard the Royal Navy man-of-war *Sweepstakes*, sailing to the Patagonian coast, which he claimed for Charles II. He then took his three hundred ton ship, with her thirty six guns and her crew of eighty men through the Strait of Magellan into the Pacific. But nothing much came of this voyage except a book which he wrote afterwards.

*   *   *

Upon inspection, the *Roebuck* turned out to be a near hulk, her ancient planking seemingly held together only by numerous coats of tar. She was, in Dampier's angry opinion, completely unsuited for the task facing her. Nevertheless, he found the sorry *Roebuck* was all that the Admiralty would provide. He had no choice. It was the *Roebuck* or nothing. Dampier swallowed both his misgivings and his ire. He provisioned the ship for twenty months, and refitted her as best he could. He then took her to sea in January 1699.

Despite his ship's poor quality, Dampier departed England with high hopes. His instructions from the Admiralty called for him to take the *Roebuck* to New Holland, make his way north of New Guinea, and then cruise to the east to search for the southern continent. At the same time he was free to "steer any other course" that he considered more likely to achieve his objectives.

Dampier had planned to get into the Pacific around Cape Horn and then to land on New Holland's east coast, so far missed by all previous explorers. In this way he would be able not only to fill in the still-blank right side of the New Holland rectangle but also to check out such supposed sightings of the continent Davisland.

But Dampier abandoned this scheme when he realized that with her departure date of January the rotten old *Roebuck* would not arrive off Cape Horn before July, the height of the Antarctic winter. She could never weather the tempestuous Cape at that season. Therefore, Dampier decided to go to the Pacific by way of the Cape of Good Hope. This meant that instead of landing on the unknown eastern shore of New Holland, he would have to touch first on the barren *west* coast of that land. In spite of this alteration in his plan, Dampier still intended to make his way via New Guinea to New Holland's eastern coast and then to strike out into the Pacific for the continent. Optimistic as always, he was sure that he would eventually find Terra Australis.

But Dampier soon found that he faced problems even more serious than the poor condition of his vessel. The ship's sailing master, who was responsible for implementing the orders of the captain, turned out to be a drunk who nearly ran the *Roebuck* aground on her first day out. Dampier's other officers, all Royal Navy, despised their commander as a former buccaneer, and sneered at his seamanship. The ship's first lieutenant, George

Fisher, was the most brazen in his contempt. He continually mocked Dampier, often expressing his derision openly in front of both officers and men.

In these disconcerting circumstances Dampier only made matters worse. He had no talent for command. Choleric and intolerant, he began responding to his first lieutenant and to his other officers with equal scorn. As the leaky old *Roebuck* rolled through the Atlantic, the tension between Dampier and his first officer grew white hot. Dampier, fearing that Fisher would try to seize the ship, took to carrying pistols cocked and ready for use.

With dissension rampant among the officers, discipline soon began to break down within the crew as well. The men became surly. They complained openly of living conditions. They muttered threats of mutiny.

Finally Dampier could endure it no longer. One day, with Fisher's insults ringing in his ears, he struck his lieutenant with a cane and had him put in irons. Dampier then made for the Brazilian port of Bahia and had Fisher thrown into a Portuguese prison. This forceful, if illegal, action had a sobering effect on the rest of the officers and crew of the *Roebuck*. There was no dissent when Dampier took the ship to sea again and pointed her toward the Cape of Good Hope.

Without Fisher's disturbing presence to hamper him, Dampier sailed the leaking and rolling *Roebuck* seven thousand miles from Brazil and around the Cape of Good Hope. He reached the western coast of New Holland on July 31, 1699. Dampier, who knew this region well from his earlier visit with the men of the *Cygnet*, named the barren country after himself: Dampierland. The *Roebuck* then set out northward along this grim coast.

At one point, with his crew suffering from thirst, Dampier went ashore for the purpose of capturing a native and forcing him to show the white men where they might find fresh water. Soon enough Dampier and his party came across a group of aborigines. The Europeans approached, intent on trapping one of the band. Suddenly the suspicious blacks began to make threatening noises and gestures. Dampier fired his gun into the air, thinking to cow the menacing locals. But to the aborigines the gun seemed only a noisemaker, not at all dangerous. Imitating the sound of the musket—"Pooh! Pooh! Pooh!," according to Dampier's account—the black warriors charged. Dampier now had to fire his weapon in earnest. He wounded one of the attackers and sent the rest flying away in terror. The men of the *Roebuck* were still thirsty, however.*

For five weeks the *Roebuck* cruised northward along this barren New Holland coast. With food and water constantly in short supply and his men beginning to suffer from scurvy, Dampier decided to interrupt his mission temporarily. He turned the *Roebuck*'s bows to the northwest and made for the island of Timor in the Indies, where England's Dutch allies maintained a strong garrison. There he refreshed his crew and refitted and resupplied his old vessel. Then he set off for New Guinea.

After arriving off New Guinea's north shore in December 1699, Dampier sailed along the mountainous coast toward the east, encountering a very large island which he named New Britain.

Although it was Dampier's plan to round New Guinea to the unknown east coast of New Holland and then strike out into the Pacific, where he expected to find Terra Australis, he suddenly found himself thwarted by circumstances beyond his control. First, despite the repairs made at Timor, the *Roebuck* was leaking worse than ever. Second, the crew, afraid of foundering in the increasingly unseaworthy vessel, was threatening to end the perilous voyage by mutiny. Dampier reckoned that he had no choice but to turn back.

Retracing his course, Dampier reached Timor again in May 1700. The Dutch shipwrights did their best to make the *Roebuck* seaworthy again, but it was clear that the old ship had only a little more voyaging left in her spongy hull. She was certainly not fit for still another thrust into the unknown Pacific. Given the situation, Dampier, now unwell himself, decided to make for home. The *Roebuck* set out west across the Indian Ocean and then around the Cape of Good Hope into the Atlantic.

In February 1701 the *Roebuck* arrived off Ascension Island in the South Atlantic. There the crumbling ship finally fell apart and sank. All those aboard, however, managed to reach the island, where they remained until April 1701, when a convoy of East Indiamen, bound for England, took them aboard.

---

*Whatever else his failings, Dampier's reluctance to engage in the slaughter of natives tells something about his relatively humane character.

When he reached England in August 1701, Dampier, to his shock, found himself facing a court-martial. His first lieutenant, Fisher, had escaped from his Brazilian prison and somehow scrambled back to England, where he had told his story to a sympathetic Admiralty that vowed to prosecute Dampier should he ever return to England. Upon his arrival home, therefore, Dampier was haled before a panel of Royal Navy officers to answer charges brought by Fisher.

Inevitably Dampier, the outsider, was found guilty. Declared unfit to command a Royal Navy vessel, he was fined all the pay due him. Thus Dampier again found himself without funds and once again saved himself by writing a book, an excellent account of his journey aboard the *Roebuck*. Entitled *A Voyage to New Holland*, the work aroused great interest.

Although Dampier was now over fifty years old, more adventures still lay ahead of him as a result of a worldwide war that had just broken out between Louis XIV and the coalition headed by England and Holland. This war, known as the War of the Spanish Succession, had its roots in the complex dynastic politics of the day.

In 1700, while Dampier was in the Pacific with the *Roebuck*, the king of Spain had died without a direct heir to the immense Spanish dominions that stretched from the far Pacific to America to Italy. In his will the Spanish monarch had left his throne to the youthful Philip of Anjou, the grandson of Louis XIV of France.

The "Sun King," as Louis was called, already ruled over a vast empire, which included the wilderness of Canada and Louisiana, as well as French possessions in Africa and India. Louis's superb army, numbering four hundred thousand men, dominated the European continent. The French fleet, though not so powerful as the army, posed a formidable threat to any potential antagonists. Other European nations trembled at the prospect of this mighty France taking control of the Spanish Empire by unifying the monarchies of both nations under Louis XIV and his grandson Anjou.

The enemies of the Sun King—not only the Protestant powers of England, Holland, and Denmark but Catholic Austria, and several principalities of the Holy Roman Empire as well—united in opposing the accession of Anjou to the Spanish throne. They warned that they would go to war if Louis upset the precarious balance of power by allowing his grandson to take the crown offered him.

Louis, drunk with visions of his own glory as exemplified in the grand palace of Versailles, disregarded the warnings. Philip of Anjou became king of Spain in 1701. War thereupon broke out between France and Spain on one side and the grand alliance of England, Holland, Denmark, Austria, Prussia, and much of the Holy Roman Empire on the other.

Although the leader of the anti-Louis coalition, William III—King of England and leader of the Dutch state—died in 1702 (after a fall from his horse), his death had no effect on the war. The childless William was succeeded by his deceased wife's sister, Anne, who prosecuted the hostilities with as much fury as if William had survived to conduct it.

The anti-Louis coalition fought what was essentially a land war, marked by the marches, sieges, feints, and occasional bloody battles characteristic of eighteenth-century combat. Nevertheless, there was some action at sea as privateering expeditions were mounted against Spanish commerce, especially in the Pacific, where the Manila galleons still carried rich cargoes of silver and Asian goods.*

Accordingly, not long after the outbreak of the War of the Spanish Succession, William Dampier, who had just written his book after suffering the indignities of the Royal Navy court-martial, was offered command of two privateering vessels commissioned to capture Spanish shipping in Pacific waters. He accepted the mission.

After departing England in 1702, Dampier's ships arrived in the Pacific without incident and then spent months in fruitless wandering in search of prey. The two ships returned home again in 1707, having taken no prizes of note. Citing Dampier's lack of skill as a leader of men, many blamed him for the failure.

The war was still on, and another privateering enterprise was being prepared for the Pacific. *This* voyage was to be led by a proven commander, Captain Woodes Rogers, already renowned for his privateering exploits. Rogers, recognizing that few men

---

*Privateering, in this era, was essentially legalized piracy. Armed merchant ships were issued licenses, called letters of marque, to attack enemy commerce. Backed by speculators, a privateering enterprise could be extremely profitable, depending on the kinds and numbers of prizes taken.

knew more about the Pacific than did William Dampier, enlisted the old buccaneer in his venture.

Rogers sailed in 1708, with Dampier as pilot and navigator. The collaboration proved extremely successful. Relieved of the responsibilities of command, Dampier was able to provide Rogers with expert guidance. Rogers, knowing how to fight his ships, captured a number of rich Spanish prizes. The expedition reached England again in 1711, having circumnavigated the globe and having made a profit in excess of two hundred thousand pounds.*

Home again, Dampier wrote still another successful book, as did Rogers. Dampier was now more famous than ever. He was still not rich, however, for in spite of the enormous success of the Rogers privateering venture, the prize money was tied up in litigation as the backers and participants in the journey wrangled over shares.†

Meanwhile, the War of the Spanish Succession was drawing to a close. In England the Tories, who opposed the war, had come to power in 1710 and had begun making secret overtures for a separate peace. They succeeded in negotiating a truce in 1712 with France. England's Dutch allies were enraged but could do nothing. In effect, England's withdrawal from the war meant an end to the conflict since the other allies could not continue alone. It also ensured the survival of Louis XIV as king of France.

With the Treaty of Utrecht in 1714, the War of the Spanish Succession officially came to an end after thirteen years of struggle. Although the Sun King's grandson was permitted to retain the Spanish throne, the treaty, signed by an aging Louis XIV, permitted him to do so only on condition that Spain and France maintain separate monarchies.

With the end of the war William Dampier's career also came to an end. In 1715, at the age of sixty-four, worn by the exertions of his vigorous life, he died in London. His accounts of his travels, literate and scientific at the same time, not only revived interest in the Pacific but also greatly influenced subsequent

---

*The expedition had also rescued, at the Juan Fernández islands, a marooned Scottish sailor, Alexander Selkirk. This man, set ashore after a dispute with his captain, had spent four years alone on a barren island when the Rogers expedition rescued him. Daniel Defoe later pirated his story for his novel *Robinson Crusoe.*
†The legal dispute continued for another eight years before being resolved by the Admiralty.

generations of English writers. In *Gulliver's Travels*, Swift has Gulliver refer to his "Cousin Dampier," and he places the land of Lilliput in the Pacific. Coleridge also read Dampier, and referred to him as "a rough sailor, but a man of exquisite mind."

It would be only a question of time before English ships returned to the Pacific to search for the southern continent. But first a Dutch lawyer, rich and influential, and no longer young, made one last stab at finding Terra Australis for Holland.

25
THE LAST DUTCHMAN

The year of Dampier's death, 1715, was a demarcation point in the history of the European powers and their colonies. Louis XIV died at the age of seventy-six, bringing down the curtain on a turbulent era dominated by royal France. The dust had also settled from the War of the Spanish Succession, and the real winners and losers in that conflict were now discernible. Nor were they necessarily the military victors.

In this watershed year, too, still another war—unrelated to the struggle over the Spanish throne, but one that would affect the future of the world in nearly equal measure—had been decided militarily, although it was not formally ended for another six years. Known as the Great Northern War, this conflict pitted the formidable military strength of Sweden against a coalition of states that included the newly emerging Russia of Czar Peter I, later called the Great.

The Europe of 1715 prefigured the world of the next two hundred years. France, shattered by the recent war and ruled by a conservative regent on behalf of a minor king, no longer dictated to the rest of Europe. With its armies crushed, its fleet wounded, and its national wealth depleted by Louis XIV's wars, the French state was temporarily paralyzed. But with its large and energetic population, productive economy, talented people, huge American, Indian, and African empire, and favorable geographic position—facing both the Atlantic and the Mediterranean—France was to rebound. Within a generation it would again take its place among the great powers.

Spain, already deep in decline, had also lost as a result of the war. With few sources of production, saddled with debt, and stretched by a far-flung empire whose wealth had finally begun to peter out, Spain would never again rank among the first-class powers. Nevertheless, as the possessor of vast dominions, it remained a major political player on the world's stage.

Sweden, too, was among the losers. Once the terror of the north, Sweden had been bled to death by its mad young king, Charles XII, on the plains of Russia. Although in 1715 the Great Northern War still sputtered on officially, in reality it had already been decided against Sweden. In the decades ahead Sweden would recede into the background.

The Turks were also in decline, beginning to sink under a corrupt and often inert government that had ignored technological advances in war and weaponry. Hopelessly out of date, the Ottoman Empire would take a long time to die, but the janissaries would never again struck fear into European armies.

A few European nations were little changed by the collisions of the previous fifteen years. Italy was still a conglomerate of petty states contended over by the major powers. Most of Germany was still part of the Holy Roman Empire, held together by nothing more than half-forgotten ties to the Hapsburg rulers of Austria. The Balkans were divided among the Austrians, Hungarians, and Turks. Denmark clung to its seagoing past.

Some states had gained in the struggles just concluded. Among these was Russia, created almost single-handedly by Peter the Great. Rich in resources yet economically backward, vast yet surrounded by enemies, Russia had crushed the armies of Sweden in the Northern War, thus gaining access to the Baltic and becoming, for the first time, a part of Europe. Still, unable to control its conservative clergy or its dangerously independent nobility, Russia would remain a muscle-bound giant well into the future.

Austria, too, was a winner. Vienna's armies, grown powerful during the War of the Spanish Succession, dominated Central Europe and intimidated the Turks to the south. Austria had also gained the former Spanish Netherlands as booty in the just-concluded war. Always a strong continental power, Austria now—temporarily—overshadowed France itself.

But it was England that had gained the most in the years of conflict. On land its armies, under John Churchill, the duke of Marlborough, had achieved impressive victories over the formidable French. At sea England's armed fleets had sailed the oceans unchallenged, protecting a mercantile empire that by 1715 stretched across the Atlantic to the colonies of North America and across the Indian Ocean to the English East India Company's commercial enclaves in India. Moreover, this empire was supported by a relatively firm political structure.

Queen Anne, the last of the Stuarts to reign, had died, childless, in 1714. Parliament had then invited Elector George Louis of Hanover in Germany, to take the throne of the land that was now being called Great Britain.* The German-speaking elector, a good Protestant, reigned as George I in full recognition that Parliament ruled the country. Thus Britain, a democracy devoted to property and business, prospered despite the new bitter political partisanship between the factions already known as Tories and Whigs.†

If Britain had won the most in the struggle with Louis XIV, then—by one of the bitterest of ironies—its ally Holland had lost the most. Holland had entered the war as one of the world's great powers. At the war's end, although one of the victors, the Dutch state was irredeemably reduced. A number of factors contributed to this descent.

Much of the struggle had taken place on Dutch territory, which had suffered severe damage as a result of military action. More important, with its soil at stake, Holland had had to expend many precious lives to fend off invasion. Proportionately, therefore, Holland, with fewer than three million people, had lost more men than any other combatant. This loss of manpower proved catastrophic. In the postwar period the Dutch state lacked sufficient skilled hands to restore its productivity.

The conflict had also exacted a terrible toll on Dutch sea power. Hundreds of vessels and thousands of sailors were lost during the war. With their resources necessarily devoted to the

*The throne of Scotland had been united with that of England, Wales, and Ireland in 1707. In this manner the United Kingdom and Great Britain came into being.
†Another complicating factor in Britain's political life was the continuing claim of the Stuart heir James III to be the legitimate king of England. Though he had many supporters, the Pretender, as he was called, was never well regarded by Britons. When he invaded Scotland in 1715 to regain the throne of his ancestors, the effort was easily defeated. Still, the Stuarts made mischief for decades.

land war in Flanders, the Dutch had not been able to replace
their lost ships. By 1715 Dutch sea power had declined precipi-
tously. Nor were the Dutch well positioned to rebuild their diminished sea power. In this postwar era ships were being
constructed with deeper hulls and broader beams to carry more
cargo and weaponry. But Dutch shipyards could not design their
craft with such proportions, for they would have been too deep
in draft to use the shallow Dutch harbors. The Dutch found
themselves severely handicapped in the competition to fabricate
bigger, faster, more powerful vessels.* Even in the design of rigging the Dutch had fallen so far behind other nations that a
Swedish traveler could write: "[Dutch] rigging is made after the
old fashion, with large blocks and thick cordage, heavy and
clumsy in every respect."

The long war had also crippled the Dutch economy by in-
terrupting commerce and nearly destroying the profitable fishing
industry. Holland could not hope for a quick recovery in either
area, for there was now little capital available for investment since
the government and the banks had exhausted their resources in
order to fight the war. It is estimated that in 1715 the national
debt of the Dutch republic stood at 148 million guilders, five
times what it had been in 1688. The Dutch now had to follow
the course of their ancient enemy Philip of Spain and borrow at
high interest rates just to service the debt occasioned by war.

Despite their reduced circumstances, however, the Dutch
clung tenaciously to their trading empire, regarding these overseas
territories as their best hope for restoring the national fortune.†
The Dutch East India Company still operated at a high volume, but
for the company the expansionist era was finished. The demand for
spices was continuing to fall. The company had lost many of its vessels to French privateers during the war, but it was a natural calamity
that had dealt the harshest blow. In 1699 a severe earthquake and
volcanic eruption had nearly obliterated the company's headquar-

---

*Because of the nature of the Netherlands—low, tidal, and sandy—Dutch harbors were
always silting up and needed constant dredging. Much of this work had been neglected
during the war. In any case, considering the equipment available to the Dutch engineers
of the day, there were limits to the depths that dredging could achieve. In the era of
bigger ships the Dutch merchant fleet suffered from this handicap as well.
†The decline of Dutch power was never reversed. Whereas, during the 1690s, the Dutch
could assemble about a hundred men-of-war each year, manning them with twenty-four
or twenty-five thousand men—apart from privateers and merchant vessels—in the second
half of the eighteenth century, they managed a war fleet of only seventeen sail, crewed
by no more than three thousand men.

ters settlement of Batavia in Java. Many of the company's warehouses and installations were destroyed. In the aftermath of the disaster an epidemic carried off many valuable employees, and the town became a hotbed of fever. Batavia rose from the ashes but never regained its commercial preeminence.

In the wake of its reverses the Dutch East India Company, reflecting the mood of the Dutch nation as a whole, adopted conservative policies aimed at achieving small but risk-free profits. Gone were the days of expansion into the Pacific. The company was no longer willing to gamble its scarce capital on speculative ventures, no matter how lucrative the potential gain.

Thus in 1717 the masters of the company rejected a suggestion that it create a colony in New Holland. The proposal, made by an experienced employee, Jean Pierre Purry, pointed out that all anyone *really* knew of New Holland was its barren coastlines. Its eastern shore or its interior might be overflowing with gold. It would take only a small amount of company backing, Purry declared, to establish a Dutch presence in New Holland before the British or French did so. At the very least Purry's idea made political sense, for British or French control of New Holland would inevitably threaten the now-shaky Dutch supremacy in the Indies. But the company, no longer willing to wager even a little to gain a lot, turned a deaf ear to Purry's program.

Meanwhile, as the Dutch East India Company pulled in its horns, the other Dutch trading company—the West India Company, established in 1621 to conduct trade in Africa and America—began to take on more economic importance. This company had lost New Amsterdam and other possessions during the Dutch republic's mid-century wars with England, but it had generally prospered even though it never reached the profit levels or achieved the political power of the Eastern enterprise. During the War of the Spanish Succession, however, the West India Company sustained relatively fewer shipping losses than the company in the East. As a result, during the postwar period the West India Company actually became more remunerative and far more enterprising than its older counterpart.

It was for this reason that a sixty-two-year-old Amsterdam lawyer chose the West India Company to sponsor his scheme to restore Dutch fortunes by making an all-out effort to find Terra Australis for Holland. Jacob Roggeveen had spent many years in the service of the East India Company and retired with much wealth and honor. He could have spent his declining years in ease, but the question of the southern continent nagged at him.

Terra Australis had been a subject of conversation in his family for many years. In 1696 Roggeveen's father had offered the East India Company a plan for the discovery of the continent, but war had intervened. When the elder Roggeveen died, the younger Roggeveen vowed to accomplish his father's dream if he ever had the resources to do so.

Jacob Roggeveen had immersed himself in old charts and maps. He had read thoroughly the reports of Tasman and other Dutch navigators. He knew that in the early seventeenth century the Dutch man-of-war *Orange* had reported a large landmass off the Pacific coast of South America. Roggeveen had read the works of the Portuguese pilot Quirós, who had been convinced beyond question that he had found the continent, and familiarized himself with the writings of the English buccaneer-scholar William Dampier. He was particularly intrigued by the claim of the English pirate Edward Davis, as recounted by Dampier, that he had sighted a large body of land west of Chile. Roggeveen speculated that this Davisland was probably an arm of the Pacific continent, perhaps the same land described by the lookouts of the *Orange*.*

The key to locating the elusive continent, as Roggeveen saw it, was to continue on a westward course far into the Pacific while keeping well south of the Tropic of Capricorn. Previous voyagers, he thought, had drifted too far north toward the equator or had failed to penetrate far enough to the west.

Well aware that the Dutch East India Company lacked the energy to sponsor any new, expensive Pacific explorations, Roggeveen made his case to the West India Company. Arguing that Terra Australis would be a New World, full of riches to help Holland regain its place in the world, he won the company's backing for his voyage. Although elderly by the standards of the day and far from renowned as a sailor, Roggeveen proposed to lead the expedition in person. He intended that the glory of the discovery, as well as a goodly share of any profit, should come to him and his family.

---

*By Roggeveen's time Davisland had been mentioned by so many writers that its reality had become virtually unquestioned. Its distance west of Chile varied, some accounts talking of five hundred miles while others put the distance at five hundred *leagues*—fifteen hundred miles. The discrepancy did not seem to concern Roggeveen.

On August 21, 1721, Jacob Roggeveen set out with three ships—the *Arend, the Thienhoven,* and the *Africaansche Galey*—bound for the Horn. After reaching the Drake Passage at the beginning of the Antarctic summer, the ships began to beat their way around the Cape.

Fighting freezing winds, fogs, blinding snow, and hail that slammed like bullets against the wooden planks of the vessels, Roggeveen's ships struggled for weeks toward the Pacific. At one point they were driven beyond latitude 62 degrees south. In the gray seas the mariners sighted huge icebergs rising like white cliffs from the churning waters. Roggeveen was aware that these islands of ice almost always reached the open water after breaking off from some mainland. He regarded the presence of icebergs as an additional indication that an immense land existed in these icy waters.

Having rounded the Horn at last, Roggeveen, anxious to escape the horrendous weather in these high southern latitudes, turned north for the Chilean coast. Reaching the Juan Fernández Islands, which lie offshore at approximately latitude 33 degrees south, the Dutch explorers rested for several weeks and then set out on a course generally west by northwest to look for Davisland.

After keeping to this course for approximately two thousand miles, well past the supposed location of his objective, Roggeveen not only failed to come across Davisland but sighted no land whatever. He concluded that the English pirate Davis, the buccaneer Dampier, and others who had reported seeing Davisland must have been "rovers from truth as well as rovers after the goods of the Spaniards." Still, he pressed on in the hope that he might yet sight the continent farther to the west.

At last, on April 5, 1722, Easter Sunday, the lookouts sighted land. Roggeveen's heart leaped. The land ahead lay at the latitude cited by Dampier and others as the location for Davisland, although much farther to the west.

Nearing the strange shore, the Dutch saw smoke rising from a number of fires. Smoke meant people. The country, seen through telescopes, appeared to be well watered, hilly, green with grass, and dotted here and there with trees. But as the Dutch ships came closer, the hope that they had sighted the southern continent faded. As Roggeveen reports in his journal, this territory did not accord with descriptions of Davisland. Most significant, it was only of "moderate elevation." Adds Roggeveen:

" . . . neither could it be the land which the aforementioned discoverers declare to be visible 14 to 16 miles beyond it and stretching away out of sight being a range of high land which . . . Dampier conjectured might be the extremity of the unknown southland." Roggeveen soon realized that instead of the continent, he had happened upon an island, a solitary Pacific outpost. He gave it the name it has borne ever since: Easter Island, in honor of the date on which it was first sighted.*

Seeking to anchor, the Dutch ships approached the coast. With an onshore wind blowing steadily, the ships crept cautiously ahead, carefully sounding all the while. As the mariners examined Easter Island through their telescopes, they began to make out what appeared to be huge stones. After a time the Dutch realized to their amazement that these were "idols" of astonishing size. Around the great figures they could discern natives prostrating themselves as if in prayer.

As the ships continued to seek an anchorage, a brave Easter Islander, rowing a skiff, came out from the shore and clambered aboard the *Arend*. One of Roggeveen's officers, Carl Behrens, describes in his journal what then ensued:

> We took [the islander] aboard our vessel and gave him a piece of linen cloth to wrap about his body, for he was quite naked; and we offered him beads and other trinkets, all of which he hung around his neck together with a dried fish. . . . We gave him a glass of wine to drink. . . . But he only took it and tossed it into his eyes. . . . Our musicians treated him to a specimen of each one of their instruments; and whenever any person took him by the hand he began at once to caper and dance about. We were much pleased to see his enjoyment; but we did not come to an anchor that day, and therefore let him go back to the shore. . . . But he parted from us unwillingly . . . cast his glances toward the land and began to cry out loudly. . . . I make no doubt that . . . he

---

*Easter Island has an area of only forty-five square miles. It lies twenty-three hundred miles west of Chile. According to later anthropological studies, it was first settled about A.D. 400 by Polynesians from the Marquesas. It is thought that the island was at one time relatively heavily wooded but that most of the wood was utilized in the transporting and erection of the famed monolith heads, most of which were carved in the period A.D. 1000 to A.D. 1600. To judge from the Dutch descriptions, the island still had some trees in the early 1700s.

was appealing to his god, as we could see great numbers of heathen idols erected on shore. . . .

Soon other islanders began visiting the Dutch ships and were suitably impressed, especially by seeing their reflections in the Dutch mirrors. They also stole some caps as well as one of Roggeveen's tablecloths.

After finally coming to anchor, Roggeveen led a landing party ashore on April 8, three days after first sighting Easter Island. The Dutch were nervous as they rowed toward the beach, for on the previous nights the natives had been seen making fires before their great stone heads. Would the Dutch be received with hospitality or hostility? Behrens describes the scene as the Dutch waded onto the beach: "Entrusting ourselves into God's hands, we landed with 150 men, soldiers as well as seamen. Our Admiral [Roggeveen] went along. . . . [Suddenly] some of [the natives] made as if to snatch our firearms from us. . . . we fired a volley, whereupon they ran away, being greatly frightened. Many of them were killed and many lay wounded. Future generations will tell stories of our deeds. . . . "

Despite the killings, the Dutch and the natives somehow managed to repair relations, for Behrens goes on to give his impressions of the Easter Islanders, garnered over the next few days:

The people were very happy, well-built, strong of limb, and swift of foot, friendly and pleasing in their manners. In color, they were light brown, almost like Spaniards, yet there were some amongst them who were darker skinned; others, on the other hand, had fair skins and yet others were reddish in color, as if burnt by the sun. We found no articles of furniture in their huts, except for red and white blankets which served as both garments and mattresses. . . . In the region in which we found ourselves, there was a village of about 20 houses. The people appear to carry no weapons, but to rely on their gods, or idols, great numbers of which had been erected on the beach. The natives would . . . worship these images, hewn out of stone and fashioned like the heads of men so artistically that we were much astonished.

The remarkable statues caused "deep wonder" in the Dutch, according to a log entry by Roggeveen. Standing on stone platforms that lined the shore, with their backs to the sea, the great figures often rose more than thirty feet high and weighed more than fifty tons. All had elongated heads. A number of them also sported tops that reminded the Dutch of hats but that were probably representative of the islanders' own hairstyles. Most of the statues also featured abnormally long ears, again like the islanders'. Most of the native people, according to Roggeveen, had "mutilated" their ears by pulling the lobes down almost to shoulder level, and piercing them to hold heavy ornamental rings. In addition, the Easter Islanders, like most Polynesians, were often heavily tattooed.

Roggeveen, unimpressed with the local canoes and huts, which he describes as "flimsy," puzzled over the islanders' apparent ability to raise the great heads: " . . . we could not understand how it was possible that people who lacked both solid timber for scaffolding and also strong ropes, could have erected such idols. . . . " The Dutch made little effort to solve the mystery. They did not even bother to question the people about their methods of construction and transportation or even about the purpose of the huge figures. They had not landed on Easter Island to study the native culture. Their purpose was to replenish water supplies and gather provisions. This they accomplished in short order. After a stay of less than a week they sailed on.

Roggeveen gives the impression that he felt relieved to leave the mysterious island behind, as if, for all its fascinating strangeness, the windswept land was also somehow repellent, a repository of primitive secrets that the stolid Dutch lawyer would rather not contemplate. In any event, he resumed the voyage. Striking out to the northwest and following a course taken by numerous other mariners, he made for the island-dotted latitudes just south of the equator.

At bottom a hardheaded realist, Roggeveen was now convinced that there was no southern continent in the waters where he had hoped to find it. If indeed such a continent existed, he concluded, it must lie far to the south of Capricorn and much farther west of Easter Island as well, in unknown waters that his little fleet—ill provisioned and showing signs of scurvy—was not prepared to visit. Roggeveen thus decided to head toward well-traveled seas, where he would readily find water and fresh supplies of meat and vegetables.

In May 1722 the Dutch ships reached the Tuamotu Archipelago. Here Roggeveen lost the *Africaansche Galey* when she ran aground on a reef. All of her crew were saved, however, and the surviving ships sailed on. A few days later, on June 2, the Dutch went ashore at one of the nearby Tuamotus to obtain water and fresh victuals. Suddenly, as the men were filling their casks, a war party of natives attacked the Dutch sailors with stones, killing ten of Roggeveen's men. The rest fled back to the ships.

Unable to obtain fresh vegetables, Roggeveen's crews now began to suffer the tortures of scurvy. Although this condition was always dreaded on any long sea journey during this era, most voyagers—apparently regarding the disease as inevitable and therefore too commonplace for special notice—usually afforded only a few lines to it in their logs. But Roggeveen's journal-keeping officer Carl Behrens, who was more soldier than sailor, was so appalled by the effects of scurvy aboard the Dutch vessels that in his later narrative of the journey he gave an unusually detailed and graphic account of the misery that scurvy caused the crews. His description is no doubt apt for any other ocean voyage of that time:

> No pen can describe the miseries of life on our ships. Only God knows what we have suffered. The ships reeked of death and the sick, and the stench alone was enough to make you ill. The stricken wailed and lamented unceasingly and their cries would have moved even stones to pity. Some of the afflicted became so thin and emaciated that they looked like walking corpses and death blew them out like so many candles. Others became very fat and were blown up like balloons. These poor devils soon went out of their wits. They were also afflicted with dysentery and passed nothing but blood, except for two or three days before they died when they passed a horrible mess that looked like gray sulphur. This was a sure sign that their hour had come. Others again were unable to walk and had to slide along the decks on their buttocks. All were overcome by a fearful melancholy. . . . There is no remedy except to eat fresh food. . . . Those who were not seriously ill with scurvy,

like myself, were still left very weak. . . . My teeth were
loose in my gums, which were swollen up almost as thick
as my thumbs, and my body was covered with swellings
the size of a hazelnut, red, yellow, green and blue in
colour. From this it can be seen that even the healthy
were sorely afflicted. . . .

Full of pity for his suffering men, Roggeveen abandoned all
thought of further exploration. He gave orders to make for the
Dutch East Indies and "salvation."

Pressing west, the ships passed through the invitingly lush
islands of the Samoa and Society groups. Despite the apparent
friendliness of the islanders, the Dutch, recalling previous native
attacks, lingered only to replenish water supplies and to obtain
whatever scarce provisions were available.

Roggeveen and his men were anxious only to find a safe
haven. They drove on, sailing into the seas north of New Guinea,
the by-now-classic route to the Spice Islands. At last the two surviving ships arrived in earthquake-ravaged Batavia. It was the end
of September 1722.

It had taken Jacob Roggeveen just over one year of voyaging
to become convinced that Terra Australis did not exist—at least
not where it was supposed to exist. Now, after all his disappointment and suffering, Roggeveen was to endure humiliation as
well.

The nabobs of the Dutch East India Company were enraged
when they found that Roggeveen had crossed the Pacific without
their permission. Company officials, apparently scorning Roggeveen's documents from his backers in the West Indies Company, seized his ships. They sent him and his men back to
Holland under guard. The company's officers in Java also impounded his record of his discoveries, declaring sarcastically that
they saw no value in them.

Back in Holland, Roggeveen, defeated by the Pacific, passed
into obscurity. He died a few years later in peaceful retirement.
With Roggeveen's failure, the Dutch imperial tide ceased to flow.
No Dutch master would ever again search for Terra Australis.
England now took up the quest for the southern continent.

26

JENKINS'S EAR AND THE COMMODORE

In the winter of 1740—seventeen years after Roggeveen's failure to find Terra Australis—a powerful British fleet was preparing for a voyage to the Pacific. Its mission, however, was not to explore but rather to savage Spanish shipping and possessions in the great ocean in order to punish "Spanish arrogance" and defend Britain's "right" to trade freely in the Spanish colonies.

The roots of this latest conflict between Britain and Spain stretched back four decades to the start of the eighteenth century, when the nature of world trade underwent a major shift.

In that era spices had begun to lose their commercial luster. Instead Europe craved sugar, and plantations had begun to spring up everywhere, especially in the American possessions of the Spanish Empire.

Because sugar cultivation required many hands, from cane cutters to overseers, Spanish colonial officials had begun to import thousands of slaves from Africa to work the plantations. The Spaniards relied on foreign trading companies to conduct this abominable business since Spain possessed no suitable African territories of its own.

Under long-standing Spanish policy, foreign trading companies conducted their business with the empire under a contract known as the asiento. This agreement, which applied not only to the commerce in slaves but to other imported goods as well, was customarily issued to the favored trading company of a favored nation. In addition to granting its holder the exclusive right to do business with Spanish colonies, the asiento spelled out tariffs, duties, and schedules.

By the beginning of the eighteenth century the asiento had become a coveted license, for all the European trading and manufacturing nations—Britain, France, and Holland—were deeply committed to what they called the mercantile system, a belief that national power depended on accumulating a surplus in trade by selling more goods to others than one had to import. Under the mercantile system trading nations strictly limited imports while requiring their colonies not only to furnish raw materials but also to buy only goods manufactured in the mother country. The system virtually assured the home country a favorable balance of trade. Because possession of the Spanish asiento was icing on the mercantilist cake, a golden prize that ensured soaring profits, the mercantilists vied shamelessly to win it, even though it required its holder to engage in slaving.*

When the War of the Spanish Succession ended in 1715, victorious Britain shouldered Holland aside and demanded that defeated Spain grant it the asiento, until then held by France. With no real alternative Spain capitulated. British merchants soon initiated a brisk trade with the Spanish Empire under the terms of the asiento, which, in addition to fabricated goods, required British traders to furnish Spanish America with 144,000 slaves over thirty years.

Within a few years after the British gained the asiento, the commerce with the Spanish Empire became critically important to Britain not only because of the profitable legal trade in slaves and goods but also because its merchants, under cover of the asiento, had established an even more lucrative traffic in contraband with the Spanish colonies.

Although it created enormous profits for some from slaving,

---

*Ironically, the mercantile system could not be effectively applied by Spain, since the mother country produced few goods for its colonies. Spain had to look to others to supply its colonies with manufactured goods as well as slaves. Thus the asiento.

commerce, and smuggling,* the asiento also helped to bring about, if indirectly, one of Britain's worst financial panics, a collapse that ruined many a businessman and might have shattered British democracy except for the leadership of one extraordinary man.

In 1711 some shrewd London merchants, anticipating a victorious end to the War of the Spanish Succession and the awarding of the asiento to Britain, had formed a joint-stock company to trade with Spanish America when the asiento became a reality. They called their enterprise the South Sea Company.

For the first few years after the war the company prospered modestly. Then, in 1718, the Hanoverian king, George I, became governor of the enterprise. Soon after this Parliament permitted holders of government bonds to convert these securities to company stock. To many it seemed that the government was backing the South Sea Company.

Investors rushed to buy shares. The price of the stock increased tenfold in a brief time. Then word began to filter out that the company could not make good on earlier promises of huge profits. Investors also discovered that the government was not after all a guarantor of the company. The South Sea Bubble collapsed with a roar. Thousands of speculators lost everything. Banks tottered. The stocks of other trading companies plunged. Ruined men killed themselves. It was learned that government ministers had been bribed to promote the company stock. A wave of popular fury threatened to engulf both the crown and Parliament.

In the midst of this crisis a brilliant and bizarre personality strode onto the stage. He was Robert Walpole. A veteran of the parliamentary battles of the day, Walpole, at forty-four seemed to some a grotesque figure. He was short of stature and immensely fat, and his face was enveloped by a series of double chins, but he was a consummate politician, a brilliant organizer, and an eloquent debater. Most important, he was untainted by

---

*In addition to furnishing access to legitimate commerce, the asiento had always been used by its holders as a cover for smuggling restricted goods into Spanish colonies. It was also a means by which traders could connive with local merchants and officials in Spanish colonies to evade import duties. The illegal traffic made possible under the asiento was almost always more profitable than the legal trade. It certainly was so with the British.

the South Sea Company scandal. He had resigned from the Whig ministry in 1717 and had since warned often against the rampant speculation in the South Sea Company. He was the one well-known figure in British ruling circles who retained any semblance of public confidence.

With characteristic gusto, Walpole flung himself into the bubble fray. He convinced Parliament and the country's investors that it was more important to restore the integrity of British financial institutions than to fix blame for the bubble. He worked out a complex plan to salvage the ruin. In effect he had the Bank of England and the East India Company assume responsibility for the larger blocs of South Sea Company stock. Slowly financial equilibrium was restored, and Britain returned to "business as usual."

In solving the South Sea bubble crisis, Walpole came to be regarded as Britain's "essential man," the only minister who could command the public trust. By 1721 he found himself the chief administrator of the realm—in effect, Britain's first prime minister.

A thoroughgoing mercantilist, Walpole supported British trade, not only with Spanish America under the asiento but also with the American colonies and with India, where the East India Company had now firmly established itself. With his eye thus fixed on business, Walpole aimed to keep the country out of war, assiduously resisting pressures to join in the hostilities that continually embroiled the rest of Europe. In the main he succeeded in keeping the peace. Despite some armed wrangles in colonial waters and some territorial disputes (such as Spain's unsuccessful attempt to regain Gibraltar), Britain managed to avoid costly general conflicts. As a result, the nation flourished in the aftermath of the South Sea Bubble. Through most of the 1720s and well into the 1730s, trade boomed and manufacturing grew immensely. The British merchant fleet expanded. Great fortunes were made. British sterling, it seemed, ruled the world.

During these years of thriving commerce, the siren song of the Pacific never quite died away. Investors, merchants, and politicians, meeting in London coffeehouses, often mused about the supposed riches of Terra Australis. Dampier's books still circulated, as did a volume called *The Book of Voyages,* published by one John Harris in 1705, calling for English exploitation of the southern continent. The more recent reports of Roggeveen's voyage to the Pacific also excited interest. Respected men like the famed privateer Captain Woodes Rogers never ceased calling for British bases in the Pacific in order to ensure Britain's dominant position in the world. There were also some who feared that the ancient rival, France, already rising from the ruin of the War of the Spanish Succession, would find the southern continent before Britain did.

Walpole, however, resisted the notion of Pacific exploration as he resisted war. If other nations wished to expend their wealth in pursuit of a Pacific empire, he seemed to say, let them. Britain already possessed more than enough profit-making enterprises overseas.

Yet under the placid and flourishing surface, all was not entirely rosy with Britain's mercantile system, particularly as it pertained to Spain. As possessors of the asiento British merchants had turned significant profits during the 1720s by legal—and illegal—trade with Spanish colonies. But the Spaniards had become increasingly resentful of British smuggling and had begun to retaliate by tightening customs at colonial ports, by replacing corrupt officials with honest ones, and by seizing illegal cargoes. As if to show it meant business, Spain had also allied itself once more with a resurgent France.

By the 1730s many British merchants began to view these Spanish policies as hostile acts or, at the very least, threats to "free trade" and "freedom of the seas." Anti-Spanish murmurings were heard in Parliament. Walpole serenely ignored the mutterings. He even managed to disregard a growing number of unfriendly encounters between Spanish coast guards and British merchantmen.

One such incident took place in 1731. In that year an English master mariner, Robert Jenkins, was bringing home his brig, the *Rebecca,* from the West Indies when a Spanish guard vessel stopped him on the high seas. According to Jenkins, an armed party of Spaniards boarded the *Rebecca* and proceeded to search it, ostensibly looking for evidence that Jenkins had been trading illegally. According to Jenkins, not only did the dons treat the British flag with disdain, but one of them even cut off one of Jenkins's ears. When the *Rebecca* arrived in England, Captain Jenkins stated his grievance to all who would listen. Although Jenkins's tale added to the growing ill will against the Spaniards, his complaint soon faded from the public mind.

Then, in 1735, a new and eloquent voice joined the parliamentary choir, and suddenly the muted mutterings against Spain swelled into a chorus. The new voice belonged to twenty-seven-year-old William Pitt, scion of a family that had made a fortune in the Indian trade. Elected to Parliament as a Whig, young Pitt soon proved himself a forceful advocate for what he termed the "rights" of British merchantmen. Although Walpole, too, was a Whig, Pitt became the prime minister's severest critic. He lashed out at Walpole for alleged corruption. He berated Walpole for refusing to uphold British honor against "Spanish arrogance." In a remarkably brief time Pitt succeeded in stirring British passions. Many clamored for war with Spain. Stolidly Walpole resisted the pressure, arguing that war would only drive Spain into the arms of France. To sabotage Walpole's policies, Pitt resurrected Captain Robert Jenkins and brought him before Parliament to retell the story of his missing ear. Jenkins was heard by a rapt audience. The MPs gasped in horror when he held up a transparent glass bottle in which floated an ear, preserved in alcohol.

All at once pamphleteers were demanding vengeance for Jenkins's ear. A majority of the British public—perhaps weary of twenty boring years of peace and prosperity—supported the war party. In 1739 Walpole yielded at last. Parliament declared war on Spain and the War of Jenkins's Ear began.*

Although the formidable British war fleet had deteriorated greatly during the more than two decades of Walpole's peaceful tenure, British strategists were nevertheless confident that the Spanish Empire would fall easily if assailed from the sea. The Admiralty devised a two-pronged strategy. One large force would conduct what a later age would call amphibious operations against Spanish strongholds in the Caribbean. At the same time a second, smaller fleet would make its way into the Pacific to attack the west coast of Spanish America as well as Spanish shipping in the great ocean.

---

*Despite the collapse of his policies, the king would not accept Walpole's resignation, and he had to preside over a war that he did not support. It was not until 1742 that Walpole was defeated by a vote of parliament. In 1742 he was created earl of Orford and ceased to be prime minister. He died in London in 1745. As for Captain Jenkins, he later served as captain of a ship in the East India Company's service and, following his seagoing days, was named company supervisor at St. Helena.

In the opening months of the war the Caribbean phase of the conflict proved wildly successful for the British as their forces captured and dismantled key Spanish fortresses at Portobelo and at the mouth of the Chagres River on the isthmus. Encouraged by this early success, the Admiralty began planning for a knockout assault on the great Spanish stronghold of Cartagena.*

Meanwhile, as the Royal Navy won initial victories in the Caribbean, eight British ships, six of them men-of-war, were preparing at Portsmouth to carry the War of Jenkins's Ear to the Pacific.

In command of the Admiralty's Pacific fleet was an awkward, taciturn career officer who, at the age of forty-three had already served twenty-eight years in the Royal Navy. He was George Anson, a hawk-nosed, red-faced man whose shyness in social situations often gave the impression of coldness.

Born in 1697 in Staffordshire, Anson was the second son of a prominent family. With little talent for letters and no interest whatsoever in the church, young Anson decided to make his career in the Royal Navy. At the age of fifteen, he enlisted as a midshipman. Anson had discovered his true calling. He found that he could set a course, fix a position, and map a coast with the best. Moreover, he was brave, a good seaman, and resolute in adversity. His men respected him. Inevitably he won rapid advancement.

In 1724, still only twenty-seven, Anson was named captain of a man-of-war, the *Scarborough,* a powerful guard ship stationed off the coast of South Carolina to intercept pirates. In 1737 Anson was given command of a major fighting ship, the sixty-gun *Centurion,* and sent to patrol the Guinea coast of West Africa.

Upon the outbreak of the War of Jenkins's Ear, the Admiralty confidently chose Captain George Anson to lead the British thrust into the Pacific. He took over his command in November 1739. In January 1740, while engaged in assembling his force at Portsmouth, Captain Anson was promoted to commodore, a rank more suitable to the leader of a fleet.

Although he was an experienced and talented officer, Commodore Anson collided with one obstacle after another in readying his squadron for sea. The Royal Navy, allowed to deteriorate

*This attack failed miserably, as did a similar operation against Havana.

over the previous two decades of peace, had become a muddle of inefficiency and corruption. As a result, necessary work on Anson's flotilla was accomplished at a snail's pace. Stores, provisions, and ammunition for the voyage trickled in. Anson fumed. Months dragged by before the carpenters finished their work. Provisions were delivered at last: poor-quality salted horsemeat and pork, certain to rot in storage casks, and bread as hard as rock. Aware that these stores were the best that he could obtain from venal administrators, Anson accepted them. At the same time he vowed to himself that if ever the opportunity came his way, he would root out the decay that was undermining British naval might.

The most formidable obstacle that Anson faced at Portsmouth was the scarcity of recruits to serve aboard his vessels. Life aboard wooden ships, even for officers, had always been terrible. Food and water had always been foul, scurvy a torment, and the lash of discipline harsh. The life had always been dangerous, too. A man might fall from the rigging, be washed overboard, or be killed in combat. But in Anson's time conditions had grown even worse, primarily because ships had become much larger and needed more men to work them. In the navy of 1740 it took five or six hundred men to handle a sixty-gun warship. This was three times the crew needed only fifty years earlier. These men had to live crowded belowdecks, where there was no ventilation. Fevers spread like wildfire. The ship reeked of rotten meat, bilge water, and unwashed bodies. It also stank of the vats of urine into which the mariners relieved themselves. (The piss water was used to douse fires, thus saving the fresh water.) With so many men living under such wretched conditions, fights were frequent, rules difficult to enforce. The harsh discipline of the past had escalated to a kind of mindless cruelty. In the navy of Anson's time, crewmen could be flogged, keelhauled, kept in irons for months, or made to run a gauntlet of tarred rope ends for the smallest of infractions. It was little wonder, then, that few went to sea willingly in 1740.

Anson, struggling to ready his ships at Portsmouth, resorted to any means available to secure crews. He sent press gangs ashore to kidnap likely-looking lads. He took seamen from the merchantmen that entered the harbor. He had his officers scour the local jails. He sent recruiters into the countryside to snare farm boys. The Admiralty even drafted partially disabled sailors and soldiers from the Chelsea Hospital on the Thames to crew the squadron. Five hundred of these veterans—some of them well up in their sixties, others crippled, and a few suffering from dementia—were marched to Portsmouth and ferried to Anson's ships. Not surprisingly, all those who were able to do so deserted at the first opportunity. Still, some two to three hundred of the hospital patients remained aboard, physically unable to drag themselves away.*

The Admiralty also sent Anson 210 recently recruited marines. These were the opposite of the hospital inmates: mere boys who had never fired a musket or spent a day at sea.

In September 1740, manned by muttering ancient mariners and raw youths, the fleet put to sea. Anson's squadron consisted of his flagship, the *Centurion*, 60 guns and 500 men; the *Gloucester*, 50 guns, 350 men; the *Severn*, 50 guns, 350 men; the *Pearl*, 40 guns, 250 men; the *Wager*, 28 guns, 140 men; and the sloop the *Tryall*, 16 guns and 80 men. In addition to the six warships, there were two supply vessels, the merchantmen *Anna* and *Industry*.

Although Anson's mission was supposed to be a secret, the Spanish enemy had long ago gotten wind of it. Thus, when Anson finally departed for the Horn, a Spanish war fleet also sailed. The Spaniards were under orders to get to the Pacific ahead of Anson and there confront the British before they could do any damage along the coast of South America.

It was early March 1741 when Anson's force at last approached Cape Horn. So far the voyage had been relatively uneventful except for the fact that dozens of seamen had died of "fevers and fluxes" belowdecks. But as the ships passed through the Le Maire Strait to round Tierra del Fuego, they were hit by the first of a series of tumultuous storms that tossed them about like toys. Although Commodore Anson had anticipated bad weather rounding the Horn at that time of year, neither he nor anyone else could have imagined the violence of wind and wave that now assailed the British task force.†

*To combat it epidemic desertion, some commanders kept seamen aboard while their ships were in port, often manacling them to ensure against escape. Locked up aboard ship, however, men were often allowed visits from wives or the paid ladies of the port. Hammocks, slung between the big guns belowdecks, served as many a conjugal bed and as sites for more profane encounters. In this manner the phrase "son of a gun" supposedly originated.

†The story of the voyage comes from Anson's own notes, descriptions, logs, and other reports and from a book, written from Anson's papers and issued under the name of Richard Walter, chaplain of the *Centurion*.

Through March, April, and May, except for a few brief interludes, tempests lashed the sea into heaving mountains of foam. Day after day the ships struggled westward. Frequently they rolled so much that men were hurled overboard or thrown about below, cracking skulls and breaking bones. Repeatedly they had to lie to under reefed sails or bare yards. When they tried to make way against the roar, sails often blew out with a crack of canvas and spars. The rigging froze. Men, trying to work in this frigid hell, suffered frostbite and lost fingers and toes to the cold. Seams opened in the hulls. It was impossible to keep dry below-decks as the vessels continually shipped freezing water. Yet the fleet persisted, despite the ice that covered the decks and hung in long shards from the rigging and despite the seas that crashed incessantly over the bows.

Frequently, in the violence and gloom of the storms or in the blackness of the windy nights, the ships lost sight of one another. But somehow they regrouped again, signal lanterns winking across the roiled waters. But one day two of the men-of-war, the *Severn* and the *Pearl*, lost contact with the rest of the fleet and were not seen again. Anson thought they had gone down.*

Inevitably, as the British squadron fought on, scurvy broke out, adding to the suffering of the crews. Soon men were dying every day. The number of dead was particularly high among the elderly pensioners aboard. In April a total of forty-three men died aboard the *Centurion* alone. In May the number doubled. Still the ships pressed on westward toward the Pacific. By now they were scattered over the tempestuous sea, no longer able to hold their formation. But each captain knew to rendezvous at Juan Fernández off the coast of Chile if his ship survived the Horn.

It was the end of May when Anson's flagship, the *Centurion*, reached Pacific waters and headed north toward Juan Fernández. On June 9, 1741, two hundred exhausted men out of an original complement of almost six hundred dragged themselves

---

*They had been blown back into the South Atlantic. Battered, beaten, and hopelessly out of touch with the rest of the fleet, the two ships made their way home, a fact that Anson learned only much later. A third ship of the fleet, the storeship *Industry*, was also making her way home at this time, but she had been sent back by Anson before the fleet began the struggle around the Horn, after transferring all her provisions. The Spanish fleet that had been sent to intercept Anson when he reached the Pacific likewise never made it around the Horn. It had already been dispersed by the horrendous weather and, unlike Anson's ships, never managed to regroup.

on deck to view the green valleys of Juan Fernández. It was the first land they had laid eyes on for months. Wrote the *Centurion*'s chaplain, Richard Walter: "Even those amongst the diseased, who were not in the very last stages of the distemper, crawled up to the deck, to feast themselves with this reviving prospect."

It was generally believed at this time that the best way to cure the sick after a long sea voyage was to get them ashore as soon as possible. As soon as the *Centurion* was brought to anchor, Anson had his few healthy crew members set up tents on the dry land. Then, with Anson himself bearing a hand, about 180 of the sick were ferried ashore in boats. There they were fed on seal meat as well as the turnips and watercress that grew wild near the anchorage. Most of the sick men began to recover within a week. Meanwhile, Anson worried about the fate of the rest of his fleet.

Then, coming in separately, some of the other ships began to arrive at Juan Fernández. The sloop *Tryall* came in first, then the man-of-war *Gloucester* and finally the supply ship *Anna*.

Anson had only four vessels left to him out of his original fleet of eight, and of the four remaining ships only three were men-of-war. To make matters worse, all the ships were in wretched condition, as were their few surviving crewmen. While his men regained their health at Juan Fernández, Anson considered his best course. It was clear that given his reduced numbers, he could not fulfill the part of his assignment that called for attacks on land installations along the Pacific coast of South America. He barely had enough seamen left to work the ships. He could not afford to lose more in land attacks that he was too weak to win. But he decided that the fleet *could* still capture Spanish prizes. Having survived the terrors of the vicious Horn, the commodore now meant to surmount the dangers of the vast Pacific.

27

THE HERO

To prepare for his Pacific campaign, Anson put every able-bodied man to work reprovisioning and repairing his surviving ships. Concluding that the storeship, *Anna* was too battered to be of any further use, Anson had her broken up, and her tackle, sails, masts, rigging, and ironwork used to repair the *Centurion*, *Gloucester*, and *Tryall.* By mid-September 1741, having spent three months on Juan Fernández, the truncated British flotilla was once again ready for action.

On a clear September day Anson's lookouts on Juan Fernández spotted a Spanish sail on the horizon. The *Centurion* went out to chase her, but the quarry got away. Fortunately, however, the *Centurion* then happened upon another Spaniard, a merchant. This vessel soon struck. Boarding the Spaniard, Anson learned, for the first time, that a Spanish fleet had been sent to intercept him but that the Spaniards, scattered by bad weather, had given up the chase. According to those aboard the captured merchantman, Spanish officials thought that Anson, too, had been defeated at the Horn. Anson was much encouraged by this intelligence. He realized that the presence of British warships in the Pacific would come as a shock to the enemy.

Eager to take advantage of the element of surprise, Anson brought the Spanish merchantman back to Juan Fernández. There he added the guns from the broken-up *Anna* to the Spaniard's own ordnance.* Anson now had four well-armed vessels with which to operate. Wrote Chaplain Walter: "And now the spirits of our people being greatly raised, and their despondency dissipated by this earnest of success, they forgot all their past distresses . . . and [they] labored . . . in completing our water, receiving our lumber, and in preparing to take our farewell of the island."

When all was ready, Anson ordered his ships to make their way separately along the coast and take whatever enemy prey came their way. They would reunite with their prizes at a prearranged spot near the equator. In this way, Anson explained, the British could inflict maximum damage at little risk to themselves.

The plan worked well. All four British men-of-war made it to the rendezvous, and they had three more prizes with them as well. The loot, however, was not much. The British had captured cargoes of "steel, iron, wax, pepper, cedar" and other goods of little use or value. Furthermore, Anson now had prisoners to feed. He also found that his sixteen-gun sloop, the *Tryall*, was no longer seaworthy. He transferred her guns and crew to one of the captured Spanish merchants, thereby gaining what amounted to a new frigate, and scuttled the *Tryall*.

Concluding that he had to dispose of his burdensome prisoners, Anson decided to mount a shore raid on the nearby port of Paita in Peru. He counted on surprise to compensate for his thin ranks. Approaching the town after dark, Anson sent several boatloads of armed men ashore. The British raiders marched boldly into Paita, beating their drums as if they were a thousand strong. The defenders fled. Anson then put his prisoners ashore and calmly ransacked the town. The British also looted the local custom house, and when the governor refused to reveal where the town's cattle had been hidden away, they burned the port. They also sank all but one of the anchored merchantmen in the harbor. That one Anson added to his fleet, giving him seven vessels, only two of them British men-of-war: the still-powerful *Centurion* and *Gloucester*.

It was February 1742. Anson now maneuvered to capture what had become known as the Manila Galleon, a great ship that sailed across the Pacific every year from Acapulco to the Philip-

---

*In this era virtually all merchant vessels carried *some* armament, even if only light cannon to ward off pirates.

pines, carrying silver worth millions. The galleon always departed Acapulco in March in order to reach Manila in time to do its business and then to leave again in July on the seasonal winds back to Mexico.

To intercept the galleon, Anson stationed his squadron in a wide arc approximately forty miles off the coast of Mexico. From March 1 until March 23 the British lay in wait. But the magnificent prey never appeared. Anson concluded—correctly—that the Spaniards, by now aware of the British off their coasts, had canceled that year's sailing. The advantage of surprise was gone. If the Manila Galleon remained in port, Anson knew, so would every other Spanish trader, and prey would be scarce in these waters. With his water running low and his prospects few, Anson lifted what was, in effect, his seaborne siege of Acapulco.

He then decided that if he could not find Spanish prey in American waters, he would cross the Pacific to the Philippines, where the Spaniards did not expect him. Anson found a safe place on the coast where he took on water. He also scuttled all the ships in his fleet except his big men-of-war, the *Centurion* and the *Gloucester*. Then, with all his surviving crewmen aboard the two warships, he sailed down to latitude 13 degrees north and set out to cross the Pacific.

Having committed his ships to this immense journey, Anson ran into the worst of weather patterns for a sailing vessel: failing winds. The northeasterly trades that almost invariably blow in the equatorial latitudes suddenly went awry. Day after day the winds were either contrary or light. At the end of seven weeks, which was the usual time required to cross the Pacific, Anson's two ships had made barely two thousand miles, a mere quarter of the distance to the Philippines.

Both of Anson's vessels were rapidly deteriorating, having developed serious leaks and sprung masts. The *Gloucester's* mainmast was so badly damaged that it was on the point of falling down altogether. It had to be cut away, and a jury mainmast rigged up. To make matters worse, scurvy had again broken out. The only saving grace was that rain fell regularly to supply drinking water. Still, Anson had no choice but to struggle on.

The weeks crawled past. Men sickened and died in their hammocks. At the end of July a westerly storm opened a new and deadly leak in the *Centurion's* bow. As a result, her men and officers had to man the pumps constantly. The *Gloucester* suffered even worse. The storm tore away her jury-rigged mainmast and opened so many leaks that her holds filled with seven feet of water. Of the seventy-seven men still alive aboard her, fifty were too sick with scurvy to work. After inspecting her, Anson's carpenter determined that she was beyond repair. Anson made the hard decision to abandon the ship. After taking her crew and salvageable stores aboard the *Centurion*, she was scuttled. It was August 16, 1741. The *Centurion* had been struggling across the Pacific for ten weeks.

At last, on August 26, the *Centurion*'s lookouts sighted land ahead: the green island of Tinian, just north of Guam. Here the ship came to anchor. As on Juan Fernández so many months earlier, Anson set his sick ashore, where they found healing fruit, wild grass, coconuts, and fresh water. They also discovered a single Spaniard and a work party of "Indians"', who had come from Guam to slaughter some of Tinian's wild cattle. The British captured the Spaniard and his boat. The natives were set free.

After seeing to it that all his sick men were made comfortable, Anson, who had a case of scurvy himself, established his headquarters on the island, leaving the ship anchored and manned by about half his remaining crew. The British passed several peaceful weeks at Tinian, resting and gathering provisions. Anson was cured of his scurvy. Then a new calamity struck.

A nocturnal storm swirled down on the island. Throughout the night the winds howled and the rain pelted down, doing much damage to the shore camp. But the worst damage was revealed with the coming of daylight: the *Centurion* was no longer in the harbor. Had she been driven out to sea by the tempest and sunk? Had she been wrecked on some unknown shoal?

Anson had to anticipate the worst. If the *Centurion* were indeed lost, the men left to him would be in a desperate plight. Marooned on an island seldom visited, they were not likely to be rescued. Perhaps even worse, they were vulnerable to attack by Spanish warships from the Philippines. Somehow Anson maintained his facade of calm and steadiness, though Chaplain Walter noted that like the rest of them, the commodore "had doubtless his share of disquietude."

Anson called his people together and proposed a plan to bring them all to safety. The small boat that had carried the Spanish work party from Guam was still available. They would haul it ashore, Anson said, and modify it, adding some twelve feet to its keel length.

They had the skilled hands to do the job: two carpenters and a blacksmith, each of whom had all his tools ashore. Anson said he was certain that once rebuilt, the Spanish boat would be big enough and sturdy enough to bear all of them to the Portuguese colony of Macao, eighteen hundred miles away in China. From there, he declared, they could make their way up the Pearl River to the nearby port of Canton where the East India Company maintained a trading facility, and where they would find British merchants to take them home. The men set to work to rebuild the Spanish boat. Anson himself helped cut down trees and saw them into planks.

Whether Anson would really have tried to make it to China in such an overcrowded, barely seaworthy craft will never be known, for nineteen days after the *Centurion*'s disappearance, a lookout spotted her returning and came running down to the camp with the joyful news. Chaplain Walter describes the moment: "The lookout . . . saw some of his comrades, to whom he hollowed out with great exstasy, 'the ship, the ship.' The Commodore, on hearing this pleasing and unexpected news, threw down his axe, with which he was then at work, and, by his joy, broke through for the first time the equable and unvaried character which he had hitherto observed."

Once more the *Centurion* anchored in the bay. Her crew told how the storm had torn the ship from her moorings, driving her from the harbor into deep water. She had been dashed about crazily in the storm-tossed darkness, her anchor hanging, her gunports awash, taking on heavy seas. When the tempest finally abated, she was far out at sea. The crew struggled to get control of her. First they wrestled her dangling anchor back aboard, a process that took a day and a half. Then they pumped out her hull. Finally they managed to get sail on her and to beat back to Tinian. Shorthanded, fighting leaks, they had taken many days to get back.

Anson decided to tarry no longer in Tinian but to take the damaged *Centurion* on to Canton for refitting. She reached Canton safely in November 1742. For the next six months she lay in port undergoing repairs. Finally, in April 1743, the *Centurion* went to sea again.

Anson had told port officials and his own men that he intended to head the *Centurion* home. However, he had a very different plan in mind. He intended to return to the Pacific and capture the Manila Galleon. He reasoned that because no galleon had sailed from Acapulco in the previous year, thanks to the presence of his fleet off the Mexican coast, this year's galleon was probably carrying *twice* the normal cargo of silver in order to make up for the missed voyage. Moreover, he assumed the galleon had left Acapulco in March, the usual departure time, and would be arriving in Philippine waters in June. Anson turned the *Centurion*'s bows northeast to the Philippines, intending to take up a position athwart the galleon's sailing route.

Arriving in good time, the *Centurion* lay in wait for three weeks. At last, at first light on June 20, 1743, the long-sought sail appeared on the eastern horizon. Anson made for her immediately.

Although the galleon must have sighted the British warship, she kept coming—a course that confounded the men of the *Centurion*. Did the galleon intend to fight instead of fleeing? Had her master perhaps mistaken the *Centurion* for a Spanish escort? Or was it possible that the Spaniard simply could not believe that he would be attacked in what were essentially home waters? The galleon finally heaved to under topsails and hoisted colors with "the standard of Spain flying at the top-gallant masthead." The Spaniard wanted a fight.

The *Centurion*, closing, answered the challenge of the Spaniard by raising the British flag and Anson's personal pennant. Through his glass Anson could see the galleon clearing for action, her crew hurling live cattle and loose cargo overboard into the sea.

Coming within range, the *Centurion* fired her light forward chase guns. The galleon returned the fire with her stern chase guns. The *Centurion* now overhauled her quarry. The battle was about to be joined.

Anson had devised a novel tactic to make up for his depleted numbers. Lacking enough men to fire a full broadside, he had trained his crew to fire the ship's cannon in sequence, rather than in one grand salvo. Now, standing calmly on his quarterdeck with drawn sword, Anson gave the order to commence firing on the galleon, using the new system.

One after another the *Centurion*'s big guns roared forth yellow fire and shot. To keep up this "rolling fire," Anson's men had to resort to extraordinary physical exertions. While two seamen, stationed at each piece, loaded and cleaned the barrels after each shot, the ship's few gunners dashed from cannon to cannon, sighting and firing at the Spaniard. Although this was incredibly fatiguing, especially under the tension of combat, the *Centurion* managed to keep up a running bombardment of the galleon, one shot booming out after another.

The *Centurion*'s peculiar firing pattern confused the Spaniards. The standard Spanish practice in battle was to lie down on the decks under protective nettings, take a broadside, and then leap to their guns to return fire. But under the continuous onslaught of the *Centurion* the Spanish response was disorganized. To make matters worse for the flustered Spaniards, thirty British sharpshooters stationed high in the *Centurion*'s rigging poured a murderous spray of lead down on the galleon.

At some point the netting over the Spaniard's deck caught fire. Her crew cut it away and tossed it, still burning and hissing, into the sea. Now the British marksmen swept the galleon with even more rapid and effective small arms fire.

All at once another fire broke out aboard the Spanish ship, this time in the rigging. Anson feared that unless he could bring the battle to a rapid close, he might lose his prize to the flames at the last minute. The British redoubled their fire and closed further in order to board.

The Spanish still fought desperately, though blood from the galleon's dead and wounded was now pouring from the scuppers. The shouts of Spanish officers could be heard over the crashing of cannon, the cracking of muskets, and the screaming of the wounded. Suddenly the two ships came together with a shivering impact. The galleon—much larger than her attacker, with three times the crew—loomed over the *Centurion*'s starboard quarter. The British began to board their quarry.

All at once it was over. The galleon surrendered. The dead and dying littered her decks. Except for the cries of the wounded and the crackle of flames in the galleon's rigging, an exhausted silence fell over both vessels. The fighting had lasted an hour.

Word came that the *Centurion*, too, had caught fire—in an area near the powder room. If the powder went up, both ships would be blown to pieces. The British fought to douse the flames. In the end the fires were quenched aboard both the *Centurion* and the Spaniard. Anson and his men could now examine their prize.

She was *Nuestra Señora de Covadonga*, a powerful fighting ship that mounted thirty-six heavy cannon and another twenty-eight lighter guns. She carried a crew of 550 men. She also carried a great fortune in her hold: 1.3 million pieces of eight and 35,000 ounces of pure silver as well luxury goods of all kinds. Although she had taken a pounding in the battle, with sixty-seven of her crew killed and another eighty-four wounded, she was still seaworthy. Anson, who had lost only two men killed and sixteen wounded, put a prize crew aboard her. Then, having no other option, he crammed her four hundred or so survivors into the stinking hold of the *Centurion*.

Exulting in victory and good fortune, the British victors sailed the *Centurion*, and her prize, back to Canton, where they arrived in late July 1743. Anson landed his prisoners and sold the galleon after first transferring her treasure to the *Centurion*. He then spent almost six months in port while the *Centurion* received a proper refitting. In January 1744 the *Centurion* again set sail. This time she *really* headed for the Cape of Good Hope and home.

In June 1744 the *Centurion* anchored at Spithead. She had been away nearly four years and had circumnavigated the globe. Anson and his men were greeted with much acclaim. It was estimated that the *Centurion* had brought home a treasure worth more than four hundred thousand pounds.*

By the time the *Centurion* dropped her anchor in English waters after her epic voyage, the War of Jenkins's Ear had escalated into a larger conflict called the War of the Austrian Succession. As a result, Britain was again locked in combat with France as well as Spain.

The war began when Maria Theresa, daughter of the Austrian ruler, Charles VI, assumed the throne after her father died without a male heir. Philip V, king of Spain, disputed Maria Theresa's succession, claiming that as the closest male relative of the

---

*Anson's share, which under the rules of the day, gave a captain one-eighth of the loot captured, made him rich for life. But every man shared in the prize money, officers and crewmen alike, and all the survivors were well satisfied with the bonuses they received.

deceased Charles, he was the legitimate heir. France supported Spain, while Britain—already fighting Spain in the War of Jenkins's Ear—lined up on the side of Austria. Prussia allied with France and Spain, while Holland joined Austria and Britain.

By the time Anson returned from the Pacific, the War of the Austrian Succession was in full conflagration. Though primarily a European land war, the conflict also pitted Britain and France against each other at sea, in the North American wilderness, and even in India. Given command of the British Channel fleet, Commodore Anson once again became a hero when on May 3, 1747, off Cape Finisterre, he led his forces to victory over a large French convoy bound for the Indies.

Despite such naval victories, however, the War of the Austrian Succession ended indecisively in 1747, although by the terms of the peace treaty, Maria Theresa was confirmed as ruler of Austria. For Britain and France, however, the war had reignited the old imperial rivalry. Both nations were now resolved to expand their empires in North America and in India. It was only a question of time before they would clash again to decide the imperial future for both nations.

In the meantime, accounts of Anson's Pacific voyage had once again fired the imagination of the British public. Tales of the southern continent were again circulating, and nautical adventures were in fashion. One of the most popular of these was a memoir called *The Narrative of the Loss of the Wager*, by John Byron, who had been a seventeen-year-old midshipman aboard one of Anson's ships, the *Wager*, when she was wrecked on the rocks of Chile after rounding the Horn.

In his narrative Byron told how, fighting against seemingly insuperable odds, he had found his way back to England after the *Wager*'s loss, surviving ill treatment by natives, a year of living among savage islanders, and cruel imprisonment by the Spaniards. Byron's tale, a romantic echo to Anson's epic Pacific cruise, portrayed the commodore's feat not only as a glorious example of British seamanship but also as proof of British superiority at sea.

Commodore Anson knew better. After years of hard service he was acutely aware of the underlying weakness of the Royal Navy, clearly revealed in his own Pacific venture and even in the victories recently achieved in the War of the Austrian Succession. He had not forgotten the horrendous conditions under which his fleet had sailed to the Pacific. He was well aware of the dishonesty of the naval administration ashore. He knew firsthand the incompetence of naval officers who had achieved advancement through favoritism rather than merit. He was still mindful of the cruel deaths his crews had suffered aboard his ships during his voyage of 1740–44. Probably better than any other officer in the British navy, Anson knew from personal experience that with France rebuilding its own fleet in anticipation of a new imperial war, the Royal Navy required a complete overhaul. Some romantics might be dreaming of an easy British conquest of the Pacific, but Anson knew that Britain first needed a war fleet capable of conquering the French. Fittingly, Anson became the builder of that fleet.

28

TO THE SOUTH LAND

The indomitable Anson, who had been created a life peer (Lord Anson, Baron of Soberton) in recognition of his victory off Cape Finisterre, was appointed first lord of the Admiralty in 1751. He now possessed the power to set in motion his long-contemplated reforms of the Royal Navy.

He began by mounting a campaign against corrupt suppliers, replacing them with honest tradesmen. He fired navy administrators who took bribes from contractors. He compelled the dockyards to render accounts to the Admiralty. He revised the Navy Discipline Act, instituting courts-martial with uniform procedures. He carried out frequent inspections of the fleet and began a system of regular oversight by senior officers. He established an official corps of marines. He improved the lot of seamen by moderating discipline, ordering fairer distribution of prize money, and providing better food and living conditions aboard British ships.*

Anson also focused on training, insisting upon constant ship-

---

*Life aboard a wooden ship still remained difficult: cramped, wet, dangerous, and often exhausting. The discipline was still harsh by later standards. Provisions still went bad on long voyages. Men still got scurvy and fevers or fell from the rigging. Press gangs still had to be used on many occasions to fill out the complement of ships. Nevertheless, Anson's reforms, while directed mostly against corruption and incompetence in the higher echelons of the Royal Navy, created a more humane environment for the men of the forecastle.

board drills, exercises at sea, and fleet maneuvers. But perhaps the most important change he initiated was the encouragement of promotions on the basis of merit rather than birth or family. Under Anson's regime, an officer of talent could anticipate advancement even if like Captain Cook, he was the son of a farm laborer. With the door of opportunity thus open, many of England's best men chose naval careers, and the Royal Navy was soon filled with bold young officers. Because of the many reforms brought about by Anson, the Royal Navy rapidly achieved a remarkable state of efficiency and became in fact, as well as legend, far superior to the naval forces of the other sea powers of the day.

During this busy period after the War of the Austrian Succession, which both Britain and France recognized as a mere lull in their rivalry, public interest in the Pacific continent continued to rise, not only thanks to Anson's own Pacific voyage and to young Byron's memoirs but also because of a Scottish scholar's reissue of an earlier book on the southern continent. The volume was *The Book of Voyages*, published in 1705 by John Harris. It had been largely forgotten for almost four decades until the Scotsman, John Campbell, found in it "clear evidence" of the reality of Terra Australis and had it reissued in 1744. In the new edition Campbell argued that the discovery of the Pacific continent—or the South Land, as it was now coming to be called—would furnish Britain with "new trade . . . [and] greatly increase our shipping and seamen, which are the true and natural strength of this country."

A convinced mercantilist, Campbell asserted that exploitation of the South Land would give Britain dominion over the greater part of the world. Moreover, he said, from his study of previous voyages he *knew* that the missing continent lay in the unexplored waters between New Zealand and the Pacific coast of South America. He suggested that the Royal Navy seize the Juan Fernández and Falkland islands and use them as bases for a systematic search for the South Land. He also urged British settlement of New Holland, which he said the Dutch had foolishly scorned.

Campbell's arguments fell on receptive ears. By 1750, as Anson went about the reformation of the Royal Navy, numerous British merchants, shipowners, and officials were persuaded that Britain had to mount an all-out effort to find the South Land—

or see the French win the prize. Rumor had it that French mariners were already seeking the Pacific South Land. One heard, for example, that as long ago as 1739, a French navigator named Jean Baptiste Charles Bouvet de Lozier, had touched on what appeared to be a foreland of the Pacific continent in the latitudes far south of the Cape of Good Hope. Since that time Bouvet had been petitioning to return to those waters in order to confirm his discovery. The War of the Austrian Succession as well as the prospect of still another war with Britain had so far barred the Frenchman's project. But could any British merchant doubt that France meant to have the South Land for its own?

Before Britain could meet this Pacific challenge, however, an undeclared war with France broke out in 1754. The struggle, a kind of unofficial conflict of outposts centered on America and the Mediterranean, began badly for Britain. In the opening months of the hostilities the French occupied a strategic strong point at the confluence of the Allegheny and Monongahela rivers in America and thereby gained control of the important Ohio River. They then built a fort on the site, naming it Fort Duquesne. When the British, under General Edward Braddock tried to take the fort in the following year, they were annihilated. Other British thrusts against French strongholds in America also failed. In the Mediterranean the British also lost at Minorca.

In 1756 the undeclared struggle became part of a much larger conflict. Later called the Seven Years' War, it pitted Britain and Prussia against a coalition of France, Austria, Sweden, Saxony, and Russia. In Europe it was a land war, ostensibly to retake the province of Silesia for Austria after its earlier conquest by Prussia. In the rest of the world it was a contest between Britain and France to determine which nation would dominate North America and India.*

In 1757, with British fortunes at a low point, William Pitt, Walpole's old antagonist, became secretary of state with responsibility for military and foreign affairs. Now forty-nine, Pitt, nicknamed the Great Commoner, was passionately certain of his own competence. "I know I can save this country," he declared to Parliament, "and that I alone can." He adopted a strategy based on using superior British sea power to win command of the sea and then to destroy French trade and bases.

---

*In America the conflict was called the French and Indian War.

Under Pitt's energetic direction, British squadrons block-aded the French coast. The tide of war turned rapidly in Britain's favor. French forts fell to British forces in North America. When Fort Duquesne was taken, it was renamed Fort Pitt and its nearby settlement rechristened Pittsburgh in honor of Pitt.

In 1759 Quebec fell to the British, while the Royal Navy crushed the French fleet at Lagos and off Quiberon in the Bay of Biscay. In the Caribbean British troops took Guadeloupe. In India Clive had already won the Battle of Plassey, making the East India Company master of almost all southern India.

In 1760 the British occupied Montreal, and the conquest of Canada was all but complete. In India the British capture of Pon-dicherry assured their dominion there. Desperate, France now maneuvered to bring its old ally Spain into the war on its side.

Pitt, acutely aware of this possibility, now proposed that Brit-ain extend the war by attacking Spanish possessions. By so doing, he argued, Britain would not only end the war but increase its empire even further. When the Cabinet rejected his proposal, Pitt resigned, telling the House of Commons that he would not govern unless his advice prevailed.

Three months after Pitt's resignation Spain declared war. The Royal Navy and British land forces now deployed against the Spanish Empire along the strategic lines previously urged by Pitt. Martinique, Grenada, St. Lucia, St. Vincent, Havana, and Manila were captured. Britain had triumphed.

The war formally ended in 1763, with the Treaty of Paris. Under the terms of the treaty, Britain won Canada, Nova Scotia, Cape Breton, and a number of West Indian islands. It was also assured dominance in India. In exchange, Britain ceded back to Spain the Philippines and Havana, as well as a number of Car-ibbean islands. In the European war Britain's ally Prussia was the victor, winning formal possession of Silesia.

The big loser in the war was France. It had lost Canada and most of its influence in India.

As a result of the great struggle, the ships of the Royal Navy cruised unhindered on every ocean of the world. The British Empire stretched around the globe.* Yet even now, prostrate af-

*The author of British sea power, Lord Anson, had died, at the age of sixty-five, a year and a half before the British triumph at the Treaty of Paris. Except for one brief interval he had been first lord of the Admiralty for eleven years. His work was widely recognized at the time of his passing. Despite his exalted position, the shy and taciturn Anson had

ter its defeat and laboring under a crushing social inequity, France could not be counted out as a rival to British interests, for it still possessed a numerous and remarkably energetic populace, as well as significant natural wealth. France had created one empire, and if it had now lost it, it might still build another by claiming the southern continent of the Pacific.

This was the thesis of a formidable French intellectual, Charles de Brosses. A well-known scholar, de Brosses had published a history of Pacific voyages in 1756, in the midst of the Seven Years' War.* In his book de Brosses, who had never made any kind of sea journey, claimed not only that Terra Australis existed but also that many seamen, most notably the Portuguese pilot Quirós, had touched upon it. De Brosses called on the French government to mount a national effort to discover the South Land. He argued that rather than leave the quest to private trading companies, which would only exploit its people and misuse its resources for their own profit, it was the obligation of the state to search for the new land. He says: "The most celebrated of monarchs will be he who gives his name to the Southern World. This enterprise can only be carried out by a King or a State. It is beyond the resources of an individual or a company."

With the respect accorded him by French intellectuals, de Brosses found a receptive audience for his ideas. In fact, even before the diplomats signed away the French Empire in the Treaty of Paris, at least one young Frenchman, a distinguished officer in the late war, had begun to implement his message.

He was thirty-four-year-old Louis Antoine de Bougainville, a colonel in the French Army, who proposed to establish a French colony on the Falkland Islands, which the French called Iles Malouines. Pointing out that most navigators regarded the Falklands, situated in the far reaches of the South Atlantic, as the key to the Pacific and its continent, Bougainville, early in 1763, volunteered to found a French settlement there at his own expense.

---

never really managed to fit into the upper levels of English society. One wag said of him: "He has been around the world, but never in it."

*De Brosses, a Dijon magistrate, was in his late forties at the time he published his book. He was a close friend of Buffon and other famed French thinkers. It was de Brosses who first coined the geographical divisions of Australasia and Polynesia adopted by later geographers. He also wrote extensively of Africa and of its cults. Curiously, he brought the word "fetish" into general use, applying a Portuguese word for charms to African magical articles.

Bougainville, who had served as chief of staff to Montcalm at the Battle of Quebec, was a man who carried weight with the French government, and he received permission to proceed.

No doubt Bougainville was familiar with the traditional belief that the French voyager de Gonneville had already touched on the southern continent in the sixteenth century. Certainly he had heard the report of the French captain Bouvet, who in 1739 claimed that he had reached a dismal, fogbound promontory of the South Land.

Bougainville outfitted two small men-of-war for his Falklands enterprise: the *Aigle* which carried twenty guns, and the *Sphinx*, which mounted twelve. Then he embarked a total of twenty-seven would-be colonists on these two vessels. Among these hopeful settlers were five women and three children. All of them were Acadian refugees, people who had been cruelly displaced from their Canadian homes by the conquering British. They were also people, according to Bougainville's later account, "who ought to be dear to France, on account of the inviolable attachment they have shown as honest but unfortunate citizens."

On September 15, 1763, some three weeks before the formal signing of the Treaty of Paris, Bougainville sailed from St. Malo. After stopping at Montevideo to take on board horses and cattle for his colonists, he went on to the Falklands.

On February 3, 1764, the *Aigle* and the *Sphinx* entered what Bougainville called "a great bay" which "seemed very convenient to me for forming the first settlement." Here the Acadians went ashore. In his later report Bougainville said that in examining the nearby land, he could discover "no sign that these parts have been frequented by any nation." The neighborhood, he declared, seemed to offer good water, fish, and waterfowl, but it was also surprisingly devoid of wood for fuel or construction.

In March the French built huts "covered with rushes" to shelter the twenty-seven new residents. Bougainville also erected a little fort nearby. He then "solemnly took possession of the isles in the King's name." Finally, on April 8, 1764, he sailed again for France, intending to fetch more settlers as well as additional tools, lumber, and building materials.

Meanwhile, in Britain MPs, admirals, and merchants were fretting over French activity in the Southern Hemisphere. Like their French counterparts, the British admirals also saw the Falklands as the strategic key to the Pacific and its unknown continent. Was it feasible for the Royal Navy to take possession of the Falklands? Were there other islands in the South Atlantic that might serve equally well as naval bases? The Admiralty was particularly interested in claiming "Pepys Island," supposedly sighted by early English mariners and supposed to lie somewhere between thirty-three degrees south and fifty-five degrees south in the South Atlantic.

There were other questions as well in the minds of the British admirals. For example, was it possible to locate the Northwest Passage through Canada back to Atlantic waters from the Pacific side of America? Was the Strait of Magellan, after all, a better route to the Pacific than the stormy passage around the Horn?

To answer these questions and a number of others, the Admiralty decided to undertake an exploratory expedition to the South Atlantic and then on to the Pacific. As commander they chose a colorful captain, John Byron, whose men called him Foul Weather Jack.* He was the same man who, as a seventeen-year-old midshipman, had survived the wreck of the *Wager* during Commodore Anson's voyage into the Pacific and had then written a popular account of his four-year odyssey back to England. Now, twenty years later, John Byron was to command the first British thrust to gain the South Land.

Byron's top-secret orders called for him to search the South Atlantic to verify or discredit the existence of Pepys Island. He was then to survey the Falklands, go on to the Pacific make his way northward to Drake's New Albion, up the California coast, and proceed even farther north in search of a Northwest Passage. If he found such a waterway, he was to follow it back to the Atlantic. If he did *not* encounter such a strait, he was to cross the Pacific and return to England by way of the Cape of Good Hope. All the while he was to keep a weather eye out for the South Land.†

To carry out his formidable tasks, Foul Weather Jack Byron was given two ships: the copper-sheathed frigate *Dolphin*, carrying thirty-two guns and 150 officers and men, and the sloop *Tamar*, with a complement of 115. Both ships and their crews were in

---

*Byron achieved his nickname because according to those who served with him, he seemed always to be running into rough seas and stormy weather.
†At this time Parliament was offering a reward of twenty thousand pounds to any Briton, sailing a British ship, who found a way between Hudson Bay and the Pacific. Members of the Royal Navy, were not eligible to collect the prize.

excellent condition, but no one aboard except Byron had any idea of the real purpose of the coming voyage.

Foul Weather Jack departed on his highly secret venture on June 21, 1764, three months after Bougainville had established his Acadians in the Falklands. By late October 1764, after a hiatus in Rio, the *Dolphin* and the *Tamar* were nearing the South Atlantic, and Byron assembled all hands to reveal their true mission. In his later report he describes his speech in these words: "[I told them] I was not, as they imagined, bound immediately to the East Indies, but upon certain discoveries, which it was thought might be of great importance to our country, in consideration of which . . . the Admiralty had been pleased to promise them [the crew] double pay, and several other advantages, if during the voyage they should behave to my satisfaction."

With no protest from men or officers, Byron made a cursory search for Pepys Island and convinced himself (correctly) that there was no such place. He was now supposed to go on to the Falklands. But he was in great need of wood and fresh water, which he could not obtain on those bleak islands. Therefore, he decided to go first to the Strait of Magellan, where he knew he would certainly find the supplies he needed.

Proceeding to the strait, the British spent the New Year of 1765 at Cavendish's old Port Famine, replenishing water casks and wood bins. The ships then sailed back eastward to the Falklands, where they arrived on January 12, 1765. For the next two weeks the British carried out observations but did not chance upon the small French colony previously established by Bougainville. Nor did Byron discover that the energetic Bougainville was also in the islands at this time, after having returned from France on January 5, 1765, with supplies—if not more colonists—for his settlement.

Bougainville, who did not detect the presence of the British either, had found his Acadians "healthy and content," although during his absence their numbers had been reduced from twenty-seven to twenty-four. After landing the goods that he had brought from France, Bougainville decided that his colonists could use still another load of timber for fuel and building materials. He also had it in mind to obtain some "young trees" for replanting on the Falklands. He set off for the Strait of Magellan to obtain the wood and living trees he wanted.

In the meantime, Byron, after formally claiming the Falklands for Britain, had also sailed once more for the strait, where he was to rendezvous with a Royal Navy cargo ship and replenish his stores. Entering the strait on February 18, 1765, several days ahead of Bougainville, Byron met his supply vessel and began taking on provisions.

When the unsuspecting Bougainville sailed into the strait, he was astonished to see three ships already there. Byron, too, was surprised. Thus neither Byron nor Bougainville showed his colors, and there ensued some tense moments as the British and French tried to discern each other's identity and intentions. When Byron's store vessel attempted to move nearer the *Dolphin*'s protective guns, she went aground. At this point Bougainville, apparently realizing that he had encountered British warships, showed his colors. In a gentlemanly gesture he also offered to assist Byron's grounded storeship. Byron refused the French help. The French passed farther into the strait and began cutting wood. The British freed their storeship and completed revictualing. Then they, too, went on farther into the strait, sailing past the anchored Frenchmen without acknowledgment.

Bougainville carried his wood and trees back to his Acadians and then returned to France, where he reported his encounter with Byron. The British, he thought, had been surveying the Falklands on their way to the Pacific.*

Meanwhile, Byron had emerged onto the Pacific in April 1765. Now, despite his orders to sail northward to search for a Northwest Passage, Foul Weather Jack decided that he would strike out westward into the Pacific in an effort to rediscover Mendaña's Solomon Islands and to find Terra Australis.

Byron touched on numerous previously discovered islands, but he located neither the Solomons nor the South Land. After reaching the Mariana Islands in late July 1765, Byron apparently decided that he had had enough of the Pacific. He pointed his two ships for home. On May 9, 1766, the *Dolphin* and the *Tamar* reached England again. Byron had circumnavigated the globe, but the voyage had added almost nothing to the world's knowl-

---

*When the French informed the Spanish government of the British interest in the Falklands and of Byron's presence in the strait, the Spaniards registered a strong protest to the British government. But they also protested Bougainville's colony, arguing that the islands really belonged to Spain. The protest soon bore fruit. France agreed to withdraw Bougainville's settlers at the earliest opportunity and to recognize the sovereignty of Spain over the islands. In the interim Bougainville's colonists were to be left in peace until arrangements could be made to evacuate them.

edge of the Pacific. Moreover, Foul Weather Jack had accomplished few of the tasks set out for him by the Admiralty.*

Despite Byron's disappointing cruise, Admiralty interest in Terra Australis burned higher than ever, fanned by French competition and by new scholarly writings. In 1766 one John Callender published still another tome on the South Land. Although plagiarized from the French thinker de Brosses, the work convinced many that a national effort was needed to seize the South Land for Britain. In addition to Callender's, a far more respected voice had also begun clamoring for an all-out search for Terra Australis. This was the voice of Alexander Dalrymple, a knowledgeable geographer and "hydrographer" for the English East India Company. Dalrymple was not only convinced that the South Land existed, but also sure that its discovery would be as significant as Columbus's encounter with America.

After Byron's report on Bougainville's activities it seemed obvious to the Admiralty that France was bent on regaining its place among the maritime powers by sending an expedition to the Pacific in search of the South Land. The lords intended to plant the Union Jack there first.

---

*Byron went on to a lengthy and honorable career in the Royal Navy. In 1769 he was appointed governor of Newfoundland, and he became an admiral in 1775. In July 1779 he fought an engagement with a French fleet off Grenada. Typically the action produced few results. Byron died in 1786. Today he is remembered most for his adventures as the young midshipman on the ill-starred *Wager* during Anson's Pacific voyage. He was also the grandfather of the poet Lord Byron. In one of his works the poet has this to say of his grandfather: "He had no rest at sea, nor I on shore."

29

THE *DOLPHIN* AND THE *SWALLOW*

HMS *Dolphin* was soon being readied for a new Pacific voyage, this time under the command of a cautious career officer, Captain Samuel Wallis. A man in his forties, Wallis was one of those drab but devoted souls for whom orders and the "navy way" were Holy Writ. An officer who had risen during the Anson years, Wallis was dependable rather than brilliant, dogged rather than daring. He had experienced combat. He knew how to handle a ship. Careful of the health of his men, he was also a disciplinarian who never flinched at flogging a man for a breach of regulations. His navy career, like his character, had been steady, unspectacular, and "by the book." The Admiralty was sure that Wallis, unlike Byron, could be counted on to carry out his instructions to the letter.

Perhaps the only question about Wallis was his health. From time to time during his career he had fallen ill of one ailment or another, and some thought these bouts of illness exacerbated by a certain gloominess in his character. Still and all, it was agreed that reliable Samuel Wallis would provide the sure hand needed on a Pacific voyage which was, after all, a hazardous undertaking whose demands no one could predict.

Wallis was to have as his flagship the *Dolphin*, which had performed flawlessly under Byron. The Admiralty chose as consort a battered sloop named the *Swallow*. In contrast to the nimble *Dolphin*, the poor old *Swallow* was slow and clumsy. With her worm-eaten wooden hull and unreliable seams, the *Swallow* hardly seemed proper company for the sleek *Dolphin*. The Admiralty thought so, too. Thus the plan was to allow the *Swallow* to make only the first leg of the voyage: to the Falklands. There her complement was to transfer to a new copper-bottomed frigate like the *Dolphin*, which would be awaiting them. The *Swallow* would then return to England. In the meantime, however, she was the only escort the Admiralty could spare. Captain Wallis, always compliant, accepted the Admiralty decision without protest.

Chosen to captain the *Swallow* was the youthful but experienced Philip Carteret, who had served as first lieutenant of the *Tamar*, Byron's consort in the recent circumnavigation. Carteret had also put in time as first lieutenant aboard the *Dolphin* herself. Having inspected the *Swallow* carefully, he accepted command of her only because of the Admiralty's promise to provide a more suitable vessel at the Falklands. In addition to the *Dolphin* and the ghastly-looking *Swallow*, a storeship was to accompany the expedition during the first phases of the journey.

Wallis's general instructions were to find Terra Australis and annex it. Specifically, he was to sail to the Pacific via the Strait of Magellan and to search for land in the high latitudes well to the south of the Tropic of Capricorn. He was to continue his search as far west as longitude 120 degrees.* If Wallis found the long-sought land, he was to claim it and then return as quickly as possible around the Horn. If unforeseen circumstances made this impossible, he was to proceed to the East Indies to refit and then make his way home via the Cape of Good Hope.

Although the Admiralty was confident that Wallis would encounter Terra Australis before he got as far west as longitude 120 degrees, the planners had provided alternative orders in case he did not. In such an unlikely eventuality Wallis was to turn to the northwest and continue searching for land in latitude 20 degrees south. If the sought-for land *still* did not appear, he was to call off the search, make his way to the East Indies, refit, and then continue homeward around the Cape to report.

Wallis and the *Dolphin*, with Carteret's *Swallow* and the store-

---

*It was understood that this longitude could only be estimated since no accurate method of measurement yet existed.

ship trailing behind, set sail from Portsmouth on August 22, 1766, only three months after Byron's return. During the Atlantic crossing, the *Swallow* often fell far behind the *Dolphin*. Her difficulties were duly recorded in a lively journal kept by the *Dolphin*'s sailing master, George Robertson. In his entry for November 4, 1766, for example, Robertson noted that the *Swallow* and the storeship could "hardly keep up" even though the flagship was creeping under close-reefed topsails. Robertson soon began to worry that the *Swallow* and the storeship would delay the *Dolphin* so much that she would arrive in the strait too late for the southern summer. Nevertheless, the *Swallow* fought on, gamely trailing the *Dolphin* until the ships reached the Falklands. Here Carteret had to endure a bitter disappointment: There was no copper-sheathed frigate on hand to take the place of the *Swallow*.*

After waiting a decent interval in the hope that the *Swallow*'s replacement would appear, Wallis decided that he had no alternative but to depart the Falklands with the *Swallow* as escort. It was too risky for the *Dolphin* to sail these waters alone. The *Swallow* would just have to do her best to accompany the *Dolphin* through the Strait and over the Pacific after that. Thus, after unloading the storeship and sending her home as planned, the *Dolphin* and the *Swallow* made for the Strait of Magellan.

Although it was now the new year of 1767—summer in the strait—the ships had to battle daily gales that hit them head-on from the west. Buffeted incessantly, the *Swallow* fought to keep way. The flagship often had to heave to while her poor consort inched up to her.

On February 21, 1767, Carteret suggested that it might be better for the *Dolphin* if the *Swallow* gave up and returned to England. Wallis rejected the idea. As he wrote later, "[Since] . . . the Admiralty had appointed *Swallow* to accompany the *Dolphin*, she must continue to do so as long as . . . possible. . . . [The *Dolphin*] would await [the *Swallow*] and attend her motions, [so] that if any disaster should happen to either of us, the other should be ready to afford such assistance as might be in her power."

---

*The exchange frigate *had* called at the Falklands some time earlier, but her master had not received the Admiralty orders to turn her over to Carteret.

Carteret and the *Swallow* fought on. February slipped into March. Once again Carteret urged Wallis to send him back to England, this time pointing out that his poor sloop would "so much retard the *Dolphin* as probably to make her lose the season for getting into high southern latitudes." He then volunteered to come aboard the *Dolphin* as a subordinate officer if Wallis thought his previous experience of the Pacific "necessary to the success of the voyage." The *Swallow* could return home under her second-in-command. Wallis refused the offer, again noting that his instructions were that *two* ships were to voyage into the Pacific. He would do all in his power to adhere to his orders. The ships went on.

At last, on April 11, 1767, after four months of battling wind, wave, and current, the *Dolphin* sighted the Pacific exit of the strait. The *Swallow* was lagging far behind as usual. But now Wallis confronted a most unusual circumstance. Instead of the steady westerlies that usually blew at this end of the strait, the wind had diminished to fitful breezes. This presented Wallis with something of a dilemma. In order to get safely beyond the dangerous rocks at the strait's outlet and enter the open sea, the *Dolphin* would have to put on all her sail in the fickle wind. But this would mean leaving the laboring *Swallow* even farther behind in the strait. After consulting with his officers, Wallis concluded that he had no choice but to get out of the strait while the getting was good. About this time—midday of April 11—the *Dolphin*'s Sailing Master Robertson scurried aloft and saw the *Swallow*, a dozen or more miles astern, churning in heavy seas, still hours behind. Accordingly the *Dolphin* raised all sail to weather the rocks ahead. She soon cleared the strait. At this point Wallis was inclined to heave to and wait for the *Swallow*. But now fog settled down, together with "a rising sea." The *Dolphin* could not tarry near a lee shore to allow the *Swallow* to catch up. Wallis ordered the *Dolphin* steered to safety in the open Pacific. When the *Swallow* finally escaped the strait, she found herself alone on the ocean.*

* * *

*Although Wallis has been criticized for leaving his consort, it was in reality a prudent decision. If Wallis can be criticized for anything, it is for failing to designate a place of rendezvous, should the ships become separated.

Unable to locate the *Dolphin* after exiting the strait, Carteret thought about the safety of his ship. The *Swallow* was now in desperate need of repair. Her crew badly needed a rest. Carteret, therefore, set off northward with the aim of taking shelter at Juan Fernández off the coast of Chile.

"From this time," he reported later, "I gave up all hope of seeing the *Dolphin* again till we should arrive in England, no plan of operation having been settled, nor any place of rendezvous appointed." He tried to hearten his men by telling them that "although the *Dolphin* was the best ship, I did not doubt that I should find more than equivalent advantages in their courage, ability, and good conduct."

To his chagrin, Carteret found Juan Fernández occupied by a Spanish force. Unwilling to risk a clash, Carteret passed on. He pointed the *Swallow*'s battered bows north and west, hoping to find another refuge. The ship, wallowing in the ocean day after day, encountered only the emptiness of the Pacific. The single island sighted in these waters was a rocky dot that offered no anchorage. Carteret named the place Pitcairn Island after the young officer who first spotted it.

In the grip of the trade winds and with scurvy beginning to plague her crew, the unlucky *Swallow*, leaking and trailing a mess of marine growth, crept to the west at about latitude 15 degrees south. Eventually she came upon sprinkles of islets and atolls, but none of them offered usable shelter. The *Swallow* plowed on for weeks before she finally reached what are today called the Santa Cruz Islands, six thousand miles out in the Pacific.

It was August 12, 1767. Almost four months had passed since Carteret had lost contact with the *Dolphin*. His men were weakened by scurvy. His ship was leaking worse than ever. Carteret decided he had little option but to take refuge in these large islands, to which he now gave an English name: the Queen Charlotte Islands. As the *Swallow* moved to anchor, however, curly-haired black warriors, brandishing weapons and howling threats, paddled out to the ship in canoes. The Englishmen tried to communicate their peaceful intent, but the natives replied with hostile gestures. Desperate for water and fresh victuals, Carteret sent a landing party ashore. Unnerved by the swarming natives around their boat, the Englishmen fired on the islanders, who retaliated with a fierce attack on the strangers. A number of Carteret's men, as well as some natives, were killed in the fight. Wisely Carteret raised his anchor and fled.*

Blundering on farther west, the *Swallow* soon reached another island chain. These were the long-lost Solomon Islands, though Carteret did not realize that fact. The *Swallow* by now was in horrendous shape. But again native hostility made it impossible to anchor. Stoically Carteret pressed on.

On August 26, 1767, having left the Solomons behind, the *Swallow* arrived at the great island that Dampier, in 1700, had named New Britain. Here Carteret took the ship into a deep inlet that Dampier had called St. George Bay. Very soon, however, the young English captain found that this waterway was not a bay after all but a strait separating Dampier's New Britain from another island just north of it, which Carteret now dubbed New Ireland. Here at last, in the waters between the two islands, Carteret found an anchorage. The men collected fresh fruits and vegetables and filled water casks. They also repaired the *Swallow*'s worst leaks. But this region was soon denuded of provisions, and Carteret sailed on farther west and north through a scattering of atolls and small isles which he called the Admiralty Islands. He did not stop, however, for these waters, too, were teeming with hostile warriors who constantly menaced his vessel.

The *Swallow*'s condition was now critical. Her canvas, yards, and tackle were rotting away. Marine growth almost covered her hull. She was once more taking water through her seams. Her crew was exhausted and scurvy-ridden. It was clear to all aboard that to survive, the *Swallow* required a proper overhaul and her crew needed decent care and rest. These things could only be obtained at a civilized port, and the nearest of those lay in the Dutch East Indies, still more than a thousand miles farther west. Indomitable even now, Carteret was determined to bring his sloop to the safe harbor she needed. The *Swallow* pressed on westward.

Meanwhile, the *Dolphin* and her crew were in excellent shape. With her copper sheath the frigate's hull remained sound. Her rigging and other equipment were in good repair. Though Captain Wallis himself was ill from time to time, the ship's complement remained well and morale was high.

*This Santa Cruz group was where both Mendaña and Quirós had tried and failed to establish Spanish colonies 150 years earlier. Carteret suspected as much.

Unfortunately, however, the *Dolphin* had been unable to keep strictly to the mission given her by the Admiralty—that is, to search for Terra Australis by sailing west to longitude 120 degrees in the high latitudes of the South Pacific.

Like so many others, the *Dolphin* had found herself incapable of bucking the South Pacific's "roaring forties." Captain Wallis had exercised his judgment as master and had changed course to the northwest in order to make way. For two months after this alteration the *Dolphin* had plowed over empty seas. Then, in early June 1767, she finally sighted land: the southern arc of the Tuamotus. Navigating through this chain, Wallis named various islands after members of the royal family. The ship then passed again into open ocean.

On June 18, 1767, at sunset, lookouts saw land on the horizon. Some aboard the *Dolphin* thought it a broad coastline, perhaps the shore of a continent. Had they found Terra Australis at last? Judging that the land lay some seventy miles away, Wallis made for it through the night.

When the nocturnal mist lifted the next day, the men of the *Dolphin* discovered hundreds of canoes around the ship, all filled with handsome natives staring in wonder at the new arrival. The *Dolphin's* company made signs of friendship, and a number of warriors climbed aboard. In the excitement, one of the *Dolphin's* goats butted a visitor, and the event so unsettled the man that he leaped overboard, followed almost immediately by the rest of his companions. The natives, however, soon returned to the ship, where they exclaimed in delight over the European devices they found aboard.

As their vessel closed with the land, the men of the *Dolphin* admired the loveliness of this coast that they had happened upon. They were also delighted by the beauty of the inhabitants, especially by the women whom they could glimpse on the beaches.*

Now the *Dolphin* began looking for a safe harbor. As the ship skirted the shoreline, sending her boats to sound and scout ahead, the native canoes continued to swarm about like so many excited water bugs. According to George Robertson, the presence of so many armed warriors, all shouting, singing, gesturing,

---

*The land was not a continent but the paradisical island of Tahiti, soon to become the most famous of all "South Sea islands."

and paddling, was a hindrance to the sailors and marines working in the ship's cutter as the sailing master looked for a suitable place to anchor.

As the *Dolphin*'s boats spent one whole day and then another searching along the shore for a suitable anchorage, the native mood seemed to darken. It was as if the local inhabitants, having expected their visitors to land, were becoming increasingly suspicious of the strange white men conducting their mysterious offshore rituals. Soon with the British unable to communicate their need to find a safe harbor and with native distrust mounting, a fidgety unease began to spread among both newcomers and locals. Inevitably, on June 21, only three days after the *Dolphin* had first sighted this lovely land, there was a clash.

On that day Robertson took the cutter into a likely-looking bay, while the ship stood off. As he sounded, Robertson says in his journal, more than two hundred canoes, with upwards of fifteen hundred warriors in them, crowded about. In addition, Robertson notes, the shoreline was packed with hundreds of women and children, all shouting incomprehensibly. In such circumstances, says the sailing master, "we had some reason to be a little afraid." Unable to sound because of interference, Robertson's boat turned away to make for the ship. Upon this, he says, the people onshore set up a loud cry and "those in the canoes began to hoot at us—and several of them attempted to board us, and seemed greatly enraged when they found we would not land."

Now, as Robertson's craft sought to reach the *Dolphin*, the warriors appeared to threaten bodily harm to the Englishmen. Robertson ordered his marines to level their muskets at the menacing warriors. They were ignored. Robertson then had one of his marines fire a warning shot "in the hopes of frightening them, without doing any more hurt." The paddling warriors were undeterred, however, and, in Robertson's view, were now "fully resolved to board us, which if they had, their prows would have certainly sunk our boat."

Fearing destruction of the cutter and harm to his nervous men, Robertson ordered two of his marines to shoot to wound two natives as they climbed aboard. The marines fired, killing one warrior and wounding the other. It was enough. The shocked canoeists "steered off," and the sailing master's boat returned safely to the *Dolphin*. But blood had been spilled.

Soon after this Robertson finally came upon a treelined bay known as Matavai. There, on June 23, 1767, the ship anchored.

On the very next morning, however, according to Robertson's journal, native warriors in hundreds of canoes launched an attack on the ship as she rode at anchor. Stones rained down on the *Dolphin's* deck "like hail," says Robertson. The stones left several of the British tars "cut and bruised."

The men, says the sailing master, then retaliated with "a few round and grape shot" from the ship's cannon. The roar of the guns and the destruction wrought by the missiles, according to Robertson, "struck such terror among the poor unhappy crowd that it would require the pen of Milton to describe. . . . " The attackers fled to the interior jungles, leaving harbor, beaches, and villages deserted. Once more white strangers had killed to get their way. The English, it seemed, were following the path previously trodden by the Portuguese, Spaniards, and Dutch in the Pacific by making implacable enemies of the indigenous people.*

---

*Although the incident with the cutter and the attack on the anchored *Dolphin* were the bloodiest clashes recorded by Robertson, they were not the only hostile acts that took place in these early days of contact between the English and the natives. Even before the attack on the ship and the shooting in the cutter, a watering party from the *Dolphin* had been pelted with stones and fruit. The ship had also fired her big guns before this, intending to frighten off stone-throwing warriors. One stone thrower had apparently been wounded in that episode.

30

PARADISE—AND INFERNO

With the natives driven away, the British newcomers secured their ship and drew much-needed water from a nearby river. Then, on June 26, one of the *Dolphin*'s junior officers, deputizing for Captain Wallis, went ashore and took possession of this beautiful place, naming it King George III Island in accordance with his captain's instructions.*

Now, as the Europeans established themselves in Matavai Bay, the local people reappeared. According to Robertson, some four to five hundred islanders assembled one morning near the river that emptied into the bay. Warily they waved boughs of plantain as a sign they wished to make peace. They presented the British with a pig and other gifts. In turn, says Robertson, the British left nails and other goods on the riverbank as presents for the locals.

From this point on relations improved rapidly although there were still occasional signs of nervousness. (The British, for example, destroyed seventy to eighty canoes that lay unmanned onshore. They did this, explains Robertson, to make certain that they could not be used for any new attacks.)

Despite such incidents, the European sailors and the smiling

*From this name it would appear that the British had now surmised that their lovely find was not a continent after all.

natives were soon fraternizing. The islanders supplied the new-comers with hogs, chicken, and fruit. The British took their sick ashore. Captain Wallis issued strict instructions to his men to avoid any further violence against the native people.

By the first week in July the British had established a camp ashore and raised a tent on an island in the river. Exploration parties sent out by Captain Wallis confirmed that the *Dolphin* had indeed found a magnificent island, with hills, trees, rivers, groves of fruit, and a delightful climate. The British had also learned the native name of their lovely discovery: Tahiti.

As the Europeans and Tahitians grew increasingly easy with each other, Captain Wallis, who was ill again with a "bilious colic" and often had to remain aboard ship, gave his tars liberty, twenty men at a time.

Free of the ship's discipline, the men of the *Dolphin* found Tahiti a kind of paradise, peopled by lovely innocents and possessing a climate that turned the land into a garden of earthly delights.

It was the Tahitian women, however, who did the most to create the illusion of paradise for the British sailors. The young beauties of the island usually wore only a gaily decorated and tight-fitting skirt, of a fabric made from beaten tree bark. This garment covered only the lower body, leaving breasts and tawny waists naked. The girls also were in the habit of anointing themselves with fragrant palm oil and ornamenting their flowing black hair with shells, flowers, and feathers. The result was ravishingly sensual, especially to young men who had been cooped up on a dank ship for months. Adding to the effect was the fact that the Tahitian girls regarded sex as natural, to be enjoyed as freely as the sun and sea. They took pleasure in displaying themselves to the British lads.

In his journal Robertson makes clear the hunger that the Tahitian lasses aroused. The very sight of them, he says, "made all our men madly fond of the shore, even the sick. . . . " In another entry Robertson illustrates how easy it was to find sexual joy on Tahiti: "This day, some of the young girls ventured over to the liberty men, and our honest hearted tars received them with great cheerfulness and made them some little presents which gained the hearts of the young girls, and made them give our men a signal which they would have willingly obeyed, had they not been immediately ordered on board. . . . "

Such meetings between sailors and girls soon became daily events, and when Robertson's "honest hearted tars" discovered that the gift of an iron nail would assure a night's bliss with one of the island's gleaming Aphrodites, the young sailors almost tore the *Dolphin* apart to obtain these "little presents." The sailing master describes this alarming turn of events:

> " . . . the carpenter came and told me every cleat in the ship was drawn, and all the nails carried off . . . the boatswain informed me that most of the hammock nails was drawn, and two-thirds of the men obliged to lie on the deck for want of nails to hang their hammocks."

When Captain Wallis recovered from his "colic," he was told of the damage being done to his vessel, and he issued orders limiting the number of men allowed to go onshore. He did this, he said later, "to preserve the ship from being pulled to pieces. . . . "

But no rules and no threat of punishment could restrain the men of the *Dolphin*. Day or night they sneaked ashore, risking a flogging for the favors of the island women. Nor was there any way to keep the native girls from swimming out to the ship and climbing aboard for a night of love.

The sailors were not alone in enjoying the pleasures of Tahiti. Captain Wallis, now able to spend time ashore, was also charmed by the Tahitians, especially by a local "queen" named Purea, who took a special shine to the *Dolphin*'s master. Described as a very large woman, stout and strong, Purea entertained Wallis and his officers on several occasions. During one of Wallis's shore visits, the powerful Purea lifted the captain bodily over some puddles, supposedly to keep him from soiling his shoes and stockings. On another occasion she had four of her lovely attendants give the embarrassed, but willing, Wallis a massage.*

The British were continually astonished by the beauty of the islanders. Many were also amazed that there were no signs of disease among the people—not even the malaria so common on other islands. For their part, the Tahitians were fascinated by the

---

*Purea was not really a queen in any European sense, but a sort of combination grande dame and clan leader. The British, however, thought her a monarch.

tools and fashions of their visitors. At one point Purea came aboard the *Dolphin* and was astounded by the size of the ship and its equipment. A telescope especially intrigued her. Her young men found the European swords a source of wonder. The *Dolphin*'s doctor also became a figure of awe when because of the heat, he removed his wig and sent the Tahitians into rapt admiration.

The British also spent time rambling about. They found so many orchards and plantations that it seemed to them that the islanders had only to reach out and pluck the fruit of their gardens to provide for their wants. As if to contribute their own bit to Eden, the British planted peach, plum, cherry, lemon, and lime trees on the island.

Like all idylls, however, this Tahitian interlude had to come to an end. After five weeks Wallis ordered the *Dolphin* prepared for sea. Learning that the English now meant to go from their shores, "Queen" Purea and her "subjects," especially the young girls, were openly distressed. Purea begged the English visitors to stay awhile longer. But Captain Wallis was adamant. When Purea realized that, for all her entreaties, Wallis did indeed leave, Robertson says, "she immediately burst out in tears, and cried and wept in such a manner that few men could have helped pitying her. . . ."

On July 27, 1767, the *Dolphin* sailed, carrying away with her many a sailor sorrowing over a lost island beauty. She also took away memories that later, in the cold light of Europe, blossomed into the myth of Tahiti as the last habitation of natural man.

Before striking westward, the *Dolphin* visited the island of Moorea, which lies near Tahiti. The ship also touched the islands north of Tonga. Wallis named one of these islands after himself.

The *Dolphin* was now lying more than six thousand miles out in the Pacific and only 15 degrees south of the equator in waters far to the north and west of the supposed location of Terra Australis. Nevertheless, Wallis was satisfied that he had done all possible to carry out his mission. It was no fault of his that the *Dolphin* had not been able to beat to westward in the high latitudes of the Pacific. He decided the time had come to set out for home. If he had not found Terra Australis, he had found heaven on earth.

*   *   *

Meanwhile, the *Dolphin*'s lost consort, the *Swallow*, was enduring an inferno of misery. By late 1767, as the *Dolphin* was carrying home her glowing reports of Tahiti, the *Swallow* was limping along the northern coast of New Guinea, still trying to reach a place of refuge in the Dutch East Indies. Unfortunately, as she rounded New Guinea, she was seized by monsoon winds and driven off course to Philippine waters.

It took weeks for her indomitable captain, Philip Carteret, to get her heading south again. Finally he succeeded, and once more the *Swallow* muddled on toward the Dutch East Indies.

On December 17, 1767, with half her crew dead or dying of scurvy and fevers, the *Swallow* entered the Dutch port at Macassar on the island of Celebes. To Carteret's fury, Dutch officials refused to help him. In desperation he put aside his Royal Navy pride and begged for assistance. He pointed out that his men were too sick to work and his ship was leaking too badly to make it to a British colony. Relenting a bit, the Dutch sent a committee aboard the *Swallow* to examine her condition. The committee's ensuing report details the wretched state of the ship:

> [The ship] had now only a strength of 25 healthy men, officers included, as a result of the shortage of victuals and fresh water, and of the great discomfits they had endured in the course of the 16 months of voyage, with steady storms accompanied by much cold weather. . . .
> The Captain requested us to see the sick members of his crew, whom we found in a deplorable and lamentable state. . . . infected by scurvy to such a degree that the teeth of most men were loose or had fallen out; their gums were black and swollen and their legs as blue as lazuli. . . . The ship was very dirty inside and on the outside overgrown with grass, moss, and shaggy vegetation. . . .

The Dutch sent Carteret and his wallowing vessel on to the nearby port of Bonthain, a small facility where the British could obtain provisions and plug the worst of their ship's leaks. For five months, while the monsoon made it impossible to sail, the *Swallow* lay at Bonthain. During this time most of her surviving crew recovered. But the ship herself continued to rot away since only the most cursory repairs could be effected at Bonthain. If she were to make it home to England, the *Swallow* would require a complete overhaul, available only at the Dutch East India Company headquarters at Batavia.

At last, in May 1768, the *Swallow* sailed from Bonthain to Batavia. There she anchored while Carteret and his men, with grudging help from Dutch officials, began working to replace her rotten, wormy planks, caulk her seams, scrape the worst growth from her bottom, and enlist stranded British sailors to replace those crewmen who had died on the journey.

In this same month of May 1768, as the *Swallow* found refuge at Batavia, Captain Wallis and the *Dolphin* reached England. Not a single man had perished on the *Dolphin*'s homeward voyage. And now Captain Wallis and his men began to tell about their adventures. Not surprisingly their tales focused on the island paradise they had discovered in Tahiti. Few in England gave any thought to Philip Carteret and the crew of the *Swallow*. Most presumed that the ship had gone down somewhere in the South Pacific. None could have guessed that the dogged Carteret and the men of the *Swallow* were still afloat halfway around the globe.

For four months Carteret and his men worked on their ship at Batavia, repairing her as best they could. Then, in September 1768, with Batavia suffering from another of the epidemics that seemed to erupt regularly in the town, Carteret decided to up anchor and head for England. Despite the best efforts of her crew and carpenters, the ship was still in miserable condition, her ribs soft, seams uncertain, many of her worm-eaten planks still unreplaced, and much of her standing rigging worn. The Dutch of Batavia reckoned that she would never see England again. Nevertheless, Carteret and his men sailed, preferring the hazardous waves of the sea to the pestilential air of Batavia.

For six months the *Swallow* labored through storms and calms. Seven more of her men died. The crew had to crank the pumps almost constantly. Marine growth encrusted the hull. Yet the ship persevered.

In March 1769, against all odds, Carteret dropped the *Swallow*'s anchor in the Thames. She was home. It was thirty-one months since she had first set out as consort to the *Dolphin*. Wallis and the *Dolphin* had already been home for ten months. Like the

Dolphin, the old *Swallow* had circumnavigated the world. But she had done it only by virtue of her crew's heroic determination and her commander's stubborn devotion to duty.

By the time Carteret brought the *Swallow* back to England, stories of the Pacific paradise found by Wallis and the *Dolphin* had already spread like wildfire. If the Admiralty was disappointed with Wallis's performance, it betrayed none of it. Apparently the Royal Navy believed, with Wallis, that he had done his best, and if he had not solved the mystery of the southern continent, at least he had brought back exciting news of great possibilities.

Carteret, on the other hand, had brought back nothing except proof of British resolution and courage in the face of stupendous odds.*

The drawing rooms of London rang with talk of the new Eden out there in the Pacific, where naked beauties lolled complacently under perennially blue skies, where no man had to labor for the fruit that lay everywhere to his hand, and where joy, peace, and comfort were the natural condition of innocent humanity. One of the tales that got around most involved staid Captain Samuel Wallis and the stout Tahitian "queen," Purea. In the drawing rooms Purea's tears upon the English captain's departure became evidence of a romantic attachment between the two, instead of an expression of Tahitian courtesy. Among the idle of London Purea was transformed into a royal beauty weeping tears of despair over the loss of her brave but duty-bound lover, the handsome Captain Wallis. That the story was nonsense mattered not at all. From now on Terra Australis would not be the only magnet drawing men to the Pacific. Tahiti, both its reality and its romance, would also act as a Pacific lodestone.

For the hardheaded men of the Admiralty, however, Terra Australis remained the great prize, the imperial Holy Grail. The

---

*True to his own code of honor, Philip Carteret never publicly blamed Captain Wallis for having deserted him at the Pacific exit of the Strait of Magellan. Nor did Carteret ever complain because the expected frigate failed to rendezvous with him at the Falklands, thus forcing him to make do with the pitiful *Swallow*. Though little recognized publicly, Carteret was well appreciated by the lords of the Admiralty. Two years after his return home he was advanced to post rank, and later commanded the *Druid* and the *Endymion*, both of which were a far cry from the poor old *Swallow*. In 1794 he retired with the rank of rear admiral. He died at Southampton two years later.

Wallis, however, achieved little more advancement in his career. He never returned to Tahiti either.

Admiralty had already begun preparing still another Pacific expedition even before Wallis had returned with the *Dolphin* and his report of Tahiti. It had decided that, whether or not Wallis found Terra Australis, a second voyage would be needed. It could either locate the continent, if Wallis had failed to find it, or could solidify British claims if Wallis had succeeded.

There was still another reason for this new British thrust into the Pacific: A French expedition was already there, searching for the southern continent. Moreover, the leader of this French effort was a man well known to the British for his resourcefulness and intelligence. He was the remarkable Captain Louis Antoine de Bougainville.

31

THE SULKY WOMAN

Captain Louis Antoine de Bougainville was thirty-seven in 1766, when he set out to find the Pacific continent. He had already filled his life with more accomplishment and excitement than most, in the process gaining a well-deserved reputation for civility and sang-froid.

Bougainville was born into a bourgeois family. His father was a notary who gave him an excellent education and pointed him toward the profession of law. But the intelligent, handsome, well-mannered young Bougainville found the law boring, and in 1753 he joined the army. A year later he published a paper on the calculus, revealing a wide-ranging mind. In 1755 Bougainville was in London as a member of the French embassy staff. While there, he was accepted into the prestigious Royal Society in recognition of his contribution to mathematics. During the Seven Years' War, Bougainville served as aide-de-camp to Montcalm, taking part in the French capture of Ticonderoga and in the defense of Quebec.

It was only after his illustrious career in the army that the versatile Bougainville, now a colonel, had become interested in the sea. Although prior to 1763 he had never commanded a ship, he had apparently learned navigation and seamanship while crossing the Atlantic on a number of missions during the Seven Years' War.

In the aftermath of the French defeat, Bougainville had
sharpened his sea skills during his two journeys to the Falkland
Islands and in his excursions into the Strait of Magellan. He had
also discovered in himself a yearning to explore. Thus, when
France decided to send an expedition into the Pacific, he was
the natural choice to lead it.

The purpose of Bougainville's Pacific voyage, which was an
official undertaking of the French government, was stated in his
written instructions:

> [M. Bougainville is to] examine in the Pacific Ocean as
> much of and in the best manner he can the land lying
> between the Indies and the western seaboard of Amer-
> ica, various parts of which have been sighted by navi-
> gators and named Espiritu Santo, New Guinea, etc. . . .
> Since knowledge of the islands [of the Pacific] or
> continent is very slight, it would be very interesting to
> perfect it; furthermore, since no European nation [has]
> any settlement on, or claim over, these islands, it can
> only be to France's advantage to survey them, and to
> take possession of them if they offer articles of value to
> her trade. . . .

In other words, Bougainville was to find and claim the southern continent, or any other territory of value, if he could. He
was also ordered to locate some island "close to the Chinese
coast, which could be used as a commercial center" for French
traders.

In addition to exploration of the Pacific, Bougainville was
given a diplomatic mission: Before proceeding to the ocean, he
was to terminate the Falklands colony that he had earlier established for Acadian refugees by formally handing over the settlement to a Spanish governor and garrison. France and Spain had
reached an amicable adjustment on the question of the islands.
First, France would recognize Spanish sovereignty. Second, any
of Bougainville's colonists who wished to remain would be permitted to do so under Spanish rule. Finally, Bougainville, who
had established the settlers with his own money, would be re-
imbursed by the Spanish government for his expenditures. The
politicians had already signed treaties to this effect. All that remained was for Bougainville to finish up the business. He could

then get on to his more important tasks in the Pacific.

Bougainville was given two ships for his enterprise: a frigate, the *Boudeuse* (Sulky Woman), which mounted twenty-six guns, and a small cargo vessel, the *Etoile* (star), which was to act as a storeship and consort. The *Boudeuse*, which Bougainville was to command, was a much-used veteran, and Bougainville harbored doubts about her seaworthiness. He felt more confident of the *Etoile* and told himself that should the *Boudeuse* prove incapable, he could finish the voyage aboard the storeship.

Bougainville intended his Pacific venture to be a scientific one.* The scholar de Brosses, whose writings had spurred the French effort in the first place, helped plan the expedition. De Brosses worked with Bougainville to choose instruments, goals, and scientific personnel. The French Academy of Sciences also provided advice. The royal naturalist, Philibert de Commerson, was recruited as the chief science officer.

Assigned to the *Etoile*, Commerson enthusiastically boarded her with an array of instruments, books, and equipment. He also brought with him his "valet," an effeminate young man named Baret who spoke little and shared M. Commerson's quarters. This arrangement raised eyebrows even among Bougainville's broad-minded French naval officers, since Commerson—a widower for some years—seemed more than a little fond of the youth.†

When all was ready the *Boudeuse* and the *Etoile* set sail from the port of Nantes on November 15, 1766, three months after the Englishmen Wallis and Carteret had set out on their Pacific journey in the *Dolphin* and the *Swallow*.‡

Almost at once Bougainville's ships were damaged by a storm off the French coast and had to put into Brest for repairs. On December 5, 1766, the *Boudeuse* issued forth again, leaving the *Etoile* behind for additional refitting. It was understood that the storeship, with her scientists and her instruments, would follow as soon as she could and would rendezvous with the *Boudeuse* at the Falklands or at Rio.

Two months later, on February 1, 1767, in accordance with the French-Spanish agreement, the *Boudeuse* met two Spanish

*In addition to geographic knowledge he hoped to test out various methods "toward finding the longitude at sea." None worked well enough to be useful.
†Despite his initial excitement Commerson soon discovered that he hated shipboard life. In his journal he soon described the *Etoile* as a "hellish den."
‡Many of the Pacific voyages undertaken in the 1760s and 1770s overlapped in time.

frigates at Montevideo. In company with the Spaniards, she then departed for the Falklands, where Bougainville was to turn over his colony to the new Spanish governor, who was traveling aboard one of the Spanish vessels.

The *Boudeuse* and her escorts arrived at the islands on March 23, 1767. Eight days later, on April 1, Bougainville conducted a ceremony during which the Spanish flag was raised over his colony. Most of Bougainville's Acadian families chose to remain on the island despite the change in sovereignty.

With the official termination of his colonial enterprise, Bougainville had nothing to do but wait for his storeship, the *Etoile*, to join him as arranged. April and May passed, but the *Etoile* did not appear. At last, on June 2, 1767, Bougainville upped anchor and set out northward for Rio de Janeiro, which he had appointed as an optional rendezvous should the *Etoile* not be able to get to the Falklands for any reason.*

Reaching Rio on June 21, 1767, Bougainville was relieved to find the *Etoile* at anchor and stuffed with provisions. He learned that the *Etoile* had sailed two months late from France and had suffered severe damage in her transatlantic passage. Although she had tried to reach the Falklands, she was leaking so badly that she had turned back to await Bougainville in Rio.

At Rio Bougainville found the local Portuguese violently hostile. Resenting their French visitors as allies of the hated Spaniards, the people not only refused help to Bougainville but even attacked his men, in one incident murdering the *Etoile*'s chaplain. Thus, after a stay of only three weeks and in spite of the southern winter, Bougainville sailed his two ships out of Rio and returned to the friendly Spanish port of Montevideo. There the two French vessels anchored on July 31, 1767, to await the return of spring in September.

Once again the Frenchmen had bad luck. The *Etoile* was rammed by a Spanish warship in the harbor and further dam-

---

*With the departure of Bougainville, France, keeping its faith with Spain, made no further attempts to plant a colony on the Falklands. The British, however, continued to claim the islands on the basis of Byron's 1765 visit. The British also placed a small colony there, naming it Port Egmont. The British finally evacuated Port Egmont in 1774. Spanish sovereignty over the islands ended when Spain lost control of its South American empire, and the Spaniards eventually left the islands in 1811. In 1832 the British, ignoring Argentine claims of sovereignty descending from Spain, again occupied the Falklands (the Malvinas to the Spaniards), and they do so to this day, despite the 1982 invasion by Argentina, repulsed by a British counterinvasion.

aged. Now Bougainville had to endure more delay while Spanish carpenters patched his storeship. Thus it was November 1767, almost a full year after sailing from France, before the *Boudeuse* and the *Etoile* (still leaking to some extent) could depart Montevideo for the Strait of Magellan.

By early December the ships were fighting their way through the strait in the teeth of fierce winds. On December 18, 1767, they anchored in what is now Bougainville Bay, near present-day Puntas Arenas, on the north side of the strait. Bougainville gave his weary crews an interval of rest, during which time the Frenchmen sighted the fires of Tierra del Fuego to the south and Bougainville himself visited that bleak coast. Commerson, the naturalist, also took advantage of the rest period to go ashore and collect plant specimens.

After twelve days the ships resumed the struggle westward. The weather continued furious and bitterly cold. On New Year's Day 1768, the ships anchored once more, while four inches of snow blanketed their decks. The French remained at anchor for two weeks, hoping for an improvement in the weather. But the gales did not abate, and Bougainville finally renewed the weary task of beating west toward the Pacific.

Now as the French toiled deeper into the channel, they came across debris left behind by Wallis's *Dolphin* and Carteret's *Swallow*, which had made the same difficult journey some eight months earlier: discarded tools, rubbish, wood shavings, and dead campfires. They also found initials and names carved on trees with the date 1767. With so much evidence of a prior British passage to the Pacific, Bougainville worried that the English might have already beaten him to Terra Australis. But he pressed on, and finally, on January 26, 1768, after fifty-two days of effort, his ships emerged onto the Pacific. The French sailors rejoiced. Emulating Magellan, they sang a Te Deum.

Bougainville had intended to head north to Juan Fernández after reaching the Pacific, but finding the winds unfavorable for that course, he decided to stand to the northwest and begin searching for Davisland. Through most of February 1768 Bougainville swept northwest and west across the huge waters of the Pacific. Though the *Boudeuse* and the *Etoile* kept lookouts constantly aloft, Bougainville had no more luck finding Davisland than had Roggeveen almost fifty years earlier. In his journal Bougainville expressed his skepticism about its very existence, noting that he had seen only open water where it was supposed to lie. "I have passed over David's Land without sighting it," he wrote wryly.*

On March 22, 1768, the French found themselves among a group of low-lying islands in 18 degrees south.† Unable to anchor because of rough surf and reefs, the ships crept through the maze in a westerly direction. On one low island Bougainville sighted men whom he described as "bronze" in color. At first he thought them European castaways in need of rescue, but when dozens more of these bronze men appeared, armed with pikes, Bougainville decided that they were neither European nor in need of help. He sailed on.

Continuing to pick his way through these low islands, Bougainville sought a place to anchor, but dangerous reefs frustrated all his efforts. Toward the end of March he headed to the west-southwest "to get out of this labyrinth of islands . . . where neither water nor refreshment can be found, as it is impracticable to disembark on most of them." But before the ships could escape from the islands—which Bougainville named the Dangerous Archipelago and claimed for France—the weather turned so "horrible" with incessant rain that, according to Bougainville: "The poor sailor cannot get himself dry, and since humidity is the most active agent of scurvy, we shall soon be infected with it; the storekeeper's clerk and one of my blacks are very ill with it."

To escape the rain, and hoping to find an island that might offer rest and fresh provisions, Bougainville now came about almost 180 degrees toward the south-south*east.* Soon lookouts sighted high land rising out of the sea. As the French approached, they saw that the steep land was an isolated island, a mere dot, but that the region beyond was lush and extensive. Making for that farther shore, the French observed nocturnal fires, a certain sign that the place was inhabited and, therefore, could offer respite and food for the relief of the scurvy-ridden sailors.

On April 4, 1768, the *Boudeuse* and the *Etoile* closed on their destination: a volcanic island of extraordinary beauty. For two days the ships coasted the shoreline seeking a safe harbor, while smiling natives, among them "some pretty and almost naked

---

*He called it David's Land in his journals and on his charts. The suspicious English later accused him of doing this on purpose, in order to mislead their navigators.
†They were the Tuamotus.

women," came out in canoes to greet the new arrivals. Though the islanders would not come aboard the ships, they engaged in friendly communication with the French. And now Bougainville learned the name of the island: Tahiti.

On the morning of April 6, 1768, the ships reached the northernmost point of the island. If the French had rounded this northern cape, they would have come to Matavai Bay, where Wallis had anchored the *Dolphin* less than a year earlier. But Bougainville saw surf boiling over the reefs ahead and judged that there was no good anchorage nearby. The French came about and made their way back down the coast again toward a previously noted inlet in the vicinity of the low-lying land that linked the two mountainous ends of the island. Although this bay, which the local people called Hitiaa Lagoon, offered relatively poor shelter, the French concluded that it would serve, and here the *Boudeuse* and the *Etoile* dropped their hooks. Crowds of canoes had accompanied the ships into the lagoon, almost blocking their progress. Now, with the big vessels anchored, the canoes swarmed about, the people joyfully crying:"*Tayo, Tayo!*" which Bougainville says meant "friend." "They all asked nails and earrings of us," he reports in his journals.

Now the French mariners drank in the beauty and frank sexuality of the native women, finding them every bit as appealing as had the British tars some months earlier. Bougainville describes the effect of the beautiful Tahitian women on his men, noting that even as his lads were trying to lower the anchors of their ships at Hitiaa Lagoon, they could not take their eyes from the hundreds of canoes around them, all filled with chanting and smiling islanders:

> How could one keep at work in the midst of such a spectacle, 400 Frenchmen, young sailors who for six months had not seen a woman? . . . In spite of all our precautions, one young woman came on board onto the poop, and stood by one of the hatches above the capstan. This hatch was open to give some air to those who were working. The young girl negligently allowed her loincloth to fall to the ground, and appeared to all eyes such as Venus showed herself to the Phrygian shepherd. She had the goddess' celestial form. Sailors and soldiers

hurried to get to the hatchway, and never was capstan heaved with such speed.

Despite the warmth of their welcome, the Tahitians showed some initial reluctance to allow Bougainville to establish a camp onshore for his sick. He assured the chieftains that he and his men would remain on the island for only eighteen days. However, he insisted, time ashore was essential to treat the sick and to obtain water and supplies. The French were then permitted to set up their camp.

Now the natives and French began exchanging social visits and goods. The French entertained their hosts with a string concert and a fireworks display. The Tahitians diverted the French in their own inimitable fashion. Even Bougainville was offered sexual hospitality. He writes of the incident: "The chief offered me one of his women, young and fairly pretty; the whole assembly sang the marriage hymn. What a country! What a people!"

The French soon realized that they were not the first Europeans to visit the island, for the Tahitians knew what guns were. In addition, trifles such as clothes, nails, glass, and utensils, which could have come only from a European source, were found in the houses of the people. Bougainville, aware that the British were also searching for the southern continent in these waters, surmised that a British expedition—probably the one that had left its traces in the strait—had visited Tahiti before him. But he seems to have made no immediate attempt to confirm his suspicions by asking the islanders. Perhaps he was distracted when the native propensity for theft threatened to rupture relations between the Tahitians and their visitors.

From the first moments of contact, light-fingered Tahitians had been annoying the French by making off with their goods: an officer's pistol one day, a hat another day, carpenter's tools. The islanders found such articles irresistible. Bougainville was lenient about the thievery, writing: "No doubt curiosity towards new objects awoke in them violent desires, and anyhow there are rascals everywhere." But he also realized that unless the thefts ceased, some French sailor would eventually kill or injure a would-be thief. He ordered guards set over the camp and the ships. Still, the stealing continued, and the retaliation that Bougainville had hoped to avoid became a reality.

On April 10, only four days after the French ships had anchored, a Tahitian was found shot to death. Bougainville tried but failed to find the murderer among his men. Two days later three more Tahitians were killed, this time by bayonets. Bougainville had four suspects arrested. By now he had already decided—partly at the request of the local chiefs—to cut his contemplated eighteen day stay in half. He made this decision not only to preclude further violence between his men and the Tahitians but also because the French were experiencing trouble with their lagoon anchorage, which Bougainville describes as "detestable." The ships had already dragged their anchors more than once, and at one point the *Boudeuse* had rammed the *Etoile*. Though the collision was minor, Bougainville worried that a second crash might have disastrous results or that the ships might go aground on the reefs. Thus, he reckoned he had two reasons to depart as soon as possible. Moreover, most of the sick were recovered, and the reprovisioning of the ships was almost complete.

Bougainville ordered preparations made for sailing. On April 14, the *Etoile* was warped out beyond the reef. Meanwhile, men worked through the night to finish the watering of the *Boudeuse*, still anchored in the lagoon.

Now, apparently as a gesture of goodwill, the French planted a garden of corn, beans, peas, wheat, and other vegetables. Bougainville also presented the Tahitians with turkeys and geese, expressing the hope that the fowl would reproduce and furnish the inhabitants with new sources of food. True to his mission, Bougainville also had prepared an Act of Possession. Carved on an oaken plank this "document" claimed the island for France and named it New Cythera. Bougainville had his officers witness the claim by signing their names to a paper, which was then sealed in a bottle and buried with the carved plank.

On April 15 the *Boudeuse* prepared to join the *Etoile*, waiting beyond the reef. Tahitians, weeping in their canoes, sang farewells. At this point a high-ranking Tahitian named Ahu-Toru, boarded the *Boudeuse*. The brother of one of the island's chief men, Ahu-Toru asked to sail with the French to see their country. Bougainville agreed, reasoning that Ahu-Toru could serve as guide and interpreter in the days ahead. The *Boudeuse* raised her anchors.

At this last moment the flagship almost came to grief. Though she got safely to open water, the wind suddenly fell and the ocean swell threatened to drive her back onto the reef. She escaped only when her boats, assisted by an offshore wind, managed to tow her out of danger.

Finally away, the ships set out to the west, making their way through a scattering of islands in the neighborhood.* Bougainville confirmed his surmise that a British ship had arrived at Tahiti when Ahu-Toru freely named the British *Dolphin* as the visiting vessel. He also said the British, too, had left the island as friends.

Although Ahu-Toru urged Bougainville to land on some of the islands that the ships were passing, the French commander rejected the idea. Instead, with the weather fine, he ordered his ships to make all sail to the west, for it was there that the continent had to lie, if it lay anywhere at all.

*These were later known as the Society Islands.

32

AUTOUR LE MONDE

By early May 1768 the French found themselves among a new group of islands, some thirteen hundred miles to the west of Tahiti. Here, as at Tahiti, many canoes came out to the ships, but the people seemed wilder and far less attractive than the Tahitians. Moreover, Ahu-Toru could not make himself understood. Uncharacteristically harsh, Bougainville described these islanders as "savage" and "hideous."*

The French ships now lay approximately seven thousand miles out in the Pacific and about one thousand miles south of the equator. Bougainville now contemplated playing it safe by changing course to the northwest, rounding the northern coast of New Guinea, and making for the Moluccas. This was the route taken by most European navigators who had preceded him in these waters. But the doughty Frenchman rejected this course, even though the provisions taken aboard in Tahiti were now running low. Instead he decided it was his duty to continue searching westward for Terra Australis. The *Boudeuse* and the *Etoile* crept on through a labyrinth of reef-ringed islands west of the Samoans. Day after day the ships had to avoid dangerous shoals, skirt surf-beaten islands, and keep a sharp eye out for the squalls that

*The French had now reached the Samoan group. Bougainville gave them the name Navigators Islands.

might spring up and drive them aground. "My God," exclaims Bougainville in his journal, "how much patience this navigation requires!"

Nevertheless, there were some advantages to this westerly track. In these island-strewn seas Bougainville could send parties ashore for water and fresh food from time to time, and by pressing on directly to the west, the French ships were able to avail themselves of favorable winds. All in all Bougainville considered hunger, thirst, and perilous waters a price worth paying for the chance to find Terra Australis.*

So the French went on to the west, holding at approximately fifteen degrees south. They soon passed the Hoorn Islands and came to that vast sweep of ocean and islands today called Melanesia. The indigenous people here were black, with woolly hair and nose rings that struck the French as barbarous. Further, their behavior was wildly unpredictable, sometimes cooperative but often fiercely xenophobic. At one island, for example, the natives, mesmerized by gifts of cloth, helped the French obtain wood. On another isle a French landing party was viciously attacked with stones and arrows. Whatever the reception, however, Bougainville, following his orders, made sure to claim the atolls and islets that came his way in the name of Louis XV.

As the expedition continued west, the weather worsened once more, and scurvy again appeared among the men. Bougainville fretted: "This is not living, it is dying a thousand deaths." To make matters worse, another disease also appeared among the French toward the end of May, when approximately twenty men of the *Boudeuse,* and another dozen in the *Etoile,* began complaining of "chancres." It was certain that the men had contracted this illness in Tahiti, the only port during the voyage where they had had sexual contact. One of those found to be suffering from this "venereal distemper" was Bougainville's Tahitian passenger, Ahu-Toru. From him Bougainville now learned that the islanders, who worried little about this disorder, called it the British illness. Bougainville speculates in his journal that the crew of the *Dolphin* first planted the infection in Tahiti: "I do not know whether the Tahitians owe to the English, as well

---

*Obtaining sufficient supplies of fresh water had been, and continued to be, a problem for the French mariners, despite the often copious rains encountered and despite distillation equipment aboard the ships. Apparently the rainfall was either too much or too little, and the distilling machines worked poorly at best.

as the discovery of iron, the introduction of the venereal diseases which we found established there."*

By now the French vessels had left the New Hebrides chain behind and had sailed through the strait that separates Quirós's Espíritu Santo from the island of Malekula to the south. Bougainville had recognized these extensive territories as Quirós's old landfall and had found himself wondering if Quirós's discovery was indeed part of a continent or if the true continent lay still farther west. Another question also teased his mind: How far off was New Holland? There was only one way to answer both these questions: Continue sailing to the west. As Bougainville puts it: "[To solve the problem of the continent] it would be necessary to follow the same parallel for a distance of more than 350 leagues. I [took] this course, although the state and the quantity of our supplies warned us to seek promptly some European settlement."

Keeping along the parallel of 15 degrees south, Bougainville plunged into the virtually unknown waters west of the Santa Cruz chain. He would either find the long-sought continent or come upon the eastern coast of New Holland. Today called the Coral Sea, this region of the ocean was marked by shoals and reefs that could spell disaster. For this reason lookouts were now more vigilant than ever to spot any peril ahead—or to sight the shores of Terra Australis.

Sometime during these critical days Bougainville inquired into yet another puzzle, one far less momentous than the enigma of the southern continent. This was the affair of Commerson's effeminate "valet."

From the beginning of the voyage, there had been suspicions aboard the *Etoile* about "M. Baret," the faithful servant of the expedition's chief scientist. But the formidable man of science, Commerson, and the diffident youth, Baret, had managed to fend off all inquiries, and Bougainville had studiously avoided the matter. Clearly, on the captain's part, it was a case of turning a blind eye. For months, on the passage through the strait and across the Pacific, Bougainville had succeeded in seeing no evil

---

*The British vehemently denied the charge that they introduced venereal disease to Tahiti. Instead they countercharged that it was the French who did so. The argument raged for many years.

and hearing no evil of young Baret and his eminent employer.

When the French had arrived in Tahiti, however, the blinders had been wrenched from Bougainville's unwilling eyes. "M. Baret," after months cooped up aboard the *Etoile*, had taken the opportunity at Hitiaa Lagoon to go ashore. Immediately the natives had identified "him" as a woman. Delighted at the sight of a European female, though she was garbed in a man's outfit, they had begun pointing and calling out, "*Vahine! Vahine!*"— their word for "girl."

Bougainville was no longer able to ignore the subject after this public exposure. If Baret was not the homosexual lover of Commerson, as some had suspected, was "he" the naturalist's mistress? Bougainville vowed to get at the truth at some later, more convenient time. That time arrived as the French ships picked their way through the Coral Sea. Bougainville, discovering that he had some business to transact aboard the *Etoile*, had himself rowed over from the *Boudeuse*. After disposing of his more commonplace affairs, he called "Monsieur" Baret before him.

Baret readily acknowledged that she was, as the Tahitians had discerned, a young woman. She said that her name was Jeanne and that she was twenty years old. She went on to unfold an astonishing story. She was an orphan, she told Bougainville, and had been deprived of her rightful inheritance by a lawsuit. With no family to protect her, she had begun wearing men's clothing as a defense against the unwanted attentions of predatory males. She had also found that it was easier to obtain employment by impersonating a young man. Still, it was as a female that she had first entered the household of the distinguished Commerson. A widower, he had retained her four years earlier as governess to his son. She would not divulge whether any personal relationship had developed between the scientist and her. Nor, apparently, did Bougainville inquire. Baret also insisted that only a thirst for adventure had induced her to join the expedition by playing the part of Commerson's valet.

It is probable that the worldly Bougainville did not entirely swallow the girl's story. But he was a man disposed to tolerate the foibles of others. Thus, although Commerson certainly must have connived at Jeanne Baret's impersonation, Bougainville deliberately ignored this aspect of the matter. Having uncovered as much of the story as he wished to know, he probed no further, clearly satisfied that the girl's imposture was revealed and explained, at least officially. The matter was thus left pretty much as before. Baret and Commerson continued to share quarters. Bougainville laconically recorded the brief facts in his later report. He did, however, permit himself to make one of his wry observations on the affair: "One must agree that if the two ships had been wrecked on some desert island in this vast ocean, fate would have played a strange trick on Baret." One of the expedition's officers, after Bougainville's official confirmation of Baret's true identity, also made a pertinent comment: "I believe that this girl will be the first of her sex to have circumnavigated the globe."*

The French ships forged on until they were well into the Coral Sea off present-day Australia. Then, on the afternoon of June 6, 1768, the ships, having already avoided one series of dangerous shoals marked by foaming breakers, came upon definite signs of peril: surf, rocks, crashing breakers, and thunderous seas. What lay ahead of the ships was a geographic phenomenon never before glimpsed by Western mariners: many miles of reefs, sandbars, rocky outcrops, and half-submerged islands, a labyrinth of coral and shallows certain to wreck any sailing ship that approached too near it.†

Bougainville realized that the maze lying before his vessels must put an end to any further voyaging to the west. "This . . . discovery," he wrote, "was the voice of God, and we were obedient to it."

On June 7, 1768, having come within a hundred miles of the unknown east coast of New Holland, Bougainville came about to the north-northeast, intent on getting his vessels away from this dangerous lee shore. He also concluded that the east side of New Holland was a cluster of islands, outlying a land "where there is not even water to drink and the approaches to which bristle with shoals and reefs."

---

*Young Jeanne Baret not only survived the voyage but disembarked with Commerson in France. Although it is almost impossible to doubt that Commerson and Jeanne Baret were lovers during the voyage, the affair did not lead to a permanent liaison. Baret later married another, younger man. Commerson, apparently never able to forget his governess-valet, left her a goodly sum in his will.
†It was the Great Barrier Reef, which stretches for well over a thousand miles along the northeastern shore of Australia.

On June 10, working northward well off the labyrinthine reefs to his larboard, Bougainville sighted the eastern point of New Guinea. But with hunger now worsening every day aboard the ships, he decided not to take the time to search for a strait between New Guinea and New Holland, although he believed that such a passage probably existed. Instead he resolved to return to "civilization" as soon as possible by doubling the eastern cape of New Guinea and following its northern coast to the Moluccas. The French ships began fighting their way northward through bad weather and a new series of shoals, reefs, and islets off the eastern end of New Guinea.*

Hunger now became so bad that the men ate a pet dog and a goat. Bougainville had to forbid them to eat the leather from the yards.

At last, on June 20, after two weeks of struggle, the ships were through these dangerous waters. But Bougainville, still fearing to come too close to the reefs along the New Guinea shoreline, continued northward until the ships reached another group of large populated islands. These were the Solomons, discovered by Mendaña two hundred years before, but not seen since (except by Carteret in the *Swallow* in 1767). Bougainville did not recognize the islands as the Solomons, but they appeared to offer the possibility of relief for his men. Unfortunately his ships were unable to anchor because of contrary winds and tides and because of the hostility of the Melanesian natives, whose furious attacks could be stopped only by lethal musket fire.

Turning west from the Solomons, the French sailed on. Hunger and scurvy aboard the ships were now worse than ever. After passing by the large island that now bears his name, Bougainville and his men spotted an uninhabited cove. There they finally anchored on July 6, 1768.

Bougainville believed that he had now reached Dampier's New Britain. In fact, it was the separate island of New Ireland. The French named their quiet refuge Port Praslin. There they found wood and water but disappointingly little fresh food with which to cure their scurvy. It was clear that they would soon have to depart after filling their water casks and repairing some recent damage.

---

*Bougainville called this archipelago the Louisiades, the name by which it is still known.

Yet if Port Praslin yielded little in the way of provisions, it presented Bougainville with a new puzzle. Foragers discovered the remains of a European campsite nearby and signs that a British ship had visited this place sometime earlier. Was it, perhaps, the *Dolphin*, the British ship that, according to Ahu-Toru, had preceded the French to Tahiti? From the debris left behind, there was no way of telling.*

Though Bougainville wanted to get under way again from Port Praslin as soon as possible, storms and even an earthquake prevented the French from departing. It was not until July 24, 1768, that they were able to set sail. Bougainville again left behind an inscription, claiming the island for France.

Bougainville now had but one goal: to reach safety in the Indies. The ships continued toward the west. Hunger and disease tortured the crews. To make conditions even worse, the French had to fight off native attacks almost daily. On some days, according to one French officer, the water around the ships was red with blood. By August 11 the French were nearing the northwest extremity of New Guinea. The Moluccas still lay several hundred miles farther west. One man died of scurvy. Forty-five others were incapacitated by the agonizing disease. Lamented Bougainville: "Each day brings new victims. What food, Good Lord, is ours? Small quantities of putrid bread, and meat whose smell could be supported only by the most dauntless. . . . In any other circumstances . . . it would all be thrown into the sea."

Finally, at the end of August, the French reached the Moluccas. Raising the beautiful island of Ceram on September 1, they were bitterly disappointed to find the place deserted by the Dutch as a result of a local revolt. On the next day, however, they anchored at the nearby island of Buru, where the Dutch were still in business and where they paid dearly for lifesaving stores. Much refreshed, the French vessels soon moved on to the Dutch East India Company's headquarters at Batavia, on the island of Java. There Bougainville came to anchor on September 28, 1768.

At Batavia, which Bougainville first called "one of the finest colonies in the universe," the French were well received and their sick taken to hospital. Bougainville learned that the British

---

*The British ship was the poor *Swallow*. The brave Carteret and his men had also visited the bay some four months earlier, as Bougainville later discovered.

sloop *Swallow* had departed only twelve days before the French arrival. Thus was solved the mystery of the British vessel at Port Praslin. It was not, after all, the sleek *Dolphin* whose traces the French had uncovered there but another craft, described by the Dutch as barely seaworthy. The French were curious to behold this British vessel in whose wake they had sailed, and Bougainville expressed the hope that he might yet catch up to her.

While at Batavia, Bougainville was much impressed by Dutch wealth, inducing him to express his own imperialist hopes for France: "Oh my country, Awake! . . . Neptune has not sworn you an eternal hatred. Is he not actually well disposed toward Venus' favorites? But it is only by regular devotion that one obtains the favors of the Gods."

Although the French were now well provisioned and receiving medical care, many of Bougainville's mariners suddenly began coming down with a new disorder: the dysentery that was endemic in Batavia. As the plague spread among his crewmen, Bougainville decided to depart as soon as possible. On October 18, 1768, the *Boudeuse* set out for the island of Mauritius, in the Indian ocean. The *Etoile*, still undergoing repairs, was to follow as soon as she could.

Reaching Mauritius safely on November 8, Bougainville was soon joined by his escort. After further refitting and medical treatment for his crews, Bougainville sailed for home on December 12, 1768. Again he left the *Etoile* behind to finish her repairs.

On January 9, 1769, the *Boudeuse* reached the Cape of Good Hope, where Bougainville learned that the British *Swallow* had sailed only three days earlier. Bougainville departed for the Atlantic, in the wake of the *Swallow*, on January 17, 1769. The French explorer wrote in his journal that he soon "hoped to join M. Carteret." Sixteen days later, on February 4, 1769, the *Boudeuse* arrived at Ascension Island, only to learn that Carteret had already moved on.

Bougainville was now intent on overtaking Carteret. The *Boudeuse* had played tag with this elusive *Swallow* long enough. He tarried only a brief time at Ascension Island and sailed again on February 6. In his journal Bougainville expressed his hope that "our next anchorage will be in our own country."

Nineteen days later, on February 25, 1769, the *Boudeuse* finally caught up with the *Swallow*. She was indeed a sight. Trailing long tendrils of marine growth from her hull, she was barely floundering in the rough Atlantic seas. Bougainville hailed her. With perhaps a tincture of Gallic swagger as well as his usual courtesy, he offered to furnish any help the Englishmen might need. Captain Carteret refused Bougainville with the pride of a Royal Navy officer. He made it clear that the *Swallow* would reach home waters on her own. But Carteret did turn over to Bougainville some letters entrusted to him at Capetown and destined for France. He also presented Bougainville with an arrow, an artifact taken during the *Swallow*'s Pacific voyage. Bougainville received the gift with graceful thanks. He kept to himself, however, the fact that he, too, had recently crossed the Pacific, often in the *Swallow*'s wake.

After some further pleasantries, the *Boudeuse* sailed on, leaving the *Swallow* behind, "as if she lay at anchor." Remarks Bougainville of Carteret's command: "His ship was very small, went very ill . . . how much he must have suffered in so bad a vessel may well be conceived." Though he did not say so specifically in his journal, Bougainville was all but certain that the beat-up British sloop could not have located Terra Australis. She was simply incapable of enduring the rigors of the far South Pacific where, undoubtedly, the continent was to be found.

The *Boudeuse* arrived home at Saint-Malo on March 16, 1769. The *Etoile*, left behind at Mauritius, came in a month later. The frigate had been away for twenty-eight months, the *Etoile* for twenty-nine. During all this time, despite the scurvy and the hunger that had tortured his crews, Bougainville had lost only nine men.

Bougainville was a sensation. He was the first Frenchman to have circumnavigated the globe. All France hailed his feat. But he had not, after all, discovered the southern continent. Thus, as charming as Tahiti surely was and as glorious as the voyage had certainly been, the mystery of Terra Australis Incognita remained unsolved.

Still, Bougainville *had* raised the curtain a little higher in the Pacific, as had the two Englishmen Wallis and poor Carteret. At least now geographers knew where *not* to seek the South Land. Nevertheless, the question remained unanswered, and there were even some skeptics who dared to suggest that the Pacific continent might not exist at all. This was a premise rejected by most scholars, who remained convinced that Terra Australis was still Incognita only because navigators and sailors had failed to look in the right part of the vast Pacific. One geographer was so sure of Terra Australis that he yearned to sail there in person and thus win immortal fame as "the Columbus of the Pacific."*

*Bougainville himself never sailed to the Pacific again. Although he later proposed leading an expedition to the North Pole, the French government refused him the necessary aid. In the reign of Napoleon I, Bougainville was awarded the Legion of Honor for his exploits. He also became a senator and count of the empire. He died in Paris on August 31, 1811, just shy of his eighty-second birthday.

33

THE SCHOLAR AND THE SAILOR

"A continent is wanting on the south . . . to counterpoise the land on the north and to maintain the equilibrium necessary for the earth's motion." These were the words of Alexander Dalrymple, a Scottish man of letters and the official hydrographer of the English East India Company.

Fat, choleric, dogmatic Dalrymple was the day's most influential writer on the undiscovered South Land. He had read all the journals of past explorers and had pondered long upon their experiences. As a result of his studies, he had concluded that not only did Terra Australis exist, but he alone knew where to find it. Moreover, he knew what he would find there: civilized people, temperate climate, and great natural wealth. When Alexander Dalrymple expressed such opinions, thoughtful men took him seriously, for he was no crank but a distinguished man whose career had won him the respect of scientists and mariners alike.

Born in 1737, Dalrymple came from an old and honored Scottish family. After receiving only a modest early education, fifteen-year-old Alexander was sent out to Madras as an apprentice in the East India Company. There his real education commenced. In the employ of the company he became a skilled geographer, navigator, and astronomer. He also began studying the voyages of Portuguese, Spanish, and Dutch explorers in the Pacific, many of which were documented in the company archives. These researches convinced him that earlier sailors had often sighted the coasts of Terra Australis but had failed to investigate properly.

In 1758, at the age of twenty-one, Dalrymple was named deputy secretary of the company at Madras. Between 1760 and 1764 he made several journeys from Madras to the East Indies with the objective of extending the East India Company's operations to that part of the world, especially Borneo. In 1765 Dalrymple returned to England with the purpose of gaining government support for further development of trade in the Indies.

At the same time he was bubbling with enthusiasm for Terra Australis, whose discovery, he argued, would ensure the growth of British commerce well into the future. By 1766, when Foul Weather Jack Byron returned from Britain's first, disappointing thrust into the Pacific, Dalrymple was already regarded as the most knowledgeable man in England on the subject of the Pacific.

In 1767 Dalrymple put his theories into a privately printed book entitled *An Account of the Discoveries Made in the South Pacifick Ocean Previous to 1764.* The book sets forth all his arguments for the existence of the southern continent: the need for balance in nature, the "conformity of hemispheres," the reported existence of "fair-haired people" in the islands of the Pacific, and past sightings.

Dalrymple wrote that he was persuaded that Terra Australis lay in the Pacific somewhere about latitude 40 degrees south. He estimated that the vast South Land stretched over some fifty-three hundred miles from east to west and probably had a population of more than fifty million people. He postulated that Tasman's New Zealand might be the western coast of the continent. The discovery of the continent, he maintained, required a new Columbus, a man of "conception" and "perseverant resolution." Dalrymple left little doubt that he viewed himself as that new Columbus.

Dalrymple's book created a stir. His arguments seemed compelling. Certainly his credentials as a geographic expert were impressive, and no one could deny that there was ample room in the unexplored South Pacific beyond Capricorn for Dalrymple's great South Land. Moreover, the volume appeared just when the race to find Terra Australis Incognita was heating up.

Only a year earlier, his fellow Scotsman John Callender had

published a plagiarized version of the Frenchman de Brosses, who had entreated his own king to sponsor a national search for Terra Australis. Even as Dalrymple's book was circulating, Wallis and Carteret were en route to the Pacific, as was Bougainville. France and England were again in urgent competition.

Many Englishmen feared that if France was first to find the great South Land, it could use it as a base to win control of the Pacific and much of Asia as well. It therefore behooved Britain to send additional expeditions into the Pacific in the wake of Wallis and Carteret, as Dalrymple proposed, for even if Wallis and Carteret found the continent, it would certainly take more than one voyage to establish British supremacy there. Dalrymple was able to find much favor within decision-making circles in England.

But it was not just because of its *political* message that Dalrymple's book was influential. In the new age of "science" then dawning, the Scotsman's theses were buttressed by scholarship that lent them credibility. In the second half of the eighteenth century intellectuals in all the Western nations were avidly investigating the nature of such phenomena as heat, sound, electricity, optics, and astronomy. Not surprisingly in a world still largely unexplored, geography was also a major area of study.

To advance scientific inquiry, scholarly associations had sprung up throughout Europe. Perhaps the most prestigious of these was Britain's Royal Society. Founded under the patronage of Charles II in 1662, its full title was the Royal Society of London for Improving Natural Knowledge. By Dalrymple's time the Royal Society had become the chief instrument for research and the repository of scientific knowledge for the British government. Sir Isaac Newton had been its president early in the eighteenth century. The great astronomer Edmund Halley, discoverer of the comet, was one of the society's most respected members. The weekly meetings of the Royal Society were often exhibitions of formidable intellect. To be a "fellow" of the society was proof of expertise in one or more learned disciplines. Alexander Dalrymple was a fellow of the Royal Society. This fact alone proclaimed that he knew what he was talking about when he argued for a concentrated effort to discover the South Land.*

*It is remarkable, considering the scientific advances already achieved in Dalrymple's time, that the concept of the Pacific South Land hung on so tenaciously among geog-

Dalrymple's association with the Royal Society also seemed likely (in his own estimation at least) to provide him with the opportunity to become the Columbus of the Pacific. Even as Dalrymple's book was impressing London in 1767, the Royal Society was at work on a project that seemed to suit his hopes exactly: a voyage to the South Pacific to observe the planet Venus.

This undertaking had been the brainchild of Edmund Halley. Several years earlier the great astronomer had noted that in June 1769 Venus would move across the face of the sun, providing a perfect opportunity to observe the planet and expand knowledge of the solar system. Pointing out that this "transit of Venus" would not recur for more than a hundred years, Halley had proposed that the Royal Society sponsor an expedition to the South Pacific, where the phenomenon could be observed best. The fellows of the Royal Society were fired with enthusiasm for Halley's scheme, and by 1767 planning was well under way.

Although as a geographic scholar Dalrymple was expected to participate in the venture, his own ambition was to command the enterprise. In November 1766, while the project was in its earliest stages, the young scholar had written to Lord Shelburne, Britain's secretary of state for the Southern Department, setting forth his qualifications to lead the Pacific voyage. He told Lord Shelburne that he had already had five years' experience in travels through "seas unknown" and thought himself "qualified to be usefully employed in such an undertaking."

This letter had had little effect, apparently, for three months later, on February 12, 1767, Dalrymple again brought the matter before Lord Shelburne, this time through an intermediary, the famed economist Adam Smith, who was a friend of Dalrymple's prominent older brother. Wrote Smith to Lord Shelburne:

---

raphers. The notion of a giant southern continent had first been put forward by scholars who knew nothing of gravity and thus postulated the need for a counterweight in the southern half of the globe to keep the earth from turning over under the weight of the great northern landmasses. But gravity and its role in governing a planet's position in space had been known since Newton's work in the late seventeenth century. Thus it would seem Newton had rendered obsolete any idea that the continent was "needed" to balance the earth. Still, geographers clung to the continent's existence. It would appear that the Pacific continent was more faith than science, even among scholars such as Dalrymple. It was as if having read so much about it, conjectured so long upon it, and dreamed so often of its supposed riches, scholars could not bear to part with it, despite Newton. Moreover, the Pacific was so vast and so little known, and so much of the earth itself remained unexplored in the eighteenth century, that the existence of a new New World in the Pacific seemed far from implausible.

... whether the continent exists or not may perhaps be uncertain; but supposing it does exist, I am very certain you will never find a man fitter for discovering it, or more determined to hazard everything in order to discover it.

The terms he [Dalrymple] would ask are, first, the absolute command of the ship with the naming of all the officers, in order that he may have people who both have confidence in him and in whom he has confidence; and secondly that in case he should lose his ship by the common course of accident before he gets into the South Sea, that the government will undertake to give him another. These are all the terms he would insist upon.

It is not clear how, or if, Lord Shelburne replied to Smith's letter. It is clear, however, that Dalrymple was demanding no less than total control of a Royal Navy vessel, something that the Admiralty would certainly hesitate to grant to a man with no rank or navy experience, even if he was a well-known geographer. In any event, for the Royal Society the subject of the leadership was less than urgent in 1767. Far more important was the need to obtain sufficient financial backing for the project. For this the society turned to its royal patron, George III.

In a memo sent in February 1768 the society pointed out to the king that accurate observations of the transit of Venus would do much to improve the study of astronomy, "on which navigation so much depends." The memorandum also pointedly noted that the other powers of Europe, including France, intended to take full advantage of this scientific opportunity and argued that it would "cast dishonour" upon Britain should it "neglect to have correct observations made of this important phenomenon."

The society then asked the king for four thousand pounds, plus ships to "convey and return the Observers." The fellows also reminded His Majesty that the Royal Society had been founded for "the improvement of natural knowledge," and thus it was their "duty" to bring this great matter to the king's attention. The king readily granted the funds, and the Admiralty was instructed to provide the transport required.

Even now there was no serious discussion of a commander for the venture, and Dalrymple himself apparently made no further efforts in that direction. Possibly he expected that the seeds he had already planted, watered by his celebrity, would bear the desired fruit. Nor did the Admiralty seem in any hurry to choose a ship and crew. Time enough for that, the navy seemed to say, after the scientists had finished their arrangements.

Then, on May 20, 1768, while the Royal Society fellows were in the midst of their preparations, Captain Samuel Wallis and the *Dolphin* returned from the Pacific. Wallis had not sighted the continent, but he gave so glowing a report of Tahiti that it was agreed that the island would provide the perfect location from which to observe the transit of Venus.

With the return of Wallis, the Admiralty began to look with considerably more interest upon the society's expedition. It suddenly seemed to the lords that a new Pacific voyage should do more than merely observe the transit of Venus. Bougainville, the Admiralty knew, was still at sea. Perhaps, unlike Wallis, he had succeeded in locating the elusive continent. If so, Britain had to move quickly to establish its own claim. The Admiralty also considered it essential to reinforce Wallis's claim to Tahiti. Thus it was decided that the Royal Society's Pacific voyage should include political as well as scientific objectives, and the Admiralty made it clear that from this time on the program would come under its jurisdiction. The ship chosen for the venture would be an armed vessel of the Royal Navy, commanded by an officer of the Royal Navy. Now that Dalrymple's chance to lead the mission had evaporated, he withdrew from the project.

But, since the commander of the expedition had to be Royal Navy, the scientists urged the Admiralty to appoint a "scientific-minded" officer. In fact, one of the organizers for the Royal Society, a certain Dr. Bevis, recollected having read something by a naval officer who just might fit the bill. Bevis could not recall the man's name offhand, but he remembered that this unknown officer had once submitted a paper to the Royal Society, something about observations of a solar eclipse. A sailor with such a scientific bent should be considered for command of the Pacific effort. Bevis rummaged through his files and found the officer's report. The author was James Cook.

Bevis's colleagues quickly agreed that Cook was perfect for the job: an expert navigator, a cartographer, and an astronomer. The Admiralty concurred.

* * *

A strapping, six-foot-tall figure with sharp brown eyes and bushy brows, Cook was thirty-nine years old in the summer of 1768. Despite his relatively advanced age, Cook had been in the Royal Navy for only twelve years, having volunteered just before the outbreak of the Seven Years' War. Cook was a thoroughgoing professional, and his naval career had been sure and steady, if not brilliant. He was no self-promoter, but a solid and unpretentious performer. He preferred to do the job before him and then move on without fanfare. As a consequence, he had sometimes been underrated by a few shortsighted superiors.

Still, Cook had done well in the Royal Navy, thanks to the reforms of Commodore Anson. Thirty years earlier James Cook, the son of a Scots-born farm laborer, could not have dreamed of a life as a Royal Navy Officer. Born in Yorkshire on October 27, 1728, Cook was the second of nine children, five of whom died before reaching adulthood. Unlike many, James was sent to school, where he learned to read, write, and do some mathematics. At the age of thirteen, he had to give up school and go to work for a grocer-haberdasher. In return for room and board, the boy clerked and kept the establishment's books. But at fourteen, he ran away to sea, signing on as cabin boy aboard the collier *Freelove*, a ship that plied between Newcastle and London. For seven years young Cook applied himself to the study of navigation, mapmaking, and astronomy, while saving as much of his pay as possible. Cook's ability and industry so impressed his employer that the young man was promoted to first mate aboard another collier, the *Friendship*. Again he proved his competence. Although only twenty-seven years old, Cook was about to be named a captain when he took a step that astounded all who knew him: He volunteered as a lowly seaman in the Royal Navy. It was the era when Anson's reforms were revitalizing the sea service, and Cook must have felt confident that his merits would bring him advancement, the more so because war with France was then imminent. And so it proved.

When the Seven Years' War broke out, Cook first served aboard HMS *Eagle*, on which, after two years, he rose to master's mate. He was then transferred to HMS *Pembroke* and participated in the British capture of Quebec, a victory achieved chiefly because the Royal Navy was able to carry Wolfe's army up the St. Lawrence River to the city, past dangerous shoals and rocks. This feat so astonished the French governor that he wrote: "The [Brit-

ish] have passed sixty ships of war where we dare not risk a vessel
of a hundred tons by night and day."

The British had been able to accomplish this daring ascent
thanks largely to Cook's skill in plotting a safe course upriver for
the fleet. Nor did the young officer's contribution to the victory
go unrewarded. In recognition of his part in the battle, Cook's
superiors presented him a purse of fifty pounds, a considerable
sum at the time.

In 1760 and 1761, with the war winding down, Cook was
employed in charting the coasts of Newfoundland and Labrador
for the Royal Navy. At the end of October, 1762, Cook, now
thirty-four, took a leave to marry Elizabeth Batts, the twenty-one-
year-old daughter of a London merchant. This year was
important to Cook for another reason: He received his first Royal
Navy command, the schooner *Grenville.*

For the next few years Cook charted Canadian waters for the
navy. While so engaged in 1766, he observed an eclipse of the
sun and later submitted his observations to the Royal Society,
greatly impressing Dr. Bevis. The Admiralty was also pleased with
his work, calling it "admirable." When the navy and the Royal
Society agreed that James Cook was the officer needed for their
joint enterprise in 1768, Cook was promoted to lieutenant. He
was ordered to choose his own vessel, enlist his own crew, and
make his own preparations for the expedition.*

Lieutenant Cook chose as his ship a 368-ton collier called
the *Endeavour.* She was not fast, but she was sturdy and offered
several advantages. She had snub bows, which gave her a stability
that would serve well in the open ocean. With her tough hull
and masts, designed to haul heavy loads of coal in rough seas,
she was capable of taking almost any strain. Wide of beam and
deep, she provided plenty of room for both crew and passengers
as well as any scientific equipment and specimens that might be
taken aboard. To give her even greater hull strength and especially to make her proof against the wood-boring teredo worm,
Cook had the ship's bottom sheathed with a second level of
planking and nails. Cook then chose a crew of eighty-three: sev-

---

*By taking command of the expedition, Cook actually lost some of his naval pay. As a
Royal Navy engineer he was paid 10 shillings a day, but as a naval lieutenant he would
receive only 5 shillings. The Royal Society, however, more than made up for this deficit,
awarding Cook 100 guineas, altogether with another 120 guineas a year as reimbursement
for his purchase of personal equipment and supplies.

enty-one sailors and officers and twelve armed marines. The Royal Society contingent numbered eleven, including two botanists, an astronomer, and an artist. The most imposing of the scientists was a young man of twenty-five, the wealthy and brilliant Joseph Banks, who was an ardent naturalist and botanist. Able to indulge his scholarly bent thanks to his wealth, Banks had made only one previous ocean journey, to Newfoundland. In a grand gesture of enthusiasm, Banks had contributed ten thousand pounds to help defray the Royal Society's expenses for the venture. He was considered the leader of the *Endeavour*'s scientific staff.*

Though accustomed to having his own way, Banks deferred to Cook as chief of their common enterprise, making it clear that he not only respected the older man but also found him "excellent company." It was not long before a strong friendship developed between the two.

The voyage was expected to take two years or more. Cook stuffed the *Endeavour* with barrels of the salt meat and biscuit that were the customary naval rations. Concerned about scurvy, he also took aboard live animals to provide occasional milk, eggs, and meat. In addition, he filled the holds with copious amounts of pickled food.

By August 1768 the ship was ready. Wrote one observer to the famed naturalist Linnaeus: "No people ever went to sea better fitted out for the purpose of Natural History, nor more elegantly."†

As the sailing date neared, Cook received secret written orders from the first lord of the Admiralty, Admiral Edward Hawke. Keenly aware that Bougainville was still in the Pacific and that the French were intent upon finding the South Land, Hawke meant to have Terra Australis for Britain. Thus he gave Cook

---

*Though it is difficult to estimate exactly, it is probable that Banks's contribution would be the equivalent today of something like $2 to 2.5 million. Banks was later elected president of the Royal Society.

†For all the scientific instrumentation that she carried, the *Endeavour* did *not* carry the most important navigation instrument of the day, the recently invented chronometer of John Harrison. This instrument, for which Harrison was eventually awarded a twenty-thousand-pound prize, could be relied upon to keep accurate Greenwich time at sea, thus allowing navigators for the first time ever to fix longitude precisely. The Admiralty apparently failed to recognize the fact that Harrison's chronometer would have been of special value in the exploration of unknown seas. As a result, Cook had to fix his longitude by the so-called lunar method. Although the lunar system was often unreliable and cumbersome, Cook had long ago mastered it and, as a result, was able to chart the voyage ahead with remarkable accuracy with regard to longitude.

explicit directions on how and where he was to search for the
South Land after the scientists aboard HMS *Endeavour* had completed the observation of Venus in Tahiti. Wrote Hawke: "You
are to proceed southward in order to make discovery of the continent above mentioned until you arrive in the latitude of 40
degrees, unless you sooner fall in with it; but not having discovered it or any sign of it in that run, you are to proceed in search
of it to the westward until you discover it or fall in with the eastern side of the land . . . now called New Zealand." In other
words, Cook was to scour the great ocean south of the track
followed by Wallis in the *Dolphin* and to go as far to the west as
necessary, even as far as New Zealand. He was also to make
friends with the people of the continent and take possession of
"convenient" lands with the consent of the inhabitants, if any.

Although the main object of the venture was the discovery
of Terra Australis, Cook was to survey any other lands he happened upon. He was free to explore as far and wide as he judged
feasible to gain his objectives. Moreover, he was allowed the option of returning either around the Horn or the Cape of Good
Hope, as he saw fit. Thus Cook's assignment was specific in regard to goals and vague when it came to methods of achieving
those goals.

On August 26, 1768—only weeks after the *Dolphin*'s return
and while Bougainville's ships were still struggling toward safety
in the Dutch East Indies and while Carteret's wretched *Swallow*
was making her slow crawl homeward—HMS *Endeavour*, James
Cook, master, sailed out of Plymouth, bound for paradise and
Terra Australis. Only a few representatives of the Admiralty and
a few fellows of the Royal Society came down to wish her bon
voyage. Alexander Dalrymple was not among them.

34

THE *ENDEAVOUR*

The crew of the *Endeavour* thought Lieutenant Cook sharp and just, a master who knew his job and would brook no nonsense. As for Cook, he understood that seafaring men required plain rules, straight talk, and firm handling. Above all, they needed occupation. Cook kept his lads busy at the hundred and one tasks that had to be done every day aboard a wooden vessel.

A dozen or more times on each watch the men had to climb into the rigging to take in or let out canvas according to the sailing conditions. Gunners had to practice handling the *Endeavour*'s ten large and twelve small cannon. The marines were required to drill daily. While lookouts constantly scanned the horizon, men polished brass, spliced sheets, repaired rigging, sloshed the decks with salt water, replaced planks, manned pumps, and hauled powder and shot.

Occupied, the men complained little, except about the food. The usual provisions—salted meat, oatmeal, and ship biscuit—were wretched fare, and with no proper storage, they soon became all but inedible. The *Endeavour*'s crew also groused because their captain insisted that they also had to consume such *unnatural* concoctions as carrot conserve, pickled onions, and sauerkraut. Who knew but that such stuff might weaken a man and give him "fluxes"?

Cook was testing a theory that a diet that included some

form of preserved vegetables could help ward off the dreaded scurvy. To the mariners, however, sauerkraut seemed less palatable than maggoty salt beef, and at the start of the voyage some refused the odd stuff pressed on them by their captain. Exasperated, Cook sentenced a marine and a sailor to a dozen lashes each for turning up their noses at a ration of onions. Then Cook hit on a more effective method of inducing his sailors to eat their vegetables. He tells about it in his journal:

> The sauerkraut, the men at first would not eat it, until I put into practice a method I never once knew to fail with seamen—and this was to have some of it dressed every day for the cabin table, and permitted all the officers, without exception, to make use of it, and left to the option of the men either to take as much as they pleased or none at all; but this practice was not continued above a week before I found it necessary to put every one on board to an allowance, for such are the tempers and disposition of seamen in general that whatever you give them out of the common way—although it be ever so much for their good—it will not go down, and you will hear nothing but murmurings against the man that first invented it; but the moment they see their superiors set a value upon it, it becomes the finest stuff in the world and the inventor an honest fellow. . . .

No doubt the men continued to mutter over their ship biscuit and salt meat, but sauerkraut, onions, and carrot conserve were now as delectable as they were formerly unpalatable.

And so the *Endeavour* crossed the Atlantic, a happy ship. The scientists worked charting the night sky, cataloging specimens taken ashore and at sea, and making records of atmospheric phenomena. Cook and his officers took their meals with their learned colleagues, and bonds based on shared adventure were forged around the captain's table.

After crossing the Atlantic, Cook gave his crew a few weeks of rest at Rio de Janeiro, proudly recording in his log that not a single man had come down with scurvy, thanks to his preserved vegetables.*

---

*Cook was by no means the only ship's captain who harbored ideas about how to treat

Continuing her journey, the *Endeavour* sailed southward from Rio along the coast of South America and made her way around Cape Horn, which Cook considered the easiest route. She reached Pacific waters at the end of January 1769, and Cook pointed her bows west by north to bring her to Tahiti as directly as possible.

By March 1, 1769, the *Endeavour* lay almost eighteen hundred miles west of the Chilean coast at approximately 40 degrees south. This was the area of the ocean, just below Capricorn, where some theorists, including Dalrymple, expected to encounter evidence of a continental landmass. But Cook and his officers observed no driftwood in the water, no clouds on the horizon, and no ocean currents that might signal land nearby.

On April 4 lookouts sighted the first islands of the Tuamotus. On April 11 the *Endeavour* raised Tahiti, easily recognized by its distinctive volcanoes. As the *Endeavour* made for the island, the Tahitians came out in hundreds of canoes to greet the ship. Swarming about, the natives, men and women alike, waved green boughs in near-ecstatic greeting and offered fruits and vegetables for trade. The British sailors goggled at the island girls.

It was April 13 when the *Endeavour* dropped her hook in Wallis's old anchorage, Matavai Bay, in plenty of time for the survey of Venus. Now the islanders clambered aboard, charming the British with their glistening beauty.

Cook was too wise to attempt to rebuff the visitors to his ship, but he insisted on taking care of first things first. Despite the distracting presence of the Tahitians, Cook saw to it that his

---

scurvy. Almost all captains understood that fresh food, vegetables and fruits especially, would cure scurvy, and it was for that reason that they so often seized opportunities to go ashore and obtain fresh provisions. The problem was to find some form of food that could be kept relatively fresh aboard ship. The English privateer Hawkins, as well as the Dutch masters Schouten and Le Maire and Roggeveen had stored lemons on their ships, and this was a practice followed by many other Dutch captains. The idea of using sauerkraut originated with the well-known surgeon and healer, Sir John Pringle, who had observed that scurvy was almost unknown on German and Scandinavian ships that plied northern waters. Those vessels carried barrels of uncooked sauerkraut as part of the regular rations of their crews. Pringle therefore proposed that British ships, too, provide sauerkraut to their men. Because of Cook's own interest in warding off scurvy and because his endeavor was largely scientific in nature, the Admiralty agreed to allow Pringle to stock Cook's vessel with sauerkraut as well as other pickled vegetables.

It remained for a contemporary of Pringle's, Dr. James Lind, to prescribe the most efficacious means of warding off scurvy: lime or lemon juice, which could easily be stored in casks. His suggestion about the use of lemon juice was adopted by the Admiralty in 1795, a year after his death. In time the antiscorbutic of choice aboard British ships was lime juice, hence the derisive term "limey" for British sailors.

ship was snug. Then a camp, with a makeshift fort, was established ashore, and an observatory built for the astronomers. Only after completing this business did Cook permit his eager crew liberty. Before doing so, however, he issued a stern warning: The Tahitians were to be treated "with every imaginable humanity."

With this the mariners were let loose in paradise, and they soon availed themselves of all its pleasures. Like the crews of Wallis and Bougainville, Cook's tars were enthralled by the open sexuality of the Tahitians. Liaisons between the island girls and the newcomers sprang up like wild flowers. Officers and men alike succumbed to the "natural and easy" beauty of the islanders. Even Banks found that his eighteenth-century rationality crumbled before his desire for "a very pretty girl with a fire in her eyes."

Despite the sexual ferment, however, the observation of the transit of Venus went off without a hitch on June 3, 1769, and Cook could now take his time having the ship refitted and reprovisioned for the rest of the voyage. Clearly, neither the scholars nor the sailors were in any hurry to depart.

As the overhaul of the ship went forward and the men continued to amuse themselves ashore, Cook and his scientists tried to learn about Tahitian society, conversing often with local chieftains. At one point they thought they had encountered Tahiti's paramount chief, a young man whom the other leaders treated with great respect. They eventually discovered that the deference paid to the youth was more religious than political, though its exact nature eluded the Englishmen.

Cook, Banks, and some others also visited a number of holy structures in the interior. They called these sacred buildings temples, though they were really burial grounds. The Englishmen also found Bougainville's camp, as well as other evidence of the French visit, including tools left behind by, or stolen from, Bougainville's men. Cook, as was his custom, also charted the Tahitian coast in some detail. Yet the Europeans sensed that they were far from uncovering the mysteries of Tahiti. Cook wrote of this after visiting a huge stone "temple": "The mysteries of most religions are very dark and not easily understood even by those who profess them."

In the course of his talks with Tahitian leaders, Cook heard that a civil war had recently taken place, resulting in the fall of

"Queen" Purea, the lady who had wept at Wallis's departure. Though the details remained vague, it was clear that there had been bloodshed. In his journal Cook expressed little surprise at finding that war and wrath existed in paradise as they did elsewhere.

Only one thing marred paradise for the British: The islanders stole anything they could get their hands on, from Banks's snuffbox to another scientist's opera glasses. They stole a musket and a quadrant despite the presence of a sentry nearby. Cook himself had his stockings taken from beneath his head as he dozed, though he swore later that he had *not* fallen asleep. At one point the stealing so exasperated one of the *Endeavour*'s crewmen that he shot a Tahitian dead. Deep apologies followed, and somehow Cook managed to mollify his hosts. The incident was forgotten, never to be repeated. Yet the thievery did not abate. It was part of Tahitian culture, as deeply ingrained in the people as their sexuality. The Englishmen managed to endure it, though they never became accustomed to it.

For three months Cook, the Royal Society scholars, and the British tars enjoyed the hospitality of the Tahitians. But inevitably, with the *Endeavour* repaired and resupplied, the day of departure arrived. Cook ordered the shore camp struck, and the men reembarked. At muster aboard ship, however, officers discovered that two crewmen were absent. They had taken to the mountains with native girls, intending to remain behind when the ship sailed. Cook sent a party of marines to hunt down the missing pair. Sailors of the king could not be permitted to desert, even for love in Eden. In short order the marines located the miscreants and brought them back. Cook made little of their offense but put them to work to cure their lovesickness. On July 13, 1769, after ninety-one days, the *Endeavour* finally sailed.

Cook had aboard two Tahitians who had volunteered to accompany the British. They were a chieftain named Tupaia and his boy servant. With Tupaia as guide, the *Endeavour* visited seventeen or eighteen other isles in the seas around Tahiti. Tupaia told him that there were about one-hundred thirty such islets and atolls in the neighborhood, most of them inhabited. Cook and his men found the people of these islands every bit as welcoming as the Tahitians. In accordance with his orders from the

Admiralty, Cook went ashore on one of these dots in the ocean and took possession of the group, which he named the Society Islands in honor of the Royal Society.

On August 9, with his ship in excellent condition and all his men well, Cook turned the *Endeavour*'s bows to the southward. It was now time to begin the search for the great South Land.

On September 2, 1769, the *Endeavour* reached latitude 40 degrees south. According to his instructions, Cook was to look for Terra Australis by sailing westward along this parallel—unless he detected signs that the continent lay farther to the south. But Cook saw nothing around his lone ship but open ocean. Moreover, the sea was rolling in unending swells from the south, a strong indication that no landmass lay in that direction. In addition, stormy weather argued against cruising any farther southward. Cook turned the *Endeavour* to the west, in the direction of Tasman's New Zealand.

For more than a month the *Endeavour* plowed across waters never before sailed by Europeans. Cook kept the ship as close to the fortieth parallel as sailing conditions permitted. Night and day, clear or cloudy, lookouts strained for any sign of land. Week after week the desolate ocean rolled beneath the *Endeavour*'s nail-studded hull. No land appeared.

Then, on October 6, 1769, while the ship was in approximately latitude 38 degrees south, one of the lookouts sighted a coast ahead. Cook was sure that the land before him was the eastern side of New Zealand. But was this beautiful country a part of Terra Australis? It was Cook's job to find out.*

Two days later the *Endeavour* anchored in a sheltered bay. There were signs of habitation in the area, including plumes of smoke as if from village fires. Cook took a party ashore for water and to have a look around. The Englishmen beached their boats and went off to fill their water casks, leaving four ship's boys to guard the skiffs. Suddenly, after Cook and the men had gone off, a number of warriors appeared and began shouting and

---

*The *Endeavour* had reached the eastern coast of New Zealand's North Island, approximately at its midpoint. Cook had no idea that New Zealand consisted of two large islands, separated by a strait and stretching more than fifteen hundred miles from north to south. All he knew was that Tasman had coasted the western shore and had rounded its northern end. But how wide it might be, how far it might stretch away to the south, or whether it was attached to some greater landmass were matters still unknown. The *Endeavour* was the first European ship to touch on New Zealand's eastern shore.

shaking their weapons at the lads by the boats. One of the *Endeavour* youngsters, unnerved, fired his musket. A native fell dead. The others fled. Cook and the shore party came running, but the clash was over. The Englishmen returned to the ship. Cook was acutely aware that this initial encounter with the New Zealanders was likely to lead to more bloodshed unless he could establish communications.

On the next morning Cook led another detachment ashore. This time he took with him his passenger Tupaia, hoping that the Tahitian would be able to make himself understood by the local inhabitants. As Cook had expected, a group of warriors again appeared on the beach. Tupaia spoke to them. They understood his words and identified themselves as Maoris. They appeared uninterested in the gifts offered them. Suddenly a Maori warrior ran forward and grabbed a sword from one of Cook's startled officers. For all his good intentions Cook felt that he had to punish such audacity immediately or Maori truculence might escalate into a bloody melee. Cook ordered his marines to fire on the thief. The man fell dead. Terrified, the Maoris fled the beach, and the frustrated Cook returned to the *Endeavour*.

That very afternoon two canoes appeared near the anchored *Endeavour*. Cook sent some of the ship's boats after them, hopeful that he could still establish friendly relations if only he had an opportunity to show his peaceful intent. But when the English sailors tried to stop the canoes by firing a musket, the Maori paddlers attacked the nearest English boat. Cook's men fired in self-defense and killed several of the warriors. The surviving Maoris then leaped overboard and swam for shore. But the English managed to pluck three young New Zealanders from the water and brought them aboard the *Endeavour*.

At last, with Tupaia's linguistic help, Cook was able to make contact. After giving gifts to the sullen trio of captives, Cook tried to explain the nature of his visit. But perhaps understandably after so much bloodshed, he got only a surly response. On the next day Cook set the three ashore under the eyes of two hundred armed Maoris, who gathered on the sand and glowered at the *Endeavour*'s boatmen. Cook quickly recalled his boats to the *Endeavour*.

He now decided that since he had made so inauspicious a start, any further effort at friendship in this region would be futile. Better to move on. He sailed from this hostile harbor, which he named Poverty Bay because he had been unable to replenish stores there.

The *Endeavour* now turned southward along the coast, seeking an anchorage populated by less xenophobic people. But the Englishmen met with antagonism at every landfall. Finally, after passing a great bay that Cook named Hawke Bay in honor of the first lord of the Admiralty, the *Endeavour* reversed course, for Cook was now in great need of some haven in which to refit, rest, and obtain fresh supplies. Since no such refuge appeared to lie to the south, he would search to the north again. The *Endeavour* made her way back, past her original landfall at Poverty Bay, and around a great cape.* There the British found another wide bay. They anchored and tried once more to make friends.

Luckily the Maoris of this region seemed less inimical than those of Poverty Bay. Though they often hurled stones or howled threats when the British came ashore, the warriors refrained from actual attacks, and there was no bloodshed. The *Endeavour's* men were even able, on occasion, to trade with the local people for fresh food. More often, however, they had to go into the countryside on their own to gather wild fruits and vegetables. Cook named this relatively hospitable shelter Bay of Plenty.

After a brief stay the *Endeavour* continued to the north. She reached another pleasant bay on November 9, 1769, and there the British were greeted with near cordiality.† Unlike the people to the south, the Maoris in this vicinity evinced great curiosity about their visitors. They accepted the gifts proffered by Cook. The British were able to trade for water, fresh vegetables, wood, and meat. Cook and his scientists were invited to visit one of the fortified villages that stood nearby. Cook, much impressed by this stronghold, wrote in his journal that the Maori outpost was so well built that "a small of number of resolute men might defend themselves a long time against a vast superior force, armed in the manner as these people are."

While anchored at this place, the scientists observed another heavenly event: the transit of Mercury across the sun. Cook gave this inlet the name it bears today: Mercury Bay.

Once more the *Endeavour* resumed her northward journey.

---

*Now New Zealand's East Cape.
†Perhaps by now Cook and his men had learned how to approach the Maoris without alarming them.

Keeping close to the coast, the Englishmen continued contacts with the natives. Most of these were friendly until the ship anchored in a beautiful harbor that Cook named Bay of Islands. Again the local Maoris proved hostile. On one occasion a throng of warriors suddenly surrounded Cook and Banks when they went to the beach with an armed escort and were dispersed only when Cook ordered muskets fired over their heads. Despite the ill will displayed by the locals, Cook managed to avoid an open clash. Again he thought it better to continue on to the north.

Then, in mid-December 1769, the *Endeavour* ran into a gale that drove her far off the coast. Suddenly Cook found the wind blowing steadily out of the west. A great ocean swell also began coming from that direction. These were unmistakable signs that the *Endeavour* had passed beyond the northern limits of New Zealand and was once more in the open ocean. To confirm this, Cook turned to the west, virtually into the wind. The *Endeavour* soon sighted the northern cape of New Zealand. Rounding this headland, she began heading southward along New Zealand's western shore, where the Englishmen noted lofty peaks, forest-clad mountains, and the smoke of Maori settlements everywhere.

On January 14, 1770, the *Endeavour* anchored in what Cook called "a very broad and deep bay or inlet." He thought it a most suitable roadstead at which to repair the ship and replenish supplies. The anchorage also seemed a good place for Banks and his associates to gather specimens. The surrounding land was thick with vegetation, and the birds sang, according to Banks, "with the most melodious wild music I have ever heard." Moreover, after some initial "heaving of a few stones against the ship," the people proved friendly. A lively trade sprang up. The British even managed to overlook the fact that the local Maoris were cannibals who left gnawed human bones lying here and there throughout the vicinity. Cook named this anchorage Queen Charlotte Sound.

One day while the *Endeavour* lay at Queen Charlotte Sound, Cook, with only a single marine as escort, went forth to reconnoiter the land. To do so, he climbed a nearby height that promised a long view of 360 degrees. Reaching the summit, he saw to his delight that instead of coming to a dead end, the "bay" where the *Endeavour* was anchored continued far to the east, joining again with the open ocean. In fact, as Cook's eyes made plain, the "bay" was a strait that separated the northern part of New Zealand from the land to the south. Northern New Zealand was an island.*

Now Cook wondered if the southern part of New Zealand was also an island. Or could it be part of the Pacific continent? It was his task to find out. On February 6, 1770, refitted, reprovisioned, and scraped clean, the *Endeavour* made her way into the strait that Cook had spied from the hill. Characterized by swirling currents and racing tides, the waterway proved a perilous passage. At one point the ship barely escaped a tidal race that almost drove her upon the rocks. But at last she sailed into the open sea. Now, just to make absolutely certain that the land to the *Endeavour*'s port side was indeed an island, Cook pointed his vessel northward again and coasted that part of New Zealand's eastern shore not previously passed. When the *Endeavour* came to land sighted earlier, all doubt was dispelled: The northern part of New Zealand was definitely an island.

Cook turned south again. Passing Queen Charlotte Sound, he made for New Zealand's southern reaches. Despite increasingly bad weather, the *Endeavour* rounded the southernmost point of the country in mid-March 1770 and began working her way up the western coast again. The truth was now incontrovertible: New Zealand was not part of any continent, but two large islands, separated by a narrow strait. On March 24, 1770, the *Endeavour* again anchored in Queen Charlotte Sound. She had circumnavigated both of New Zealand's islands.

With April now approaching, the bitter southern winter would soon descend. Cook and his men had already accomplished much. They had carried out their Tahitian mission. They had claimed new lands for His Majesty's government. They had greatly expanded knowledge of the South Pacific. They had discerned the nature and shape of New Zealand. They had proven that no continental landmass lay to the east of those islands—at least for two thousand miles. It was time to think of going home.

---

*Tasman and Visscher had not discovered this fact, for they had not dared to probe too deeply into the "bay," fearing to be driven aground. The strait, which separates the northern half of New Zealand from the southern half, is today known as Cook Strait.

35

HAZARDOUS HOMECOMING

All aboard the *Endeavour* agreed it was time to head for home. But which route should they take? If they sailed east from New Zealand, back toward Cape Horn, they might still be able to prove, or disprove, once and for all the existence of Terra Australis. Cook himself would have preferred to go that way. But he also knew that to do so, the *Endeavour* would have to navigate in the high latitudes of the South Pacific during winter. This was risky at best but made even riskier by the fact that, having already endured much hard use, the ship was no longer as sound as she had been a year earlier.

The alternative was to head north from New Zealand to New Guinea, then on to the Dutch East Indies, and homeward via the Cape of Good Hope. Unfortunately, if the *Endeavour* sailed this course, it would bar any further discoveries in the South Pacific.

In the end Cook prudently and unilaterally decided against voyaging back across the Pacific to the Horn. But he then convened a council of officers to consider how best to employ the *Endeavour* on her homeward journey in the other direction. Out of this council, Cook reported later, a bold plan emerged: From New Zealand the *Endeavour* would first make her way to the unknown eastern coast of New Holland. She would then "follow the direction of that coast to the northward or what other direction it might take us until we arrive at its northern extremity, and if this should be found impractical, then . . . endeavour to fall in with the lands or islands discovered by Quiros.''

On March 31, 1771, the English expedition set out. Nineteen days later the *Endeavour* raised the eastern coast of New Holland just north of what is now Bass Strait, the waterway that separates present-day Tasmania from the mainland. The ship coasted northward, looking for a suitable place at which to anchor. Heavy surf and winds kept the Englishmen from going ashore at several likely spots, but at last, on April 29, 1770, having reached latitude 34 degrees south, Cook found a sheltered cove and came to anchor.

Although this arid region seemed less inviting than the greener territory just passed to the south, Cook, in company with Banks and a squad of marines, went ashore to look about. They soon spied bands of natives in the area: naked black men armed with spears and throwing sticks. Cook and Banks were amazed that these people seemed to take no notice of them but continued about their business (some fishing and others apparently cooking over a fire) as if the British did not exist. Perhaps there was an element of "magical thinking" here, as if the natives were saying to one another, "These strangers are demons. Ignore them and they'll go away."

But Cook and his party did not disappear. They continued to observe the blacks at their occupations, and eventually two of the younger black men stationed themselves on a rock and made threatening gestures at them. Cook and his companions tried to placate the menacing warriors but failed. At last Cook had a musket fired to frighten off the natives, who seemed to be growing dangerously agitated. The black warriors withdrew, although they seemed less than terrified by the noise of the gun.

While the *Endeavour* was anchored here, Cook inspected the fine harbor and sent men inland to find fresh water for the ship's casks. The men also gathered wood. The inhabitants of the country showed themselves from time to time, and Cook made new overtures to them. But Tupaia was unable to establish any contact. The local people also scorned gifts. Occasionally they hurled spears at the strangers, as if to express irritation at their protracted presence.

Despite the hostility of the inhabitants and the inhospitable country, Banks and the other men of science were enthralled by this wild country, finding everywhere hitherto unknown plants, which they gathered and cataloged avidly. Cook acknowledged the botanical richness of the area by naming the anchorage Botany Bay. He also hoisted the Union Jack and formally took possession of the land for the British crown.*

The *Endeavour* then sailed on northward. Cook charted the coast and gave names to many geographic features. As the ship went on, the shoreline to larboard seemed to grow drier and less attractive with each mile. By night, however, the tropical moon softened the harsh landscape.

In early June, as the *Endeavour* followed the seaboard northward, she suddenly found herself in the dangerous waters covering what was later called the Great Barrier Reef, a huge tidal shelf studded with abrupt coral outcroppings, sharp rocks, and hazardous shoals.

It was near sunset on June 10, 1770, when Cook, who had not at first realized the extent of the reefs and the peril to his ship, decided that he had no choice but to extricate her as quickly as possible from these deadly shallows. Despite the onset of night, he ordered the *Endeavour* to make for deeper, safer water offshore, even though this meant that she would have to wend her way through a labyrinth of reefs that could tear her bottom out.

In accordance with his orders the *Endeavour* came about. Slowly, sounding all the while, she began making her way toward the open sea. The sun sank. A bright moon spilled light on the path ahead. The sea was calm, and a gentle offshore breeze was blowing as the ship worked her way toward the deeper water already visible ahead. After several hours Cook, apparently confident that the worst was over, went below.

Suddenly, just before 11:00 P.M., the ship gave a terrifying lurch. Her bottom crunched over a submerged reef not detected by the leadsman. She seemed to rise from the water, her hull grinding and splintering against razor-sharp coral. Tilted at a sickening angle, she lodged fast.

Cook was on deck in moments. He immediately saw the mortal nature of the crisis. Even if the *Endeavour* got free of the reef, her hull might be so damaged that she would sink. If this happened, many would drown, for the ship lacked enough boats to take all her complement. Moreover, even if some men managed

*Botany Bay is now Sydney.

to get to land, their survival in such barren country was doubtful. Cook decided that he had no alternative but to try at once to get the ship off the coral. It was now high water. When the tide ebbed, she might settle even more firmly on the reef, never to come free again.

Cook issued his orders. First he had anchors rowed out and fixed in deep water. Then he set the men to the capstan to push against the planted anchors in an attempt to haul the *Endeavour* off the coral. But strain as the men would, the ship would not budge. Now water was pouring in through the damaged hull. So far the pumps were able to control the leaking, but for how long? Cook ordered guns, ballast, and other heavy gear thrown over the side in an effort to lighten the *Endeavour.* The sweating crew jettisoned between forty and fifty tons of material. Still, she hung fast. Now with the falling tide she ground further on the sharp edges of the coral. The men redoubled their efforts at the pumps and capstan to no avail.

The tide turned again, and now the ship started to take water into her hull faster than the pumps could suck it out again. Cook later recalled this moment: "This was an alarming, and I may say terrible circumstance, and threatened immediate destruction to us as soon as the ship was afloat." Nevertheless, he knew she *had* to be freed from the reef. Only if she was afloat could she be kept alive. Thus, with the rising tide, the sweating men at the capstan hauled like demons against the planted anchors.

At last she moved a little—and then a little more. Her bottom ground against the coral. Then, as suddenly as she had crashed twenty-three hours earlier, she came to life. She gave a roll—and was free.

But now seawater was pouring in through the gash in her hull. The crews worked furiously at the pumps to keep her afloat. So great were their efforts that the pumps even gained a little on the gushing leak. Cook knew that the only hope was to staunch the *Endeavour's* wound. He had already decided to try a time-honored sealing method called fothering. This consisted of filling a large sailcloth bag with wool and the unraveled strands of old hempen ropes (a material known as oakum and often used for caulking purposes). The bag would then be lowered over the side and dragged along the ship's bottom, until suction pulled it firmly into the hole, plugging the leak.

A fothering bag was lowered over the side near the gushing hole. All aboard held their breath as the bag was sucked under. It worked. The plug lodged in the hole like a cork. But the danger was not past. Because no one could tell how long the oakum stopper might hold, Cook sent a boat off to sound out a safe route to land and to look for a place to beach the ship and repair her.

Within hours a small river was found on the coast. The *Endeavour* was warped up this stream, and here she was careened. The expedition was saved.*

While the carpenters worked to make the *Endeavour* whole again, the men roamed over the countryside, and the scientists collected specimens, including three kangaroos shot by a hunting party of marines. These odd animals, never seen before, excited tremendous interest among the naturalists. They studied the carcasses with the amazed enthusiasm of schoolboys.

During this interval the British also encountered more bands of aborigines. Though these people seemed less belligerent than the blacks of Botany Bay, Cook was still unable to communicate with them, for they showed no sign of understanding the words spoken to them by Tupaia. It was clear that linguistically as well as racially the aborigines of New Holland differed vastly from the Polynesian Tahitians and Maoris.

By July 4, after a stay of three weeks at the river, the carpenters had finished mending the *Endeavour*, at least as far as was possible under the circumstances. She would float and could be sailed securely, but only an overhaul in a shipyard would really restore her damaged hull. Nevertheless, she was ready for sea. However, contrary winds kept her at anchor for more than a month. Finally, in early August 1770, the *Endeavour* made her way back through the maze of reefs that guarded the coastline until, after a passage that Cook called "the most dangerous navigation that perhaps ever ship was in," she reached the open sea again.

Although the *Endeavour* was again taking water and had to be pumped out constantly, Cook was bent upon finding out whether there was really a strait between New Holland and New

---

*Cook named the stream after his ship, the Endeavour River, and a nearby headland Cape Tribulation. Upon examination of the ship's hull it was discovered that the fothering bag had been helped by a large chunk of coral that had also lodged in the hole.

Guinea. If such a passage existed, he meant to sail through it.

Thus Cook continued northward through tricky waters, sounding constantly and using boats to tow the vessel when feasible. On more than one occasion the ship again came close to disaster. More than once she had to be turned away from sudden reefs, foaming with surf and breakers, or pulled from the grip of raging tides that threatened to drive her aground again. Yet she crept on, driven by Cook's determination to find the passage he sought (and thought existed) or to prove once and for all that New Guinea and New Holland were joined by a land bridge.

It was August 21, 1770, when at noon the strait came into view. Cautiously, preceded by her boats, the *Endeavour* made her way into the shallow waterway that separates New Guinea and New Holland. This passage, too, was strewn with shoals and coral heads, but they were nothing like those that had endangered the *Endeavour* during the weeks just past.*

Once well into the channel, Cook took a party ashore on a small nearby island which he named Possession Island. He formally claimed for Britain the entire east shore of New Holland from thirty-eight degrees south to the northern tip of the country, which he christened Cape York. Thus he asserted British sovereignty over the more than two thousand miles of coast that the *Endeavour* had passed, naming the whole territory New South Wales.

With this business complete, the *Endeavour* passed on farther west through the narrows and then found the coast of New Guinea. At last the worst dangers were past, and the reality of the Torres Strait was established. Cook wrote that he felt "no small satisfaction" at proving "that New Holland and New Guinea are two separate lands or islands, which until this day hath been a doubtful point. . . . "

Much in need of a complete overhaul, the *Endeavour* now pressed on to the Dutch East Indies, and on October 10, 1770, reached Batavia. There Cook learned just how much battering the *Endeavour* had sustained during her voyage. In some places

---

*This passage, the Torres Strait, is some 150 miles wide at its narrowest point. Thus neither New Guinea nor Australia is visible from the opposite shore. For this reason, Torres who had sailed through the passage near the New Guinea side, had never sighted what is now Australia. The men of the *Endeavour*, entering at the southern end of the strait, could not see the New Guinea coast from their position, though, unlike Torres, they knew full well that it lies to the north, and not very far either.

coral had worn the planking of her hull down to a quarter inch of thickness. Worms had chewed through timbers. The sails were nearly useless, the pumps almost worn out, seams open. By mid-November, however, the Dutch carpenters and chandlers had made her whole again. Cook planned to sail for home in late December, with the monsoon.

But now, waiting for the wind, Cook's crew began to suffer from the same sickness that had devastated Bougainville's and Carteret's crews during their layovers at this unhealthy port. For Cook's men, the epidemic that seized the ship was a cruel paradox as well as a tragedy. Until that point not one of the *Endeavour*'s complement had died of disease, thanks to Cook's insistence on antiscorbutics in the crew's diet and his requirement that the mariners keep both themselves and their ship scrupulously clean. But now, with the worst hazards of the journey supposedly past, dozens of men fell desperately ill. Seven died, including the Tahitians Tupaia and his boy servant. When the *Endeavour* finally escaped Batavia on December 26, 1770, and started for the Cape of Good Hope, many of her crew were still hovering near death. It was only after the crossing of the Indian Ocean that the plague lifted, and by then another twenty-two mariners had perished.*

After a month's respite at the Cape of Good Hope—from March 10, 1771, to April 10, 1771—the *Endeavour* headed out on the last leg of her journey. It was July 13, 1771, when she reached England again. Her cruise had lasted thirty-five months, and Cook was hailed as a hero. But he was characteristically modest about his achievements. He acknowledged his failure to discover the "much-talked-about Southern Continent (which perhaps does not exist)." Still, he wrote, he was "confident that no part of that failure can be laid to my charge."

In fact, Cook's voyage had accomplished a great deal. If he had not located Terra Australis, he had mapped the east coast

---

*Another man, Lieutenant Hicks, died before reaching home, from tuberculosis. His condition had not been contracted on the voyage but had afflicted Hicks long before sailing with Cook. In the midst of all the medical problems aboard the *Endeavour*, there seems to have been little concern about venereal disease, the affliction that had so troubled Bougainville's men after their stay in Tahiti. It may be that with the seriousness of the plague aboard the ship, VD did not worry the *Endeavour*'s men much. It is more likely, however, that the British tars did not contract VD at Tahiti, but, unlike the French sailors, already had long-standing cases before they ever laid eyes on the Tahitian girls.

of New Holland, and he had taken possession of it for Britain. He had proved that New Guinea was separate from New Holland.

He had circumnavigated New Zealand and established a British claim to those islands. He had shown that New Zealand was not, after all, a part of Terra Australis, as previously conjectured.

He had set the stage for another voyage, one that would prove or disprove once and for all the existence of the southern continent. But perhaps the most enthralling result of Cook's voyage—at least from the point of view of eighteenth-century Europe—was his confirmation of the existence of the island paradise of Tahiti, first described by Wallis and Bougainville. The learned men who had accompanied Cook and, in his laconic way, Cook himself, reported rapturously about Tahiti and Tahitians upon their return to civilization. After Cook's voyage all Europe found itself enchanted by Tahiti, the South Seas, and the beautiful "noble savages" who lived there.

36

THE NOBLE SAVAGE

Home again in England, Cook was reunited with his wife, Elizabeth, whom he had not seen for three years.* The couple's two sons, James, now eight, and Nathaniel, six, were well and strong, but Elizabeth, four, had died three months earlier, and the youngest, Joseph, a baby when Cook had sailed, had not survived infancy.

Even with journey's end, Cook had duties to perform as the *Endeavour*'s master. He dismissed the ship's company with thanks and praise. He submitted recommendations for promotion of many of his officers. He turned over his journals and logs to the Admiralty and reported to the Royal Society. He wrote letters of condolence to the kin of those who had died on the voyage. Only then did he take formal leave of his ship at Woolwich, where she had been moved for refitting, and permit himself to enjoy the acclaim that was already being showered on him, Banks, and all the men of the *Endeavour*. Cook was the perfect hero. Ruggedly handsome and self-effacing, he accepted the adulation with typical composure. He knew better than anyone else what he had accomplished.

---

*Both Cook and his wife were reticent about their relationship. Yet they seem to have been an affectionate, if undemonstrative, couple, well suited to each other and well adapted to the seafarer's life.

In early August, three weeks after the *Endeavour*'s return, Cook received the Admiralty's first official response to his journals and logs—documents he had sent up to the lords upon his arrival in England. The Admiralty wrote Cook: "Their Lordships extremely well approve the whole of your proceedings and . . . they have great satisfaction in the account you have given them of the good behaviour of your Officers and Men and of the cheerfulness and alertness with which they went through the fatigues and dangers of their late voyage." The communication went on to praise Cook's reports and informed him that the promotions he had requested for his officers were confirmed. Their lordships also made it plain that they intended to employ Cook again.

Two weeks later Cook, now approaching his forty-third birthday, was officially elevated to the rank of commander. He had already been given the news by Banks, who was a friend of the first lord, the Earl of Sandwich, and he had written to Banks of his satisfaction at the advancement, saying that "it is better conceived than described."

On August 14, 1771, Commander Cook received another honor: an audience with King George III. At this meeting Cook outlined his journey, using maps and charts to illustrate its finer points. In reply the king presented Cook with his written commission as a commander. After his talk with His Majesty, Cook could not refrain from preening in a note to a friend: "I had the honour of an hour's conference with the King the other day who was pleased to express his approbation of my conduct in terms that were extremely pleasing to me. . . . "

A genuine celebrity now, Cook, along with his wife, dined out on a number of occasions with the great of the day. He impressed all. Author James Boswell, who came to know Cook well, described him as "a plain, sensible man with an uncommon attention to veracity."

If Cook received accolades, his learned friend Joseph Banks, whom many regarded as the chief figure in the venture, swam in a *sea* of adulation. Like Cook, Banks enjoyed a private interview with His Majesty. He received an honorary degree from Oxford. Sir Joshua Reynolds insisted that young Banks sit for his portrait. The newspapers were full of Banks. With his ebullient personality, wealth, and family background, he became the lion of the social season in London. Dr. Samuel Johnson invited him to lunch.

At gatherings of all kinds, the exuberant Banks held forth about the beauties of Tahiti, Polynesian society, and the oddities he had observed in the Pacific. He enjoyed showing his listeners some of the hundreds of artifacts that he had carried off from the other side of the world. These exotic articles, ranging from weapons and coral ornaments to native cloth and carvings, fascinated all who beheld them.

Banks's tales and Cook's sober recollections added to the earlier impressions created after Wallis's and Bougainville's cruises and soon the fashionable world was seized by a veritable mania for Tahiti, the Pacific Eden. In the drawing rooms of Mayfair and the salons of Paris, cultivated men and women talked knowingly of lovely Tahitian women who adorned their natural nakedness with flowers and of Adonis-like men who lived carefree lives, hunting, fishing, and making love.

The idealization of the Tahitians as inhabitants of an enchanted isle was at least in part a reaction to a civilization built on the extremes of artifice. The upper-class Europe of the 1770s was devoted to elegance, wit, style, and seduction. For those cramped in such a world, visions of a free, natural life in Arcady held much appeal. Tahiti came along just as the wealthy of Europe were yearning for a new golden age of innocence and beauty.*

Much of the noble savage vogue was due to misinterpretation of Tahitian mores. For example, after Wallis returned to England, accounts of his activities in Tahiti appearing in such London papers as the *St. James Chronicle* or the *British Evening Post* had sentimentalized the flower-bedecked women and the powerful men of Tahiti, describing them as unspoiled children and ignoring suggestions that they were also thieves, possibly cannibals, and benighted worshipers of idols. Romance carried the day.

One widely circulated anecdote illustrates the London

---

*The French philosopher, writer, and political theorist Jean-Jacques Rousseau had inspired much of this nostalgia for a golden age with his essays in the 1750s. He often depicted the sciences and arts of Europe as "corrupting instruments." In much of his writing, Rousseau counseled that impulse and feeling were more valid than rationality—a viewpoint then much at odds with general attitudes in the Age of Reason.

hacks' propensity for making fairy tales of the Tahitian experience. According to this story, Captain Wallis (miraculously transformed into a dashing young officer) and the Tahitian "queen"
Purea (now changed to a lovely young "princess") fell madly in
love during the captain's sojourn in paradise. But the lovers were
tragically separated when the brave Briton had to sail away. This
fable of Wallis and the forsaken Tahitian princess was based on
reports that the lady wept when her English visitors had departed. Surely, the publicists of London concluded, she wept for
love.*

In France, too, the press romanticized Tahiti after Bougainville's return. One influential French paper, *Mercure de France*,
carried a rapturous article by Bougainville's science chief, Commerson, the same gentleman who had smuggled Jeanne Baret
aboard the *Etoile*. He wrote: "Tahiti is the only place on earth
where there are people without vice, where inequality of rank
does not exist and where people live without jealousy and discord." Going on to paint these paragons of innocence as "happy
people, born under eternally blue skies and fed on the choicest
fruits of the earth," Commerson declared: "[The whole island]
knows only one God, the God of Love. Every day they make of-
ferings to him, the whole island is his temple, the men are his
high priests and the women sacrifice themselves on his altar."

Paris relished such effusions. Nor was Commerson alone in
describing Tahiti as utopia. A memoir by another of Bougainville's veterans was equally lavish: "If happiness consists in an abundance of all things necessary to life, in living in a superb land
with the finest climate, and enjoying the best of health, in
breathing the purest and most salubrious air, in leading a simple,
soft, quiet life, free from all passions, even from jealousy, although surrounded by women, if these women can themselves
disperse happiness, then I say that there is not in the world a
happier nation than the Tahitian one."

Although fascinated by accounts of Tahiti, the French took
even greater delight in the living Tahitian, young Ahu-Toru,
whom Bougainville had brought back with him. This youth was
a perfect example of the noble and innocent islander. He smiled

---

*In reality, the tears shed by the Tahitians upon the departure of Wallis and his men,
though genuine, were primarily a form of politeness in the Tahitian culture.

easily. He loved French wine and food—and ladies. He soon became an idol of Paris society. With his wide-eyed manner, Ahu-Toru seemed to jaded Parisians the embodiment of Rousseau's "natural man." Ahu-Toru, as entranced as he was entrancing, played his part to the hilt, posing for artists, wearing costumes, and appearing at Parisian galas.*

Bougainville himself had written an excellent account of his journey. Though he was no romantic, he had nevertheless helped promulgate the idea of a Pacific paradise by focusing much of his story on the charms of Tahiti, which he had named New Cythera after the birthplace of Venus.

For some Frenchmen the noble savage craze, coming at a time when the fury of common people was beginning to boil beneath the ornate surface of French life, offered an opportunity to comment on social ills. One of these was the philosopher Denis Diderot, who seized on the revelations of Tahiti to criticize European civilization as a scam to cheat humanity of its natural happiness. In a "letter" to Bougainville, Diderot "pleaded" with the explorer to leave the Tahitians in peace: "Ah! Monsieur de Bougainville, steer your vessel far, far away from the shores of these innocent and fortunate Tahitians. They are happy and you can only bring harm to their happiness. . . . " The "letter" then went on to express the author's revulsion for European society and its injustice.†

In England, where there was burning public interest in Pacific exploration, it was thought that Cook's logs and journals—together with the reports of his predecessor, Wallis—should be edited for release to the public. But the Admiralty did not for a moment entertain the idea of allowing Cook, a rough sailor after all, to tackle this literary task. Instead, Dr. John Hawkesworth, one of the literary lights of London, received the commission to write the official account of Cook's voyage for the princely fee of six thousand pounds.

---

*He tired of it all within a relatively short time, however, and yearned for home. Bougainville obliged his Tahitian guest by spending a considerable amount of money in an effort to return Ahu-Toru to his island.
†Diderot was not the only proponent of reform in prerevolutionary France to use the noble savage as a vehicle. In 1782 a play entitled *Zorai* on the theme of the superiority of a savage, but just, society over that of civilized men was produced in Paris. Set in New Zealand, the play was a virtual propaganda piece, full of antigovernment speeches and calls for liberty and equality. The government of Louis XVI, regarding it as a plea for revolution, promptly banned it.

Hawkesworth understood little about geography, less about botany, and virtually nothing about ships and sailors. Apparently unimpressed by the plain facts in Cook's journals, Wallis's logs, and Banks's papers, he sat down to write, and embellished wildly. A true believer in the noble savage concept, Hawkesworth, writing in the first person as Cook, was soon adorning Cook's straightforward story with flights of elevated fancy that included philosophical speculation, mythological references, and invented sentiment.*

The romance of the South Seas, it seemed, had triumphed over nature, reality, and even common sense. Yet there were skeptics. Some London wits had great fun with the noble savage. Dr. Johnson declared that he found little attractive in the concept. Moreover, he could not see how one learned very much from careening around the world. And why, he asked, had young Banks expended so much energy in capturing insects? After all, there were plenty of such creatures in England. Banks did not need to go to the Pacific if he wanted bugs.

One of the scoffers was Horace Walpole, who, after viewing drawings of the Pacific islanders, offered this verdict : " . . . a parcel of ugly faces, with lubber lips and flat noses, dressed as unbecomingly as if both sexes were ladies of the highest fashion; and rows of savages with backgrounds of palm trees."

In addition to the mockers, there was a coterie of critics who regarded praise of the Tahitian way of life as an implied indictment of Christian values. To these sober few the exponents of the noble savage seemed to be condemning the Ten Commandments, the church, and the Bible, while urging people to em-

---

*Hawkesworth eventually produced three volumes, each illustrated with engravings and maps. In addition to telling the story of Cook's voyage, Hawkesworth focused on other voyages before Cook. These included the story of Wallis's journey, with an account of the supposed romance between Wallis and "the Tahitian princess." By writing—or to be more precise, paraphrasing—in the first person, Hawkesworth's work, when finally published, appeared to give Cook's endorsement to the noble savage idea when in truth, Cook was generally scornful of the notion. Cook confessed himself "mortified" when he read the prose that Hawkesworth's volumes attributed to him. In fairness to Hawkesworth, it should be noted that under his arrangement for production of the volumes, the commanders involved were to read and approve those parts of the text attributed to them as he produced them. Somehow this part of the process was skipped, though Hawkesworth forwarded his copy as arranged and subsequently came to believe that the commanders involved had seen and approved his work. He was perhaps understandably bitter when he discovered that his flowery prose had merely "mortified" the man, Cook, whom it was intended to immortalize.

brace the communal life practiced by the natives of the new Eden in the Pacific.

Nevertheless, despite these undercurrents of scorn, the noble savage found a warm place in the hearts of the majority. Rose-colored visions of Tahiti and the Pacific became the common coin of the day, a dream shared throughout most of Europe.*

What was the reality of Tahiti in the eighteenth century? Although much of the record has been distorted, it is still possible to discern the outlines of the pristine culture encountered by Wallis, Bougainville, and Cook.

Many of the people certainly possessed a vigorous Polynesian beauty. They were usually taller than most other Pacific natives and taller than most of their European visitors as well. Their eyes were invariably dark, and their long black hair was lustrous with sweet-smelling oils. To such natural good looks, the Tahitians, and virtually all other Polynesians from New Zealand to Easter Island added the adornment of tattoos. It was not unusual for a young Tahitian, man or woman, to sport complex designs on the face, legs, and back. The Tahitians also attached great importance to the shape of the head, and every baby had his or her skull massaged until molded into the desired form: sloping brow and flat back. Moreover, the Tahitians tended to view obesity as a mark of desirability. The slim girls regarded as most beautiful by the European sailors often became enormously fat as they grew older.

The religion of Tahiti was apparently animistic in its basic form, with many spirits regarded as sacred under the rule of a Supreme Being. As intrepid sailors in their magnificent seagoing canoes, the Tahitians also seem to have worshiped the sun and a god of the sea. In daily life the Tahitians were surrounded by ghosts and by the shades of great men of the past who had to be propitiated, sometimes by human sacrifice.

Tahitian political life was apparently organized according to traditional forms that were already ancient by the time Europe-

---

*The Tahitian vogue continued for many years. In the late 1770s a Tahitian named Omai became the toast of London. He sat for a full-length portrait by Sir Joshua Reynolds, met with King George, whom he referred to as King Tosh, and became the pet of the London ladies, whom he treated with natural gallantry. Omai, who loved the theater, eventually became the subject of a play himself.

ans reached the island. Led by chiefs, priests, and important
men, whose role was primarily advisory, the Tahitians, like many
other Polynesians of the Pacific, were divided into clans, or
castes, having to do with hereditary occupations, such as wood-
carvers, fishermen, or navigators. The Tahitians apparently relied
on general popular assemblies as the means for deciding peace
and war, taboos, and disputes.

They were also adept at building and sailing very large, seagoing vessels propelled by both paddles and sails. Wood carving
was an advanced art. The Tahitians were also great builders of
"marae," the stone platforms that were used for burial places
and for religious rites that may have included blood sacrifice.

Like other Polynesian peoples, Tahitians practiced infanti-
cide in periods of scarcity. They carried on blood feuds among
themselves. Murder was not unknown. Nor was conflict between
clans. Tahitians occasionally attacked the people of nearby islands. They lived in superstitious fear of devils and spirits. There
is some indication that they even resorted to cannibalism in time
of war or under religious stress.

Yet if Europeans thought Tahiti and a few other islands harbored noble savages, they also supposed the rest of the Pacific
populated by "ignoble barbarians." The black natives of New
Guinea and Melanesia, with their nose ornaments and face paint,
were regarded as barely human cannibals bent on murdering any
stranger who happened among them. Even less noble to civilized
Europeans were the naked aborigines of New Holland, described
so disparagingly by Dampier and the Dutch navigators. Even
Cook had failed to reach these primitives, who decorated themselves with streaks and spots of white paint and "ate even the
slimy things that crawled upon the ground."*

Cook himself, of course, never subscribed to the noble savage mania. He was too grounded in reality for such highflown
sentimentality. Yet he did not trouble himself by trying to dispel
the myth of the Tahitian paradise that his own labors had helped
to create. It was not in him to spend his energy in correcting
misinformation. Moreover, he seemed to realize that it was futile

---

*This revulsion toward the "primitive" aborigines almost resulted in their extinction in
Australia. Settlers came to gun them down as "vermin." In Tasmania the aboriginal
people were exterminated.

to try. In any case he was far too busy with other pursuits.

While Hawkesworth was preparing his version of Cook's journal, Cook, with the support of the Admiralty, was thinking about a new exploration. As magnificent as his voyage had been, it had not, after all, settled the question of the southern continent. If Tahiti was Eden, then Terra Australis might be an *empire* in Eden. The Scottish scholar Alexander Dalrymple still believed in the southern continent and said so openly even after Cook's return. Britain still meant to find the South Land. Moreover, Britain's rivals were every bit as anxious as the Admiralty itself to find Terra Australis.

In fact, even before Cook and Banks had returned to the plaudits of the world, both the French and Spanish had despatched new expeditions into the Pacific to hunt for the elusive continent.

37

AFTER BOUGAINVILLE

Jean François Marie de Surville was a bold mariner, a canny businessman, and a faithful servant of France. Born in sea-washed Brittany sometime around 1715, Surville grew up with the sight, sound, and smell of the Atlantic as part of his daily experience. Like many another Breton lad, he shipped out for the Indies at the age of twelve or thirteen. Employed on the ships of the French East India Company, young Surville rose steadily in rank and accumulated a modest fortune in the process.

Like other Frenchmen in overseas trade, Surville was devastated by the French defeat in the Seven Years' War of 1756–63. The conflict had all but driven the French East India Company out of business, spelling near ruin for many French merchant seamen. Without a functioning company to spread the risks, few French shipowners dared operate in the East.*

Unlike many of his colleagues, however, Surville refused to accept the eclipse of the French eastern trade as permanent. Although nearing fifty at war's end, the optimistic Surville became a free-lance trader of sorts, operating primarily in European waters. By 1766 he was the owner and master of his own ship, the 650-ton *St. Jean Baptiste.* With such a sturdy, well-armed,

---

*The French East India Company was still nominally in existence after the war but had virtually ceased to operate in the face of British domination of the seas.

and capacious vessel, he felt sure that even as an independent he could still make a grand profit in the Indies, despite Britain's ascendancy. Motivated by this conviction, he persuaded a group of investors to back him on a speculative trading mission to India and China. To demonstrate his confidence in the venture, Surville put a significant amount of his own money into the enterprise.

Having loaded the *St. Jean Baptiste* with European manufactured goods to be exchanged for silks and luxury items in China and India, and provisioned for a three-year cruise, Surville sailed from Brittany in June 1767, the very month that the Englishman Captain Samuel Wallis and his ship, the *Dolphin* were dropping anchor in Tahiti.

After rounding the Cape of Good Hope and calling at the French-held island of Mauritius some six hundred miles east of Madagascar, the *St. Jean Baptiste* rode the monsoon to the thriving Coromandel Coast on the eastern shore of India. There Surville spent several months trading from port to port, intending to go on to China after finishing his business.

During this time Surville, like every other merchant then in the Indies began to hear reports of magnificent new discoveries in the far-off Pacific. Tahiti was the name most often mentioned, for by now the *Dolphin* had passed through the Indies on her way home, leaving in her wake rumors of that paradisical island. Bougainville's men had also talked of Tahiti in Mauritius after their Pacific voyage. Inevitably these accounts became distorted as they spread by word of mouth. By the time they reached Surville in India, Tahiti had been transformed into a golden land somehow confused with Terra Australis.

Surville, by nature an optimist, appears to have leaped to the conclusion that Tahiti was either part of the great South Land or an outlying island of the continent. On the basis of this surmise he now made a momentous decision: He would take the *St. Jean Baptiste* to the Pacific—to Tahiti, if he could find it—and there trade for gold. He would also claim Terra Australis for France.

Like virtually every French navigator of the era, Surville believed implicitly in the continent. He also believed that French possession of Terra Australis would more than make up for the loss of Canada and India. Furthermore, Surville shared with other Frenchmen the belief that the French navigator Binot Paulmyer de Gonneville had *already* touched on the mysterious South Land in 1504.

Thus, for Surville, a passage into the Pacific in search of the continent offered both personal and financial rewards. If Surville could locate the continent, he would naturally become rich. But he would also cover his own name with glory by presenting France with a new empire.

Adding to Surville's confidence was his belief that other French mariners recently had seen territory supposed to be part of the continent. The most intriguing of these sightings had occurred as late as New Year's Day 1739. On that date a veteran captain, Jean Baptiste Charles Bouvet de Lozier, exploring the high southern latitudes for the French East India Company, had encountered a high, snowy region, surrounded by icebergs. Bouvet had managed to get within twenty-five or thirty miles of the land before the icebergs blocked his progress.

Bouvet had named the country Cape Circumcision in honor of the January 1 feast day marking the circumcision of the infant Jesus. He had taken special notice of the fact that the sea around Cape Circumcision was full of kelp and teeming with seabirds, almost certain signs that his two ships were near extensive land. He had also been much impressed by the fact that his cape was surrounded by icebergs of huge size, "like so many floating islands," which must have originated from glaciers on some nearby landmass.

Bouvet had continued for some weeks more to investigate the seas around Cape Circumcision. But hampered by fog, bad weather, and illness among his crews, he had had to return to France in mid-1739. He was convinced, however, that he had "passed close to a continent."*

Thus for Surville, thirty years after Bouvet, the reality of the southern continent seemed beyond dispute. In June 1769, Surville departed the east coast of India, bound for the Pacific and, he hoped, Tahiti.

For four leisurely months the *St. Jean Baptiste* cruised in stages: through the Strait of Malacca, to the China seas, past Borneo, and then off the north shore of New Guinea. By October she was in the Pacific, just north of the Solomons.

---

*Bouvet's "extensive land" was the small fog-shrouded South Atlantic island now called Bouvetoye after its discoverer. Cape Circumcision is the northwestern arm of the island. Because Bouvet had reckoned his longitude wrongly, his find would be lost for many years until rediscovered in 1806 and then named for its discoverer.

Following a course opposite that taken by Bougainville in the previous year, Surville made his way along the Solomon chain. Many of his crew were sick with scurvy and in dire need of water and food. But Surville was unable to locate a good anchorage in the Solomons that was safe from hostile natives. He decided to make for the island of Espiritu Santo in the New Hebrides chain some five hundred miles to the southeast. Unfortunately an error in navigation headed the *St. Jean Baptiste* too far to the south, and she sailed past her intended destination.

It was now November 1769, and Surville was essentially lost somewhere in the Coral Sea. His charts were inaccurate, and he had no way of determining his longitude. He could merely estimate his position. According to his best reckoning, the only land that might be within reasonable sailing distance was the coast discovered by Tasman some 125 years earlier and named New Zealand. This country, vaguely marked on his maps, apparently lay some fifteen hundred miles farther to the south and east of the *St. Jean Baptiste.*

Surville adopted a course he thought certain to bring him to New Zealand. The *St. Jean Baptiste* would sail south until she reached the latitude of New Zealand as indicated on the charts and then turn due east. Unless the maps were hopelessly muddled, the French vessel *had* to strike New Zealand.

For more than a month the anguished French followed the route laid down by Surville. Every day men died of thirst and scurvy. At last, on December 12, 1769, driven by the prevailing westerlies, the *St. Jean Baptiste* raised the north cape of New Zealand. Managing to double the cape, she came to anchor on December 17, 1769, in a broad bay on New Zealand's northeastern coast.*

By a remarkable coincidence, Cook's *Endeavour* had been rounding the north cape of New Zealand in the opposite direction just as Surville was doing so. At one point the two ships lay only a few miles apart. Had the visibility been better, they might even have spotted each other. In any event, by the time the weather cleared, they had drawn far apart again.

Finally anchored off what appeared to be an abundant coast, Surville and his scurvy-ridden crewmen went ashore to find water and fresh food. They soon encountered local Maoris who greeted

*It was probably the haven later named Doubtless Bay by Cook.

them with friendliness. Surville gave presents to these tattooed warriors. In exchange he obtained fruits, vegetables, and meat. The surviving members of Surville's crew began to recover from the scurvy that had already carried off a third of their number. The French also began to refit their ship, which had suffered considerable damage from bad weather.

Soon, however, the French became embroiled in a series of furious clashes with their hosts. The hostilities began when Maori warriors seized one of Surville's boats after it had gone adrift. Surville tried to force its return by burning villages, canoes, and food stores. He also kidnapped a local chieftain to whom he had only recently presented gifts of friendship.

The Maoris retaliated. They attacked any Frenchmen who came ashore. They threatened to massacre all aboard the *St. Jean Baptiste*. The unexpectedly vehement wrath of the local people brought home to the French the mortal danger in which they now found themselves had blundered. Surville called a council of officers, and it was decided to make for the safety of the open sea.

Surville and his officers also agreed that once they were away from New Zealand, their best course would be to continue eastward across the Pacific, riding the favorable westerly winds in the high latitudes. In this manner, they believed, they might yet reach Tahiti, which Surville apparently still confused with the South Land. If they failed to find their objective, the council concluded, the company could then continue on to a safe port in Peru.

Taking the captive Maori chief with him in irons, Surville sailed from New Zealand on December 31, 1769. For weeks the *St. Jean Baptiste* pressed eastward. Driven by the roaring forties, she passed over thousands of miles of ocean. Far from finding the South Land, Surville and his men saw no land at all. After three months of such voyaging, ten men, including the Maori chieftain, were dead of scurvy. Surville began to fear that he would soon lack hands to work the ship and decided to forgo any further search for Tahiti or the continent. He changed course to the northeast toward Peru and, he hoped, refuge.

On April 7, 1770, with only a handful of men still strong enough to crew her, the *St. Jean Baptiste*, now a near wreck, arrived off the Peruvian port of Chioca. In his anxiety to inform the Spanish port officials of the condition of his ship and people, Surville had a boat lowered so that he could be rowed ashore to tell his tale. As the skiff crossed the bar in heavy surf, it capsized. Surville and two companions drowned. The suspicious Spaniards took the French vessel on to Callao. There she was interned with her surviving crew.*

The unfortunate Surville was not the only Frenchman to seek the continent in the wake of Bougainville. In October 1771, two years after Bougainville's return to France and while Surville was still thought to be alive somewhere in the Pacific, another French voyager also struck out for the great ocean. This intrepid navigator and former naval man was a planter on the isle of Mauritius, named Marc-Joseph Marion, Sieur du Fresne.

As was the case with Surville, the chain of events leading to Marion's Pacific enterprise grew out of a series of circumstances that were only peripherally related to exploration. Marion's venture began when Ahu-Toru—the Tahitian whom Bougainville had brought back to France with him—started longing for his island home after eleven months as the toast of Paris. The humane Bougainville had no desire to keep the homesick Tahitian in France against his will. Bougainville and a few friends came up with a plan: They would send Ahu-Toru to Mauritius, where French officials, using money donated by Bougainville and his associates, would charter a local ship to carry Ahu-Toru on to Tahiti.

The first half of Bougainville's program went off without a hitch, and Ahu-Toru reached Mauritius safely in mid-1771. Here Marion, one of the leading men of Mauritius, became intrigued by the project to return the Tahitian to his homeland, seeing in it an opportunity to realize his own ambition to follow his father's example as a voyager in the Pacific.†

A man of forty-seven at the time of Ahu-Toru's arrival in Mauritius, Marion had had a brilliant career in the French Navy. He had first gone to sea in 1735, at the age of eleven. During the War of the Austrian Succession (1740–48), he had served aboard French privateers operating in the English Channel. In the midst of that war, Marion, though only twenty years old, had achieved command of his own small vessel, the privateer *Catin*.

---

*The Spaniards of Peru held the *St. Jean Baptiste* and her French crew for three years, finally allowing her to sail again in April 1773. She arrived home in Brittany in August of that year a virtual wreck, carrying little cargo of value to her owners.
†Marion's father, Julien, had captained a merchant vessel in the Pacific trade during the early years of the eighteenth century when France had held the much-coveted asiento, the monopoly on trade with the Spanish colonies.

After a number of adventures as a privateer, Marion, at age twenty-three, had been commissioned a first lieutenant on a regular navy man-of-war, the *Invincible*, and had acquitted himself gallantly. In 1747 Marion was taken prisoner and spent some time in the custody of the Royal Navy at Plymouth.

Following the war, Marion had entered the service of the French East India Company as an officer in the China trade. He had soon achieved command of the company's ship *Diligente*. With the eruption of hostilities with England in 1756, he had returned to the Navy and won the prestigious Order of St. Louis for his service.

In the aftermath of the Seven Years' War Marion went back to the French East India Company until the company became inactive in the mid-1760s. In 1766 Marion, already a major landowner on Mauritius, won the post of harbormaster at the island's main town, Port Louis. By the 1770s he had amassed considerable wealth and prestige. Despite his success, however, Marion was restless. With the French East India Company all but moribund after the Seven Years' War, there seemed little likelihood of achieving his dream of taking a French vessel into the Pacific.

When the Tahitian Ahu-Toru arrived in Mauritius in 1771, Marion saw his chance. As long as a French craft was to be used to return the Tahitian chief to his island, Marion asked, why not seize the opportunity to look for the South Land as well? Marion brought this idea to the governor of Mauritius. He suggested leading the enterprise himself and even adding some of his own money to Bougainville's to defray the costs, provided the government allowed him to use two of the king's ships. The governor agreed. Thus, as Ahu-Toru waited ashore for transit home, Marion worked out an expanded program: First he would sail as far south as possible into the Indian Ocean. He would then turn eastward, cross the Indian Ocean into the Pacific at a latitude south of New Holland and Van Diemen's Land (Tasmania), and explore the mysterious land of New Zealand.* Only then would he go on northeastward to Tahiti to return Ahu-Toru to his people. After Tahiti, Marion would turn westward again and travel back along the twenty-first parallel as far as possible. Finally

---

*Marion, of course, did not know that both Cook and Surville had already visited New Zealand.

he would return home via the Solomons, New Guinea, and the Moluccas.

By following this route, Marion thought, he would certainly find evidence of the continent if it lay in "Australasia" as postulated. He would also enlarge upon Bougainville's discoveries, assess British activity in the Pacific, and, most important, establish new French territorial claims in the ocean. Marion intimated that he might even manage surreptitiously to obtain some spice plants in the Moluccas for replanting in Mauritius.

Marion was given two ships for the venture: the *Mascarin*, a transport vessel that would serve as the flagship, and the *Castries*, a small man-of-war that mounted sixteen long guns.

Then Marion learned that his passenger, Ahu-Toru, was sick, suffering from smallpox contracted during his stay on Mauritius. Marion sailed hastily from Mauritius on October 18, 1771, in the hope that clean salt air would restore Ahu-Toru's health, although his ships were not yet fully provisioned. But a week later, when the *Mascarin* and *Castries* dropped anchor at Madagascar to obtain supplies still needed, Ahu-Toru was worse. In a few days he was dead.

Despite the demise of the Tahitian—and with it the removal of one of the main reasons for his voyage—Marion was determined to carry out his mission. Thus, according to plan, he sailed from Madagascar to the Cape of Good Hope, where he obtained fresh supplies and made last minute repairs. On December 28, 1771, the *Mascarin* and the *Castries* set out to the southeast.

38

SEEKERS SOUTHWARD

On January 13, 1772, twelve hundred miles south of the Cape of Good Hope, Marion's ships sighted a group of tiny fog bound islands. As the French vessels maneuvered in poor visibility about these specks, the *Castries* rammed the *Mascarin* and suffered severe damage to her bowsprit and forward rigging.*

Although Marion ordered his carpenters to mend the *Castries* while under way, it was soon clear that the job could be done only at a proper anchorage where timber was available. Moreover, until her forward rigging was replaced, the *Castries*'s maneuverability would be much hindered. For this reason Marion altered his plan. Instead of pressing farther into the dangerous, iceberg-laden waters ahead, to latitude 55 degrees south, the ships would turn toward the east at approximately 46 degrees south, some seven hundred miles short of Marion's original southerly goal. All aboard the French vessels agreed with Marion's decision, and the ships changed course accordingly.

Now, proceeding eastward across the Indian Ocean along the forty-sixth parallel, the *Mascarin* and the *Castries* encountered another island group about fourteen hundred miles directly south of Madagascar. Marion's second-in-command, Julien

*The islands are called the Marion Islands.

384

Crozet, landed to take possession of the islands for France. While ashore, Crozet suddenly spotted a pigeon flying overhead, leading him to conclude that the long-sought continent could not lie much farther off—probably to the southeast. He urged his commander to head in that direction, but Marion would not risk the damaged *Castries* in the rough seas farther south, and the two vessels continued east.

On March 3, 1772, less than two months after leaving the Cape of Good Hope, the *Mascarin* and the *Castries* raised Van Diemen's Land (Tasmania). There they anchored, hoping to repair the *Castries*. Though the area's inhabitants first greeted the French with friendliness, relations soured when Marion apparently violated a taboo by using a native fire to light one of his own. Exploding into fury, the local people attacked the Frenchmen with stones. Marion and another officer were hurt in the assault. With their modern weapons, however, the French forced the islanders to retreat. The French then spent several days searching the countryside for fresh water and suitable timber to use in repairing the *Castries*. Disappointed on both counts, Marion decided to press on to his next goal: New Zealand.

The two French vessels reached New Zealand's western coast in mid-April. They turned northward, rounded the North Cape, and, heading south again, coasted the eastern shore until they came to a beautiful, bay, full of small islands. They dropped their hooks there on May 11, 1772.*

At this pleasant anchorage the French found copious sources of fresh water. Even more important, they discovered a nearby pine forest that would furnish excellent timber for making the long-delayed repairs to the *Castries*.

Marion established two camps. One was on the mainland, where working parties would cut timber and carpenters would fashion the new mast, spars, and other woodwork needed by the *Castries*. The second camp, set up on a small island in the bay, was for treatment of the sick.

The Maoris, curious and friendly, frequented the French ships and both camps. Trade began. Marion, anxious to preserve amicable ties with the Maoris after his bad experience with the

---

*This place was the Bay of Islands, visited by Cook almost two years earlier and named by him.

people of Van Dienen's Land, spent much of his time with the natives. But one day, for reasons never determined, relations went tragically awry.

On June 12, 1772, Marion and sixteen of his men took a ship's boat to the mainland to gather oysters and net fish. This was an activity that the French often engaged in as a means of varying their diet. When night fell, Marion did not return to the ships. But there was little concern. His officers supposed that their commander had decided to stay overnight at one of the Maori settlements.

At dawn the next day the *Castries*'s longboat, manned by eleven men, went ashore as usual to fetch water and wood for cooking. Although the boat did not return within the normal time, there was again little worry aboard the ships, for it was assumed that the men had been distracted by other business.

Then, at approximately 9:00 A.M., lookouts spotted one of the missing longboat's crewmen swimming frantically toward the anchored *Castries*. The man was bleeding badly from a number of wounds.

Pulled aboard, the sailor gasped out a tale of horror: After beaching their boat, he and his mates had scattered to collect wood. Suddenly howling Maoris had attacked them with spears, clubs, and knives. The victims had never had a chance, wept the bleeding survivor, but were hacked to pieces in moments. He had escaped only by running deep into the woods and hiding. He had watched in terror as the Maoris had cut up the bodies of his dead companions and carried the pieces off to be devoured.

The French officers heard the survivor's story with dread. They now surmised that Marion and his party had suffered a similar fate the day before. Prudently the officers decided to evacuate both the shore camp, where the carpenters were working, and the island camp of the sick. Boats manned by armed mariners were dispatched immediately to rescue the Frenchmen ashore. At that moment the Maoris launched an attack on the French boats and ships, but the Frenchmen beat them off with musket fire, killing a number of them. The French then brought all their men safely back to the ships, suffering no casualties in the process.

In the aftermath of the battle a council of officers concluded that despite the inexplicable fury of the Maoris, the expedition had no choice but to remain in the bay in order to finish repairs to the *Castries* and complete reprovisioning. The ships lingered at anchor while armed parties took aboard barrels of fresh water and numerous cords of firewood. From time to time the French lobbed a cannonball ashore, to cow the Maoris. On one occasion they fired one of their cannons at a canoe, blasting it and its crew of eight or ten warriors out of the water. The French also continued to refit the *Castries*, but without safe access to the good timber of the interior they had to jury-rig some repairs as best they could.

During this period Marion's second-in-command, Crozet, sought to verify his suspicions about the fate of his commander. He sent a heavily armed party ashore with orders to discover, if possible, what had happened to Marion and the other missing Frenchmen. Entering a nearby village, the French raiders surprised a chief who was wearing Marion's scarlet and blue cloak. The chief and his young men fled, but a search of the houses turned up the bloodstained garments of other officers and men. The infuriated French burned this village and another one in the vicinity. They also destroyed two war canoes.

Having confirmed Marion's brutal death, Crozet made up his mind that, with so many of his men killed and with the *Castries* still crippled, it was best to forgo any further search for the southern continent. On July 14, 1772—more than a month after hostilities with the Maoris had erupted—the French ships sailed from the bay, which Crozet now named Treachery Bay. After first heading northeast to the Tonga Islands in order to pick up the trade winds, the French ships came about and headed west for home. On September 20 they arrived at Guam, where they rested for two months. They sailed again on November 19, heading for Mauritius, and arrived there safely early in the new year of 1773.

Despite Marion's failure, hopes were high among French officials at Mauritius that another navigator—a Breton nobleman named Yves Joseph Kerguélen-Trémarec—would at last claim the South Land, for he seemed to have already touched on it. Kerguélen, with two ships, the *Fortune* and the *Gros Ventre*, had first sailed from Mauritius in January 1772—three months after Marion's departure—to look for the continent in the high latitudes of the Indian Ocean. On February 13, 1772, he had come upon land at approximately 50 degrees south, about two thousand miles south of Mauritius.* Convinced that he had found a promontory of the South Land, Kerguélen had given his discovery the name South France. Then, because of bad weather and sickness, he had retreated to Mauritius, planning to explore South France further in the following year. Thus, when Crozet brought the battered remnants of the Marion expedition back to Mauritius in January 1773, French disappointment was tempered by hope that Kerguélen's South France would indeed turn out to be the southern continent.

With the advent of the southern spring in October 1773, Kerguélen went back to the land he had seen the year before. With good weather he now found, to his bitter disappointment, that his South France was not a continent but only another foggy, lonely island in the endless sea. To express his chagrin, Kerguélen changed the name of his discovery from South France to Desolation Land.†

Although the voyages of the French mariners Surville, Marion, and Kerguélen fell far short of their grand objectives, that fact was not apparent to other nations with an interest in the Pacific. To the British Admiralty, for example, the French ventures in Bougainville's wake appeared to constitute a serious challenge to British plans for Pacific supremacy.

Spain, too, perceived itself threatened in the Pacific. Though no longer the feared nation of an earlier era, Spain still disposed of great wealth and controlled enormous Pacific coast domains in the Americas. This Spanish Empire depended upon free passage of the Pacific. Spain feared that if Britain or France discovered the southern continent or established a maze of bases on the islands of the Pacific, the Philippines would be isolated. To forestall this possibility, the Spaniards determined to make an effort of their own to seize Terra Australis as well as any strategically located Pacific islands.‡

---

*This was twenty days after Marion and Crozet had found the Crozet Islands some thousand miles to the west.
†It is today called Kerguelen Island in honor of the navigator who, though he did little else, discovered it.
‡Although both the French and British closely guarded information about the islands and other lands discovered in their Pacific voyages, regarding them as state secrets, Spanish diplomats in London and Paris managed to obtain the information they needed to mount their own Pacific enterprises. The Spanish ambassador to London, for example, pur-

Thus, in October 1770, while both Cook and Surville were still in the Pacific, the viceroy of Peru, Manuel de Amat y Jumient, sent two ships into the western ocean to search out Davisland and the southern continent. These vessels were the sixty-four-gun ship of the line *San Lorenzo*, captained by Commodore Felipe González, which had just delivered troops and military goods to the port of Callao, and the frigate *Santa Rosalia*, which just happened to be in Callao at the time.

In accordance with his orders, Commodore González sailed his two warships far out into the western ocean. He encountered no land, however, until November 16, 1770, when he sighted the strange and lonely island that the Dutchman Roggeveen had discovered almost fifty years earlier and had christened Easter Island. Going ashore on November 20, a Spanish party claimed the place for Spain, renaming it San Carlos in honor of the Spanish king Carlos III. The Spaniards remained only five days on "San Carlos Island" before sailing on westward for another two days to be sure that no land lay beyond. They then turned back and reached the South American coast again on December 15, 1770.

In his report on "San Carlos Island," Commodore González expressed the opinion that earlier navigators, glimpsing the island on the horizon, had mistaken its hills for a continental landmass, thus giving rise to the myth of Davisland. He also said the inhabitants of the place, numbering about three thousand souls, were "docile." Like others before him, he noted the many statues "of monstrous size" that decorated its shoreline. Though he described the island as treeless and rocky, he still considered it a worthy addition to the empire.

With Roggeveen's Easter Island now a renamed Spanish possession—at least according to the laws of Spain—the Peruvian viceroy decided to undertake a thrust at Tahiti as well. However, the viceroy first published a decree announcing that Spain still claimed the Pacific and all it contained in accordance with Balboa's discovery in 1513. Satisfied that he had now reaffirmed Spain's prior rights, the viceroy ordered the frigate *Aquila* to go to Tahiti. There her commander, Domingo Boenechea, a career officer, was to investigate the island thoroughly, find out what

chased an account of Wallis's voyage to Tahiti, as well as a description of the island from one of the *Dolphin*'s men.

treasures it had to offer, and ascertain whether the British had established a colony on the island, as many Spaniards suspected. He was then to claim Tahiti for King Carlos.

Boenechea sailed from Callao on September 26, 1772. With favorable trade winds he arrived in the Tuamotu Archipelago in late October, 1772. He sighted Tahiti, farther to the west, on November 8. Unfortunately the *Aquila* ran aground on a reef during the approach to the island, and several days were lost while she was worked free. At last, on November 19, 1772, the *Aquila* anchored safely off Tahiti.

Boenechea remained at Tahiti for a month. During this time he charted the coast and satisfied himself that the British had not established a permanent presence there. For once relations between Spaniards and a native population remained cordial, although the Spanish sailors apparently did not fraternize with the Tahitian girls to the same degree that the British and French had. On December 20, 1772, the *Aquila* weighed anchor and Boenechea departed, taking with him four Tahitians who had volunteered to return with him to Spanish America.

Because of the damage the *Aquila* had suffered when she ran aground on the reef, Boenechea thought it prudent to forgo a planned revisit of Easter Island.* Thus, after examining the isle of Moorea in the vicinity of Tahiti, he set off for South America and arrived at the port of Valparaiso on March 8, 1773.

Although the Spanish voyages to Easter Island and Tahiti had been carried out with professional thoroughness, they did not extend Spanish influence in the Pacific. Spain could control neither of the islands that her navigators had touched on, and the Spaniards had accomplished no more in the Pacific than had the French.

In far-off Britain, however, the Admiralty was not aware of this. To Whitehall the Pacific seemed to be swarming with Spaniards and Frenchmen. Thus it was decided to send Cook on a second journey to the Pacific.

Although French and Spanish competition for the South Land supplied much of the impetus for Cook's new expedition,

---

*The viceroy had instructed his commander to revisit "San Carlos" either before or after going to Tahiti to examine it more thoroughly and to obtain the consent of its people for establishment of a Catholic mission there. Boenechea had decided to go to Tahiti first.

the scholar Alexander Dalrymple had played a large part, too. Even after Cook's return from his first voyage, the choleric Dalrymple had continued to maintain that a resolute scouring of Pacific waters would finally reveal the South Land to the world. He had written to the Royal Society insisting that the continent existed. Although he knew better than to attack Cook or to belittle his achievement, Dalrymple did write another book setting forth new "proof" that Quirós, the Portuguese navigator, had visited Terra Australis. In doing so, he implied that Cook, like all who had traversed the Pacific before him, had looked in the wrong places for the southern continent.

The imperturbable Cook, secure in the Admiralty's approval and the public's admiration, did not try to refute Dalrymple. Instead, in his straightforward, meticulous way, he said he agreed with the Scotsman in one respect: He could not say absolutely that no continent lay in the Pacific far south of Capricorn, for no ship had ever sailed those waters. Cook made it clear that he would happily lead such an enterprise, designed "to put an end to all diversity of opinion about a matter so curious and important."

Cook was growing weary of life ashore, tired of his role as hero celebrity. Exploring had entered his blood. He yearned to be away again under sail. The Admiralty was pleased by Cook's eagerness to go back to the Pacific. Their lordships wanted no further investigations of paradise, however. They wanted Cook to go to the Pacific again for one purpose only: to settle once and for all the question of Terra Australis.

39

BEYOND CAPRICORN

In preparing for his second Pacific voyage, Cook was even more science-oriented than he had been in readying his first. He welcomed aboard as chief naturalist a German scientist of considerable reputation, Johann Reinhold Forster, who was attended by his eighteen-year-old son, Johann Georg. A second naturalist, two astronomers, and an artist were also engaged.

Initially Joseph Banks, the scientific hero of Cook's earlier enterprise, had planned to participate in this new effort. The ebullient Banks had leaped into the venture with typical enthusiasm. With his great wealth he had put together his own sixteen-member team of naturalists, artists, and botanists. But a snag had developed over accommodations. Banks had wanted Cook to use a large East Indiaman for this voyage in order to quarter his scientists and their instruments comfortably. Cook, mindful of his near disaster on the barrier reef, had chosen two smaller ships. When he tried to restructure one of these vessels for Banks's people, the result proved unsatisfactory to both the scholars and Cook's officers. Banks had then withdrawn—without rancor—from the enterprise, and Cook had appointed Forster to head the scientific staff, making it clear that he would just have to make do with the accommodations.

One important goal of the expedition was to test a new chronometer designed to keep time under all conditions. The Admiralty hoped that the chronometer would allow perfect calculations of longitude, previously impossible because of the unreliability of seagoing clocks. If this instrument worked well in the Pacific, the Admiralty intended to put it aboard all its vessels.*

Cook had not only decided to use two ships for his new cruise, but also specified that they be of the *Endeavour* type, and he gave cogent reasons for his choice: "[The ships] must not be of great draught but of sufficient capacity to carry a proper quantity of provisions and stores for the crew, and of such construction that [they] will bear to take the ground, and of such a size that [they] can be conveniently laid on shore if necessary for repairing any damage or defects, and these qualities are to be found in North Country built ships, such as are built for the coal trade, and in no other."

The Admiralty accordingly provided him with two recently built colliers, which were rechristened for the voyage: the *Resolution*, of 462 tons, and the *Adventure*, of 340 tons. Cook captained the *Resolution*, while command of the *Adventure* went to a career officer, Tobias Furneaux, who had sailed in the *Dolphin* with Wallis. The ships had a complement of 118 men, and Cook provisioned them for thirty months.

Cook had been allowed to devise his own program for settling the question of the southern continent. Like Cook himself, the scheme had the virtues of simplicity and thoroughness. In brief, he would take his two ships to the Cape of Good Hope. He would then sail south from the Cape and try to find Cape Circumcision, that vague land which the French navigator Bouvet had encountered in 1739. If he found Bouvet's land, Cook meant to determine whether it was part of the southern continent or an island. If it turned out to be an island, or if Cook could not find it, he would continue south as far as he judged useful. Then,

*The chronometer did work extremely well, and Cook came to call it "our never-failing guide." It always told the time at the prime meridian—0 degrees longitude—which ran through Greenwich, England. With a sextant, Cook could determine the local time. He could then convert the difference. Since one hour equals 15 degrees of longitude, Cook, and after him all navigators, could determine than longitude by converting time to degrees. For example, if Cook was three hours earlier than Greenwich, he knew that he was in longitude 45 degrees west. Latitude, of course, was never a problem since mariners could reckon that by the altitude of the fixed stars. Bougainville had also tested a chronometer but it had proved unreliable.

if he still had not met with the continent, he planned to turn eastward and, still keeping as far south as possible, cross the Pacific past the southern tip of South America and back to his starting point. By thus circumnavigating the globe in these far southern latitudes, Cook was sure he would come upon the southern continent—if it existed outside the icebound South Pole.

When all was ready, the *Resolution* and the *Adventure* sailed from Plymouth Harbor on July 13, 1772.*

Cook's expedition arrived safely at the Cape of Good Hope on October 30, 1772. The ships took on provisions and prepared for the great push into the unknown. Three weeks later—on November 22, 1772—the *Resolution* and the *Adventure* set sail southward to search for Bouvet's Cape Circumcision.

Day after day the ships plowed southward. As they passed beneath the Tropic of Capricorn, the ocean turned gray. Cold fogs descended, obscuring bowsprits and topsails. Ice formed on the rigging. Soon, as they neared 50 degrees south, the two sturdy vessels found the wind-tossed seas dotted with floating ice. They fought on. It was the Antarctic summer, but as Cook wrote in his log, snow blanketed the decks, and iron cold drained the strength of the men. Cook ordered extra clothing furnished to his crews.

On December 12 Cook noted the first really large icebergs. Some rose fifty feet or more out of the sea. These masses of ice, often two miles around, were stunning to the eye, according to Cook's log, "but conveyed to the mind an idea of coldness, much greater than it really was. . . . " Had these huge bergs broken off some relatively nearby landmass? Or had they drifted to these lonely seas from some polar glacier? The only way to find out was to push south.

On January 17, 1773, at 11:15 P.M.—still daylight—the expedition crossed the Antarctic Circle at 65 degrees south. Cook

---

*At this very moment, halfway around the world, the French expedition originally organized by Marion was preparing to leave New Zealand for home after furious hostilities with the Maoris had taken the lives of Marion himself as well as more than two dozen of his men. The survivors of a still earlier French expedition—the one headed by the drowned Surville—were still being held by Spanish authorities in Peru. The Spaniards, having claimed Easter Island in 1770, were preparing to send their frigate *Aquila* under Captain Boenechea to Tahiti. That voyage, however, was still some two and a half months in the future.

noted that they were undoubtedly "the first and only ship[s] that ever crossed that line."

Still they pushed on until they reached latitude 67 degrees, just to the west of what is now Enderby Land in Antarctica. Here the ships were blocked by an enormous ice field and pulled back north of the Antarctic Circle.*

Now, according to plan, Cook turned more directly east toward the Pacific. Still keeping as far south as possible, the ships continued in a zone of intense cold, immense blocks of floating ice, and unpredictable fogs. A pallid sun lit the days for twenty hours at a time with an eerie, otherworldly cast.

On February 8, 1773, a wool-thick fog descended. Cook's consort, the *Adventure*, disappeared into the soup and did not reply to light or sound signals. Cook did not worry much, however, for it had been agreed that in case either of the two ships lost touch, they would lay by for three days to give each time to locate the other. So far this system had worked well. But this time, when the blinding fog lifted, the *Adventure* could not be found. Still, Cook was only mildly concerned, for he and Captain Furneaux had also made provision that in case they could not join up again after a separation, they would rendezvous at Queen Charlotte Sound in New Zealand. Confident of the qualities of the *Adventure* and her captain, Cook went on, guiding the *Resolution* like a ghost ship through mountains of ice that floated blue-green in the pale sunlight.†

In the middle of March 1773, with no sign of the southern continent anywhere and with the southern winter now looming, Cook declared that the time had come to get to safer waters. He turned the *Resolution* to the northeast—out of the icefields—toward New Zealand. After reaching Dusky Sound on the southwestern corner of New Zealand, on March 25, 1773, the *Resolution* lay at anchor for seven weeks while her men recuperated from their exertions. Then she set out for Queen Charlotte Sound to the north, the appointed place of reunion with the *Adventure*.

It was May 18, 1773, when the *Resolution* reached Queen

---

*Cook had already concluded that Cape Circumcision was no part of a continent. He had now gone farther south than any mariner before him, and he had not encountered Bouvet's cape, probably because it was an island easily missed in the vast ocean.
†Cook had come back north of the Antarctic Circle by now, and thus the Antarctica, probably lay some 300 to 350 miles farther to the south.

Charlotte Sound and found Captain Furneaux and the *Adventure* already there. Furneaux reported that after becoming separated from Cook, he had coasted the southern shore of Van Diemen's Land (Tasmania), intending to make his way north to New Holland. Contrary winds had thwarted him, and he had made directly for the rendezvous. Furneaux said he believed that Van Diemen's Land was actually part of the New Holland mainland. Anxious to check this notion for himself, Cook tried to sail the *Resolution* back west to Van Diemen's Land, but bad weather blocked him, and he quickly returned to New Zealand again.

While at Queen Charlotte Sound, the two English ships were visited by Maoris seeking to trade. The women offered their bodies in exchange for such coveted European commodities as bottles, pots, and iron goods. Cook disapproved but did nothing to stop this traffic. The naturalist Johann Forster, however, made a terse comment in his journal: "It seems that [Maori] ideas of chastity are quite different from ours, for an unmarried girl may have as many lovers as she pleases, without in the least losing her reputation. . . . [Yet the natives] only lowered themselves to this abominable traffic in their women when the need for iron tools had been created in their midst." Firmly on the side of the noble savage, Forster was convinced that in the years to come, the European influence in the Pacific would "do great harm" to the inhabitants of the islands.

Under Cook's original plan, the ships were to spend the southern winter safely anchored in Queen Charlotte Sound. But now he altered that program, saying he saw no real reason to avoid winter sailing—as long as they stayed out of the bitter-cold high latitudes. He gave orders for the *Resolution* and the *Adventure* to strike out into the ocean east of New Zealand. Keeping to the temperate middle latitudes around 40 and 45 degrees south, Cook said, the ships would run eastward for three thousand miles. If they encountered no landmass, they would turn north for Tahiti, where they would refit. They would then return to New Zealand for still another eastward passage in the summer months, this time in higher latitudes, and all the way to Cape Horn. In this manner, Cook declared, the voyagers would be able to cover all the vast waters below the fortieth parallel between New Zealand and South America, an area of fourteen million square miles. If Terra Australis existed, it had to be somewhere in that blank on the globe.

On June 7, 1773, just before the southern winter, the *Resolution* and the *Adventure* sailed eastward from New Zealand. Two weeks later scurvy appeared on the *Adventure.* One man died, and twenty others were ill. Cook had the sick dosed with extra rations of sauerkraut and lemons. For some reason, the sickness did not abate. Nevertheless, the ships plowed on. Now, though the ships were in latitudes well north of the Antarctic, Cook found the weather far rougher than he had anticipated. Constantly hammered by heavy seas, the expedition struggled on. Says Forster of this passage: "The name Pacific Ocean, in my opinion, can only apply to those waters lying between the two Tropics, for only there is the wind constant, and the weather good."

On August 1, 1773, after seven weeks of battering and with no sight of land, Cook decided that in spite of his earlier optimism, the winter cruise had to be cut short. Both the *Resolution* and the *Adventure* were beaten up. More important, the *Adventure* was reporting many sick men aboard. Prudently Cook suspended any further search for the continent and ordered his ships turned north toward Tahiti, for a period of rest.

On August 25, 1773, having threaded their way through the Tuamotu Islands, the *Resolution* and the *Adventure* dropped anchor at Matavai Bay in Tahiti. Although it had been four years since Cook had visited Tahiti, and six years since Wallis had first stumbled on the place, the Tahitians received the British as dear old friends and lavished special hospitality on Cook and his lads. Within days the sick men of the *Adventure* began to recover.

Cook noted that Tahiti was already much changed since his earlier stay. The Tahitians now used European tools, including weapons. European disease, especially venereal disease and influenza, had ravaged the population. The people now included a number of children with fair hair and European features.* In

---

*The English sailors cannot be blamed entirely for this circumstance. Certainly Bougainville's men and probably some of the Spanish sailors brought to Tahiti by Boenechea had also contributed to the half-breed population of Tahiti. The English and the French might wrangle over who brought venereal disease to the islanders, but there can be little doubt that both contributed to changes in the island's racial composition. Curiously Cook seems to have made little of the Spanish visit to the island the year before, although there was a rumor that a Spaniard was still living somewhere on Tahiti.

addition, it seemed to Cook that there were fewer people and domestic animals than there had been during his first sojourn. He also learned that civil wars had recently erupted among the clans as some islanders who had previously obtained European muskets had used them in an attempt to grab power.

Cook attributed most of the negative alterations in Tahitian life to European influences. Yet in spite of such troubles, the island was still an Eden filled with beautiful, complacent women, plentiful food, ease, and fair weather.

Thus it was with heavy hearts that, after first making brief visits to neighboring isles, the men of the *Resolution* and the *Adventure* bade farewell to Matavai Bay, on September 17, 1773, having stayed only three weeks. As the ships set sail, they had aboard two adventurous natives who had volunteered to accompany the Englishmen. Aboard the *Resolution* was a man named Odiddy, from Bora-Bora. Aboard the *Adventure* was the young Tahitian called Omai.

Heading west by south after leaving Tahiti, the *Resolution* and the *Adventure* called at a number of hitherto unknown islands, among them a chain later named the Cook Islands. There, on October 1, the girls of one village entertained the Europeans with some "harmonious singing." The British reciprocated by playing bagpipes—to the delight of the local people. During this time the British also touched on some other islands, where they were received with such warmth that Cook named the group the Friendly Isles.*

On October 7, 1773, Cook once more headed for New Zealand, in order to launch the next leg of his program: a sweep across the far South Pacific from New Zealand to Cape Horn. After raising the eastern coast of New Zealand on October 21, the *Resolution* and the *Adventure* again lost touch in stormy weather. According to previous arrangement, the two ships were to rendezvous at a place called Ship Cove. When the *Resolution* reached this anchorage in early November, the *Adventure* was not there. After waiting for more than two weeks, Cook began to worry that he might miss the summer sailing season. Finally he wrote a message for Furneaux and left it in a bottle. Then, on November 25, 1773, Cook struck out into the Pacific bound on

*They are today called by their native name: Tonga.

a last quest for Terra Australis in the grim waters near the bottom of the world.*

By early December 1773 the *Resolution* lay beyond the Antarctic Circle—in latitude 67 degrees south. Once again the days were long and great icebergs reared up around the ship. Once again the cold was so severe that it laid a crust of ice over the rigging and hardened the canvas so the sails could hardly be worked.

Cook had now adopted a new stratagem for searching out land in these eerie southern seas: He had begun zigzagging over the ocean. First he plunged southeast toward the pole and went as far as conditions would allow. When the ice and cold became too much, he turned again *north*east to recover and then once more headed south. In this way the *Resolution* was covering vast areas of the ocean. Thus, after reaching 67 degrees south, *Resolution* retreated once more until—on January 11, 1774—she lay in latitude 48 degrees, at which point Cook zigzagged again to the *south*east.

For the next three weeks the ship made her way through a labyrinth of floating ice islands. Often she had to battle snowstorms that swirled out of the south. Sometimes she was engulfed by fogs so thick that the sailors could not see from one end of the icy deck to the other. And for twenty hours a day a disk of sun spilled a pale light over silent blue-white ice and green-black sea.

On January 30, 1774, the *Resolution* reached latitude 71 degrees 10 minutes south, the farthest south ever attained by *any* ship. But now mountains of ice barred the way. Wrote Cook: "I think there must be some [land] to the south behind this ice; but if there is, it can afford no better retreat for birds, or any other animals, than the ice itself, with which it must be wholly covered. . . . Since . . . we could not proceed one inch farther to the south, no other reason need be assigned for my tacking, and standing back to the north."

According to his chronometer, Cook's longitude on this day was 106 degrees west of Greenwich. Thus he lay but a few miles

*The *Adventure* arrived at Ship Cove only a few days after Cook's departure. She never again caught up with the *Resolution* though she experienced adventures of her own.

off the coast of the Antarctic continent in the vicinity of what is now called Ellsworth Land and barely twelve hundred miles from the Pole itself. But blocked by ice to the south, he turned north again.

At this point he was all but certain that no continent existed in the Pacific, for he had now crossed most of the great ocean and had seen no evidence of it. If a southern continent existed at all, he thought, the greatest part of it must lie within the polar circle, where the sea was so icebound that the land, if any, would be inaccessible.

Cook's program had called for him to circumnavigate the globe in the high southern latitudes and then return home by way of the Cape of Good Hope. Now, after retreating again from the Antarctic ice, he had only to go on past the Horn into the Atlantic to complete his mission. But Cook decided to delay this last segment of his voyage in order to explore more of the Pacific. He explained his thinking in his journal: "I was of opinion that my remaining in this sea some time longer would be productive of some improvements to navigation and geography as well as other sciences."

Instead of passing on to the Atlantic, therefore, Cook headed north, to investigate some of the other lands previously reported in the Pacific, particularly those supposed to lie west of Chile. Cook also hoped to chart Easter Island. Then, after another stopover at Tahiti to reprovision and perhaps to hear some word of the *Adventure*, he intended to sail westward again to explore the lands discovered by Quirós. Only then would the *Resolution* turn east and run past Cape Horn to the Atlantic, to close her circumnavigation of the Southern Hemisphere.

By February 1774, once more in the milder latitudes of the Pacific, Cook was convinced that no large body of land lay off Chile. The *Resolution* made for Easter Island. Suddenly the company faced an unexpected crisis: The seemingly indestructible Cook, upon whose leadership all had come to depend, fell grievously ill with a "bilious colic." In agony Cook kept to his cabin, where he could be heard groaning with excruciating abdominal pain.*

Although he continued to issue orders despite his illness, Cook was unable to eat the ship's ordinary rations, and the sur-

---

*To judge from the symptoms, it is likely that Cook was experiencing a gallbladder attack.

geon worried that he would weaken and die. To forestall this calamity, the doctor had a pet dog belonging to Forster slaughtered to provide a nourishing soup and bits of fresh meat for the captain. The canine fare seemed to do the trick. Cook, to the relief of all, began to recover. On March 4, 1774, he was back on the quarterdeck. A week later, March 11, lookouts sighted Easter Island, and Cook ordered the ship anchored.

The British, who had been continuously at sea since leaving New Zealand some eleven weeks earlier, were ravenous for fresh food. They rejoiced mightily when a party of Easter Islanders paddled out to the *Resolution* and presented the sailors with bunches of bananas as a welcoming gift. Wrote Forster, "The joy which the sight of these fruits produced in us can hardly be described. Only people as miserable as we were can have any conception of this. The men, in their happiness, began shouting all at once to the natives in the canoes. . . . "

But after going ashore, the men of the *Resolution* found that Easter Island was no Tahiti. It was windswept and barren, and its people grew little food. Besides a few bananas, their thin gardens produced only potatoes and some scrawny chickens. Wrote Cook of Easter Island: "Here is no safe anchorage, no wood for fuel, nor any fresh water worth taking on board."

Though gratified that his native passenger Odiddy could comprehend the language of the Easter Islanders, Cook found the place oppressive and the people far less attractive than other Polynesians. As Cook and his officers walked around the island, they discovered what was left of paved roads. They came across the ruins of an old harbor and many tumbled-down villages whose buildings were made of stone. To the British, it seemed as if the island had fallen under some curse.

Like all visitors before and since, Cook and his men were amazed by the statues of Easter Island. They counted some 150 figures in all stages of completion. But all the sculptures appeared to be long neglected. Many lay about in a half-completed state. It was as if the whole enterprise had been abandoned suddenly. Cook himself thought that the great stone heads were not idols, as the Dutch lawyer Roggeveen had suggested, but "monuments of antiquity" that had been erected to mark the burial places of great personages.

Forster—in an opinion Cook shared—was sure that the heads had not been carved by the island's current inhabitants, for these people could not explain how they had been made or their meaning. Forster saw the monuments as the products of a "more civilized people" who had fled long ago.

With so little available in the way of fresh provisions at Easter Island, Cook determined to get under way again as soon as possible. Accordingly, on March 16, after a stay of only five days, the *Resolution* sailed from Easter Island.*

Although bound for Tahiti, Cook first detoured to the northeast to visit waters just south of the equator. On April 6, 1774, following a brief relapse into illness, he happened upon the high islands known as the Marquesas, last visited by Mendaña in 1595. Though the British remained only five days, Cook was much impressed with the beauty of the Marquesans, calling them "the finest race of the South Seas." After charting the islands' exact position, Cook turned the *Resolution* southward to Tahiti and raised the island on April 22, 1774. Anchoring at Matavai Bay, Cook and his men were once more received with affection.

The British now learned that the Tahitians were in the midst of a war with the neighboring island of Moorea. Cook was greatly interested in observing the assembly of a Tahitian war fleet, made up of hundreds of war canoes, manned by thousands of warriors. Forster, too, found the mobilization fascinating and described the scene in his journal: "No fewer than 150 war canoes, 50 to 90 feet long, were gathered here. . . . They consisted of two canoes connected by 15 to 18 strong planks tied amidships. . . . These canoes carry a minimum of 144 oarsmen and eight helmsmen." Forster added that each canoe also carried 15 to 20 armed men who apparently did the actual fighting.

Although the pleasures of Tahiti were tempting and he was curious about the Tahitian way of war, Cook had no intention of lingering in paradise. On June 4, after a stay of six weeks, Cook, having heard no word of the *Adventure*, pointed the *Resolution* westward again, to find the land that Quirós had named Espiritu Santo.†

---

*Although Cook's crew and the scientists hiked across the island they did not, apparently, see the crosses erected in the center of the island by the Spaniard González in 1770, when he had claimed the place for Spain and named it San Carlos. There were, however, signs that Europeans had visited the island recently. Among these were European hats and scarves worn by the natives, apparently left behind by González.

†During his stay in Tahitian waters, Cook returned his passenger Odiddy to his home. He also spent less time than usual at Matavai Bay, instead removing from Tahiti on May 14 to anchor, for the last segment of his stay, at the nearby islands of Huahine and Raiatea.

By mid-July the *Resolution* was sailing through Quirós's Santa Cruz Islands, approximately three thousand miles west of Tahiti. Most recently visited by Bougainville, these isles were populated by Melanesians who struck Cook as the "most ugly, ill-proportioned people I ever saw, and in every respect different from any we have met with in this sea." Using his chronometer, Cook plotted the exact position of the islands and then gave the more southerly group the name they still bear, the New Hebrides.

The Melanesian folk of these waters, who had greeted Quirós with fury 170 years earlier, showed themselves equally hostile to Cook's men when in early August a watering party landed on the isle of Erromango. The British were no sooner ashore than the natives attacked. In a clash reminiscent of the fights between the old Spaniards and the ancestors of these black warriors, the British fired on their attackers, while the islanders, howling with rage, assailed the Europeans with spears, rocks, and arrows and tried to drag the ship's boats onto the beach. Men were wounded on both sides. The British fled, and Cook withdrew the *Resolution* farther south, where he continued to chart the islands in the chain.

Turning north again and now skirting the western coasts of the islands, Cook made his way to Espiritu Santo. Anchoring at Quiros's old harbor in late August 1774, Cook saw how the extensive countryside had fooled the Portuguese navigator into thinking it a landmass. He saw, too, the rivers, the hills, the smoke fires of a large population, and the ample vegetation. No doubt all these had convinced Quirós that he had found the long-sought continent. To honor the Portuguese visionary, Cook named a point on the great bay Cape Quiros.

With the winter season farther south about to ameliorate, Cook again sailed for New Zealand, charting New Caledonia and other islands as he went. Reaching his old anchorage at Ship Cove in late October 1774, Cook saw clear signs that Captain Furneaux and the *Adventure* had been in the inlet and had sailed again. There were old campfires on the beach and felled trees. The bottled message that Cook had left for Furneaux was gone, apparently found by its intended recipient. Why had the *Adventure* departed without leaving her own message? The Maoris talked wildly—and confusingly—of a battle between themselves and Furneaux's men, during which a number of the *Adventure*'s crewmen had been killed. Cook thought the Maoris were exaggerating the tale.*

After refitting, the *Resolution* went to sea again on November 11, 1774. Cook intended to take her on one last eastward sweep of the waters between New Zealand and South America. This time Cook did not sail to the far south. Nor did he employ a zigzag strategy. Instead he sailed almost directly east, keeping in latitude 54 or 55 degrees south.

After a journey of five weeks, during which no land was sighted, the *Resolution* arrived at the tip of South America on December 17, 1774. The British spent Christmas in a bay off Tierra del Fuego. There Cook and his men entertained a primitive people who, according to Cook, "stank of rancid oil" and lived as best they could on shellfish and game while huddling for meager warmth around their fires.†

After departing Tierra del Fuego three days after Christmas, Cook rounded the Horn into the South Atlantic to complete his circumnavigation. Still heading east, he stopped at a little island that he named South Georgia. He then made south to latitude 60 degrees, sighting ice-covered islands, which he called Southern Thule and which are now known as the South Sandwich Islands.

Gradually the *Resolution* made her way north and east again, crossing her own track of December 1772, when Cook had

---

*As Cook learned after returning home, the Maoris had indeed killed and eaten some of Furneaux's men when a boatload of British sailors, operating ashore, got into a quarrel with some of the Maoris and shot two of them. The Maoris had massacred the British and had made a meal of them. Unable to bring back the dead or to find and punish the guilty, Furneaux had sailed on.

†As Cook and his men celebrated Christmas in Tierra del Fuego, the Spanish navigator Boenechea and his ship *Aquila*, this time accompanied by the supply vessel *Jupiter*, were once more in Tahiti. The Spaniards were returning two Tahitians whom they had brought back to Peru on an earlier voyage. Two other Tahitians had died. Also with the Spanish ships were two missionaries and two other men who were to be left on the island to convert the Tahitians. Boenechea, and presumably the missionaries, got along well with the islanders and on New Year's Day 1775 the priests celebrated their first mass on shore, to the great amusement of the natives. Boenechea also signed a treaty with some Tahitian chiefs in which the Tahitians acknowledged the sovereignty of Spain. But after cruising to nearby islands, Boenechea became ill on January 18, 1775, and he died on January 26. Two days later the Spanish ships sailed away leaving behind the missionaries and two other Spaniards. By April 8, 1775, the *Aquila* had come home again to Callao, with the *Jupiter* arriving five days later. The Spaniards did not remain long in Tahiti, however. Later in 1775 the *Aquila* returned to the island. The missionaries, though unharmed, begged to be taken home again, and the Spanish master reembarked them and their two companions and returned them to Peru in February 1776. It was the last attempt by the Spaniards to take Tahiti and its nearby islands for the Spanish crown.

searched unsuccessfully for Bouvet's Cape Circumcision. Even now Cook saw no sign of that cape, though, in fact, he passed a little to the south of the island actually found by Bouvet. At last, his mission in the south done, Cook made for the Cape of Good Hope. He had circumnavigated Antarctica, although he had not caught even a glimpse of the land itself. He had crisscrossed the Pacific above and below Capricorn. He had shattered forever the myth of Terra Australis.

On March 21, 1775, the *Resolution* anchored at Table Bay, on the Cape of Good Hope. Cook learned that Furneaux and the *Adventure* had been there in the previous year and had already departed for home.*

At Table Bay Cook met with the French mariner Crozet, who had served as second-in-command to the unfortunate Marion, killed by Maoris in 1772. Crozet spoke of the islands that he and Marion had discovered in the Indian Ocean and of his experiences in New Zealand. At Table Bay Cook also heard of Surville's drowning off the coast of Peru. But Cook spoke little of his own epic odyssey, for according to Admiralty policy, he was to keep secret all that he had learned in his voyaging.

On April 27, 1775, three weeks after the start of the American Revolution, the *Resolution* set off for home. Heading north in the Atlantic, Cook expressed his joy at having escaped from the high southern latitudes, where, as he put it, "nothing is to be found but ice and thick fog." On July 30, 1775, the *Resolution* reached England, after a voyage of seventy thousand miles, lasting three years and eighteen days. Cook had lost only four men, three by accident, and one by illness. Not a single man had succumbed to scurvy.

*   *   *

*The *Adventure* had safely reached England some eight months earlier, in July 1774. After the Maoris had massacred ten of his men in the bloody incident at Queen Charlotte Sound, in December 1773, Furneaux, unaware of Cook's exact whereabouts, despite the message in the bottle, considered it prudent to get under way as soon as possible. He set sail from New Zealand on December 23, 1773, a month after Cook's departure for the waters around the Antarctic. Furneaux, however, did not take the *Adventure* so far south. Instead, following instructions from the Admiralty, he made for Cape Horn and then across the South Atlantic to the Cape of Good Hope. At Table Bay he had refitted and then returned directly to England. Like Cook, he had also searched for Cape Circumcision and found nothing except floating ice. Upon his arrival in England, in July 1774, Furneaux was well praised for his voyage, and his passenger, the Tahitian Omai, created a sensation. Furneaux was made a captain in 1775 and commanded the British man-of-war *Syren* in the American Revolution. He died in 1781 at the age of forty-six.

Cook was now forty-six years old—and a national hero. Hawkesworth's fanciful account of Cook's first expedition, in the *Endeavour*, had come out during Cook's absence, and despite the nonsense it contained, it had made Cook's name known from the Shetlands to Land's End.

Praised everywhere, Cook now wrote a report of both his voyages. This book was every bit as popular as—and much more accurate than—Hawkesworth's labored tale. Cook was also elected a fellow of the Royal Society, a rare honor for a man with no academic credentials. In addition, he received the society's gold medal for a scientific paper on preserving the health of his crew against scurvy.

The Admiralty promoted Cook to the full rank of captain and gave him a shore assignment intended to provide a comfortable income for him and his long-suffering family for the rest of his life.

The search for the southern continent was over. Cook wrote: "I have now done with the Southern Pacific Continent, and flatter myself that no one will think I have left it unexplored." Dalrymple's dream, Quiros's quest, Mendaña's measureless land, it turned out, had no more substance than the mists that hung over the Antarctic waters in the far south summer. The sea beyond Capricorn was empty.

EPILOGUE
GHOSTS

Heroic, tragic, and often both cruel and farcical, the story of the Pacific continued well after the southern continent was a forgotten dream.

Although Cook had exploded the myth of Terra Australis, there were still empty places on the map to fill in: New Holland, Van Diemen's Land, and nearly all the immense ocean north of the equator.

Cook himself took part in the further exploration of the Pacific. He could not remain long ashore. Having done more than any other man to reveal the South Pacific to the world, Cook now turned his eyes northward. Within nine months of his return from his second voyage, he was in the North Pacific, seeking the Northwest Passage.

This notion—that a waterway might link the Atlantic and Pacific in the north as the Strait of Magellan linked them in the south—had intrigued navigators since the early sixteenth century. Thus, when the British government sponsored an expedition to confirm or disprove its existence, Cook volunteered to lead the venture. The Admiralty instructed its most famous mariner to sail to the coast of California and then to proceed northward as far as the Arctic Circle in an effort to find a likely waterway leading to the east. At the same time other ships would attempt to find a passage from the Atlantic.

Sailing from Plymouth on July 12, 1776, with his old *Resolution* and a similar craft called the *Discovery*, Cook rounded the Cape of Good Hope, passed into the Pacific, and made still another visit to Tahiti. He then traveled into the North Pacific, where, fittingly enough, he discovered what are today the Hawaiian Islands in early February 1778.*

Cook went on to the California coast, which he reached at a latitude of approximately 45 degrees. In accordance with his orders, Cook proceeded up the western American coast, surveying all the way. Passing beyond the Bering Strait, Cook got as far north as 70 degrees 41 minutes. There, well past the northwest corner of Alaska, Cook's ships encountered ice that stretched away as far as his eye could see. The expedition could go no farther. The Northwest Passage was as much a myth as the southern continent.

Cook's vessels now made their way back through icy, hazardous seas, repassing the Bering Strait, and then southward for almost three thousand miles to Hawaii, where Cook anchored again in January 1779 to refit.

On February 13, 1779, as the British were refreshing themselves at Hawaii, a party of islanders stole one of the *Discovery*'s boats. Cook, impatient for once with the Polynesian propensity for thievery, seized a local chief and announced that he would not free the man until the boat was returned. The next day, when Cook and a party of marines were ashore, the infuriated natives, demanding the return of their chief, confronted the Europeans. Cook and his marines retreated down the beach to their boats, Cook being the last to retire. Suddenly he was clubbed from behind. He fell, but he rose immediately. The crowd of natives pressed upon him. In a scene reminiscent of the death of Magellan 250 years earlier, Cook held off his assailants as long as he could while his men floundered into their boats. But overpowered, he fell—and did not rise again.

Thus ended the golden career of James Cook, acknowledged as not only the first of Britain's great explorers but a commander of extraordinary talents and a human being of remarkable understanding. He was mourned at home. Honors were paid to his memory. His widow received a pension.†

*Cook named these lovely Polynesian Islands the Sandwich Isles after his friend and sponsor Lord Sandwich, first lord of the Admiralty.
†It is generally believed that Cook would have been made a baronet had he returned

Cook was dead, but others carried on his work. George Vancouver, who had served with Cook, followed up the master's labor on the west coast of North America in 1792–94, surveying and mapping almost the entire shoreline from Cape Mendocino in California north to the Arctic.

Such daring explorers as Matthew Flinders and George Bass charted New Holland's waters in the 1790s, at last filling in the coastal maps of what was really the southern continent. It was Bass who, in 1795, finally proved that Tasmania was an island separated from the Van Diemen's Land, soon to be known as the mainland by a strait that now bears his name.

Nor did France abandon the Pacific entirely. In 1785 a brave French navigator, Jean François de Galaup, count de La Pérouse, set out to explore the Pacific, crossing and recrossing the ocean at its widest part. La Pérouse disappeared in 1788 and was never heard of again. In 1791 another Frenchman, Joseph de Bruni, chevalier d'Entrecasteaux set out to learn La Pérouse's fate. Though he did not achieve his main purpose, his voyage advanced knowledge of the Pacific. The French Revolution, however, effectively ended French Pacific exploration until the first decades of the nineteenth century.

Thus, in the years after Cook's death, with the question of the southern continent answered, the map of the Pacific continued to fill up. But the days of the quest, the leap into the unknown, were done.†

Exploitation replaced exploration. Now began the melancholy litany of the white man's lethal consumption of the people and products of the Pacific.

New Holland was early on the list.

When Cook claimed Botany Bay for Britain in 1770, no one

---

from his third journey. In any case, his greatness was recognized even more by succeeding generations than by his own. A statue of Cook was set up in the Mall in London in 1914. It was carved by the English sculptor Sir Thomas Brock, who also did the Victoria Memorial that stands in front of Buckingham Palace. Cook's real memorials, of course, are the voyages themselves and the memorable character they reveal.

†The most influential proponent of the southern continent, the Scottish scholar Alexander Dalrymple, survived the explosion of his theory and even flourished. Far from retiring in disgrace after Cook's epic voyage around Antarctica, Dalrymple continued to ply his trade as oceanographer. In 1795 he was employed by the Admiralty as hydrographer and given the task of compiling, drawing, and publishing its charts. Though he was a civilian, the Admiralty considered Dalrymple the most qualified man for the job. He died in 1808 at the age of seventy-one, much honored for his work. He was the only civilian ever employed by the Royal Navy as hydrographer. After him they were all RN officers.

had envisioned any colonial future for the place. It was too far away and too lacking in natural amenities to serve as a colony. Yet a few years later these very defects made this bleak land attractive for a very special purpose.

In 1779 British jails were overflowing. Because of the American Revolution, prison officials could not transport convicts to labor in most of Britain's trans-atlantic possessions. The decision was made to use Botany Bay as a prison settlement. In 1788 the first contingent of convicts was deposited there. Two years later a second batch disembarked. In 1793 the first free settlers began arriving. In 1795 Parliament appointed a governor. By 1829 some seventy-five thousand convicts had been "transported" to the land that was now being called Australia and the British government laid claim to the entire continent.

In the process of the whites settling Australia, the aborigines—"the most miserablist people on earth," as Dampier had called them—were almost exterminated. In Tasmania, where a penal installation was set up in 1803, the native people *were* wiped out. But Australia was not the only land exploited by Europeans.

Sealers and whalers also poured into the Pacific and Antarctic waters. They slaughtered millions of aquatic beasts to obtain oil for the lamps of the civilized world. The roughhewn killers of seals and whales wreaked destruction not only on their seaborne quarry but also on the folk of New Zealand, Tahiti, Australia, and the dozens of islands where the whaling and sealing ships customarily put in for rest and resupply. The harpooners and mariners of America and Europe turned bucolic islands, once described as paradises, into steamy hells, where native warriors stupefied themselves with the white man's alcohol and where their women sold their bodies for the white man's money. Violence and cruelty were rampant not only in the icy waters of the high latitudes but also under the palms of the sweet-smelling isles where the trade winds never cease.

Despite the hellish reality, however, the idealization of the noble savage continued. Even in the last decade of the eighteenth century most Europeans and Americans still regarded Polynesia, especially Tahiti, as the Blessed Isles, the Earthly Paradise. This vision persisted primarily because of the popularity of books and plays that insistently romanticized the South Seas. Even Cook's death became the subject of moony paintings and plays.

For fundamentalist Christians, however, the noble savage exerted less appeal than ever, and paradise seemed a place much in need of redemption. For these sturdy Christians the Pacific seemed not innocent but corrupt, an underworld of human sacrifice, free sex, thievery, and, worst of all, idolatry. Add to these the vices taught by white men, and you had the devil's playground, an inferno of lost souls.

To fight the Evil One in the Pacific, the London Missionary Society was founded, in 1795, by evangelical ministers of several denominations. The LMS had but one purpose: to bring Jesus to the South Seas.

In 1797 the first boatload of zealots from the London Missionary Society arrived in Tahiti. Over the next forty years or more, missionaries—Catholic as well as Protestant—invaded the Pacific. They covered the nakedness of the people, taught them Christ, preached against alcohol, treated their diseases, and tutored them in numbers and language. The missionaries turned the islands into beautiful backwaters, belonging *to* the world, but not quite *of* it. It is impossible to say whether the missionaries succeeded in saving their charges from destruction. They did, however, bring their own form of salvation. In time the trade in seal oil and whale oil dried up. The whalers departed. The missionaries remained. The people of paradise also remained, and they were much changed.

But the ocean was not changed. It is the same today as it was when Cook crossed Capricorn. The westerly gales still howl across the empty waters where Sarmiento and Dalrymple believed Terra Australis lay.

And if you sail those endless empty seas today and if you are in the least inclined, you can easily believe that you glimpse a sail far out on the horizon or looming in the shifting mists. You can never overtake these sailing vessels, however, for they are ghost ships: perhaps the shades of Mendaña, and Quirós, or Tasman, or Roggeveen—and all the navigators who sought the southern continent in these latitudes.

Sometimes, in the howling wind, or on the quietest of moon-watered nights, you can hear the cries of drowned mariners, the creak of long-lost ships, and the lamentations of the rejected gods who once ruled a thousand islands in this ocean.

They are all still here, for the Pacific clings to its ghosts and gives up nothing.

BIBLIOGRAPHY

Allen, Robert J. *Life in 18th Century England.* Boston, 1941.

Anson, George. *A Voyage Round the World in the Years 1740–44.* Compiled by Richard Walter. Geneva, 1885.

Armstrong, Edward. *The Emperor Charles V.* London, 1910.

Atkinson, William C. *A History of Spain and Portugal.* London, 1960.

Ayton, W. A. *Life of John Dee.* London: Camden Society, 1909.

Banks, Joseph. *The* Endeavour *Journal of Joseph Banks, 1768–71.* Edited by J. C. Beaglehole. Sydney, 1962.

Barnouw, Adrian. *The Pageant of Netherlands History.* New York: Longmans, Green, 1952.

Bates, Daisy. *The Passing of the Aborigines.* New York: Praeger, 1967.

Beaglehole, J. C. *The Exploration of the Pacific.* Stanford, CA: Stanford University Press, 1966.

———. *Life of Captain James Cook.* Sydney, 1974.

Bellingshausen, Fabian. *The Voyage of Captain Bellingshausen to the Antarctic Seas 1819–21.* London: Hakluyt Society, 1945.

Benson, E. F. *Sir Francis Drake.* London, 1927.

Bluche, Francois. *Louis XIV.* New York: Franklin Watts, 1990.

Blok, Petrus J. *History of the People of the Netherlands.* London and New York, 1912.

Bougainville, Louis Antoine de. *A Voyage Round the World.* Translated by John Reinhold Foster. London, 1772.

Boulenger, Jacques. *The Seventeenth Century.* New York, 1920.

Bourne, Edward, G. *Spain in America 1450–1580.* New York: Harper & Bros., 1904.

Boxer, Charles R. *The Dutch Sea-Borne Empire 1600–1800.* New York: Knopf, 1965.

Braudel, Fernand. *The Structures of Everyday Life: The Limits of the Possible.* New York: Harper & Row, 1981.

Brosses, Charles de. *History of Voyages to Southern Lands.* Paris, 1756.

Burrage, Henry, S. *Early English & French Voyages from Hakluyt.* New York: Scribner's, 1906.

Byron, John, A. *Journal of His Circumnavigation, 1764–66.* London: Hakluyt Society, 1964.

Callender, John. *Terra Australis Cognita.* Edinburgh, 1766–68.

Carswell, John. *The South Sea Bubble.* Stanford, Calif.: Stanford University Press, 1960.

Carteret, Philip. *Philip Carteret's Voyage Round the World, 1766–69.* London: Hakluyt Society, 1965.

Castiglione, Baldassare. *The Courtier.* New York: Everyman's Library, 1965.

Chapman, Charles. *History of Spain.* New York: Free Press, 1968.

Churchill, Winston S. *A History of the English Speaking Peoples: The New World.* New York: Dodd Mead & Co., 1956.

Cipolla, Carlo M. *Guns and Sails in the Early Phase of European Expansion—1400—1700.* New York: Pantheon Books, 1965.

Cook, James. *The Journals of Capt. James Cook on His Voyages of Discovery.* Edited by J. C. Beaglehole. London: Hakluyt Society and the Cambridge University Press, 1961.

Corbett, Julian S. *Some Principles of Maritime Strategy.* London, 1960.

Dalrymple, Alexander. *An Account of Discoveries Made in the South Pacifick Ocean Previous to 1764.* London, 1767.

–––––. *An Historical Collection of the Several Voyages and Discoveries in the South Pacific Ocean.* London, 1770.

Dampier, William. *Dampier's Voyages.* Edited by John Masefield. London: Hakhuyt Society, 1906.

Davis, Ralph. *The Rise of the English Shipping Industry in the 17th and 18th Centuries.* New York: St. Martin's Press, 1963.

Dee, John. *The Private Diary of Dr. John Dee.* Edited by J. O. Halliwell. London: Camden Society, 1842.

Dereksen, David. *The Crescent and the Cross.* New York: G. P. Putnam's Sons, 1964.

De Surville, Jean. *The Expedition of the St. Jean Baptiste to the Pacific 1769–1770 From the Journals.* London: Hakluyt Society, 1981.

Dickens, A. G. *Reformation and Society in 16th Century Europe.* New York: Harcourt Brace & World, 1966.

Drake, Francis (the Younger). *The World Encompassed.* Ann Arbor, Michigan: Michigan University Press, 1966.

Dunmore, John. *French Explorers in the Pacific, The Eighteenth Century.* Oxford: Clarendon Press, 1965.

Durant, Will, and Ariel Durant. *The Story of Civilization*. Vols. 5–9. New York: Simon & Schuster, 1965.

Elcano, Juan Sebastian. *Report to the Emperor Charles V, September 1522*. Translated by Jose T. Medina in *Magellan and His Companions*. Madrid, 1920.

Erickson, Carolly. *Great Harry, The Extravagant Life of Henry VIII*. New York: Summit Books, 1980.

Erlanger, Phillippe. *The Age of Courts & Kings*. New York: Harper & Row, 1967.

Forster, Johann Reinhold. *The Resolution Journal 1772–75*. London: Hakluyt Society, 1982.

Gibbons, H. A. *Foundation of the Ottoman Empire*. New York, 1916.

Grierson, Edward. *Fatal Inheritance—Philip II and the Spanish Netherlands*. Garden City, NY: Doubleday, 1969.

Guillemard, F. H. H. *The Life of Ferdinand Magellan*. New York: AMS Press, 1971.

Hakluyt, Richard. *The Principal Navigations, Voyages, Traffiques and Discoveries of the English Nation*. 12 vols. 1589. Reprint. Fairfield, NJ: Augustus M. Kelley, 1969.

Haley, K. H. D. *The Dutch in the 17th Century*. New York: Harcourt Brace Jovanovich, 1972.

Haring, Clarence H. *Trade and Navigation Between Spain and the Indies in the Time of the Hapsburgs*. Cambridge, MA, 1918.

———. *The Spanish Empire in America*. New York: Harcourt, Brace and World, 1963.

Harris, John. *A Complete Collection of Voyages and Travels*. London, 1705.

Hawkesworth, John. *An Account of the Voyages by Byron, Wallis, Carteret, and Cook*. London, 1773.

Hazard, Paul. *The European Mind, The Critical Years (1680–1715)*. New Haven: Yale University Press, 1953.

Hemming, John. *The Conquest of the Incas*. New York: Harcourt Brace Jovanovich, 1973.

Holland, Julian. *Lands of the Southern Cross*. London: Aldus Books, 1971.

Howarth, David. *Sovereign of the Seas. The Story of Britain and the Sea*. New York: Atheneum, 1974.

Jarrett, Derek. *England in the Age of Hogarth*. New York: Viking Press, 1974.

Kemp, P. K. *History of the Royal Navy*. New York: Putnam, 1969.

Kinross. Patrick Balfour, Baron. *The Ottoman Centuries*. New York: Morrow, 1977.

Kirkpatrick, F. A. *The Spanish Conquistadores*. Magnolia, MA: Peter Smith, 1962.

Landstrom, Bjorn. *The Ship*. Garden City, NY: Doubleday, 1961.

Las Casas, Bartolome. *History of the Indies*. Translated by A. Collard. New York: Harper & Row, 1971.

Le Maire, Jacob. *The East and West Indian Mirror*. London: Hakluyt Society, 1906.

Ley, Charles D., ed. *Portuguese Voyages, 1498–1663*. New York: E. P. Dutton & Co., 1960.

Lyons, Henry, Sir. *The Royal Society, 1660–1940*. Cambridge, England: Cambridge University Press, 1944.

Macauley, Thomas Babington. *History of England*. New York: Everyman's Library, 1960.

Macintyre, Donald. *Sea Power in the Pacific*. New York: Crane, Russak & Co., 1972.

Mahan, Alfred Thayer. *The Influence of Sea Power Upon History 1660–1783*. New York: Hill & Wang, 1968.

Marra, John. *Journal of the* Resolution's *Voyage, 1772–1775*. London, 1775.

Masselman, George. *The Cradle of Colonialism*. New Haven and London: Yale University Press, 1963.

Medina, Jose Toribio. *Juan Diaz de Solis*. Santiago, 1897.

Mendana, Alvaro de. *The Discovery of the Solomon Islands*. London: Hakluyt Society, 1901.

Merriman, Roger Bigelow. *The Rise of the Spanish Empire*. New York: Macmillan, 1934.

Mettam, R. C. *Government and Society in Louis XIV's France*. London, 1977.

Miller, John. *Bourbon and Stuart*. New York: Franklin Watts, 1987.

Mitchell, Mairin. *Elcano: The First Circumnavigation*. London, 1958.

———. *Friar Andres de Urdaneta, O.S.A*. London, 1964.

Montross, Lynn. *War Through the Ages*. New York: Harper, 1946.

Morison, Samuel Eliot. *The European Discovery of America The Southern Voyages, 1492–1616*. New York: Oxford University Press, 1974.

Motley, John L. *The Rise of the Dutch Republic*. London: Dent, 1906.

Napier, William. *Lands of Spice & Treasure*. London: Aldus Books, 1971.

Nowell, Charles E., ed. *Three Contemporary Accounts of Magellan's Voyage*. Chicago: Northwestern University Press, 1962.

———. *Portugal*. Englewood Cliffs, NJ: Prentice Hall, 1973.

Ortiz, Antonio Dominguez. *The Golden Age of Spain 1516–1659*. New York: Basic Books, 1971.

Pardoe, Julia. *The Court and Reign of Francis the First, King of France*. New York: James Pott and Co., 1901.

Parkinson, Sidney. *A Journal of a Voyage to the South Seas*. London, 1784.

Parkman, Francis. *Pioneers of France in the New World*. Boston: Little, Brown & Co., 1906.

Parks, George Bruner. *Richard Hakluyt and the English Voyages*. New York: Frederick Ungar Publishing Co., 1961.

Parry, J. H. *The Age of Reconnaissance.* London: Weidenfeld & Nicolson, 1963.

Payne, Stanley G. *History of Spain and Portugal.* Madison, WI: University of Wisconsin, 1973

———. *The Spanish Seaborne Empire.* New York: Knopf, 1970.

Penrose, Boies. *Travel & Discovery in the Renaissance.* Cambridge: Harvard University Press, 1952.

Pigafetta, Antonio. *The First Voyage Round the World by Magellan.* London: Hakluyt Society, 1874.

———. *The Journal.* Translated by J. A. Robinson. Cleveland, 1906.

———. *A Journal of Magellan's Voyage Around the World.* New York: Harper & Row, 1964.

Polo, Marco. *The Travels of Marco Polo.* New York: New American Library, 1968.

Prescott, W. H. *History of the Reign of Ferdinand & Isabella.* Philadelphia: J. B. Lippincott, 1874.

———. *The Rise and Decline of the Spanish Empire.* New York: Viking Press, 1963.

Pretty, Francis. *Sir Francis Drake's Famous Voyage Round the World.* New York: P. F. Collier & Son, 1910.

Quiros, Pedro Fernandez de. *The Voyages of Pedro Fernandez de Quiros, 1595 to 1606. Edited by Clement Markham. London: Hakluyt Society, 1904.*

———. *Documents on the Voyage of Quiros to the South Sea—1605–1606. Cambridge, England: Cambridge University Press, 1965.*

Riesenberg, Felix. *The Pacific Ocean.* Whittlesey House, 1940.

Ristow, Walter W. *Guide to the History of Cartography.* 1972.

Robertson, George. *The Discovery of Tahiti.* London: Hakluyt Society, 1948.

———. *A Journal of the Second Voyage of HMS* Dolphin *Round the World Under the Command of Captain Wallis RN in the Years 1766, 1767, 1768.* Edited by Hugh Carrington. London: Hakluyt Society, 1948.

Rogers, James E. T. *The Economic Interpretation of History.* London, 1891.

Rogers, Woodes. *A Cruising Voyage Around the World.* 1712. Reprint 1970. Magnolia, MA: Peter Smith.

Roggeveen, Jacob. *The Works of Roggeveen.* Edited by F. E. Mulert. The Hague, 1919.

Sarmiento, Pedro de Gamboa. *Narratives of the Voyages of Pedro Sarmiento de Gamboa: The Straits of Magellan.* Edited by Sir Clements Markham. London: Hakluyt Society, 1895.

Schurz, William Lytle. *The Manila Galleon.* New York: E.P. Dutton & Co., 1939.

Scott, Ernest. *Australian Discovery by Sea.* London: Dent, 1929.

Smith, Adam. *The Wealth of Nations.* London: Methuen, 1950.

Smith, Bernard. *European Vision and the South Pacific.* New Haven and London: Yale University Press, 1985.

Spear, Percival. *India, Pakistan and the West.* 3rd ed. London, New York, and Toronto: Oxford University Press, 1958.

Tasman, Abel Janszoon. *The Journal.* Edited by J. E. Heeres. Amsterdam, 1898.

Todorov, Tzvetan. *The Conquest of America.* New York: Harper & Row, 1982.

Torres, Luis Vaez de. *New Light on the Discovery of Australia.* London: Hakluyt Society, 1930.

Tyler, Royall. *The Emperor Charles the Fifth.* London: G. Allen and Unwin, 1956.

Vespucci, Amerigo. *Letters.* Edited by Sir Clements Markham. London: Hakluyt Society, 1894.

Wasserman Earl R. *Aspects of the 18th Century.* Baltimore: Johns Hopkins University Press, 1965.

Wilkinson, Clennell. *William Dampier.* London, 1929.

Wilson, Derek. *The World Encompassed: Francis Drake and His Great Voyage.* New York: Harper & Row, 1977.

Wittek, P. *The Rise of the Ottoman Empire.* London, 1971.

Wood, William Charles Henry. *Elizabethan Sea-Dogs.* New Haven: Yale University Press, 1918.

Wright, I. A. *Spanish Documents Concerning English Voyages 1527–1568.* London: Hakluyt Society, 1928.

INDEX